Hungary in the Cold War 1°

Hungary in the Cold War 1945–1956

Between the United States and the Soviet Union

by
LÁSZLÓ BORHI

CEU PRESS

Central European University Press
Budapest   New York

Published in 2004 by

Central European University Press
An imprint of the
Central European University Share Company
Nádor utca 11, H-1051 Budapest, Hungary
Tel: +36-1-327-3138 or 327-3000
Fax: +36-1-327-3183
E-mail: ceupress@ceu.hu
Website: www.ceupress.com

400 West 59th Street, New York NY 10019, USA
Tel: +1-212-547-6932
Fax: +1-212-548-4607
E-mail: mgreenwald@sorosny.org

Photographs by courtesy of the Hungarian National Museum.

ISBN 963 9241 80 6 cloth

Library of Congress Cataloging-in-Publication Data

Borhi, László.
  Hungary in the Cold War, 1945-1956 : between the United States and the Soviet Union / by
László Borhi.
    p. cm.
  Includes bibliographical references and index.
  ISBN 9639241806 (hardbound)
  1. Hungary—Politics and government—1945-1989. 2. Hungary—Foreign relations—
United States. 3. Hungary—Foreign relations—Soviet Union. 4. United States—Foreign
relations—Hungary. 5. Soviet Union—Foreign relations—Hungary. I. Title.

  DB956.4.B67 2004
  943.905'2—dc22

                                                                        2004009360

For my parents and grandparents

CONTENTS

ACKNOWLEDGEMENTS

As with all manuscripts, this too owes to colleagues and friends who read and commented on it. First of all I am greatly indebted to Martin J. Sherwin, Günter Bischof, Mark Kramer and Mihály Szegedy-Maszák, who not only shared with me their intellectual resources, but also encouraged me to pursue this project. I am greatly indebted to Joanna McGarry, who helped me put this manuscript into its final form. I also wish to thank (in alphabetical order) those who read the whole or parts of the manuscript at different phases of readiness: Magda Ádám, Csaba Békés, Magdolna Baráth, Tibor Frank, John Lewis Gaddis, Tibor Hajdu, István Kozma, György Litván, Geir Lundestad, Vojtech Mastny, Tamás Meszerics, Zsuzsa L. Nagy, Attila Pók, János M. Rainer, Péter Sipos, István Vida, Odd Arne Westad. They all claim credit for all the virtues, but I alone assume responsibility for the faults. Numerous institutions provided financial support, hospitable and generous background for the research and writing of this book. Most of all I owe gratitude to my own institution, the Institute of History of the Hungarian Academy Sciences and its Director, Ferenc Glatz, who took me to the institute as a young researcher. In addition I am highly thankful also to James Hershberg and Cold War International History of the Woodrow Wilson Center, Washington D.C., École des Hautes Études en Sciences Sociales Paris, the National Security Archives Washington D.C., the Norwegian Nobel Institute Oslo and the Russian Academy of Sciences. The Soros Foundation Budapest gave financial support for my research in Moscow. Finally I must thank the staffs of all the libraries and archives that I used throughout the long years of this project. I wish to make special mention of Magyar Országos Levéltár, the National Archives Washington D.C., the National Security Archives Washington D.C. and the Library of the Norwegian Nobel Institute. Last but not least I want to thank my wife Csilla, who supported and helped me throughout.

INTRODUCTION

"The victorious country demands to assert its rights
for the reason that the vanquished country
started war against it."
(Vladimir Dekanozov, Deputy Commissar
of Foreign Affairs, April 1949)

"Whenever a country achieves
the conditions for the liberation of the proletariat
or for socialism this will be carried out."
(Mátyás Rákosi, May 1946)

"Hungary cannot...ask or receive
our aid in the Greek manner.
They are parallel tragedies,
but cannot have parallel treatment."
(Senator Arthur Vandenberg, June 1947)

After World War II the United States believed that it could retain Soviet–
American cooperation on a liberal basis and preserve a politically pluralistic, economically open Eastern Europe at the same time. The Soviets made
a similar judgement of error. They too hoped to continue cooperating with
the West, albeit on their own conditions: an exclusive sphere in Eastern
Europe with Stalinist systems of government. What resulted was the worst
of all worlds, a Stalinist Eastern Europe and Soviet–American hostility.

In the next four decades the U.S. tried to undo the mistaken policies of
the first few postwar years, but the restoration of European unity was ultimately the function of Soviet policy just as drawing the Iron Curtain on
Eastern Europe had been Stalin's responsibility. For the East European
nations the iron curtain that descended between Stettin and Trieste was not
a figure of speech but a real experience, a real barrier that kept the East
Europeans in, and the people, goods and ideas of the Western world out.
Communist propaganda portrayed the Soviets as liberators who delivered
the East European nations from fascism and led the people onto the road
towards a better society, Socialism. But the high political and human principles on which Communist ideas were founded were rapidly compromised
by the Soviet practice of Communism. People were deprived of their basic
freedoms, even murdered in the Communist campaign for the imagined perfect society. After only a brief experience under Soviet rule few doubted
that the goal, if it ever existed, was not worth the sacrifice. For many East

1

Europeans suicidally taking on Soviet tanks was better than living under Soviet control.

Having been caught up in the struggle for continental mastery in the middle of the 20th century, Hungary, as the other small nations of middle Europe, was in the wrong place at the wrong time. In 1945 the gloomy future predicted by 19th century political thinkers came true: the Hungarian nation was engulfed in the Russian empire. Could it have been otherwise? Were the small nations of Eastern Europe masters of their destiny? Or was their fate the outcome of power politics? These questions can be examined in the larger framework of Soviet–American rivalry, which eventually led to the division of Europe. Few scholars doubt that the Soviet Union wanted predominant influence in the eastern part of the continent, but whether the imposition of Stalinist regimes was unavoidable is strongly debated.[1] Many historians think that if it wasn't for U.S. meddling in the Soviet sphere of influence, at least some of the eastern countries could have existed with more or less democratic governments in the Soviet zone. Their view is that Sovietization was Moscow's response to a foreign threat. Others claim that Moscow intended to have proletarian dictatorships from the outset, only the timing and the modality of achieving them in a politically and culturally diverse region was open to question.[2]

Traditionalist accounts of the origins of the Cold War and the Soviet conquest of East-Central Europe emphasized the Soviet Union's responsibility, which was described as an expansionist power seeking to extend its power and influence.[3] Revisionists on the other hand blamed the United States not only for the Soviet–American conflict, but also for the Bolshevization of the Soviet-occupied territories. If Washington had acted differently, they suggested, the outcome would have been better, perhaps, Soviet-controlled, but not communized *Europe Orientale*.[4] But traditionalists, revisionists and representatives of more recent approaches agree that the fate of Eastern Europe was a major bone of contention and figured prominently in the evolution of the Soviet–American conflict.

Studies of the Communist seizures of power show that they were incremental and Soviet tactics differed from country to country. At least initially East European Communist parties took into account the domestic setting of their respective countries as well as the "external" conditions. Moscow sought to avoid a dramatic showdown with the Western powers and, therefore, Communists carefully avoided talk of proletarian dictatorship. Communist takeovers were idiosyncratic. There was no blueprint for any of them, but blueprints were not necessary. Dictatorships of the proletariat could be established on a flexible basis. Karel Kaplan's description of the Czechoslovak scene characterizes the whole region: "the Communists entered the coalition with clear intention of monopolizing power by liquidating all democratic principles."[5]

This book will describe and analyze the way the Soviet Union built, consolidated and preserved its Empire in Hungary and the American response to it with the help of newly available evidence. The first part will be concerned with Soviet Empire building in Hungary and the U.S. attempt to appease the Soviet Union. The second part will consider the nature of the Soviet Empire and U.S. efforts to disrupt it.

In the last phase of World War II the Soviet Union capitalized on Great Britain's determination to preserve its influence in the Mediterranean as well as on American eagerness to conclude the war as speedily as possible in gaining "responsibility" for East-Central Europe. Although this did not necessarily mean Bolshevization, it is hard to believe that leaders in London and Washington did not count on this as a likely result of Soviet occupation. At the same time, the Anglo-Americans took care to kindle the Hungarians' fancy that they would participate in its occupation. This was exactly what the pro-Western elements in Budapest wanted to hear, since Western occupation would have been the only way to avoid what they dreaded most: German and Russian invasion. Little did they realize that Washington and London envisioned both. British and American officials urged the Hungarians to "jump out of the war" if they wanted to win the Allies' good faith. This was designed to provoke German occupation of Hungary for the sake of diverting German troops from the western front prior to the landing in Normandy. Furthermore, for the same reason, the Allies wanted to make the Germans believe that the second front would be opened in the Balkans. These policies were pursued in the knowledge that Hungary was the haven for the largest intact Jewish community in Europe, 825,000 people. When Hitler for his own reasons finally decided to invade, the result was the implementation of the final solution and the elimination of many of the nation's pro-Western elements. The large German and Hungarian military contingent forced the Soviets to fight some of the fiercest and bloodiest battles of the European war. In Budapest alone, 70,000 soldiers of the Red Army died. Hungarian civilians and the Russian military suffered from Hitler's decision to make a last stand in Hungary. On the other hand, politically Moscow benefited from the Anglo-American decision not to participate in the occupation of the Carpathian Basin and from the fact that Hungary was physically and morally devastated. Western policy towards Hungary was Janus faced. While Washington and London wanted to see democratic change for the sake of regional stability, they refused to take any responsibility for Hungary. In fact, Allied strategy, which was designed to provoke the German invasion of Hungary, failed to contemplate its consequences for Hungarian democratic elements.

The war finished off the old Hungarian political elite. Many of its anti-German and pro-Western representatives were either killed or the Germans deported them. Others, who committed war crimes, or were simply wary of their prospects under Russian rule, fled the country with the retreating German army. Morally the old regime was destroyed for entering and finishing the war on the German side. Hungary's formal ruling classes, the aristocracy and the Gentry middle-class ceased to exist as the leading political, economic or social force. Central and local administration all but disappeared. There was no army, the police and the Gendarmerie disintegrated. Likewise, the economy was in a state of disarray. What better chance could have presented itself for the only well organized political force, the Russian sponsored Communists, to reorganize politics and the economy to their own image?

Before the democratic political forces had a chance to assert themselves, the Communists were in a commanding position in local administration, controlled the newly organized police and the security forces and had infiltrated what was left of the army. Moscow was allowed to impose an Armistice Agreement on its own terms, which prefigured Soviet political and economic domination. The Soviets received Western license to control the Allied Control Commission, which allowed them to guide the Communist Party to power under the cloak of legality.

Chapters II and III will deal with the Communist road to power. This course will be shown within the triangular relationship of Budapest, Moscow and Washington. It is a question whether Hungary's Sovietization was part of a more universal course of Soviet expansion of ideological and/or imperial nature,[6] whether it resulted from Stalin's quest for security,[7] or was provoked by an expansionist or ill-conceived American policy.[8]

It would be an overstatement to claim that Hungary made the difference between harmony and antagonism between the great powers. But to a certain extent it was a litmus test of Soviet intentions towards the Western world. Eduard Mark has shown that American objectives in Eastern Europe were limited to seeking an open sphere arrangement, one that would tolerate "regional arrangements open to the economic interests of other nations that did not threaten the military security of the hegemon."[9] President Truman was willing to accept an open sphere arrangement that would have left Eastern Europe open for Western investment and trade primarily for the sake of European reconstruction. It is another matter that Moscow may have viewed even such a limited goal with suspicion. Be that as it may, the fact that the Soviets did not concede even the most insignificant issues, such as landing rights for U.S. civilian aircraft, sent the signal that cooperation with Moscow was no longer possible already in late 1945. As a matter of fact in 1946 at the latest, both parties decided that *modus vivendi* with the other was probably impossible. The Soviets invoked Leninist ideology that predicted an unavoidable showdown with the leading imperialist power,[10] while the Americans cited Soviet bad faith[11] as it manifested itself in Moscow's conduct in Iran, Turkey and Eastern Europe.

What misled historians in their explanation of Hungary's Sovietization, and its consequences for Soviet–American rivalry, was the semblance of restraint—as compared to Romania or Bulgaria—the Communists displayed in Hungary. A coalition government survived through 1947, which led some historians to seek an external *cause* for the presumed change of paradigm in Communist policy. That cause was commonly identified in America's actions, the most often cited culprit being the Truman doctrine or the Marshall Plan. The argument that the Americans caused the establishment of Stalinist dictatorship implicitly rests on the claim that there was a major shift in Soviet policy towards Hungary. This underlying assumption, however, remains to be demonstrated.[12]

It is true that in 1945 Muscovite Communists claimed that the situation was not ripe for the dictatorship of the proletariat. Yet one should not confuse means with ends. The fact that the Hungarian Communists eschewed the immediate seizure of power at Stalin's advice does not mean that they rejected the same on a longer run. Furthermore, superficial impressions can turn out to be pretentious. First of all, the Communists acted in the spirit of Stalin's exhortation, "Don't be grudging with words, don't scare anyone. But once you gain ground, then move ahead [you] must utilize as many people as possible, who could be of service to us."[13] Stalin also recommended self-restraint in proclamations towards private property and initiative, but events showed that this was a Leninist tactical measure.[14]

In their inner circles Communist leaders made no secret of the fact that initial restraint was only a temporary measure. Hungarian party leader Mátyás Rákosi once remarked that the national election of 1945 had little significance in Communist plans. In fact, Moscow was deeply involved in sharing out the portfolios, making sure the Communists controlled the Ministry of Interior. In May 1946 Rákosi announced that the construction of a proletarian dictatorship was on the agenda regardless of external or domestic conditions. The Communists thereupon decided to liquidate their political opponents, a process that reached its apex in May 1947, when the Prime Minister was forced to resign. In 1945 constitutional measures were introduced to reduce the role of the parliament where the democratic parties were in majority.[15] The fact that non-elected legislative bodies, which were not responsible to the voters curbed the powers of the parliament, was the result of clever Communist tactics and the lack of democratic experience. These measures, together with the system of party bargaining euphemistically called inter-party consultations, effectively minimized the parliament's

ability to influence politics or to represent the will of the voters. With the
parliament thus neutralized, the Communists were poised to seize power.
They had local administrations, the army, the police and the political police
pretty much under their control coupled with unconditional Russian support. It would be hard to pinpoint a critical juncture, a point of no return in
the Communists' relentless trajectory to power. The Soviets meddled in
Hungarian domestic issues in quite a particular way. They relied on their
local protégés and intervened only in cases when the Hungarian Communists were unable to prevail over their opponents on their own. At important
junctures the Kremlin decided political battles using pressure, threats and
eventually Soviet security organs. This in part explains why the numerically
powerful democratic opposition often yielded to Communist demands without a fight. In his important work on Communism, Hugh Seton-Watson dif-
ferentiated postwar East European regimes on the basis of the composition
of their governments[16] and this categorization has been used ever since.
However, because the Hungarian government and the parliament had very
limited authority in deciding political and economic issues, grouping the
people's democracies on the basis of the makeup of their governments
explains very little. Its usefulness in describing the political situation in
Hungary is highly questionable.

In general, U.S. diplomats in Hungary acted on the assumption that the
Hungarian issue should not strain Washington's relations with the Kremlin,
and seldom encouraged the Hungarians toward independent action. Whenever it was decided to oppose a Soviet measure they preferred to work
directly through Moscow. As a rule, the U.S. contested Soviet actions that
were directed against the democratic political elements, or violated the open
sphere principle and endangered existing U.S. investments. It turned out
that American diplomacy was incapable of keeping Hungary in an economically open sphere, of defending business interests or even protecting U.S.
citizens. Although U.S. diplomatic representatives in Budapest were deeply
worried by the ongoing process of liquidating democratic governance, the
principle of non-intervention in domestic affairs was rigidly upheld. Peace
depended on relations with the USSR—not on Hungarian democracy. In
addition Hungarians, like other East Europeans, had been regarded skepti-
cally and were not thought to deserve the kind of assistance Westerners
did.[17] The State Department paid a great deal of attention to Hungarian
developments, but took care not to challenge Russian primacy. Instead of
increasing diplomatic pressure in the face of growing Communist assertive-
ness they chose to back down and finally to abandon Hungary altogether.
This was not an easy choice to make as the diplomatic representations on
Hungary's behalf testify. Considerations concerning the future relations

with the Soviet Union and the lack of British support limited the room for diplomatic maneuvering.

Chapter IV will be concerned with a relatively little known feature of Sovietization, economic penetration. Economic penetration was an aspect of postwar Soviet expansionism that has received little attention, although the economic imperialism of the United States has been one of the focal points of Cold War literature. Ideology, security and even domestic rivalry in the Kremlin have been discussed in connection with the possible sources of Soviet conduct. I will discuss the economic factor in conjunction with these. Economic expansion is habitually used to prepare the ground for political conquest and is also an end in itself: the acquisition of markets, raw materials industrial capacity, agricultural base and profit. Soviet politics used it for both ends. Trade arrangements increased Moscow's political leverage while enriching the Soviet economy at the same time. The control over much of Hungary's industry and mining removed the economic pillar of independence. At the same time economic penetration ensured that the Soviet Union would have access to Hungarian natural resources such as oil, natural gas, coal, manganese and bauxite for as long as it wanted. Hungary supported the Soviet economy with deliveries in kind under various pretexts such as reparations that eventually may have exceeded one billion dollars in the decade after 1945. Simultaneously with the Soviet economic penetration the Hungarian Communist Party (HCP) came to control economic and financial policy and proceeded to centralize them. The democratically elected government had little influence on the formulation of economic policy. At Stalin's suggestion the HCP established the Supreme Economic Council, which was in charge of all affairs relating to the economy, implemented the Communist program of economic transformation and was instrumental in transferring Hungarian (and foreign) property to the Soviets.

If the argument that the United States was out to extend its economic sphere of interest into Eastern Europe were true, one would expect that this would be the field where the U.S. contested the Soviets the most vigorously. In reality Washington failed to sign a trade agreement with Budapest. Although the U.S. envisioned an expansion of its investments, it watched helplessly as the Communists gradually eliminated American investments, while Moscow built its own economic empire in the form of Soviet-owned companies. As in the political sphere, the American posture was essentially defensive. There was enough trouble with Moscow over Germany. When it became apparent that the survival of foreign investments would not be tolerated, the United States made it clear that nationalization was a domestic affair and it would not interfere with it. On the other hand, it wanted compensation for nationalized property but did not get it. Neither was Washington able to avoid American property from going into Soviet or Hungarian ownership.

There was a notable difference between this attitude and the one in Austria. The U.S. took effective measures to ensure that Austria should remain outside the Soviet sphere of political and economic influence. Of course this was made possible by the fact that Austria was in part under a Western occupation regime and Hungary was not. The motivation was powerful: Soviet control in Austria would have jeopardized the United States' position in Germany. Not only that but the Russian "possession of Austria as a satellite prior to a military offensive would [have] placed the USSR in a position to commence offensive action with her Forces already having outflanked Central Europe and Italy."[18] Hungary had no such strategic significance. Geography then was an important factor in shaping American policy in Central Europe.

Throughout history smaller political entities were pawns of great power rivalries, served as buffer zones to protect them, or as reservoirs of economic resources and even of manpower. Oftentimes rather mundane imperial purposes were disguised under the mantle of ideological salvation, which is not to deny the messianic pretenses of powers like the Ottoman Empire, or more recently the United States or Soviet Russia. Pragmatism and ideology are often allies. Turkey, which championed the cause of Islam, used the conquered lands' manpower for military purposes, its taxes to fill the pockets of its dignitaries and the treasury in Constantinople and their territory as a springboard for further expansion. Aside from Albania and Bosnia the Turks did not bother to convert their subjects to Islam. As George Lichtheim put it, an empire always needs ideology as cement to hold the empire together. For the Soviet Union dissemination of Communism may *not* have been an end in itself. Its relationship to practical matters will be examined in the chapter on the Soviet Empire in Hungary.

As opposed to the United States' "empire by invitation" in Western Europe (although not in places like Mexico or the Phillipines) as Geir Lundestad called it, Soviet presence was imposed. Throughout at least the first part of the 1950s the Hungarian leadership used the Kremlin as an external source of power to exercise domestic authority.[19] The question is why the Soviet Union did not apply the Baltic model of integration in Eastern Europe. Or, on the other hand, why it was not satisfied with the kind of friendly but relatively independent and sovereign regimes that Czechoslovakia or to some extent Hungary offered before 1948? There is not enough evidence to get a definitive answer. But on the basis of the role the Soviet Union played in the 1950s it is possible to infer the motives. I assume that the experience of a single country is somewhat indicative for the rest of the people's democracies, particularly because in the early phase of occupation

Moscow introduced a large measure of uniformity in Eastern Europe. Stalinist leaderships in Eastern Europe made sure that Soviet imperial needs would be fulfilled without reservation. The fact that the satellite states were allowed to retain their international legal sovereignty helped preserve the Soviet Union's image as a great power that rejected colonialism. In addition, the nominally independent satellites were able to promote the goals of Soviet foreign policy. Local Communist leaders were trained in the Soviet capital in the spirit of internationalism, therefore they accepted the notion that allegiance to the revolutionary movement led by the Soviet Union[20] superseded the concept of national sovereignty. In their eyes, national and Communist interest were one and the same.

In the years leading up to 1956, the political, social and economic system in Hungary imitated the Soviet system. The triumph of Communism was the purpose of all political, economic and cultural activities. According to the official political canon enshrined in 1950, Hungary was liberated by the Soviet Union in order to free it from the Nazi yoke, and to open the road for the revolutionary development to Socialism. But it may well be that ideology legitimized imperial control. More precisely, practice and ideology sustained one another. From the perspective of Soviet control the voluntary subservience of the Hungarian leadership made the real difference as compared to the period preceding the Communist seizure of power. Moscow never defined its relationship with Hungary or any other of the East European allies in legal terms. When Hungary was made part of the Habsburg Empire in the 18th century its obligations, such as its contribution to the imperial army were codified. At the same time Austria was obliged to honor the constitutional guarantees of Hungarian independence. Hungary was to be administered according to its own laws and customs. In the course of over a century, Hungary occasionally denied the military services required by the imperial court, and Vienna neglected to observe Hungarian legal customs. On such occasions, legal appeals could be made in order to redress the grievances. It is another matter that even these arrangements were insufficient to hold the Empire together. When the United States introduced military government in Cuba, the Platt amendment of 1901 codified Cuba's obligations towards the U.S. even though it contained no rights for Cuba. But even such a one sided arrangement is probably better than having none at all, because the smaller nation's rights are to some extent protected by the very fact that its obligations are codified.

Imperial dues to the Soviet Union were laid out in loosely worded bilateral agreements and embraced foreign policy, the military sphere and the economy. Moscow used its political leverage to interpret these flexible agreements the way it saw fit. By and large the USSR got what it wanted: a continuous flow of payments and access to strategically important raw

materials. Domination of Hungarian foreign trade provided additional political leverage. Hungary's economic exploitation through the mid-1950s suggests that it may have been one of the motives of Soviet expansion. The
Soviets also had unrestricted control of Hungarian territory for military purposes meaning that the Soviet Union's defensive (and offensive) perimeter
was extended to Hungary. This reaffirms the notion shared by contemporaries
and historians alike that Russia imposed its political system on Eastern
Europe because of military needs.

Although the political entities under Soviet control were putatively sovereign, the Kremlin reserved the right to meddle in their domestic affairs.
Intervention took a variety of forms ranging from military intervention to
political consultations in Moscow or even Soviet participation in the deliberations of local decision-making organs. For instance, Anastas Mikoyan
participated in the sessions of the Hungarian Political Committee in July
1956. Even for reformers such as Imre Nagy it was natural to ask for Russian arbitration in domestic disputes. The purpose of all forms of Soviet inter-
ventions was to induce moderate or radical changes in the domestic policies
of the satellites. Between 1953 and 1955 Moscow sought to alter the course
of Hungarian politics by arbitrating between the Stalinist and the reform
factions of the party. Soviet actions reflected the changes that were taking
place within the Kremlin. Yet it would be a mistake to think that the reforms
were mere responses to commands from Russia. They also stemmed from
the autonomous ideas of Imre Nagy and other reformers even though it was
Soviet interference that helped them to power in 1953.

When in 1849 Grand Duke Paskievich launched his attack on revolutionary Hungary on behalf of the Habsburg dynasty he used similar terms
to describe Czarist Russia's mission as Marshall Konev would use in 1956
to explain the Soviet Union's motive for intervening: the restoration of law
and order, the continuation of the status quo ante. In 1849 this meant both
the restoration of the balance of powers in Central Europe and the uphold-
ing of the Conservative principle of the Holy Alliance.

In 1956 the Kremlin decided on military intervention for two reasons.
First, the situation in Budapest was getting out of hand, Communists were
being killed. Second, the international situation changed: two western powers proceeded to bomb Egypt. This may have been viewed as a challenge to
the global balance requiring Moscow to put an end to the revolt that endangered the stability of its sphere of influence in Central Europe. Russia's
position in Eastern Europe was non-negotiable: the Kremlin wanted to maintain its control as it was, as an essentially closed sphere, without Western
inroads. Hence the Soviet leadership rejected U.S. proposals to open Eastern
Europe even though these included pledges meant to safeguard Soviet security interests. Undisputed control over adjacent lands was obviously prefer-

able to American promises of doubtful sincerity. Furthermore, Hungary still yielded economic benefit, for instance since 1955 it was a source of large quantities of cheap uranium. Was there a possibility then, shortly after Stalin's death, to change the status quo in Central Europe? Did the political will to do so exist in the only power that had the power to do so, the United States, which openly expressed interest in rolling back the Soviets?

Throughout the period under discussion American policy towards the Soviet Empire in Eastern Europe was fraught with contradiction. The presence of Russian power in middle Europe was deemed inimical to western security interests. The existence of oppressive totalitarian regimes subservient to Moscow was distasteful for those who were anxious to disseminate the ideas of national self-determination, democracy and economic liberalism. Although the elimination of Soviet mastery in East-Central Europe was the only way to remedy these problems, military means were ruled out. In the final analysis both the Truman and the Eisenhower administrations believed that a forceful attempt to deprive the Soviets of their holdings in the eastern part of the European continent would lead to an armed conflict between the United States and the Soviet Union. This in turn might well escalate into a nuclear conflict the cost of which would probably be too high to pay for the freedom of the Soviet satellites and for defusing the political and military tension in the heart of the continent. Nuclear war would have meant the devastation of Central Europe and destruction beyond that experienced in World War II. This was driven home particularly by the successful testing of the H-bomb in 1952, which cancelled all previous notions about war and politics. The result was that the American stance towards the region was highly ambiguous. In the final chapter I will explore these ambiguities through the discussion of American policies and their impact in Hungary: economic, psychological and covert warfare, negotiation and finally Washington's response to the Hungarian crisis in 1956.

The U.S. policy of economic embargo was meant to hinder the economic consolidation of the Communist regimes and to reduce Soviet military capabilities. Psychological warfare was aimed at maintaining hope of eventual liberation, to preserve and nurture resistance and to win over the minds of men behind the Iron Curtain. Unfortunately, however, this effort was plagued by the difficulty of holding out hope while at the same time not promising anything practical to change the status quo. Initially, organs responsible for psychological warfare introduced measures to undermine Communist regimes by way of covert warfare, sabotage and the establishment of underground resistance even at the cost of provoking a military conflict with the Soviets, that many believed was unavoidable anyway. This aggressive policy was shielded by U.S. nuclear superiority. In 1952, however, U.S. assessment of Soviet intentions changed: Moscow would attack only in case its vital interests—such as Eastern Europe—were threatened. Moreover, it became apparent that the Soviets would soon have the capacity to launch a crippling nuclear strike on American territory. This meant that aggressive psychological warfare against Eastern Europe was too danger- ous.[21] After initial hesitation the Eisenhower administration also concluded that containment was the appropriate policy to pursue on Eastern Europe. Thus, the dichotomy between the ambitious ends and the insufficient means to achieve them became apparent during the Hungarian revolution of 1956. Then the American strategy was to convince the Soviets that the U.S. har- bored no desire to exploit the situation at Moscow's expense, and thereby to allow for a mutually acceptable solution. For Washington this would have been Hungary's (and possibly the whole region's) Finlandization with ade- quate guarantee for Russian security. Simultaneously, however, the Eisen- hower administration tolerated a propaganda campaign that was designed to encourage the Hungarian freedom fighters to liberate their land. This was done in spite of the fact that armed struggle against the Russians behind the Iron Curtain was considered suicidal.

The two approaches were in conflict with one another: the harder the rebels fought, the more likely the Russians were to see the use of force as the only option, hence the less chance for them to accept change along the lines of Finlandization. In view of the unresolved nature of Germany's posi- tion, it was unlikely that the Kremlin would seriously consider changing the status of the bloc countries anyway. Propaganda revealed a more cynical aspect of American policy, one in which the ends justified the means. The stakes were high enough, since a Soviet withdrawal from Eastern Europe would have led to a significant lessening of political and military tension in Europe. There was a good chance that a diplomatic initiative would fail and in that case self-liberation would offer the only chance of success. For a short while decision-makers in Washington were led to believe that the Rus- sians were giving in. When Soviet tanks were rolling in the streets of Buda- pest on the fourth of November Radio Free Europe was still encouraging the Hungarians to fight. One wonders whether there might have been an alternative course for U.S. policy, as Henry Kissinger suggested, one that might have altered the course of events in Hungary and hence, perhaps the future course of the Cold War. But, as I argue, throughout these years it was up to the Soviets and not the Americans whether the status of Eastern Europe would change and consequently whether the Cold War would end or at least subside.

NOTES

1 Vojtech Mastny wrote that "nowhere beyond what the Soviet Union considered to be its borders did its policies initially envisage the installation of Communist regimes." Vojtech Mastny, "Soviet Plans for Postwar Europe," in Antonio Varsori, Elena Calandri eds., *The Failure of Peace in Europe* (London: Palgrave, 2002), p. 69.

2 For the most convincing recent argument see Eduard Mark, "Revolution by Degrees: Stalin's National-Front Strategy for Europe, 1941–1947" CWIHP Working Paper no. 31.

3 Traditionalist accounts include Herbert Feis, *From Trust to Terror. The Onset of the Cold War, 1945–1950* (New York: Norton, 1970); Arthur Schlesinger Jr., "The Origins of the Cold War," *Foreign Affairs*, October 1967, pp. 22–52. For a review of older and recent literature see Günther Bischof, "Eine Historiographische Einführung: Die Era des Kalten Krieges und Österreich," in *Österreich im Frühen Kalten Krieg 1945–1958* (Köln, Weimar: Böhlau Verlag, 2000), pp. 19–55.

4 Revisionist accounts include William Appelman Williams, *The Tragedy of American Diplomacy*, revised edition (New York, 1962); Joyce and Gabriel Kolko, *The Limits of Power. The World and United States Foreign Policy, 1945–1954.* (New York: Harper and Row, 1972). In one of the first accounts based on declassified U.S. sources Lynn Ethridge Davis claimed that Washington "refused to accept publicly Soviet unilateral determination of the political future of Eastern Europe and as a result failed to achieve either goal, cooperation with the Soviet Union or the implementation of the Atlantic Charter." According to Davis, the U.S. "should have abandoned its opposition to the establishment of minority governments in Eastern Europe and should have informed the Soviet Union that the United States did not intend to threaten Soviet security in that part of the world." Davis concluded that in this case "the Soviet Union might not have felt the need to enforce such complete control over Eastern Europe, at least not so rapidly." Thus, the Soviet Union was portrayed as a passive observer, rather than an active participant of affairs. See Lynn Ethridge Davis, *The Cold War Begins* (Princeton, N.J.: Princeton University Press, 1974), pp. 372–394. Geir Lundestad agreed that "the United States did work to set up democratic regimes and the principle of free trade in Eastern Europe at the expense of the Soviet Union" and "America's insistence on an important role for Washington also in Eastern Europe contributed significantly to the conflict with the Soviet Union." Lundestad stopped short of saying that U.S. policy encouraged or speeded up Bolshevization. See Geir Lundestad, *The American non-policy towards Eastern Europe, 1943–1947* (Tromsö–Oslo–Bergen: Universitatsforlaget, 1978), pp. 37–63. Later Lundestad criticized the notion that American policy alone determined the course of international relations after 1945. Geir Lundestad, *The American "Empire" and other Studies in U.S. Foreign Policy in a Comparative Perspective* (Oxford–New York: Oxford University Press, Oslo: Norwegian University Press, 1990), p. 29. For an account of U.S. policy towards Eastern Europe see Bennett Kovrig, *The Myth of Liberation—East-Central Europe in*

U.S. Diplomacy and Politics since 1941 (Baltimore and London: The Johns Hopkins University Press, 1973).

5 Karel Kaplan, *The Short March—The Communist Takeover in Czechoslovakia, 1945–1948* (New York: St. Martin's Press, 1987), pp. 14–15. In a similar vein Ivo Duhacek argued that "while February 1948 was the official putsch, in reality that date represented a consummation of a very long process that started before the end of World War II." Ivo Duhacek, "Czechoslovakia," in Stephen D. Kertesz, ed., *The Fate of East-Central Europe—Hopes and Failures of American Foreign Policy* (Notre Dame, In.: Notre Dame University Press, 1956), pp. 208–209. The same view is shared by Pavel Tigrid, "The Prague Coup of 1948: The Elegant Takeover," in Thomas T. Hammond ed., *The Anatomy of Communist Takeovers* (New Haven: Yale University Press, 1975), pp. 399–492. A Russian historian has recently written that "February had to happen in Czechoslovakia sooner or later, but the international situation speeded up the coming of the Communists to power." V. V. Marina, "Ot doverie do podozritelnosti" [From trust to suspicion] in E.G. Zadorzhiuk and V. V. Marina eds., *Febral 1948. Moskva i Praga* (Moscow, 1998), p. 41. On Romania a historian has written that the Kremlin's decision to Sovietize it was not premeditated except to the extent that it fell within the framework of long-range Soviet determination eventually to install a puppet government in Romania. Stephen Fischer-Galati, "The Communist Seizure of Power," in *The Anatomy of Communist Takeovers*, p. 31.

6 A case for the ideological motivation of Soviet expansion was made by R.C. Raack, *Stalin's Drive to the West, 1938–1945* (Stanford, California: Stanford University Press, 1995), pp. 18–72. He used German Communist sources to show that Stalin hoped to export the dictatorship of the proletariat to Western Europe. Raack's evidence is corroborated by Czech evidence presented by Igor Lukes, *Czechoslovakia Between Stalin and Hitler, The Diplomacy of Edvard Benes in the 1930s* (New York, Oxford: Oxford University Press, 1996). See especially pp. 72–74; 154; 158; 198–199. Based on his findings Lukes makes a strong case that Stalin hoped to export the proletarian revolution to the West. For an explanation of Soviet foreign policy within a dual, imperial-ideological paradigm see Vladislav Zubok and Constantine Pleshakov, *Inside the Kremlin's Cold War—From Stalin to Khrushchev* (Cambridge, Massachusetts, London, England, 1996); Hannes Adomeit, *Imperial Overstrech: Germany in Soviet Foreign Policy from Stalin to Gorbachev* (Baden-Baden: Nomos Verlagsgesellschaft, 1998).

7 For a security oriented explanation of post-war Soviet foreign policy see Vojtech Mastny, *The Cold War and Soviet Insecurity: The Stalin Years* (New York, Oxford: Oxford University Press, 1996).

8 See Zubok and Pleshakov, *Inside the Kremlin's Cold War*.

9 Eduard Mark, "American Policy Toward Eastern Europe and the Origins of the Cold War, 1941–1946: An Alternative Interpretation." *The Journal of American History*, vol. 68, no. 2, (September 1981), pp. 313–336.

10 See the Novikov telegram of September 1946. *Diplomatic History*, 1991, Fall, no. 3.

11 See for example the Clifford–Elsey report of 1946. As cited in Melvyn Leffler, *A Preponderance of Power—National Security, the Truman Administration, and the Cold War* (Stanford: Stanford University Press, 1992), pp. 130–138. In Leffler's view the Truman administration exaggerated signs of Soviet ill will and disregarded Moscow's efforts of conciliation.

12 Bennett Kovrig wrote that "The criticism that by pursuing democracy in Eastern Europe Washington rode roughshod over legitimate Soviet security interests and only accelerated the process of Sovietization is as fanciful as the notion that it was driven fundamentally by capitalist ambition [...] Nor does the balance of evidence indicate that American policy was counterproductive." Bennett Kovrig, *Of Walls and Bridges—The United States and Eastern Europe* (New York and London: New York University Press, 1991), p. 26. In contrast, according to Charles Gati the Marshall Plan provoked Russia to act in defense of its interest and introduce Stalinism in Hungary. See Charles Gati, *Hungary and the Soviet Bloc* (Durham, N.C.: Duke University Press, 1986). More recently Zubok and Pleshakov extended the effect of the Marshall Plan to the Sovietization of Eastern Europe as a whole, claiming that the United States threatened vital Soviet interests in Eastern Europe, the Sovietization of which hence came as a response. Zubok–Pleshakov, *Inside the Kremlin's Cold War*. Melvyn Leffler argued that "The Truman doctrine, the Marshall Plan and the initiatives in Germany triggered great fears" in the Kremlin, which in turn "tightened the grip on the satellites." The critical turning point was, according to Leffler, the Marshall Plan, from then on Stalin demanded "rigid compliance and subordination." Melvyn Leffler, *The Specter of Communism: The United States and the Origins of the Cold War, 1947–1953* (New York: Hill and Wang, 1994), pp. 65–66. A similar argument was made by Scott Parrish, "The Marshall Plan—Soviet American relations and the Division of Europe," in Norman Naimark and Leonid Gibiansky, eds., *Establishment of Communist Regimes in Eastern Europe, 1944–1949* (Westview Press, 1996), pp. 267–269. All authors fail to demonstrate that there was in fact a drastic change in Soviet policy after the Marshall Plan as opposed to before it.

13 Stalin gave similar instructions to other East European Communist leaders.

14 For a discussion of the role of pragmatism in the policies of ideological states see Nigel Gould-Davis, "Rethinking the Role of Ideology in International Politics During the Cold War," *Journal of Cold War Studies*, vol. I, no. I, Winter 1999, pp. 90–109.

15 A selected legislative body (Politikai Bizottság—Political Committee, not to be confused with the Political Committee of the Communist party) was entitled to act on behalf of the National Assembly and pass laws in the form of government decrees. The Political Committee was enabled to instruct the National Assembly to enact legislation in an urgent procedure without prior debate in a parliamentary committee or even the Assembly itself. It functioned similarly to the Supreme Soviet of the Soviet Union until it was replaced by an exact replica of that Soviet organ, the Presidential Council. Another body, Nemzeti Főtanács (Supreme

National Council) appointed the ministers of the government and ratified international agreements at the recommendation of the Political Committee. See on
this Gizella Föglein, *Államforma és államfői jogkör Magyarországon, 1944–1949*
[Constitutional form and the head of state's jurisdiction in Hungary, 1944–
1949] (Budapest: ELTE, 1994).

16 Hugh Seton-Watson, *From Lenin to Khrushchev—The History of World Communism* (New York, Washington: Frederick. A. Praeger, 1966), pp. 248–249.

17 See Hugh DeSantis, *The Diplomacy of Silence—The American Foreign Service,
the Soviet Union and the Cold War* (Chicago, London: The University of Chicago
Press, 1979).

18 For the statement by the State Department and the corresponding maps see Günter Bischof, *Between Responsibility and Rehabilitation: Austria in International
Politics, 1940–1950,* Part 2 (Ph. D. dissertation, Harvard University, 1989), pp.
838–839. Mussolini had already noticed the strategic significance of Austria and
commented, referring to Hitler's Austria that he who has breakfast in Vienna will
have lunch in Milan.

19 According to Stephen Krasner if a state "is subject to external sources of authority" its Westphalian sovereignty is violated. Stephen D. Krasner, *Sovereignty
Organized Hypocrisy* (Princeton, New Jersey: Princeton University Press, 1999),
p. 13.

20 No Hungarian Communist leader ever questioned the Soviet Union's leading
role in the world revolutionary movement. In later years Party First Secretary
János Kádár explicitly acknowledged the supremacy of the USSR in the international Communist movement against the challenge posed by China.

21 See Grigory Mitrovich, *Undermining the Kremlin—America's Strategy to Subvert the Soviet Bloc* (Ithaca, London: Cornell University Press, 2000).

CHAPTER I

WE DO NOT WISH TO MOVE A FINGER

When Hungary's former Regent, Miklós Horthy, was queried by an American officer about why he did not break with the Germans before he sacrificed twelve to thirteen divisions on the Russian front, Horthy replied in German: "Was konnte ich machen?" Though this response may sound banal and self-serving, it is hard to falsify even from the temporal distance of half-a-century. Hungary's course from the late 1930s encapsulated the fate of small nations caught up in Central European power politics. Hungary entered the war on the German side in part because of its own choosing and in part because of the bandwagon effect.[1] The Anschluss of 1938 destroyed any possibility of a regional anti-German alliance. Mussolini's famous dictum that he who has breakfast in Vienna will have lunch in Milan was true also for Budapest.

The situation changed drastically in 1943. Hitler's defeat was no longer an unlikely prospect. Realizing Hitler's impending doom, his allies prepared to jump off the bandwagon. Hungary's conservative political elite sought salvation through surrendering to London and Washington in the hope that Anglo-American armies would occupy Hungary, thereby forestalling a German or Soviet invasion. But the question was whether such an Anglo-American occupation of Hungary was a real possibility. The answer will reveal the deeper motives of Allied policy towards Germany's minor allies and will reflect on the origins of the Soviet sphere of influence in East-Central Europe.

The first segment of this chapter will review Hungarian foreign policy, which was founded on the prospect that Hungary would be on the Anglo-American route to Berlin. This belief was not wholly a figment of Hungarian imagination. A military strategy involving the British penetration into the Carpathian Basin was discussed on several occasions and was only finally discarded at the conference of Teheran in December 1943. The second section will discuss the equations of power politics that sealed the fate of East-Central Europe, the nations of which were not the masters of their own fate.

The United States wanted to win the war as quickly as possible even at the price of inviting the Soviets into the heart of Europe. Moscow, it seemed to Roosevelt and his advisors, had given up its revolutionary designs, but even the communization of Eastern Europe was not too large a sacrifice, if it brought lasting peace in Europe. Both in Washington and London there was a widespread notion that postwar cooperation with the Soviet Union would be possible and that the Soviets would not impose their own political system on Eastern Europe.[2] For Roosevelt it would not have mattered even if the Soviet political system were introduced in Eastern Europe. He told Cardinal Spellman that the Nazis and their smaller allies were not undeserving of their fate. To Averell Harriman the President confided "he did not care whether the countries bordering Russia became communized or not."[3] Hence it is hardly surprising that the allies accepted the Soviet occupation of that region. Secretary of State Cordell Hull assumed that the problem of Eastern Europe would be treated in subordination to the goal of preserving the cooperation of the great powers after the war.[4]

The British were anxious to preserve their position in the Mediterranean, and the Danube Basin could serve as a bargaining chip with the Russians. Between 1943 and 1944 British planners were less concerned with the countries of Central and Eastern Europe than with the Mediterranean countries of Turkey, Italy, and Greece.[5] Like Roosevelt, Winston Churchill came to believe that the Soviet Union was changing. In an unsent letter to Stalin in 1944 he wrote that "the differences in our social systems will tend to get smaller, and the great common ground we share of making life richer and happier for the mass of the people is growing every year."[6] From the perspective of power politics, however, it does not matter whether Churchill thought that the Soviets would introduce their own political system in the countries they occupied or not. We shall never know what would have happened if Great Britain and the U.S. had tried to oppose the Soviet possession of East-Central Europe. In the victory against Hitler a great deal depended on Soviet cooperation, and it is hard to blame Roosevelt and Churchill that they did not oppose Soviet occupation. Yet there was a darker side of British and American politics, which will be examined in the last section.

The Allied invasion in Normandy required that German troops be removed from the theatre of war. This could be done in two ways. First, by convincing Hitler that the invasion would be launched from the Balkans.[7] Second, by persuading Hitler's allies to jump out of the war with the policy of the stick and the carrot. Both lines were actively pursued. In Hungary's case these policies were somewhat contradictory, since a German invasion was likely to result in the destruction of the democratic elements the Allies needed for democratic reconstruction. There ought to have been a further dilemma for the allied powers. Hungary was a haven for the last intact Jewish community in Europe. The Horthy regime refused to deport the bulk of

Hungarian Jewry (with the exception of 20,000 Jews who did not have Hungarian citizenship, and were deported to Kamenec Podolsk in 1941), but it was likely that if Germany invaded Hungary, their lives would be put to great jeopardy. Yet the fate of the Jewish community did not matter in Allied calculations. The presence or absence of a couple of German divisions in Normandy may or may not have made a difference in the outcome of the war.

As a result of Hungary's occupation by the Germans in March 1944 the great majority of Hungarian Jews, perhaps as many as half-a-million people, did not live to see the Allied victory. Democratic elements were persecuted and Hungary became a battlefield where some of the heaviest fighting of the war took place. While the Wehrmacht and the Red Army were locked in lethal struggle on Hungarian soil, preparations were taking place in Moscow for the establishment of a post-Horthy political system. The final part of the chapter will discuss these preparations and the extent to which they prefigured Hungary's Sovietization.

Jumping off the bandwagon

In early 1942 Hungary's head of state, Regent Horthy, decided to alter the nation's course. Horthy felt that Hungary had been too closely tied to Germany, whose fortunes had slowly started to decline with its defeat near Moscow and the United States' entrance into the war. In fact, as the Nazi colossus was losing the war, many of its allies began to consider jumping off the bandwagon. The Hungarian political elite saw only one option: surrendering to the West, but not to the Soviet Union. For Horthy, as Nicholas Roosevelt, an American diplomat assigned to Budapest had observed, "the fear of Russia had become an obsession. Over and over he insisted that it was Russia which presented the greatest threat to Hungary and the Western world." Harry Hill Bandholz, who acquainted Admiral Horthy in 1919 as the head of the U.S. military mission in Budapest had "great confidence in his ability and good sense,"[8] but the Regent became quite irrational when it came to the Soviet Union. In private conversation Horthy used the strongest language to describe Communism: it was a cancer to be excised, a poison to be removed from the system, a vile Mafia ran by the scum of society. Moscow, he was convinced, was the center of a conspiracy whose immediate goal was to overthrow all existing institutions.[9]

In March 1942 Horthy dismissed his pro-German Prime Minister, László Bárdossy and appointed a relatively little known conservative politician of gentry origin known for his anti-German sentiments, Miklós Kállay. The regent expected his protégé to restore Hungary's freedom of action by loosening Hungary's ties with Germany and establishing contacts with the Allies. Although Kállay was hostile to Nazi Germany he also shared Horthy's anti-Soviet prejudices. Bolshevism, in his view, was "a system of terror...An Asiatic system that was opposed to and hated the West."[10] Kállay pursued the policy of "jumping out" wholeheartedly but with great caution.

When the Second Hungarian Army was destroyed near Voronezh in January 1943, Kállay decided to step up Hungary's efforts to find a modus vivendi with the Allies and sent peace-feelers to neutral cities such as Stockholm, Istanbul or Lisbon to explore the possibilities of a separate peace. This was not easy. He had to contend with strong opposition within Hungary itself, particularly from the Arrow-Cross movement, members of the officer corps and even members of his cabinet, who for ideological reasons were devoted to the German cause. Furthermore, as Romanian and Bulgarian peace-feelers also demonstrated, the British, who wanted unconditional surrender, initially refused to talk to representatives of the Axis states. Kállay's dilemma was that while the British expected deeds such as acts of sabotage to indicate Hungary's readiness to part with Hitler, pro-German loyalty had to be demonstrated and the talks had to be kept in secret in order to avert German occupation. Secrecy was obviously beyond Hungarian capability, since the London *Times* published reports of the allegedly secret activity, including an almost verbatim version of an encoded message containing Hungary's conditions for surrender. Hitler knew enough of Hungary's dealings with the enemy to demand that the (from the German perspective) unreliable premier be dismissed. The situation was further complicated by the fact that even in the eyes of the pro-Western political elite Soviet Bolshevism was as distasteful and dangerous to national survival as Hitler's Germany and Nazism. Kállay was convinced that Russian victory "was bound to mean the end of Hungary, for it was quite natural that as a drop in the ocean of Bolshevik and Slav peoples the Hungarian identity would disappear." In such a way, as he put it, there was nothing left but to turn to the West.[11] Hungary's official and semi-official representatives solicited the British and the Americans with an offer that Hungary was ready to surrender if, and only if an Anglo-Saxon army would occupy the country. This would have been the optimal solution for the Hungarians, enabling them to avoid both evils: German *and* Russian occupation.

Kállay based his policy on the assumption that the British would occupy the Danube Basin before the Russians got there. There was some justification for his assumption, since Churchill did in fact propose a so-called "Vienna option" for the second front. At the heart of this was the idea of attacking the "soft underbelly of Europe," either by a landing in the Balkans, or, by pursuing the Italian offensive through the Ljubljana gap, possibly through Budapest to Vienna. Hungarian leaders hoped that the Western allies would understand their difficult predicament and believed that the West would count on Hungary against Bolshevik expansion. One of the key participants of Kállay's secret overtures, Aladár Szegedy-Maszák, who headed the political section of the Hungarian Ministry of Foreign Affairs, recalled that Hungarian diplomats overestimated the significance the Western powers attached to the Danube Basin. Another peace-feeler, Hungary's ambassador in Lisbon, Andor Wodianer, thought that the West regarded Hungary as a kind of second line of defense against Russia.[12] In reality, the Allies had no use for Hungary's services, and showed little sympathy for the country or its people. Instead, for understandable reasons, they exploited the Hungarian initiative to defect for their own purposes. The Allies hoped to profit from Hungary's desperate situation. Policymakers in London and Washington realized that it may actually benefit them if the Wehrmacht was to invade Hungary because it would mean that Germany would be forced to take the necessary troops from the Western theater of war prior to the invasion in France.

Until the conference of Moscow in October 1943 Hungarian diplomatic sources tended to confirm the hope that Hungary would be occupied by the British or the Americans or maybe both. In September 1943, after protracted negotiations the Hungarian envoy to Istanbul, László Veres concluded a preliminary armistice agreement with the British, which was to be published only when the British forces actually reached Hungary.[13] Although the particulars of the secret dealings were not made public, the anti-German press in Hungary alluded to an arrangement with the Western allies. The readers of the liberal *Magyar Nemzet* were called upon to "brush up" their English, a book with the same title was published with great success, the social democratic *Népszava* discussed the merits of the Beveridge plan, and readers were informed of German military setbacks by *Magyar Nemzet*'s military expert.

Soon the Hungarian Foreign Ministry learned that there would be no landing in the Balkans. After the Teheran conference the Hungarian Legation in Stockholm reported that Hungary would be left in the Soviet sphere of influence: "Full Russian influence will prevail [...] in the Danube Basin and the Balkans."[14] Such information led to a belated reappraisal of foreign policy, and in early 1944 the Kállay government came round to the idea of seriously approaching the Russians.[15]

The inveterate idea harbored by pro-British politicians and diplomats that the British would beat the Russians to Hungary was fuelled by an irrational belief in Hungary's alleged geopolitical significance. This regionally widespread notion was rooted in ideas that dated back to the era of national reawakening in the 19th century, which suggested that East European states had a mission at the time of their national greatness in the Middle Ages.

Hungarians thought that their country had been a bastion protecting the Christian West from the heathen Ottomans, a mission that could be accomplished again—this time against the Soviets. A significant figure in the secret negotiations with the allies, the diplomat György Bakách-Bessenyei believed that "Western powers could not afford Russian domination of this (Hungary's) geographically important area, the gateway to Western Europe because it would be more dangerous to their safety than German influence in the area."[16] Hungary's minister in Lisbon, Andor Wodianer was also an active participant of the secret peace talks, and shared this illusion.[17] Prime Minister Kállay admitted that his belief in Hungary's geopolitical importance nourished his hopes that Hungary would fall into the Western sphere of influence: "If Hungary could have been made into a base, British and American influence would today be prevailing in the Balkans and on the Danube."[18] Little did he know that in order to preserve wartime cooperation Roosevelt was ready to sanction the Soviets' 1941 boundaries there, and even condone the extension of Russian influence in Europe.[19] With all their failings and shortcomings Kállay and some like-minded compatriots tried to avert the disaster of both German and Soviet occupation. It was not entirely their fault that they succeeded in forestalling neither.

Allied diplomacy and the fate of Hungary

Eventually the high expectations concerning Hungary's Western occupation turned out to be unfounded. Military involvement in the liberation of the Danube Basin did not fit into British or American strategy. Washington and London intended to conclude the war as rapidly as possible and this goal was not to be hampered by political considerations such as beating the Russians to the Danube. In March 1944 the U.S. Chiefs of Staff ruled that the United States would not take any responsibility in the Balkan area.[20] The question of the second front—which determined the spheres of occupation each power would control—was resolved in such a way as to allow the Soviets to occupy Eastern Europe, including the Carpathian Basin. The historian Vojtech Mastny has written that for Stalin, "military occupation of a territory for political gains was not an overriding priority until the end of the war. In their readiness to sanction in advance conquests that Stalin had not yet made, the Western powers mistook his ability to use force for determination to use it. This may not have made a difference for Poland but could have done so to the strategically less exposed Hungary, where the Red Army moved in only when the British and Americans, for their own military reasons chose to stay out, ignoring Stalin's prodding to land in the Adriatic and advance toward Hungary from the south."[21]This was a crucial issue because wartime strategy prefigured postwar Soviet political intentions.

As early as 1941, Stalin had made it clear to British foreign secretary Anthony Eden that he regarded Eastern Europe a part of the Soviet sphere of influence. "In the Eastern part of Europe as a whole the role of the USSR shall be taken into consideration as a power waging a great war of liberation [...] and being the greatest factor in the cause of preserving lasting peace in Europe and prevention of new acts of aggression by Germany."[22] Control of adjacent space and enhanced military-industrial capacity were key components of Soviet thinking about the postwar world.[23] Neither Eden, nor anyone else ever seriously contested this claim. In fact, Eden convinced himself that Russia could play a positive role in post-war Europe. In 1943 William Bullitt wrote Roosevelt that Stalin aimed to dominate Europe and if it "meet[s] no obstacle the Soviet Union flows in." Roosevelt was not converted by Bullitt's thesis and hoped to charge Russia with "keeping peace in Europe." Eden said he did not believe Bullitt and advised "to cultivate to the utmost possible extent the friendship and confidence of the Soviet Government."[24]

At the Teheran conference of November–December 1943 Churchill broached his pet idea that the German Reich should be attacked from the direction of southern Europe. This could be done either by reinforcing the Italian front or through a landing on the Adriatic coast. It was to the latter that the Hungarians attached their greatest hopes, not knowing that Churchill "never wished to send an army to the Balkans, but only agents, supplies and commandos to stimulate the intensive guerilla activity there" in the hope of yielding "measureless" results.[25] This issue deeply divided the Allies; both Stalin and Roosevelt favored the second front in Normandy with a complementary operation in southern France. For Roosevelt the prime minister's project raised the specter of alienating the Russians. Churchill argued that if the Allies would land in the Balkans, Turkey would enter the war with the Allies, while Bulgaria, Romania and Hungary would jump out of it. On the other hand he was forced to admit that the Mediterranean campaign would delay Operation Overlord, which had received a green light at the conference in Moscow in October 1943. The United States wanted to stick to the priorities decided at the conference of Quebec and was hostile to the idea of transferring resources to the Mediterranean; Roosevelt insisted on holding only the existing positions, in order to tie down an adequate number of German troops. At the Cairo conference of November 1943 U.S. representatives had opposed military operations in the Balkans and the Aegean, but Churchill managed to postpone the final word on the Teheran conference. Pending final decision, he would have been satisfied with halting the diversion of landing crafts from the Mediterranean. In Teheran

Churchill insisted on accelerating the Italian campaign to Rome, hoped to increase assistance to partisans in the Balkans and advocated the seizure of a bridgehead on the Dalmatian coast, as well as an offensive on Rhodos in January 1944. The prime minister's aim was to reach Rome and then the Pisa–Rimini line in order to be able to turn "left" (toward southern France) or "right," in the direction of the Danube countries through the Ljubljana gap. In view of the topographical difficulties and British strategic priorities the latter may have merely been a theoretical option. What Churchill wanted was to avoid operation Overlord entirely ruling out operations in the Mediterranean, and most importantly, to confront Moscow with a common Anglo-American strategy. Both wishes were to be ignored. Roosevelt, who was out to extract a Soviet promise to enter the war against Japan, would hear of no such thing.

Thus it came as a surprise that at the first plenary session of the Teheran conference on 28 November the unpredictable President proposed "a possible operation at the head of the Adriatic to make a junction with the Partisans under Tito and then to operate northeast into Romania in conjunction with the Soviet advance from the region of Odessa."[26] Churchill seized the opportunity and proposed that a committee be set up to study the plan. Here was a magnificent chance for Stalin to support Churchill in sharing the occupation of the Danube Basin. At this point a British operation in the Balkans would appear to be more realistic than it would a year later. British and American troops were advancing in Italy and the Red Army was still fighting its way through German defenses in western Russia. Although Stalin thought that a landing in the Balkans was better than a campaign through Italy,[27] he would not hear about it. He did not think it wise to scatter the forces in the Mediterranean and declared that a landing in southern France should support Operation Overlord: "It would be better to take Overlord as the basis of all 1944 operations; after the capture of Rome the troops thus relived might be sent to southern France, and in conjunction with forces operating from Corsica might eventually meet in France the main force of Overlord from the north. These would be in the nature of diversionary operations to assist Overlord." There was nothing surprising about the Soviet position. Eden had sounded out Moscow's stance on the second front in October 1943. He cabled to Churchill that "the Soviet Union would brook no change of emphasis or plan: 'Overlord' must go ahead. Molotov and Voroshilov were insistent. I am quite clear," Eden continued, "that they are completely and blindly set on our invading northern France and that there is absolutely nothing that we could suggest in any other part of the world which could reconcile them to the cancellation of or even a postponement of 'Overlord'."[28] Stalin's unequivocal stance in Teheran gave Roosevelt a chance to reiterate his earlier position, by saying that nothing could delay

Overlord, and the Mediterranean operations would do just that.[29] Further-more, Roosevelt thought that a plan should be developed for the operation in southern France. With the fate of his Balkan project apparently sealed, Churchill now saw the Italian campaign endangered as well.

The purpose of the Italian campaign was not to penetrate into the Danube Basin, but to knock Italy out of the war and to tie down the German forces that would replace the Italian units.[30] In Cairo, the British revealed that the campaign in Italy was not meant to reach Rome or the Pisa–Rimini line, but in Teheran it was decided that it should do just that, and 68 landing crafts were placed at the disposal of the drive for Rome. Thus, the fate of the Italian campaign remained unresolved. The British military leader-ship was divided over it. All agreed that it should reach the Pisa–Rimini line, but the Commander-in-Chief of the Allied armies in Italy, Sir Harold Alexander, wanted to extend the operations toward Yugoslavia, an idea that Chief of the British Imperial Staff Alan Brooke did not support. Even so, Churchill planned to divert ten divisions designated for Operation Anvil (the codename for the landing in southern France) to the Adriatic with the purpose of taking Trieste by the end of September. Roosevelt countered by referring to the views of Montgomery and Eisenhower, both of whom were in favor of Operation Anvil. In a message to Churchill on 1 July 1943, Roosevelt claimed he could not survive politically if Overlord suffered even the slightest delay.[31] Churchill appreciated Roosevelt's position, but still hoped to reach Vienna through Yugoslavia. Eventually he seemingly real-ized that the terrain was so difficult that it was impossible to go beyond the River Piave.[32] In this way a mixture of political and military arguments doomed whatever hope the nations of the Danube Basin might have had for being included into the western sphere of influence.

Seeing no better solution to preserve British interests, Churchill decided to divide Eastern Europe into spheres of "responsibility." First, in March 1944 he offered the Soviets a free hand in Romania in return for the same for England in Greece. The Soviet Union was quite receptive to the idea, which hardly came as a surprise. At the first Moscow conference in October 1943 Eden had proposed a "declaration regarding general European respon-sibility as against spheres of responsibility." Deputy Commissar of Foreign Affairs, Maxim Litvinov refused to commit the Soviet Union to such a dec-laration on the grounds that it would "give rise to the belief that there had been some such intention" on the part of the Allies.[33] The percentage agree-ment of the second Moscow conference in October 1944 extended the Soviet sphere of responsibility to Bulgaria and Hungary as well; the two powers shared Yugoslavia, while British predominance in Greece was reaf-firmed. The arrangement with Stalin reflected British views on the future of Eastern Europe. Churchill was ready for concessions in order to preserve

Greece, especially as he already felt that Eastern Europe was slipping from
his hands anyway. In June 1944 the British Post Hostilities Planning Committee predicted that Soviet influence would extend to Poland, Czechoslovakia and Hungary after the war.[34] On the first day of their meeting on
9 October Churchill explained to Stalin what was possibly the chief purpose
of his visit: British interest in Greece. Britain wanted to be the leading power
in the Mediterranean and hoped the Marshal would let the British have "the
first say in Greece in the same way as Marshal Stalin about Romania." As
Stalin agreed, Churchill produced a "naughty document," expressing Soviet
and British political influence in the Balkans in percentages. Churchill
explained "it was better to express things in diplomatic terms, and not to
use the phrase 'dividing into spheres' because the Americans might be
shocked if they saw how crudely he had put it."[35] After the initial agreement between Stalin and Churchill the Soviets, who according to Churchill
took "great interest in Hungary,"[36] wanted to change the fifty–fifty percent
deal on Hungary. Molotov claimed that "Hungary bordered Russia not
Britain." This may well have been a Freudian slip of the tongue since the
Soviet Union soon annexed Rusinsko, a territory that had belonged to
Czechoslovakia prior to 1939, which did in fact give the Soviet Union a
common border with Hungary. Eden, who saw risks inherent in abandoning
Bulgaria altogether,[37] agreed to grant the Soviets predominance in Hungary
in return for a slightly stronger British influence in Bulgaria. Although
Churchill was upset by Eden's horse trading with Molotov, he was happy
about the final outcome of his talks in Moscow, which would allow Britain
"to save Greece."[38]

Already on 31 May 1944 Churchill had informed Roosevelt of his initial proposal to the Soviets on the exchange of Romania for Greece: "the
Soviet government would take the lead in Romanian affairs while we would
take the lead in Greek affairs."[39] The prime minister claimed the Soviets
wanted to be sure that they had United States' consent to the British propo-
sition. He sought to convince Roosevelt by arguing that the arrangement
"would be a natural development of the existing situation since Romania
falls within the sphere of Russian armies and Greece within the Allied command." Somewhat disingenuously Churchill alleged that the Balkans would
not be "carved up into spheres of influence" and the agreement would "not
affect the rights and responsibilities which each of the great powers will
have to exercise at the peace settlement and afterward in regard to the whole
of Europe." The arrangement, the prime minister explained, was devised to
maintain Soviet–British harmony in the Balkans. Roosevelt saw through
Churchill's intentions and was concerned that the Stalin–Churchill deal
would lead to the division of the Balkan region into spheres of influence,
despite the declared intention to limit it to military matters.[40] Churchill's

response revealed the real motive behind his insistence on the "arrange-ment": to have a free hand in Greece and to suppress the EAM movement. British influence in Greece could be preserved, and since the Russians were about to invade Romania, they would "probably do what they wanted any-how." In order to placate Roosevelt, he proposed a trial period of three months.[41] At the end of June Roosevelt, against Hull's advice and at Stalin's insistence, sanctioned the British initiative. Then, praising the percentage agreement, he wrote to Churchill: "It is most pleasing to know that you are reaching a meeting of your two minds as to international policies."[42] Roosevelt's blessing revealed his disinterest: he condoned the agreement two days before being informed of its full content. Roosevelt suspected no foul play from the Soviets' part. Even if he did, he assumed that there was not much that could or should be done about it. Before the meeting in Moscow ended Stalin suggested to Churchill that the British land in the upper Adriatic and join the Red Army in Vienna. Acknowledging that Stalin's offer would have involved the British in difficult fighting across rough terrain, Vojtech Mastny argues that Stalin's offer may have been sin-cere, indicating Soviet willingness to share with the British their control of Hungary. Yet when such an operation had a realistic chance of success, Stalin and the rest of the Soviet leadership adamantly opposed it. Even dur-ing the Moscow conference the Soviets expressed great interest in Hungary and haggled with Eden to gain predominance there. In early October 1944 Stalin had evaded British suggestions for direct coordination of Supreme Allied Commander in the Mediterranean, Maitland Wilson's operations in Hungary and Yugoslavia.[43] In fact an operation in the Adriatic could have reached Vienna without entering Hungary. Moreover, when the offer was made some units of the Second Ukrainian Front were only around a hun-dred kilometers from Budapest. A fortnight later, for "political reasons," Stalin rejected Second Ukrainian Front Commander, Marshal Rodion Mali-novskii's request to regroup before launching his attack on Budapest—no doubt to take the city as a prize for the 7 November celebrations. Finally, the Soviet negotiating position on the Hungarian armistice terms and the Soviet role in the Hungarian ACC indicated that the Soviets were striving for the same conditions as in Romania, where they had already received full control.[44] What may have been Stalin's purpose? Perhaps he was testing Churchill on the percentage agreement. Or his invitation to the British could have been a gesture of goodwill. At Yalta in February 1945 Stalin suggested to Churchill the transfer of some British divisions from Italy to Hungary and Yugoslavia, in order to direct them against Vienna. Churchill wrote later: "it cost him nothing to say this now, but I made no reproaches. 'The Red Army' I answered 'may not give us time to complete the operation'."[45]

Be that as it may, the ball was on the Soviet side. If they wanted the small nations of Eastern Europe to be independent it was up to them to grant it. Alternatively, if they so desired, they could dominate them with little or no opposition. U.S. chargé d'affaires in Moscow, George Kennan summarized the political dilemma: "the Kremlin finds itself committed by its own inclination to the concrete goal of becoming the dominant power of East-Central Europe. At the same time it also finds itself committed by [...] past promises [...] The first of these programs implies taking. The second implies giving. No one can stop Russia from doing the taking...no one can force Russia to do the giving."[46]

Romania, Hungary and Bulgaria were not strategically significant enough for the British or the Americans to put the Grand Alliance at risk. Their importance was, however, *temporarily* elevated by the final assault on Germany. They could be induced to make trouble for the Germans, who would be forced to divert troops from the western theatre to keep them at bay, hence reducing the number of units available to fight the advancing Anglo-Americans. If, for example, Budapest could be induced to jump out of the war by the application of the carrot and the stick formula, Berlin would surely decide to hold it down with forces that would otherwise fight in France. In a nutshell, Hungary and the rest of the minor satellites were unimportant in themselves, but for a short time became militarily significant: by deserting their German ally they could reduce German resistance and hasten Allied victory over Germany.

Allied interest, it was believed, would be greatly enhanced by a German invasion of Hungary. In a callous analysis the British Joint Planning Staff Committee opined that a German invasion of Hungary would suit British interest well. During the time it would take for Germany to prepare, collect the necessary forces and occupy the country, it would receive no benefit from Hungary, and would be hard pressed to maintain its forces in the Balkans. "Moreover the diversion of German forces for the invasion and occupation of Hungary might result in a dangerous weakening of the German position elsewhere."[47] It was clear that if the Hungarian government carried out the British terms of the preliminary armistice, a German occupation of it would ensue. In a similar vein, on 23 August 1943, a day after the Joint Planning Staff Committee completed its own study, the deputy chief of the British staff prepared a memorandum for the chief of staff, Sir Alan Brooke, arguing that Hungary's capitulation would cause political and military difficulty in Germany. Furthermore, if Romania were to follow suit, Germany would be left with a crisis that could only be solved by the occupation of Hungary. If Germany would take the risk and pull out troops from elsewhere to invade Hungary, the consequent weakening of her position in other theatres would be to Britain's advantage. The deputy chief recognized that in such an eventuality no assistance could be given to Hungary.[48]

Churchill was also well aware of the advantages a break between Germany and her allies would bring. He wrote to Roosevelt that the Germans obviously attached great importance to the eastern zone and would not hesitate to divert a major part of their strategic air force to maintain their position there. Germany feared Hungary and Romania's desertion and a "violent schism" in Bulgaria. "When we remember what brilliant results have followed from the potential reactions in Italy induced by our military efforts" —Churchill continued—"should we not be short sighted to ignore the possibility of a similar or even greater landslide in some or all the countries I have mentioned? If we were able to provoke such reactions and profit by them, our joint task in Italy would be greatly lightened."[49]

When the Hungarians signed the preliminary armistice agreement with the British on 9 September 1943, the British agreed to allow the Hungarians to keep the agreement secret until it was safe to publish it. The Hungarian government was told to accept unconditional surrender at the "earliest possible moment." This was in response to the concerns sounded by the Hungarian peace-feelers that drastic action against the Germans could provoke a German invasion of Hungary, which in turn could lead to the liquidation of the Jewish population in Hungary. The historian Lewis Namier warned the Foreign Office that if the Hungarian government should prematurely break with Germany, the Germans would respond by invading Hungary and would annihilate the last remaining significant Jewish community in Europe. The only hope for the Jews was if the Hungarians did nothing until the Germans were unable to react. Denis Allen of the Foreign Office commented that "we have always paid a great deal of attention" to this issue as one of the main reasons for not urging the Hungarians to oppose the Germans openly, although the chance for a German invasion was in Allen's view slight.[50] As for the Soviet position, the Hungarians were not to be given any alternative to immediate unconditional surrender. The British agreed to a less drastic line in recognition of the fact that the Budapest government would not surrender in absence of a reasonable prospect of Allied protection against German reprisal. Immediate surrender would not be in the best interest of the Allies since it would merely lead to a German occupation of Hungary and the establishment of a Quisling government. Churchill and the chiefs of staff insisted on this position[51] even though at the Moscow meeting of foreign ministers in October 1943 Molotov insisted that a half measure by the British government could only interfere with the purpose of unconditional surrender.[52] Eden thought that the Russians should dictate Allied policy toward Hungary.[53] W. Harrison of the Foreign Office added that the tardiness of the Hungarians in implementing their offer of unconditional surrender can be explained by developments in the war since the beginning of September and particularly the not very encouraging example of Italy.

Allied forces, he wrote, "are too far away and it would be foolish in present circumstances to expect any sudden developments in Hungary." Nonetheless, the high ranking official of the Foreign Office opined that "there seems to be great force in arguments originally put forward by the prime minister and Chiefs of Staff that we should delay Hungarian volte-face until it can be *best fitted into our military plans*"[54] (emphasis added). The best timing to provoke the announcement on Hungarian unconditional surrender was for it to coincide with the invasion of Europe.[55] In November Admiral William D. Leahy, Roosevelt's personal representative on the Chiefs of Staff Committee, informed Freeman Matthews from the State Department of the Joint Chiefs' position: militarily it would significantly further the Allied cause if either Hungary or Romania, or even both, were to pull out of the war even though that would probably result in Germany occupying the two countries.[56] On 11 December 1943 the American government officially called upon Bulgaria, Hungary and Romania to withdraw from Germany's side in the war.[57]

Initially the Allies appreciated the dangers of Hungary turning openly against the Germans and gave instructions accordingly. Later, Allied intelligence and diplomatic representatives sought to convince the Hungarian peace-feelers that Hungary should demonstrate its goodwill toward the Allies with active subversion of the German war effort. On 23 May 1943 a representative of the British Foreign Office informed a Hungarian diplomat in Switzerland, György Barcza, that England did not expect Hungary to do anything that would provoke German occupation and in view of the consequences, "could not imagine Hungary jumping out" of the war. In contrast, less than three months later, on 5 August, the same person told Barcza that Hungary "should immediately follow Italy's example (i.e. jump out) shouldering the risks. If Hungary failed to draw the consequences of this situation it would mean that it was once more siding with the Germans. It would thereby forever lose her chance of being handled differently from Germany by the victors [...] (Hungary) should take this step even at the risk of temporary German occupation."[58] The same message was communicated to Barcza by an OSS representative in Berne, Royall Tyler, on 28 August 1943. Tyler, who had spent time in Hungary as the financial representative of the League of Nations, wished to persuade the Hungarians that they should withdraw their troops from Russia and turn against the Germans. The last moment for Hungary to jump out of the war "without harm would come with the Italian armistice."[59] The next day a Soviet diplomat, with whom the Hungarians sought contact to sound out the Russian terms for a separate agreement, told his interlocutor, Ferenc Honti, that there was only one option for Hungary: to break with Germany. This would risk a German invasion of the country for a while, but was a risk well worth taking. The most suitable and least risky opportunity in the Soviet diplomat's view would be at the same time as the Anglo-American landing in Normandy.[60] The possible ramifications of German invasion: the destruction of Hungarian democratic elements and Europe's last intact Jewish community seemed to pale in comparison with the strategic advantage to the Allies that could be derived from it. In fact a peace-feeler, former President of the Hungarian National Bank Lipót Baranyai, reported to the Hungarian Foreign Ministry that when he tried to explain the dangers of a German invasion to the OSS representatives in Switzerland, Allen Dulles and Royall Tyler, they told him "there was a war on, we are up to our necks in blood, a few hundred thousand lives here and there will not make a difference."[61]

After the Teheran conference the Allies accepted a plan, Operation Bodyguard, the aim of which in part was to tie down German forces in South Eastern Europe by convincing the Germans that the Allies would land in the Balkans, as well as to induce Hitler's satellites to jump out of the war. Thereby the attention of the German forces would be distracted from the 'Overlord' area, and the satellites would be encouraged to carry out acts of sabotage. Under Operation Zeppelin, the component of Bodyguard that referred to the south east European area, Hitler was led to believe that the Allies intended to march on Germany through the Ljubljana Gap and that the otherwise no longer existing 7th U.S. army under Patton was planning to land near Trieste.[62] Hitler did in fact come to believe in the prospect of a Balkan landing. This view is supported by a contemporary British intelligence report, according to which German troop concentration prior to the invasion of Hungary "show(s) anxiety regarding the whole German military position in South Eastern Europe rather than any increased suspicions regarding Hungarian unreliability."[63]

In the initial stage, the German military leadership worked out plans to occupy western Hungary up to the River Tisza and to seal it from eastern Hungary. The occupation of eastern Hungary, where there were two Hungarian armies capable of opening the frontier to the Soviets, was not initially planned, indicating that the immediate reason for the German occupation of Hungary was that the Germans expected the Allies to attack from Trieste. It was only in the second stage of the German invasion that eastern Hungary was occupied in order to defend the Carpathians. German foreign minister Ribbentrop claimed that Germany occupied Hungary because they expected parachute divisions to land in Hungary.[64] Bodyguard worked well, at least from the perspective of the Allies. An after-action report of cover and deception operations in Europe noted that Hitler stripped France of three of his best divisions. Hitler claimed on 31 August 1944 that if he had had the SS Panzer Korps in the West on D-Day, this invasion "would probably have never occurred."[65]

Following the German invasion Prime Minister Kállay fled to the Turkish embassy in Budapest and Regent Horthy appointed a puppet government under Döme Sztójay. Political opposition was stifled; anti-German elements were either arrested, or went into hiding. Jews were rounded up and deported with full speed. As a result of the German occupation and the lack of armed resistance thereto, the British lifted the bombing ban that had been in effect for Hungary, since the "Quisling government" could no longer be expected to deny the Germans the use of strategic railroads. Both the British and the Americans encouraged the Hungarians and the other satellites to turn against Germany, arguing that by doing so they could gain the sympathy of the United Nations when the war ended. Facing the rapid approach of the Red Army, however, Horthy had no other choice but to turn to the Soviets. This was a prudent move, since Eden's summary of the Western position was, "We do not wish to move a finger" for the Hungarians.

Facing the Nemesis

In the summer of 1944 Regent Horthy embarked on his final attempt to change his nation's course. He dismissed Sztójay and sent a mission to the Commander-in-Chief of the Mediterranean, General Maitland Wilson, to offer surrender and to secure Anglo-American participation in Hungary's occupation. Simultaneously, Horthy finally brought himself to contact the Russians. There was a new urgency to do this since Romania surrendered on 23 August. The strategic consequence of this surrender was that the Red Army was effectively free to advance on Hungary. In this desperate situation the Regent's spirits were significantly raised by a letter that his emissary received in September from Lieutenant-Colonel Makarov, who acted as the political commissar of the Ukrainian partisan units in Slovakia, and claimed to represent the Soviet government.

The letter purported to contain Moscow's conditions for an armistice agreement with favorable terms, no doubt to hasten the collapse of Hungarian military resistance and to strengthen the Hungarian resolve to break with the Germans. There would be no allied bombing of Hungary until the armistice delegation arrived in Moscow. Hungary's full integrity would be guaranteed. The Soviet Union would support a plebiscite on the fate of Transylvania. In areas where the Hungarians did not support the Germans the Soviets would allow an independent Hungarian military and civil administration to operate. Neither the army, nor the police nor the gendarmerie would be disarmed. Hungary's independence would be guaranteed and would be free to choose its own system of government. The letter stated that the Soviet Union had no desire to expand in Europe.[66] Yet, when the delegation headed by General Gábor Faragho arrived in Moscow with Horthy's personal letter to Stalin seeking an armistice, they were in for an unpleasant surprise: Commissar of Foreign Affairs, Viacheslav Molotov disclaimed any knowledge of the Makarov letter. Makarov, whoever he may have been, had apparently acted without the authorization of the Soviet government or the military authorities.

After unsuccessful consultations with General Kuznetsov, Soviet Deputy Chief of Staff Antonov received the Hungarian delegation on 5 October. The Hungarians informed the general that Hungary was ready to terminate military operations against the Soviet Union and to fight against Germans. Soviet forces would be allowed to maneuver in Hungary without constraints. Hungary's conditions were firstly that the Red Army should occupy Budapest as soon as possible, and secondly that the Romanians should not be allowed to participate in the occupation of Hungary. Antonov revealed the Soviet terms, which contained no trace of Makarov's conditions. Hungary was expected to evacuate all territories acquired after the 31 December 1937 within ten days after the reception of this declaration. An inter-allied committee would be sent to Hungary under Soviet chairmanship. Budapest had to severe all relations with Germany and declare war on it, with which the Soviet units would be ready to assist.[67] There was no word about guarantees for territorial integrity, the freedom to choose the nation's future government or any plebiscite on the fate of Transylvania.[68] The next day Molotov consulted with the British and the U.S. ambassadors in Moscow and sought out their views on the Soviet proposals. Both sets of representatives approved of them and sent for further instructions from London and Washington. On 11 October the Faragho delegation affirmed that the Hungarian government was willing to accept the preliminary conditions, but requested a delay of three days to declare war on Germany, while Hungarian army units would be deployed to Budapest. Molotov agreed, and on the same day the Hungarians signed the preliminary armistice agreement. However, this agreement was never carried out. Horthy's coup of 15 October was poorly organized and executed, and failed miserably. The Germans had been counting on it and managed to foil it with the assistance of their sympathizers in the Hungarian army. The SS stormed Horthy's residence and Hitler's plenipotentiary in Hungary, Edmund Veesenmayer, forced the regent to resign and to appoint the leader of the Arrow Cross, Ferenc Szálasi, as the head of state. Horthy was politically finished. Moscow would have been willing to keep him in power at least temporarily, but when he rescinded power to Szálasi, Stalin declared that Horthy had committed political suicide—"shot himself in the head," as he put it. A new "source of power" (istochnik vlasti) had to be found, who would be ready and able to sign Hungary's armistice. Moscow continued to accept the credentials of the Horthy mission, which participated in the formulation of the Armistice Agreement and the establishment of the Provisional Government. But from this point the Hungarian Communists in Moscow joined in the discussions and there was not a shadow of doubt that they would constitute a crucial element in the new political establishment. Molotov later claimed that the Soviet government "took an active part in forming the first government of Hungary in 1945. We formed it quickly enough."[69]

The negotiations began on the basis of the proposals put forward by General János Vörös, the former Chief of Staff of the Hungarian Army, who arrived in Moscow on 7 November. Molotov agreed with the Hungarian proposal to set up a Provisional Government under the leadership of General Béla Miklós Dálnoki. On 6 December the representatives of the Hungarian Communists in Moscow, Ernő Gerő and Imre Nagy met with the members of the Horthy delegation and Molotov to discuss the makeup of the government.

In the meantime, the democratic parties of Hungary began to reestablish themselves in the liberated territories of the country. Britain and the United States were eager to carry on with the preparations of the armistice and on 2 December the State Department designated the United States' future diplomatic representative in Hungary, well before the other Allies. In the Soviet-occupied territories of Hungary the Communist Gerő conferred with the representatives of the various political parties on the future government, but they made no concrete arrangements. Back in Moscow the Hungarian Communists negotiated with Molotov, as well as with deputy foreign commissar Vladimir Dekanozov and the future Soviet political representative in Hungary, Georgii Maksimovich Pushkin. On a number of occasions Stalin joined the discussions in order to sort out contentious issues and no doubt to assert his authority. One problematic issue was whether Hungary should have a Provisional Government or only a National Committee like the French. Originally the arrangement was that there would be a government headed by General Béla Miklós, the former commander of the First Hungarian Army who had gone over to the Soviets after Horthy's aborted coup. His government would be set up in Hungary, but the composition would be compiled in Moscow, and it would assist the Allied war effort. Molotov made it clear that while the war was being waged, the Provisional National Government would operate under the guidance of the Red Army, and would carry out the intentions of the Soviet authorities.[70]

A counter-proposal for a National Committee was prepared by the two officials responsible for Hungarian affairs, Pushkin and Béla Geiger. This came in response to a new Hungarian proposal presented to the Soviet Government on 27 November. The essence of this proposal was that the Smallholder Party, together with the left wing parties, the Social Democrats and the Communists should set up a Provisional Government under the leadership of the Smallholder Zoltán Tildy. This government would be composed in Debrecen, rather than Moscow, and the ministers would be appointed by the designated prime minister. Horthy would continue to be accepted as Hungary's head of state. In his absence he would be substituted by a Regency Council and the Regent's Representative. This proposal was obviously unacceptable to the Soviets, firstly because they would have been deprived of their influence on the government's composition and secondly because the Muscovite Communists would have been excluded from the government. As a counter-proposal Pushkin and Geiger recommended a National Front or Committee, partly because there was no list of candidates acceptable to Moscow, and partly because they thought that there would be tension between a cabinet made up of pro-Horthy ministers and Muscovite Communists on one hand and the Soviet authorities on the other. To complicate matters, the British and the Americans would have a chance to send their diplomatic representatives, which had the potential to cause further problems. But Stalin did not like the Geiger–Pushkin proposal. He ruled that "if Szálasi had a government, then the democratic forces could not afford to have a simple National Committee without any powers."[71] A simple National Committee would create a carte blanche for future political developments, whereas a Soviet-designed government could set Hungary's political course.

When the choice between a National Committee and a government was made, the government needed a program. Moscow's overriding priority was to induce the Hungarians to turn against the Germans as rapidly as possible in order to assist the Soviet military campaign in Hungary, which was facing stiff resistance. Therefore Stalin wanted to make the government appealing to as many people as possible, even if it meant the temporary suspension of ideological premises. He provided the guidance himself: the government program had to emphasize the protection of "small people's private initiative and the maintenance of private initiative in general." Flexibility would be shown in the question of land reform—a promise that the Soviets broke only a few months later. Revealing the true motives of his moderation Stalin instructed the Communists "not to be sparing with words, not to scare anyone. But once you gain strength you may press on [...] move as many people as possible who may be useful."[72] At Soviet instruction the government program included the promise that "The Provisional National Government regards private ownership as the basis of the country's economic and social order and will assure its inviolability." Stalin was at that point pursuing a popular front policy in so far as he encouraged Western European Communist parties to join coalition governments. Stalin's instructions to the Hungarian Communists has led one historian to speculate that the Soviet leader "initially regarded the countries of that region [Eastern Europe] subject to the same conditions of development as the West European countries liberated by the Americans and the British."[73] Stalin's wording—"once you gain strength you may press on"—and subsequent events in Hungary cast a shadow of doubt on the assertion that Stalin may have been looking towards a very slow progress towards socialism in the territories his armies had come to occupy. In fact the opposite may have been true. Stalin followed popular front strategy to divide and render ineffective local opposition and to minimize Western objection to the creeping establishment of Communist-dominated regimes subjected to Moscow, lest the USSR be drawn into premature conflict with its allies and forfeit the advantages of association with them.[74]

The new government was made up of the Hungarian generals that negotiated in Moscow, the representatives of the Communists, the Smallholders, the Social Democrats and the National Peasant Party as well as Erik Molnár, who allegedly had no party membership, but in reality was a clandestine Communist. Moscow insisted that Ferenc Erdei of the National Peasant Party receive the Ministry of the Interior even though the Smallholders claimed that post for themselves. Erdei, a talented sociologist, had long been a Communist sympathizer and even wanted to enter the Communist Party in late 1944, but was advised that the Communist cause would be better served if he stayed in the peasant party. In December the Provisional National Assembly was convened in Debrecen, the former seat of Lajos Kossuth's revolutionary government of 1849. Almost forty percent of the deputies were Communist Party members. This new legislature declared war on Germany, while Szálasi's parliament was still in session and some Hungarian units were actively engaged in fighting the Russians. All that remained to be done was to sign an Armistice Agreement, which Stalin considered to be the new government's priority, and to cleanse the country of the Germans.

The most contentious issue between the U.S. and the Soviets was the modus operandi of the Allied Control Commission (ACC) and the way Hungary would pay reparations. Learning from the Romanian and Bulgarian examples the U.S. wanted to ensure greater influence in the Hungarian ACC. Originally the U.S. wanted the three Allied governments to have "equal participation in the work of the Commission," while the Soviets wanted the ACC to work under "the general direction of the Allied (Soviet) High Command."[75] Eventually it was agreed that the Soviet Chairman would have to consult with the British and the American representatives before issuing an instruction to the Hungarian authorities. It is a different matter that the Soviets never complied with the provision. The Soviets wanted a fixed amount of reparations from all Axis countries. In Hungary's case

Moscow wanted $400 million, to be divided among the USSR, Yugoslavia and Czechoslovakia with the Soviet share to be $300 million.[76] Based on the German experience after World War I the U.S. government did not want to fix the amount in advance, so as not to exceed the Hungarian economy's productive capability. Instead an amount would be determined annually in the function of Hungary's capacity to pay.[77] Washington argued that reparations should not have the effect of destroying Hungary's national economy. The British had more sympathy with the Soviet case and accused the Americans of having more sympathy with the Hungarians' standard of living than the needs of their most important ally. Eventually as a compromise the Allies agreed in a concrete sum of $300 million, which was $100 million lower that the Soviets originally wanted. All the participants agreed that Budapest could furnish this amount without impairing the national economy.

The Hungarian Armistice Agreement was signed in Moscow on 20 January 1945. It was based on the armistice agreements with Romania and Bulgaria, which is shown by the somewhat careless wording. Thus, for example, Hungary was required to furnish naval units for Soviet use. Being a landlocked country Hungary was hardly in a position to oblige. The Hungarians were compelled to set up eight infantry units with heavy weapons and to place them at the Red Army's disposal. These were in actual fact provided, but the Soviets never used them, although the Hungarian government requested them to do so. Some of the articles were loosely worded, and Moscow took advantage of them. Article 11 for instance determined that Hungary would place at the disposal of the Allied (Soviet) High Command such currency and goods (fuel and foodstuffs) as may be required for it to carry out its functions. This provision served as the legal pretext for the maintenance of the whole Soviet army stationed in Hungarian territory. Article 12 dealt with reparations—$200 million worth of goods were destined to the Soviets, 100 million worth to Czechoslovakia and Yugoslavia together. The Allies agreed that the Hungarian commodities would be valued according to 1938 prices plus a ten–fifteen percent bonus. Soviet authorities made use of the loose wording to extract an almost unlimited amount of goods, since the clause failed to clarify how the 1938 prices should be determined. The agreement was very specific, however, in the sense that Hungary would have to pull back behind its 1937 boundaries, that the Vienna Awards of 1938 and 1940 were regarded null and void. There was no ambiguity regarding the fact that the Allied Control Commission would be headed by the Soviet representative.

The ACC operated as an organ of the Soviet military command and was subordinated to it. The Hungarian government was allowed to communicate with the Western members of the Council through the Soviet chairman only. Lacking clear provisions as to the duration of its function, the

ACC played a decisive role in Hungary's political and economic life until 15 September 1947, when the Peace Treaty came into force. By then Hungary was firmly ensconced in the Soviet zone. The ACC was entitled to collect information on all aspects of political life; the Hungarian government or the local authorities were obliged to seek the ACC's preliminary approval for each measure they intended to bring into force. The prime minister and the minister of foreign affairs served as the liaison between the ACC and the government; committee meetings were held on issues like reparation payments under the chairmanship of an ACC representative, who conveyed the instructions of the Soviet Union on the given problem. The British and American representatives were by and large neglected, to the extent that the Chairman, Kliment Voroshilov did not bother to convene a meeting with them for over a month. To a certain extent the Potsdam conference improved the situation, at least in theory, by increasing Western influence in the Bulgarian, Romanian and Hungarian ACCs.[78]

The Soviet Union rightfully regarded Hungary an enemy, which had to be occupied, not liberated. In the course of the bitter fighting in the siege of Budapest alone, the Red Army lost 80 thousand men, with a further 240 thousand wounded. They lost twice as many in taking the whole country, while the combined German–Hungarian casualties were about 60 percent of the Soviet losses. Beside the stubborn resistance mounted by SS General Pfeffen von Wildenbruch, the catastrophic Soviet losses in the siege of Budapest were caused by Stalin's politically motivated decision to take the Hungarian capital as rapidly as possible, disregarding Marshal Malinovskii's opinion. The deputy political commissar of the 4th Ukrainian Front, Colonel-General Mekhlis, who gave an optimistic assessment of the military situation, raised Stalin's hopes. Mekhlis, who was incompetent in matters of military strategy, reported that the Hungarian units were in the state of disintegration facing the Russian army. Although Chief-of-Staff Antonov stated that Mekhlis's claims were not indicative of the general situation, Stalin ordered immediate attack. In a telephone conversation Malinovskii informed Stalin that five days would be necessary for the necessary reinforcements to arrive, to which Stalin declared: "the headquarters cannot give you five days. Understand that because of political considerations we must take Budapest as rapidly as possible." Malinovskii insisted that he needed five days, claiming that in that case he would take Budapest in another five days, otherwise he would be unable to occupy the city. But the Vozhd' remained adamant: "I decisively command you to launch your attack on Budapest immediately" and slammed down the phone.[79] This episode reveals that Stalin remained well in control of the army.[80]

Fueled by thirst for revenge and incited by propaganda, many, though not all, Russian units conducted themselves as barbarians and committed atrocities against the prisoners of war and the civilian population. Their ire was directed mostly against SS men and Russian units that fought with the Wehrmacht. In many cases they tortured and executed such captives. Hence for instance Soviet soldiers shot the wounded, non-German speaking patients of a military hospital in Budapest. They threw hand grenades into the hospital's rooms, raped and stabbed several nurses. On one occasion they beat up POWs of Russian and Ukrainian nationality with swords and then executed them. In some instances they would kill German soldiers who had surrendered. Members of the SS and wounded men were forced to dig their own graves before their execution. These atrocities were not committed systematically; neither were the perpetrators acting according to a preconceived plan.[81] Instead, they were subjected to intensive official propaganda that dehumanized the enemy and called on the members of the Soviet armed forces not to spare them. On many occasions the Russians killed Arrow Cross party activists—who themselves were on a killing rampage—when they caught them. Sometimes Hungarian prisoners were spared by kindly Soviet officers. In January 1945 Marshall Malinovskii issued a decree that prohibited the killing of civilians and prisoners.[82] At the same time he had 50 thousand civilians rounded up in the course of February so as to produce the contingent of prisoners he promised to the Soviet high command and permitted his men three days' free looting in Budapest.[83] The writer Sándor Márai recalled that the Russians were "childlike, sometimes wild, sometimes edgy and melancholy, always unpredictable [...] Nearly all Russians were gentle and kind with children. Somehow it was in this, their feelings about children, that they preserved their inner bent for humanness."[84] The Soviet conduct caused despair in the midst of even those who welcomed them. The Communists of a working class district in Budapest reported that the Russians raped mothers in front of their husbands and children, with ten–fifteen soldiers raping a single woman. They shot fathers and sons, looted factories and robbed livestock. According to an eyewitness, their actions "outdid the wildest propaganda."[85]

The Nazi rampage and the ensuing Soviet occupation regime created chaotic conditions that were conducive for the construction of new structures of power. It was the Communist Party that was best able to exploit the turmoil to its advantage. Still, Hungary's prospects seemed somewhat brighter than that of Poland or Bulgaria. In Poland, the Soviet-backed Lublin government was comprised of Polish Communists delivered from Moscow, and declared itself the provisional national government of Poland in late December 1944. Within a month Moscow granted it diplomatic recognition despite Western protest. The former political elite of Bulgaria, including members of parliament, were arrested and tried in December 1944. Death sentences were meted out to one hundred defendants, all of which were executed on the same night. As the end of the war was approaching, Hungary had a coalition government and political parties of various persuasions were organizing and preparing for the arduous road to power that lay ahead.

When the war ended the traditional Hungarian political elite was shattered. Hungary had not witnessed such drastic economic, political and social change since the Middle Ages. The ruling class that led the country into war was incapable of delivering Hungary from the German alliance. As the pro-British elements of the Hungarian government slowly realized, Hungary was becoming part of the Soviet sphere of interest by late 1943. Roosevelt wanted to preserve Stalin's cooperation after the war even if it meant Soviet domination in Eastern Europe; Churchill wanted to save Greece and thereby to preserve Great Britain's status as the predominant Mediterranean power. The price was Soviet predominance in the Danube Basin. What this meant for Hungary will be examined in the next chapter.

NOTES

1 All of the following conditions applied for Hungary: when the offensive power permits rapid conquest, vulnerable states may see little hope in resisting, and bandwagon because balancing alliances are not viable; weak neighbors of great powers are more likely to bandwagon than to balance; states are tempted to bandwagon when allies are not available; the more aggressive a state's perceived intention is, the less likely others will align against it; the more similar two or more states are, the more likely they are to ally. See Stephen Walt: *The Origins of Alliances* (Ithaca: Cornell University Press, 1987), pp. 25–34.

2 On American prospects for post war Soviet–American cooperation see John Lewis Gaddis, *The United States and the Origins of the Cold War* (New York: Columbia University Press, 1972); on the transformation of the Soviet Union's image into a trustworthy and respectable ally see: Amos Perlmutter, *FDR and Stalin—A Not So Grand Alliance, 1943–1945* (Columbia and London: University of Missouri Press, 1993). For a variety of reasons including the perceived democratizing trend within Russia American diplomats remained hopeful of continued U.S.–Soviet cooperation. By the close of 1944 U.S. diplomats were predisposed to view Soviet behavior in the liberated countries of Eastern Europe as confirmatory evidence of the Kremlin's adherence to the envisioned liberal-democratic world order. See Hugh DeSantis, *The Diplomacy of Silence—The American Foreign Service, the Soviet Union and the Cold War, 1933–1947* (Chicago, London: The University of Chicago Press, 1979).

3 John Lamberton Harper, *American Visions of Europe—Franklin Delano Roosevelt, George F. Kennan, Dean G. Acheson* (Cambridge: Cambridge University Press, 1994), p. 89.

4 Quoted by Keith Sainsbury, *The Turning Point* (Oxford, New York, 1987), p. 149.

5 See John Kent, "British Postwar Planning for Europe" in Antonio Varsori and Elena Calandri eds., *The Failure of Peace in Europe, 1943–1948* (Palgrave, 2002), p. 42.

6 Cited in Martin Gilbert, *Road to Victory—Winston S. Churchill 1941–1945* (London: Heinemann, 1986), pp. 999–1000.

7 In Teheran the three Allied leaders agreed that a "cover plan to mystify and mislead the enemy [...] should be concerted." See Elisabeth Barker, *British Policy in South-East Europe in the Second World War* (London and Basingstoke: The MacMillan Press Ltd., 1976), p. 121.

8 For American perceptions of Horthy see Tibor Frank, "Diplomatic Images of Admiral Horthy—The American Perception of Interwar Hungary" in Tibor Frank, *Ethnicity, Propaganda, Myth-Making: Studies in Hungarian Connections to Britain and America, 1848–1945* (Budapest: Akadémiai Kiadó, 1999).

9 See Thomas Sakmyster, *Hungary's Admiral on Horseback—Miklós Horthy, 1918–1994* (Boulder: East European Monographs, 1994), p. 150. A French officer, General Graziani observed that "l'apprehension du Bolchevisme domine l'Amiral." It is interesting to note that Winston Churchill used similarly harsh language to describe the Soviet system.

10 Nicholas Kallay, *Hungarian Premier—A Personal Account of a Nation's Struggle in the Second World War* (New York, 1954).

11 Kallay, *Hungarian Premier,* pp. 349–350.

12 Aladár Szegedy-Maszák, *Az ember ősszel visszanéz... Egy volt magyar diplomata emlékiratából* [One looks back in Fall... From the memoirs of a Hungarian diplomat], vol. 2 (Budapest: Európa-História, 1996), p. 189 and p. 231.

13 See Gyula Juhász, *Magyar–brit titkos tárgyalások 1943-ban* [Hungarian–British secret talks in 1943] (Budapest: Kossuth, 1978), pp. 63–65.

14 Wodianer jelentése a külügyminiszternek [Wodianer's report to the foreign minister], Magyar Országos Levéltár (Hungarian National Archives, hereafter cited as MOL), Külügyminisztérium (Ministry of Foreign Affairs, hereafter cited as Küm), 192, Pol. A report from the pro-German Hungarian minister in Ankara claimed that in Eastern Europe "every country will be Bolshevized." Vörnle jelentése a Külügyminiszternek [Vörnle's report to the foreign minister], 23 November 1943, MOL, 179/Pol.

15 Some contact was made with the Soviets in Stockholm in 1943, but nothing was achieved.

16 Quoted by Stephen D. Kertesz, *Between Russia and the West*, p. 77.

17 Based on his conversation with the Polish envoy in Lisbon Wodianer came to believe that the western Allies regarded Hungary as a second line of defense against Russian expansion. Szegedy-Maszák, *Az ember ősszel visszanéz*, p. 181.

18 Kallay, *Hungarian Premier*, p. 382.

19 See Lamberton Harper, *American Visions of Europe*, pp. 81–82. On 1 October 1943 Roosevelt told Zita Habsburg, Charles Habsburg's widow that he would like to curb Russian expansion but if the Russians wanted to do so the West cannot oppose it and cannot wage war against them because "we are not strong enough not to be the Russians' friends." Szegedy-Maszák, *Az ember ősszel visszanéz*, p. 316.

20 Quoted in Robert Murphy's telegram to the secretary of state, 21 July 1944. Cited in Péter Sipos – István Vida, "The Policy of the United States towards Hungary During the Second World War," *Acta Historica Scientiarum Hungaricae* 29 (1), 1983, p. 82.

21 Vojtech Mastny, "Soviet Plans for Postwar Europe," in Varsoria and Calandri eds., *The Failure of Peace in Europe*, p. 68. Earlier Mastny had written that Stalin seemed prepared to share with the West the liberation of Hungary. On 14 October 1944 Stalin suggested to Churchill that the British land in the upper Adriatic and join the Red Army in Vienna. Vojtech Mastny, *Russia's Road to the Cold War* (New York: Columbia University Press, 1979), p. 211.

22 *War and Diplomacy—The Making of the Grand Alliance. Documents from Stalin's Archives*, Edited with a Commentary by Oleg A. Rzheshevsky (U.K.: Harwood Academic Publishers), Document 6., p. 26.

23 See Ralph B. Levering, Vladimir O. Pechatnov, Verena Botzenhart-Viehe and C. Earl Edmondson, *Debating the Origins of the Cold War—American and Russian Perspectives* (Lanham, Boulder, Oxford, New York: Rowman and Littlefield Publishers Inc., 2002), p. 90.

24 Lamberton Harper, *American Visions of Europe*, pp. 93–96.

25 Churchill to Roosevelt, 7 October 1943, in Warren F. Kimball ed., *Churchill and Roosevelt—The Complete Correspondence*, vol. 2, pp. 498–499.

26 First Plenary Meeting, 28 November 1943, Bohlen minutes, *Foreign Relations of the United States*, The Conferences at Cairo and Teheran, 1943, p. 493. (hereinafter referred to as FRUS with appropriate year and volume numbers).

27 Stalin said at the first plenary meeting, "[...] despite the fact the heart of Germany is far from the Balkans, it would be a better area from which to launch an attack on Italy." The statement appears in the Combined Chiefs of Staff minutes, but not in the Bohlen ones. Ibid., p. 501.

28 Eden to Churchill, 21 October 1943. Cited in Gilbert, *Road to Victory*, pp. 536–537.

29 The first plenary session, Bohlen minutes. *FRUS,* The Conferences at Cairo and Teheran, pp. 494–495.

30 David Hunt, "British Military Planning and Aims in 1944," in Barker, Deakin and Chadwick eds., *British Political and Military Strategy in Central and Eastern Europe* (London, 1989), p. 30.

31 For the controversy over the campaign in Italy see: Robin Edmonds, *The Big Three—Churchill, Roosevelt and Stalin* (London: Hamish Hamilton, 1991).

32 Hunt, *British Military Plans and Aims in 1944*.

33 U.S. Delegation Minutes of the Final Meeting of Moscow, 30 October 1943. *FRUS,* Conferences at Cairo and Teheran, pp. 130–131.

34 Elizabeth Barker, "Problems of Alliance—Misconceptions and Misunderstanding," in *British Military and Political Strategy.*

35 See Gilbert, *Road to Victory*, pp. 991–992.

36 Churchill's telegram to Hopkins, 12 October 1944. Ibid., p. 1005.

37 In September 1944 Eden wrote to Churchill, "if we abandon Bulgaria [...] our credit would suffer throughout the Balkans." Cited in Barker, *British Policy in South-East Europe During the Second World War*, p. 143.

38 Churchill's letter to Attlee, 3 December 1944, in Gilbert, *Road to Victory*, p. 1028.
39 Churchill to Roosevelt, 31 May 1944, in Warren Kimball, ed., *Churchill and Roosevelt—The Complete Correspondence*, vol. 3, pp. 153–154.
40 Roosevelt to Churchill, 10 June 1944. Ibid., p. 177.
41 Churchill to Roosevelt, 11 June 1944, Ibid., pp. 178–179.
42 Roosevelt to Stalin and Churchill, 11 October 1944. Ibid., p. 352.
43 Barker, *British Policy in South-East Europe During the Second World War*, p. 121.
44 See for example The Secretary of State to the Ambassador in the Soviet Union, 14 October 1944, midnight. *FRUS, 1944*, vol. III, pp. 906–907.
45 Cited in Barker, *British Policy in South-East Europe in the Second World War*, p. 125.
46 Memorandum by the Counselor of the Embassy in the Soviet Union (Kennan), September 1944. Ibid., pp. 902–924.
47 Memorandum by the Joint Planning Staff Committee, 22 August 1943. PRO CAB 121/441. I am indebted to Éva Figder for this document.
48 A vezérkari főnök helyettese a vezérkari főnöknek [The deputy chief of staff to the chief of staff], 23 August 1944, in Juhász, *Magyar–brit titkos tárgyalások 1943-ban*, pp. 219–220.
49 Churchill to Roosevelt, 7 October 1943, in Kimball, *Churchill and Roosevelt, The Complete Correspondence*, vol. 2. pp. 498–499.
50 A.W.G. Randall feljegyzése Namier professzorral folytatott megbeszéléséről [Memorandum by Sir A.W.G. Randall on a conversation with Professor Namier], 14 October 1943, in Juhász, *Magyar–brit titkos tárgyalások*, p. 271. Allen's comment appeared on the memorandum.
51 Cited in a memorandum by W. Harrison, December 1943, PRO, FO, 371-39251. I am indebted to Péter Sipos for this document.
52 Ibid.
53 Ibid.
54 Ibid. A similar view was expressed by F. K. Roberts of the Foreign Office on 16 November: The Hungarian volte-face should be delayed until it best suits the Allied war effort. A brit Külügyminisztérium feljegyzései a magyarországgal folytatott tárgyalásokról [Memoranda of the Foreign Office on negotiations with Hungary], 13 November 1943 – 22 November 1943, in Juhász, *Magyar-brit titkos tárgyalások*, p. 285.
55 W. Harrison feljegyzése [Memorandum by W. Harrison], 11 December 1943, in Juhász, *Magyar–brit titkos tárgyalások*, p. 294.
56 USNA, RG 218, C.C.S. 387 (Hungary/3-16-44). Cited in Péter Sipos and István Vida, "The Policy of the United States toward Hungary during the Second World War," *Acta Scientiarum Hungaricae*, 29 (1983), p. 90.
57 Ibid., p. 90.
58 Barcza a külügyminiszternek [Barcza to the minister of foreign affairs], 21 May 1943; Barcza a külügyminiszternek [Barcza to the minister of foreign affairs], 5 August 1943. The Macartney Papers, Bodleain Library, Oxford, Box 5.

59 Stephen D. Kertesz, *Between Russia and the West. Hungary and the Illusion of Peacemaking* (Notre Dame–London: University of Notre Dame Press, 1984). p. 77.

60 Szegedy-Maszák, *Az ember ősszel visszanéz*, pp. 345—347.

61 Ibid. p. 330.

62 Anthony Cave Brown, *Bodyguard of Lies,* vol. I (New York: Harper and Row Publishers, 1975), pp. 479–508. See also David Stafford, *Britain and European Resistance 1940–1945* (Oxford: 1980), p. 173.

63 Memorandum by F. K. Roberts, 20 March 1944. PRO, FO, 371 39258. I am indebted to Péter Sipos for this document.

64 See on this Gyula Juhász, "A magyar–német viszony néhány kérdése a második világháború alatt," [Some questions of Hungarian-German relations during World War II] *Történelmi Szemle*, vol. 27, no. 2, (1984).

65 Cave Brown, *Bodyguard of Lies*, p. 504.

66 See Juhász, *Magyarország külpolitikája*, pp. 424–425.

67 For the proceedings see: "Orosz levéltári források az 1944 őszi moszkvai kormányalakítási tárgyalásokról, az Ideiglenes Nemzetgyűlés összehívásáról és az Ideiglenes Nemzeti Kormány megválasztásáról." [Russian archival documents on the Moscow talks on forming the government, convening the provisional National Assembly and the election of the Provisional National Government] Published and introduction written by István Vida, in István Feitl ed., *Az Ideiglenes Nemzetgyűlés és az Ideiglenes Nemzeti Kormány, 1944–1945* [The Provisional National Assembly and the Provisional National Government] (Budapest, 1995).

68 Soviet planners agreed that Transylvania should go back to Romania. Stalin had already expressed this position in December 1941 during his talks with Eden.

69 *Molotov Remembers—Inside Kremlin Politics. Conversations with Felix Chuev.* Edited with an introduction and notes by Albert Resis (Chicago: Ivan R. Dee, 1993). p. 63.

70 Korom, *Magyarország Ideiglenes Nemzeti Kormánya és a fegyverszünet*, pp. 231–232.

71 Vida, "Orosz levéltári források az 1944 őszi moszkvai kormányalakítási tárgyalásokról," pp. 60–62.

72 For Stalin's remarks see Korom, *Magyarország Ideiglenes Nemzeti Kormánya és a fegyverszünet*, pp. 333–334; for their English translation, William McCagg, *Stalin Embattled, 1943–1948* (Detroit: Wayne University Press, 1978) pp. 315–316. McCagg failed to include the crucial sentence about having to press ahead once the CP gains strength.

73 McCagg, *Stalin Embattled*, p. 313. According to McCagg, Stalin may have hoped to garner Western acquiescence in his revolutionary goals and therefore, for the sake of the "greatest extension Communist power" it may have seemed prudent not to grab for power immediately, but to hold back. Ibid., pp. 69–70.

74 Mark, "Revolution by Degrees: Stalin's National-Front Strategy for Europe, 1941–1947." CWHIP Working Paper no 31. (Washington D.C.: Woodrow Wilson Center, 1996).

75 See The Ambassador in the Soviet Union (Harriman) to the Secretary of State, 13 October 1944. *FRUS*, Vol. III, 1944, pp. 903–906; The Secretary of State to the Ambassador in the Soviet Union, 14 October 1944. Ibid., pp. 906–907.

76 The Ambassador in the Soviet Union (Harriman) to the Secretary of State, 13 October 1944. *FRUS,* Vol. III, 1944, p. 903.

77 On the U.S. position regarding reparations see e.g. "The Acting Secretary of State to the Chargé in the Soviet Union (Kennan)," November 1944. Ibid., pp. 922–924.

78 On a detailed account of the operation of the ACC in Hungary see *Dálnoki Miklós Béla Kormányának (Ideiglenes Nemzeti Kormány) Minisztertanácsi Jegyzőkönyvei 1944 december 23 – 1945 november 15* [The Minutes of the Ministers' Council of the Government of Miklós Dálnoki Béla (Provisional National Government) 23 December 1944 – 15 November 1945], vol. A, edited, annotated and the introductory essay written by László Szűcs (Budapest: Magyar Országos Levéltár, 1997).

79 Quoted in Krisztián Ungváry, *Budapest ostroma* [The siege of Budapest] (Budapest: Corvina, 1999), pp. 13–14.

80 According to William McCagg "the Soviet army by its very existence constituted a threat of sorts to Stalin's power, and that its wartime prominence, *esprit de corps*, and independence" represented a threat to his authority. McCagg, *Stalin Embattled*, p. 82.

81 Ungváry, *Budapest ostroma*, pp. 265–267.

82 Ibid. pp. 268–269.

83 Ibid., p. 272.

84 Sándor Márai, *Memoir of Hungary 1944–1948.* Translated by Albert Tezla (Budapest: Corvina in association with Central European University Press, 1996), p. 47, p. 86.

85 Ungváry, *Budapest ostroma*, pp. 278–279.

CHAPTER II

THE MYTH OF DEMOCRACY

Like many alliances in history, the coalition between the Soviet Union, the United States and Great Britain broke up almost as soon as its raison d'être, Nazi Germany ceased to exist. The forces pulling apart this "strange alliance" proved to be stronger than the forces of cohesion. The desire to pursue national aspirations turned out to be more motivating than the prospect of jointly policing the world for the sake of peace and stability. For Moscow, an exclusively Soviet oriented belt of security and the pursuit of ideological goals prevailed over cooperation; economic exploitation and autarchy were more desirable than economic integration with the West. In Russian eyes the slightest hint of American interest in Eastern Europe indicated a desire to deprive the Soviet Union of the fruit of victory. Washington, on the other hand, could not and would not accept the Soviet terms for the continued existence of the Grand Alliance. Wendell Willkie's "One World" was a thing of the past soon after the war ended. Moscow isolated its sphere of influence from the outside world and introduced Stalinist dictatorships even in former allies like Poland. This combined with Stalin's encroachments on China, Turkey and Iran made it seem as though Russia was on a quest for world mastery. Having allowed the Soviet Union to ensconce itself in its own sphere, America proceeded to protect and economically strengthen the West. In the process each side came to see the other as a mortal and insatiable enemy; perhaps America had more reason to do so than the USSR, which watched the "capitalist world" with *a priori* presumption of malicious intent.

Many scholars hold that Stalin had no political strategy for Eastern Europe. Hungary and Czechoslovakia, they argue, enjoyed genuine democratic governments in the aftermath of the war and were subjected to Sovietization only in response to threatening American initiatives. In contrast, Eduard Mark argues that Stalin "had a highly developed political strategy for liberated countries throughout Europe through the establishment of national fronts." Moscow supported popular democracies where communist dominated coalitions outwardly observed conventions of "bourgeois democracy." Ultimately the purpose of this support was to minimize Western objection to the "creeping establishment of Communist-dominated

47

regimes directly subject to Moscow lest the USSR be drawn into premature conflict with its allies and forfeit the advantages of association with them. Stalin wanted Communist revolution in Europe and continued cooperation with the allies."[1] A study of the Sovietization of Hungary will shed light on the motives of postwar Soviet policy and on whether multiparty democracy was an option anywhere in Eastern Europe or not.

The political left emerged after the war as a potential agent of transformation. Its appeal extended to Western intellectuals and masses. State Department officials, many of whom believed that the Soviet Union had shunned its revolutionary ideals, captured the prevailing spirit of the old continent: "The general mood of the people of Europe is to the left and strongly in favor of far-reaching economic and social reforms, but not however in favor of left-wing totalitarian regime to achieve those reforms."[2] For Communist sympathizers the USSR was the mirror of the future. World revolution was no longer the immediate order of the day, but it remained the long-term goal and inspiration. In this view events up to 1945 were seen as capitalism working itself out, but the present stage of development was the dramatic extension of Communist power and influence.[3] In Italy, where membership in the Communist Party climbed to two million, the large masses were in a revolutionary mood in the immediate aftermath of the war. The same was true for France. The Communists exercised self-restraint because Stalin prescribed coalition tactics. Maurice Thorez, the Stalinist leader of the French Communist Party explained, "We who are Communists should not at the moment make explicitly Communist or socialist demands."[4] In Greece the Communists fought a civil war against the British-backed royalist government until their eventual defeat in 1947.

The socialist movement previously in bitter rivalry with the Communists was geographically divergent. The Italian Socialist Party was the most radical and the most fundamentally Marxist of all the European parties. The French socialists emphasized freedom and human rights instead of class struggle and became a radical, popular movement instead of a revolutionary one.[5] The British Labour Party was traditionally more moderate than its continental counterparts, pragmatic in approach. It was gradualist, not revolutionary in its pursuit of piecemeal change for example in its aim to create a welfare state, rather than a socialist society. Furthermore, it adopted a pragmatic approach, through its affirmation of democracy, parliamentary action, and social justice.[6] The post-war period saw the rise of European Christian Democracy that broke with its past of anti-socialism and anti-liberalism, by dissociating itself from confessional interest. Now it espoused democracy and carried out important economic reforms.[7] What these movements had in common was the approval of state intervention in the economy and the curbing to a greater or lesser extent of private initiative. Nationalization of certain branches of the economy was on the agenda in France and Great Britain. However, while national economies were being centralized, international economy was moving in the opposite direction, towards the liberalization of trade and the flow of capital. Under American initiative and guidance supranational cooperation, the coordination of production, open markets, free convertibility of currency and the free flow of capital and goods were the order of the day in Western Europe. France and West Germany pioneered the supranational coordination of the production of coal and steel.

Nuclear arms transformed international relations. In 1945 the nuclear physicist, Niels Bohr tried to convince Churchill and Roosevelt of the need to assure Stalin that they intended to cooperate with the USSR in neutralizing the bomb through international control. Instead the United States opted for the exclusive ownership of the bomb and hoped to take advantage of the diplomatic leverage it might yield. President Truman and his Secretary of State, James F. Byrnes believed that the bomb might be useful in settling problems like the future of the Balkan states or even that of Russian influence in the Chinese province of Manchuria. Byrnes thought that it "might well put us in a position to dictate our own terms at the end of the war."[8] In fact the opposite happened. Nuclear arms eventually enhanced Moscow's hold on its empire in Eastern Europe. Eastern Europe became all but unassailable, as Washington would not risk nuclear war to liberate it. Stalin immediately understood that a new factor had entered international relations and believed that the use of the atomic bomb in Japan was directed against Soviet interests. In a broader context the balance of power that had resulted from the Soviet victory over Germany was destroyed. Stalin sought to restore the balance by acquiring the bomb as quickly as possible. For this reason, as well as the opportunity to possess this new and potent symbol of power, Stalin devoted vast resources to building the bomb. Perhaps, as David Holloway suggests, these reasons were sufficient for Stalin to want the new weapon even if Bohr's advice to inform Stalin had been followed.[8] Hiroshima shattered many of Stalin's assumptions and calculations, his image of the United States in particular. The U.S. was no longer a harmless giant unable to threaten Soviet security, it could now endanger anyone. In fact Stalin may have interpreted Hiroshima as blackmail against the USSR.[9] Aided by espionage, Moscow used its vast intellectual and material resources to conclude its nuclear program in 1949, earlier than anticipated by western observers. Consequently Stalin and his successors were able to consolidate their gains against foreign encroachments and extended the Soviet Union's *actio radius* beyond what had been possible for Imperial Russia.

Even though at the end of the war U.S. officials did not disparage cooperation on the basis of liberal internationalism,[10] in 1945 Washington was up against the Soviets in Asia and Europe alike. In Iran, Moscow competed with Western oil companies for crude oil. The Soviets forced the Iranian government to grant a concession to the Soviet Union and refused to meet the deadline for troop withdrawal set by the 1942 Anglo-Soviet agreement. Iran's resolve to resist Moscow's designs were buttressed by the United States, which convinced itself that Iran's territorial integrity was important for Western security. Washington was ready to assume Britain's traditional role of balancing Russia in the Middle East. Although the Iranian crisis was eventually resolved peacefully, with the Soviet Union securing Teheran's promise to establish a joint Soviet–Iranian oil company, it led to hostility between the former wartime allies.[11]

The disagreement between the Western powers and the Soviet Union over the fate of Germany was one of the fundamental issues of post-war international politics. In Potsdam the victorious powers agreed to preserve German unity, with Germany to be administered as one political and economic entity by a single governing body, the Allied Control Council. Yet, in the absence of any agreement on specific programs to give meaning to the generalities agreed at the Potsdam conference, the Allied Control Council proved ineffective in governing Germany as a single unit. As a consequence the occupying powers applied their own ideas in their zone.[12] American officials placed immediate emphasis on Germany as a source of coal for the stabilization and reconstruction of Western Europe. Substantial amounts of goods were needed from the Soviet zone in order to restart coal production in the British controlled Ruhr as well as to revive light industry in the American zone. Therefore the Americans stressed the need for the economic unification of Germany. Washington expected the USSR to defer reparations until the coal industry's rehabilitation could be paid for with German exports. This thirst for coal led US officials to argue against schemes that envisioned the separation or the internationalization of the Ruhr as desired by Moscow (and Paris) in order to forestall the extension of Soviet power and influence into the "heart of Western Europe" through the device of international trusteeship.[13] France, which feared the revival of German militarism, favored the Ruhr region's detachment from Germany, seeing it as the epicenter of the great rival's industrial might.

The Soviet Union consolidated control over its own zone of Germany. Left wing political parties there were brought under Moscow's control and the Soviets established an exploitative economic presence. They transformed the economy along the Soviet model and took advantage of Eastern Germany's human and natural resources for Soviet reconstruction, while Stalin kept his options open. He pressed for a unified German state and restrained the process of Sovietization until he saw a chance for unification that suited Soviet interests. This fell short both of socialization and of free capitalist development and prescribed neutrality. Hannes Adomeit has shown that the division of Germany "may not have been the inevitable consequence of Stalin's adherence to the (revolutionary and imperial) paradigm but it was a logically consistent and *probable* result."[14] The apparent policy of Sovietization in Germany's Russian zone was self-defeating. It alarmed Russia's Western rivals and enhanced their readiness to break with Moscow and consolidate their positions in Western Europe.

If Soviet policy in Germany was sending alarming signals to the West, so was the subjugation of Eastern Europe. Perhaps it was not so much forced Sovietization that was distressing, but the prospect that Moscow would scorn Western expectations in more important regions the same way. Roosevelt and Churchill accepted Russian predominance in Eastern Europe although arguably not its Bolshevization. The Yalta agreement assigned a decisive role to Moscow with the proviso that the democratic principles of the Atlantic Charter would be upheld in the regions under Soviet control. Only a couple of months before the European hostilities were terminated, however, Churchill began to wonder about the wisdom of giving the Soviets a *carte blanche*, because Romania and Bulgaria were on their way to becoming Communist dictatorships even before the war ended. He advocated a tougher stance against the Soviets, including a refusal to withdraw the Anglo-American troops behind the agreed demarcation line. Yet Washington was not yet ready to break with Moscow. In July 1945 the Americans recognized the Communist-dominated Polish government with the proviso that the Russians ensured free elections. In December Secretary of State Byrnes held out the recognition of the governments in Bucharest and Sofia in return for a Soviet pledge that democratic elements would be included in them and that free elections would be held. At the same time Byrnes relaxed U.S. conditions to the extent that the Romanian and the Bulgarian governments would need to be transformed to satisfy American expectations.

Cooperation with the Soviet Union was still possible, but only on the "realistic" lines proposed by Kennan, whereby the continent would be divided "frankly into spheres of influence." Byrnes took the lead at the Potsdam Conference to what amounted to a "spheres of influence" settlement in Europe: each side would have a free hand in the area it dominated and would get along on that basis. Byrnes recognized that the ideologies of the U.S. and the USSR were too far apart for long-term cooperation. This recognition led to a fundamental change in U.S. policy on Germany, which would not be run on a quadripartite basis. It was agreed at Potsdam that each side could take as much as it wanted from its zone, East and West Germany would relate to each other as foreign states in trade. The way to get along was to pull apart.[15]

While Byrnes was trying to lay the foundations of future coexistence with the Soviets, Stalin, who thought that each victor's share should be proportionate to the number of soldiers "spent" and enemy killed in the war, was preparing for a preponderant role in the regions adjacent to the Soviet Union. As a recent assessment of Soviet policy put it, "although important, collaboration with the West was subordinate to the main task of building a buffer zone along the western border."[16] While U.S. officials were ready to shelve anti-Soviet prejudices for the sake of cooperation at least up to late 1945, the Soviet Union was fueled by a mixture of insecurity, feelings of inferiority and ideological hostility *vis-à-vis* the more advanced West intermingled with a sense of Russian spiritual superiority, of its global mission and necessity of autocratic rule and self-reliance. Nevertheless Stalin wanted the West as partners in preventing the resurgence of Germany and Japan, and looked upon the former as a potential source reconstruction.[17] If it is true that the Soviet Union was to be "an invincible fortress against foreign, particularly capitalist enemies,"[18] democracy was hardly an option for the countries around the USSR.

1945: Carry a stick but talk softly

It has been argued that Stalin was terrified of the Western Powers and was hardly in the mood for revolutionary exaltation. He protected the Grand Alliance and therefore supported "new type governments" against the revolutionary Communists of the underground. Stalin first "held back" and adopted a "blocist" attitude, meaning imposition of full Soviet control on Eastern Europe only after December 1947, when the West gave up the concept of unified Germany.[19] Some historians distinguished between the Soviet satellites according to the existence of coalition governments that passed from genuine, through bogus coalitions to monolithic blocs.[20]

Public statements and the composition of governments could be misleading. In Hungary the Communist penetration of national and local institutions of government and other centers of power, the piecemeal Sovietization of the economy, police and the army, the gradual elimination of democratic political elements and cultural diversity were concealed by the maintenance of uneasy coalition governance. There was no tension between the policy of Hungarian Communists and the local organs of Soviet power on one side and the policy of the Kremlin on the other, as in eastern Germany. Rather, the Soviet Union intervened on behalf of the local Communist Party in instances when they were unable to prevail over their opponents. American attempts to moderate the Communist drive for power were met with hostility and failed. Even the slightest U.S. initiative was construed as undue interference and manifestation of anti-Soviet ill will. Hungary was a restricted zone. Even after the termination of hostilities the Russians screened Western journalists and trade representatives that wished to enter Hungary, although less severe restrictions applied in the Soviet zone of Austria and Germany.[21] Special clearance was needed to cross the iron curtain into Hungary. Soviet authorities refused landing or transit rights for U.S. or British civilian airlines; often aircraft destined for the Western representatives of the ACC were denied permission to fly into Hungary. The restriction of Westerners in Hungary reflected traditional Russian suspicion of foreigners. During the war they showed the same attitude toward the American mission in the Soviet Union.[22] Thus the restrictions imposed on the Western allies may have been an early indication that Moscow considered Hungary an exclusively Soviet terrain. As Stalin's personal representative, Marshal Voroshilov put it: "This is our zone of occupation and we are going to ask information on every person that comes in."[23]

Hungarian Communists exploited the economic and political chaos in the war-damaged country. They capitalized on the division of their political opponents, (which was in part engineered by the Communists), the lack of decisive Western involvement, the irresolute, often pusillanimous political opposition and most of all Soviet support to gradually establish a Communist dictatorship.[24] There is no evidence for the existence of a "blueprint" for Communist takeover. Nevertheless from the outset the goal may have been the establishment of Communist monopoly of power, a proletarian dictatorship. Communist seizure of power was carried out piecemeal, with subtlety in order to maintain the semblance of democracy for as long as possible. Moscow wanted the best of both worlds: to preserve the benefits of cooperation with the West whilst consolidating itself in Eastern Europe. Given the widespread anti-Communist sentiment in Hungary, this gradualism avoided domestic turmoil. Eventually, however, untrammeled control in Hungary as in all of Eastern Europe was more important to the Soviet Union than the preservation of the Grand Alliance. Soviet policy in Hungary suggested that "although important, collaboration with the West was subordinate to the main task of building a buffer zone along the western border."[25] During their struggle for power the Communists made political and tactical mistakes, but were usually able to exploit their opportunities to further their cause. Their task was made easier by the fact that the West attached an affordable price tag on the loss of Hungary.

The last six months of the war left Hungary devastated. Hungarian, Wehrmacht and SS units mounted a desperate last-ditch struggle against the Red Army, and some of the war's fiercest battles were fought on Hungarian territory, which Hitler treated as an advanced line of defense.[26] Furthermore, the Germans dismantled and removed industrial equipment and inventory. All in all, 40 percent of Hungary's national wealth was destroyed: 90 per-

cent of the industrial plants were damaged, 40 percent of the rail network
and 70 percent of the rolling stock were lost.[27] Material damage could be
replaced, but the loss of human lives was beyond repair. Taking Hungary's
1941 area into account, 340–360 thousand soldiers, 80–100 thousand non-
Jewish civilians and 450–490 thousand people of Jewish descent died, a
staggering 10 percent of the population.[28]

Since many officials of the Hungarian local administrations fled the
country with the onslaught of the Russians, the Soviet army had no administration to count on. Therefore the Soviets created their own military administration within the liberated territories. Although the military administration was not supposed to work towards changing the existing social–economic order, internal Soviet documents refer to the role of the Red Army in
bringing people's democracy to Eastern Europe.[29] Soviet *kommandaturas*
were entitled to appoint managers to deserted factories and commercial
enterprises. Most industrial and agricultural enterprises as well as commu-
nications fell under Soviet military control and they were in no hurry to
return them to Hungarian administration. Railways were given back only
six months after the fighting was over. Industrial plants were returned in
July with the exception of twelve factories that continued to produce for the
Russians. The Red Army issued its own currency to pay for its purchases
and obliged the Hungarian National Bank to exchange it under the conditions set by the occupation authorities. Banknotes, which were withdrawn
from circulation, had to be turned over to Soviet authorities without compensation.[30] This meant that the Soviets only pretended to pay for what they
purchased.

Soviet brutality in dealing with the conquered peoples of Austria and
Germany is described in recent scholarship. Less has been written about
Soviet occupation policies elsewhere. There is little doubt that the atrocious
behavior of many Russian units was fueled by a thirst to revenge brutality
committed by the Axis powers on Soviet territory. It is important to remember, however, that the Soviets had been noted for their barbarity towards
conquered peoples before the German attack on the USSR took place. Thus
they looted the Baltic States in the process of conquering them in 1940.
A British diplomat in Kaunas described them as "Asiatic hordes," which
"threaten civilization [...] and bring misery in their wake."[31] Some historians argue that in many ways the work of the Soviet NKVD in eastern Poland
proved far more destructive than that of the Gestapo in the first two years of
Poland's occupation.[32]

Hungarian war propaganda mobilized for war with threats that Soviet
victory would mean an invasion of barbarians and deportation of Hungarians to Siberia. Soviet occupation vindicated Nazi propaganda,[33] although
Russian atrocities did not surpass the crimes perpetrated by the Nazis—but

not the Hungarians—themselves. Nevertheless, Soviet misconduct jeopardized the Communists' political future. The Communist Party's leader, Mátyás Rákosi complained about this to the head of the International Department of the CPSU, Georgii Dimitrov in early 1945: "Our position is made more difficult by the fact that the excesses of the Red Army are written on the Party's account […] the cases of mass raping of women, the looting, etc. are repeated with the liberation of each territory, thus, recently in Budapest. Raids are still going on, during the course of which workers, including good party members are taken to war prisoner camps where they disappear."[34] Rákosi gave the matter a working class perspective, perhaps in the hope that he could influence Soviet conduct. But such complaints were to no avail. Atrocities and deportations were carried out without regard to class, religion, gender, or ethnicity, although in the initial stage of Russian occupation ethnic Germans were specifically targeted. Civilians were murdered without apparent reason. As a typical example Soviet troops shot András Kiss, a father of eight children, when he tried to stop them from raping his wife and daughter. In the same village two married women were shot in their vineyard without any apparent reason.[35]

In December 1944 the Soviet State Defense Committee decreed the "mobilization and internment" of all ethnic Germans and German nationals in Hungary, Romania, Bulgaria, Yugoslavia and Czechoslovakia, with all persons fit for work to be sent to the Soviet Union for physical labor. Men between the ages of 17 and 45 and women between 17 and 30 years of age were eligible for deportation overseen by Lavrentii Beria. The laborers would be sent to the coal industry of the Donbass region and the metallurgical industry of the south.[36] From this time until 19 January 1945, almost 67,000 ethnic Germans were sent to the USSR, 23,000 of which from Hungary,[37] but the final figure may have reached 44,000.[38]

Most of the Hungarian deportees were civilians that were sent to forced-labor camps. While Nazi terror raged in the western part of the country, the population in Soviet occupied territories suffered from random atrocities and deportations. Thus for example in November 1944 Soviet military authorities deported three hundred civilians from the village of Hajdúnánás in eastern Hungary. In February 1945 foreign minister János Gyöngyösi asked for the liberation of sixty-five people captured in the village of Abafalva. In the village of Tiszaluc a twenty-year-old girl was taken into custody by a Russian officer who was put up in her home. She was taken to the town of Szerencs, wagonized and deported with several thousand other internees.[39] In May three Hungarian political parties petitioned Prime Minister Béla Miklós to intervene on behalf of interned, "politically reliable" party members, including six hundred former Jewish labor servicemen, who were interned in a prison camp near the town of Cegléd. The petition pointed out that their "continued captivity may result in their large scale deaths." Intervention on their behalf was urgent because the Soviets had already started to deport them to an "unspecified location" and "a large number of deaths had already occurred."[40] Sometimes whole families were taken as in the village of Pince, where Soviet troops deported 19 families including children in July 1945.[41] Soviet authorities employed the same tactic all over the country: the people they rounded up were told that they would be home soon, perhaps even by the same night.

As soon as the first Soviet troops set foot in Hungary, special NKVD units began to round up ethnic Germans and deport them to the Soviet Union. In order to establish German identity the Russians used family names. If there were not enough Germans they took Hungarians instead. They failed to consult with the Hungarian authorities or the leadership of the Hungarian Communist Party. Party ideologist József Révai pointed out that some of the deportees were proven antifascists or sometimes even Communist Party secretaries or deputies in the National Assembly.[42] The deportations caused a mixture of widespread panic, despair and public outrage and hence subverted the general aim of uniting the Hungarian nation in the struggle against Germany. Or, to put it another way, the demand for slave labor prevailed over the more immediate concern of defeating Hitler. Prisoners of war were employed in the Soviet economy from 1941 onwards. Their mass utilization started in 1945, an average of 1,833,000 prisoners were used in various branches of the Soviet economy, mainly in the construction, the armament, as well as the heating and power industries.[43] All in all up to 550–600,000 Hungarians were taken to the Soviet Union as prisoners of war, out of whom as many as 200,000 may not have returned.[44]

The rape of German women by Soviet troops has received wide scholarly attention. Norman Naimark concluded that the mass rape of German women was the ultimate assertion Soviet victory and conquest over the people that described itself as racially superior to Slavs.[45] Mass sexual offense then was a tool of power politics. Less is known about Soviet sexual conduct in Eastern Europe. In Hungary rape may have resulted from the lack of discipline and the low morals of brutalized troops. Based on incomplete figures derived from medical institutions the number of rapes committed in Hungary by the Soviet armed forces is estimated between 50,000 and 200,000. As a result the Hungarian authorities liberalized abortion, making it possible for Hungarian women to abort their unwanted offspring legally and free of charge.[46] Women tried to protect themselves by cladding in filthy apparel or trousers, but this was usually not enough to spare them. Soldiers who committed such crimes seem to have been driven by sexual lust, revenge and a desire to demonstrate power.[47] In the view of the Swiss embassy in Budapest rapes caused the greatest misery for the Hungarian population. "These atrocities are so widespread that—from the age of ten to seventy—few women in Hungary can escape this fate." The Swiss claimed that "rape against the women sometimes happens with extreme brutality. Many women would rather choose suicide in order to avoid the monstrosities. [...] The women are usually not killed, but they are kept in captivity for hours, if not days before letting them go. The misery is made even worse by the fact that many of the Russian soldiers are ill and there is no medicine in Hungary. There are cases where women serving in the Red Army or the Russian police commit rape. These women caused serious bodily harm to the men who were unwilling to satisfy their desires."[48] Men who tried to protect women were often shot. In Hungary the best known victim was Bishop Vilmos Apor, who had opposed the persecution of Jews during the war and was killed while trying to save women from being raped. In the village of Cserszegtomaj for instance two Russians showed up who "demanded women." When a policeman and the president of the local National Committee appeared at the scene, the soldiers shot at them, seriously wounding both.[49]

As their defeat drew closer and closer, the Germans and Hungarian Nazis robbed banks and stole art treasures. They removed nine billion pengős (the contemporary Hungarian money) worth of currency[50] and as part of an operation cynically named "Winterhilfe" looted Jewish owned villas. On many occasions the looters set fire to works of art they were unable to take. For instance the famed art collection in the Mauthner villa in Buda fell victim to the uniformed arsonists.[51] Much, although not all of the treasures taken by the Germans were returned to Hungary from the Western zones of occupation after the war. The same cannot be said about the "trophies" collected by the Soviets. Red Army units robbed banks and took three billion pengős (roughly 2.3 million dollars) of banknotes, 1.75 billion pengős worth of securities and fifty-five kilograms of gold.[52] Many of Hungary's wealthiest families hid their valuables in bank vaults to save them from Nazi plunderers. Specially trained Soviet trophy brigades, however, systematically looted the financial institutions, private mansions, churches in the capital city and the countryside. They even stripped the Swedish Embassy in Budapest. Red Army troops often burned, or the local population sometimes carried off, what was left in the private homes after the trophy brigades had left. Soviet trophy brigades went about their business brutally but with expertise. One is given an impression of the enormous riches the trophy brigades stole and shipped to the USSR from the list of art treasures that belonged to the Jewish Hatvany family—which hosted Thomas Mann in Budapest in 1936—and were deposited in various banks in Budapest. These included paintings from the best Hungarian artists as well as works by masters such as Greco, Tintoretto, both Cranachs, Delacroix, Manet, Degas,

Courbet, Pissaro, Renoir, Daumier, Rodin, Corot and Constable. The family managed to repurchase some of the masterpieces from Soviet officers in 1947 and smuggle them out of the country.[53] Soviet authorities also sanctioned the looting of money.

In the town of Nagykanizsa a Soviet committee opened the local Savings Bank's vault and took the contents. When asked for their entitlement to do so they showed an authorization signed by the commander of the Third Ukrainian Front Marshal Fiodor I. Tolbukhin, which entitled the committee to open and empty every vault and pay-box.[54] There were also many acts of random violence. Individuals that fell victim to robbery sometimes paid with their lives. Ferenc Keserű of Felsőpáhok was beaten to death while his home was being robbed. Other individuals in the same village were beaten up and their valuables—watches, jewelry, leather bags, food—were confiscated.[55] Sometimes the perpetrators were drunk; occasionally the locals beat them up. Soviet behavior was utterly unpredictable. The writer Sándor Márai remembered a maid reporting that "the very same Russians who had dined at their place just a little while ago, kissed the hand of the lady of the house, said goodbye graciously [...] sent back the chauffeur with a submachine gun...to their hosts, to demand that the master of the house hand over his gold wristwatch." "It occurred," Márai recalled, that "the Russian who dropped by in the morning, conversed amicably with the family, showed pictures of his family back home, sentimentally patted the heads of the children present and gave them candy, departed and then returned in the afternoon or late at night and robbed the very same family he had made friends with in the morning."[56] Endless looting, Márai thought, was not rage directed against the "fascist enemy," "But simply abject poverty: These Communist Russians were so impoverished, so miserably destitute...so completely stripped of everything needed to make life more colorful and humane that now, set loose after thirty years of privation and drudgery they threw themselves hungrily on everything that fell into their hands."[57]

Soviet troops acted with obvious disdain for Hungarian culture. In Count Erdődy's mansion, requisitioning troops demolished the parquet flooring and the wooden panels in search of the family vault with obvious disregard for the building they were robbing. They stripped the vault of its contents, such as a gala dress ornate with diamonds and emeralds and left the building in shambles.[58] The Red Army's uncivilized conduct was also noted in Austria. On one occasion the soldiers destroyed a school and left it covered with human excrement.[59] Soviet officers often established themselves in private homes, sometimes for months. One owner found that the Russians "took practically everything [...] Piano, paintings, furniture, carpets [...]. In all the rooms the remnants of grandfather's library were stacked up high: a heap of human excrement with an open book on it, another heap and another book and so forth [...] the pages that were needed for this 'activity' had been torn from them. These towers, emanating an unbearable stench, were sitting side by side like skyscrapers."[60] Soviet units used schools or country mansions as garrisons, which they completely destroyed after use. In a typical case, the fruit trees, vine props and the furniture belonging to an agricultural school in the town of Nagykőrös were used up for firewood.[61] Red Army units had their garrisons renovated. When one unit moved out it destroyed the interior so when the next contingent arrived, renovation had to be repeated since the electric cords were ripped from the walls and the window frames were removed. Chairman of the Allied Control Commission Marshal Kliment Voroshilov ruled that the Hungarian authorities could disregard renovation orders of the Soviet army except for the ones that had his own signature,[62] but in practice nothing changed.

The Red Army seized agricultural products and used them without payment. One example of this was the village of Földes, which was compelled to feed a contingent of up to 600 Russian men.[63] While Russian soldiers were consuming the country's food and cereal reserves, the Hungarian government was forced to borrow food—meat, cereals, and sugar—from the Soviet Union. The confiscation threatened the country's livestock. Révai complained that if the Red Army went on wasting the Hungarian livestock there would be famine and it would be impossible to carry out the necessary agricultural works in the spring. The HCP and the government used their separate channels to find a remedy. While the former turned to Deputy Commissar of Foreign Affairs Dekanozov,[64] the government petitioned the ACC to restrain the Soviet army's requisitioning and arrests. Unexpectedly, Voroshilov refuted all allegations, claiming that "the Soviet armed forces were operating according to the directives of the Soviet High Command and the stipulations of the Armistice Agreement."[65] When the political parties set out on their unequal quest for power, the rules of warfare still prevailed. The Communists and their sympathizers were the best representatives of Soviet interests and in return the Soviet Union lent them full support.

The optimistic assessment of Hungary's political future expressed by the OSS in October 1944, according to which Hungary would not be Bolshevized, was obsolete in a matter of one year. At the end of 1945 State Department analysts wrote that the Soviet Union was out to integrate Hungary into its security zone by gaining a decisive influence in its politics and economy.[66] Moscow's predominance in Hungarian affairs was unquestioned. Although the Kremlin did not participate in the day-to-day affairs of running the country, it influenced the course of events in important junctures decisively and always with a sense of direction. Whenever Moscow wanted to modify national politics, or to steer it onto a different course altogether,

its instructions were communicated through the head of the Allied Control
Commission, or the Soviet political representative in Hungary. Occasionally
party leader Rákosi received the Kremlin's directive personally. Soviet
decision-making was highly centralized. The role of the Chairman (or later
the Acting Chairman) of the Commission was merely to convey instructions
from Moscow. If the Chairman attempted to act on his own and the Kremlin
did not agree with the course of action, he was overruled. In such cases new
instructions arrived, which in turn were imposed on the government or on
the Communist Party.

Initially the ACC was run by Marshal Kliment Voroshilov. Voroshilov
had been Stalin's close associate and friend until their rift in 1940. Although
his prowess as a military leader was considered to be inferior to most of his
fellow generals, he acted as commissar of defense till 1940. Voroshilov's
war record was poor; he suffered several defeats around Leningrad. In 1944
Stalin removed him from the State Defense Committee, but he remained a
member of the Politburo. Since Stalin suspected him of being a British spy,
his mission to Hungary was an exile and a relief. To a certain extent the
Marshal sympathized with the Hungarians but he had little room to maneuver. Although he tried to get along with his American and British colleagues,
it was not in his competence to define policies on the entrance of Western
civilians or even to grant transit rights to Allied aircraft. Since the West
wanted greater influence in the Hungarian ACC the Allies revised the statutes
at the Potsdam conference. Based on these guidelines the U.S. proposed
that the chiefs of the British and American Missions should be appointed as
the vice-chairmen of the Commission. Allied representatives would be free
to travel in and out of Hungary and to communicate with the Hungarian
government. In effect Voroshilov rejected the U.S. proposal and the Western
missions communicated with the Hungarian authorities through the chairman of the ACC.[67]

Moscow could also work through the Hungarian Communist leaders,
who implemented the Soviet guidelines to the best of their abilities. However, in some specific issues such as the size of the reparation payments, the
treatment of the Hungarian minorities in Czechoslovakia, territorial revision
or the prisoners of war there was disagreement with the Kremlin. This was
in part because the Hungarian Communists were better informed of domestic sentiments and were aware that anti-Hungarian Soviet policies were at
odds with garnering popular support for socialism. They had only one overriding aim: the seizure of power, whereas Moscow had a variety of competing goals. Some of these goals superceded the immediate needs of the Hungarian Communists. For instance slave labor for Soviet economic reconstruction was more important than the popularity of the HCP prior to the
national election in November 1945, therefore Rákosi's request to return

Hungarian POWs to enhance his party's popularity remained unheeded. It is also true that the popularity of HCP candidates was a useful, but not indispensable prerequisite of winning the election. Moreover, electoral victory was not the only road to power.

Upon establishing itself in Hungary the HCP followed the guidelines defined in the Kremlin: patience before moving ahead with full speed. Polish Communists were also instructed to make compromises and concessions to split their political opponents in order to create favorable conditions for long-term political goals. Similarly, in Romania Vasile Luca explained that the Romanian Communist Party should not talk openly about its final purpose, but for the time being should work within the framework of "bourgeois democracy." That form of government would end once it had become safe to implement the "final purpose," and even before that "there would be limits to bourgeois democracy." In Bulgaria Dimitrov cautioned his party never to portray the struggle in class terms and to eschew all that smacks of revolution.[68] In Hungary the HCP would govern in coalition with their political rivals. Veterans of the Communist dictatorship of 1919 who desired a "premature" introduction of the dictatorship of the proletariat were silenced. No internal dissent within the party would be tolerated and the Bolshevik veterans threatened party unity.[69] Révai explained the correct line. Of petit-bourgeois origin, Révai was an archetypal Bolshevik revolutionary. Thin, bespectacled and endowed with great intellectual curiosity he was a voracious reader of philosophy and was well versed in socialist literature by the age of nineteen. He was remembered as "a terrifying opponent, who was never satisfied in winning the battle [in debate] but saw to his party's supremacy mercilessly." Révai, who wedded himself with Bolshevism in the aftermath of World War I, maintained that the dictatorship of the proletariat was necessary in 1919: it was a choice between a bourgeois and a proletarian dictatorship. Révai entered the party's Central Committee in the mid-1920s. In theoretical writings he began to emphasize the importance of a transition period as opposed to an immediate introduction of proletarian dictatorship; and in the 1930s he worked out the theory of national front governance. Arrested in 1930 for illegal Communist activity, he was sentenced to three years in jail. From 1939 he worked for the Propaganda Division of the Comintern, then edited the Soviet propaganda broadcasts to Hungary. In January 1945 Révai assumed responsibility for matters concerning propaganda, the National Assembly and local governments.[70] The party's main task in 1945, Révai explained, was to convince "our own comrades" of the correctness of the official party policy. This effort had been successful aside from the territories "recently liberated by the Red Army".[71] Révai stressed the need for collaboration between the working class, the peasantry and the intelligentsia for reasons of foreign and domestic politics.

Reconstruction, Révai argued, could not be carried out "on a socialist basis."

> "[At a time] when the Soviet Union [...] pursues a policy of coop-
> eration with the Anglo-Saxon world powers here in Hungary we
> cannot follow a policy contrary to this. Communist international-
> ism means that we align ourselves with the Soviet Union's world
> policy. And if the Soviet Union cooperates with England and
> America to maintain world peace, in Hungary we cannot make a
> policy the direct objective of which is the rule of the working
> class."[72]

Even so, the extirpation of divergent views was not easy. Ernő Gerő, the second man in the HCP hierarchy, deplored the ideological problems within the party. Ruthless, suspicious, ascetic and unable to build human contact, Gerő devoted his life to the movement. A political opponent de-scribed him "as crueler, more pathologically anti-Semitic than Rákosi. He looked like a modern Savanarola [...] he was one of those old-fashioned ascetic Communists who accepted no money, no luxuries and took no joy in life."[73] Gerő severed all contact with his parents and eight siblings; the only kinship he ever observed was his son born in Moscow. As his biographer, Magdolna Baráth observed, Gerő's Communism was messianistic, he was ready to give his life for the movement if necessary. As a youth Gerő was a sociable, witty person whose psyche was distorted by the atmosphere of ter-ror and mistrust surrounding the Communist movement combined with the tragic fate of his comrades. Incarcerated for illegal Communist activity in 1922 he was released to the Soviet Union in 1924. After graduation from the Lenin Academy he became Comintern's itinerant agent in Western Europe, a job where he made use of his exceptional language skills. As Manuilsky's close associate after 1935 he acquainted himself with the Soviet party elite. He was assigned to Spain as a Comintern instructor entrusted to politically extirpate Trotskists and anarchists. Gerő carried out his assignment assidu-ously and without questioning Soviet motives. Uncritical acceptance of Soviet interests served him well throughout his political career. Between 1939 and 1941 he was the first man in the HCP, a position he relinquished to Rákosi with a certain degree of resentment. Gerő took an interest in eco-nomic affairs and consciously strove to become the party's economic poten-tate. He had no doubt as to the correctness of the Stalinist model of econ-omy and took the lead in the Sovietization of the Hungarian economy.[74] Gerő feared that the Bolshevik hard-liners could cause political problems even though the "ultra left wing views," expressed in issues like the land reform seemed to come from those who had not yet "had the chance to find out about the Party line."[75] He obviously could not conceive that ideological disobedience could stem from anything else but a lack of enlightenment.

The HCP could count on the National Peasant Party (NPP) as a close ally in the accomplishment of their political aims, particularly the Communist version of land reform. This was because some of the peasant party leaders, like the talented sociologist, Ferenc Erdei, were either clandestine Communists or shared Communist ideals. Erdei wanted to enter the HCP, but he was only admitted as a clandestine member so as to maximize his political usefulness in the NPP. Its leadership consisted of populist writers like József Darvas (another clandestine member of the HCP), Imre Kovács or Péter Veres. Although in the 1930s some populists had drifted to the extreme right others moved towards the opposite end of the political spectrum. Rákosi counted on them in the belief that they have strong influence on the "poor peasantry and the intelligentsia."[76] In the hope of dispelling prejudice against Communist ideology, party propagandists wanted to prove that theirs was a national movement in the field of literature even at the expense of their socialist traditions. Led by József Révai and the Marxist philosopher, György Lukács, the party supported the populists in their dispute with urban intellectuals, the representatives of liberal bourgeois ideals, avant-garde and a new literary movement built on the legacy of the Holocaust, even though some of the populists propagated anti-Semitic ideas. The Communist Party's pro-populist cultural policies were motivated by its desire to maximize their support among the intelligentsia and the peasantry.[77]

The Social Democratic Party (SDP) was traditionally influential among industrial workers and by the end of 1945 the party counted half-a-million members. Most of these were recruited from the working class and to a lesser extent from the peasantry, the urban petit bourgeoisie and the intelligentsia. Although the SDP's strategic objective was the construction of a socialist state, its concept of socialism was more democratic than that of the Communists. The party's leadership was heterogeneous. Veterans like Anna Kéthly or Manó Buchinger favored loose cooperation with the Communists, others on the left like Árpád Szakasits were Communist sympathizers. Rákosi put the dilemma bluntly: "a great question within the Social Democratic Party is that of cooperation with the Communists. The left wing cooperates, the right wing is against it [and] although they don't talk about it openly it is felt in every issue."[78] Regarding foreign policy right wing elements of the SDP envisioned Hungary as a bridge between East and West, while the left wing preferred an all-out pro-Soviet line. During the interwar period the HCP–SPD relationship was less than friendly. This was to change: the Communists urged close cooperation with their erstwhile ideological enemies, or more precisely with their pro-Communist left wing. Collaboration grew out of the two parties' alignment during the last phase of the war, when they pledged joint struggle for the creation of socialism in Hungary. The "Hungarian wing" of the Communist Party, i.e. those who spent the war at home, established an inter-party committee with the Social Democrats for the coordination of their policies in such a way that the committee's resolutions would be mutually binding.[79]

In January 1945 the HCP Central Committee instructed Mihály Farkas to reinforce the agreement on behalf of the Moscow group with Sándor Rónai who represented the Social Democrats.[80] Rónai wanted to enter the Communist Party, but Farkas convinced him not to do so. Like Erdei, he could be of more use in the ranks of a rival party. Farkas and Rónai agreed to promote close cooperation between the Social Democrats and the Communists in their "joint struggle," the Social Democrats would accept the Communist position in cases where differences of opinion could not be resolved within the coordinating committee.[81] The Communists attached great importance to the joint committee. This is demonstrated by the fact that they delegated top cadres: Gerő, Révai and Farkas, while initially none of the most important Communists entered the government. This reflected the HCP's desire to keep the Hungarian faction of the Communist Party from taking part in the formulation of political strategy. Cooperation with the SDP was labeled as the decisive factor in the future of Hungarian democracy and the struggle against "audacious reaction." Past differences had to be forgotten and those who failed to heed this warning were branded as "allies of reaction."[82]

Loosely organized with little centralization or discipline, the Independent Smallholder Party (SHP) emerged as the largest political force. At the end of 1945 it had over a million members. Its leader, Zoltán Tildy, was born in a tiny village in south-western Hungary. Tildy graduated from the Reformed Church Theological Academy. As assistant minister he acquainted himself with the problems of the agrarian proletariat and the lower strata of the peasantry. In 1919 he collaborated with the local organ of the Communist dictatorship; his father-in-law fell victim to the reprisals of white terror. Endowed with magnificent oratorical skills, Tildy launched into a dual career: besides serving his Church as a minister, he became instrumental in reviving the SHP in 1930, of which he became a leading figure. His fellow politician, Ferenc Nagy recalled that without Tildy's "unselfishness, limitless energy and magnificent organizational skills long years would have passed" before the Hungarian peasantry was united into a political movement. Although he enjoyed great success as a politician—he was elected into parliament despite the handicap of the Hungarian electoral system, and was well respected as a minister—he suffered setbacks. When his publishing company went broke he was accused of financial corruption, an allegation that would recur in his career as a politician. During the German occupation of Hungary Tildy participated in the illegal anti-Nazi movement and emerged as the leader of his party. Although in 1936 he declared the "death of Marxism as an ideological and social system," in 1945 he emphasized "combative unity" with the "working class parties." Although his ideal was the Finnish model for "the satisfaction of indescribable human striving for freedom and socialism filled with spiritual content," as President of the Republic Tildy made dubious concessions to the Soviets. As his biographer put it, Tildy "was not bereft of illusions, showed himself sincerely pro-Soviet, sought cooperation with the left, particularly the Communists."[83] This may be attributable to Tildy's weakness of character, as well as his leftist political inclinations and the constraints of political reality. Tildy's lack of character is illustrated by the fact that he did not even attempt to save his son-in-law, who was executed under mostly false charges in 1948. Tildy accepted Soviet occupation as fait accompli. "Tildy was someone we could do business with," Rákosi remembered, "all the more so since he had a realistic sense of politics and did not forget about the Soviet Union."[84] Tildy regarded close cooperation with the Communists and the Russians a matter of political reality, but his performance was marked with unprincipled compromise at the expense of pluralist democracy. Rákosi described him as the leader of the left wing in a difficult situation: when he agreed with the Communists and attacked his right wing, he was seen as carrying out the orders of the Communist Party, and when he didn't he was also in dire straits with the Communists.[85]

The SHP's social base was diverse. The party recruited from all strata of the peasantry, the state bureaucracy, much of the bourgeoisie and the intelligentsia. The left wing, which represented the poor peasantry, was Communist-oriented, the center wanted an agrarian democracy, and the right believed in a Western type democratic establishment. Characteristically, it was an open secret that a prominent representative of the SHP left wing, István Dobi was a clandestine member of the HCP. Rákosi instructed him to stay in the SHP, "because it seems that it is there that he can exert the best effort for the sake of democracy." The party's second-in-command, Ferenc Nagy, was a quintessential peasant politician, who rose to national prominence from humble peasant stock. Nagy finished six grades in elementary school and labored on his parents' plot until the age of 28. Self-educated, he gained national fame with writings on the peasantry. In 1930 he was among the founders of the Independent Smallholder Party, later he helped found the Hungarian Peasant Union. Nagy took part in the anti-Nazi movement during the war and was arrested by the Gestapo. From August 1945 he was the president of the SHP, and succeeded Tildy as Prime Minister in February 1946. Like the life of many Hungarian statesmen before him, his life ended in emigration. Nagy opposed the dictatorial aspirations of the Left, in the same way that he opposed the restoration of the pre-war regime. His tendency to yield to Communist pressure may have resulted from a desire to disarm their dictatorial aspirations, but to a certain extent also from opportunism. Sándor Márai, Hungary's celebrated writer, who was on the Communist blacklist for his postwar publications, remembered that Nagy avoided him at a book fair in 1946.[86] When he visited the U.S. in 1946 Nagy was disappointed by what he saw of American farming, the spirit of which was alien to him. It is ironic that he died in the U.S., where he purchased and farmed a piece of land.

The newly found cooperation with the Social Democrats and the collusion with the Peasant Party served the Communists well when they introduced their version of land reform, which had been worked out in Moscow by the party's agricultural expert, Imre Nagy. The transformation of the uneven distribution of land had been on the agenda of progressive political forces throughout the century. Moreover, both the United States and the Soviet Union wanted to see radical land reform. All democratic parties supported it and, considering the strength of the Smallholders, it is likely that their concept would have prevailed in free debate. Under Soviet control, however, the Communist program was introduced in March 1945.

Land reform occasioned the first direct Soviet intervention in Hungarian domestic affairs. Aiming to demoralize the Hungarian army, on 7 March the Soviet State Defense Committee instructed the ACC in Budapest to have the land reform carried out immediately on the "Polish principle." Molotov hoped that rapid execution would "concentrate the democratic social strata, particularly the peasants around the government," would secure urban food supply and would strengthen the hinterland of the Russian army.[87] Thereupon on 13 March Voroshilov summoned three members of the provisional government to stress the military and political significance of the land reform. He argued that if it were carried out rapidly people would desert the Szálasi government, which was fighting with ten divisions, more hastily. Voroshilov defined the timing and the modality of the land reform, which was passed as a government decree on 17 March.[88] Perhaps it is not a coincidence that the Romanian land reform was promulgated on the 22nd. The ACC's, or more specifically Moscow's direct and inconsiderate intervention in one of the nation's most sensitive internal problems set the pattern for the future. Moscow did not even consult with its political ally, the HCP. At this point, however, few people bothered, since possibly for the last time in almost half a century, the Soviet wishes and the aspirations of many, if by no means all, Hungarians by and large coincided.

In public the Communist Party espoused the cause of "a free, independent and democratic Hungary." Hungary would be neither a "bourgeois capitalist democracy," nor, *as of yet*, socialist, but possibly something between the two, a people's democracy. In Hungary it would have been suicidal to go straight for power. The HCP was weak, with virtually no members or even sympathizers when the war ended. Nor were international conditions conducive for the propagation of the proletarian dictatorship. Explaining his party's position to veterans of the 1919 Communist dictatorship, Révai stated that "if we expected the Red Army to make a proletarian dictatorship we would not be taking into account that the alliance between the Soviet Union, Britain and the United States would fall apart." The latter two "would never recognize a Communist government."[89] Rákosi recalled that socialism in the Communist sense was initially played down for tactical reasons. "Stalin warned us," he remembered, that "mention of the dictatorship of the proletariat before the time comes plays into the hands of the enemy."[90] For the time being, however, Rákosi depicted a rosy future for Hungarian democracy. To the U.S. diplomatic representative, Arthur Schoenfeld he explained that Hungary "should look to small states like Denmark and Norway as models of political and social organization."[91]

Rákosi made a highly favorable impression on Schoenfeld, whose comment inadvertently demonstrates his contempt for the Hungarian political arena: "[Rákosi was] forceful and highly intelligent with the advantage of knowing his own mind. His knowledge of English and contact with Anglo-American press circles make him one of the more enlightened Hungarian public men."[92] A Smallholder, Miklós Nyárádi was less favorably impressed. Rákosi, Nyárádi wrote was "one of the smartest men of any political persuasion [...] His Russian training told him what to do; his own instinct of timing told him when to do it." Rákosi, who "managed to inhibit every human trait" was "ashamed of two things: he is a Jew and hence a merciless anti-Semite; he springs from a bourgeois background."[93] Rákosi, born in a family with twelve children, remembered his childhood days in the countryside fondly. Yet, he broke with his rural past and persecuted its inhabitants mercilessly after he came to power. Trained as a merchant, he entered the Social Democratic Party, but was won over to the Bolsheviks as a POW in Soviet-Russia. He had played a role in Béla Kun's dictatorship in 1919 as deputy commissar of trade and later as the commander of the Red Guard. Fleeing Hungary he ended up in Moscow and worked as a traveling commissioner of the Comintern. In 1925 he was arrested as the leader of the Communist Party's secretariat in Hungary and was sentenced to 8.5 years in prison. When his sentence expired he was tried and sentenced for his role in 1919, this time for life. In 1940 he was extradited to the Soviet Union; a day after his arrival he stood at Stalin's side at the 7 November parade. Rákosi assumed leadership of the Hungarian Communist emigration, in February 1945 he was appointed the HCP's general secretary.

In spite of all the talk about popular front tactics, the position of non-

Communist political forces was deteriorating in most East European countries. In Romania, Andrei Vishinskii forced the king to appoint the pro-
Communist leader of the Ploughman's Front, Petru Groza. In March the
establishment of Soviet–Romanian joint companies (Sovroms) furthered
Soviet economic penetration in the Romanian economy. Shortly after liberation from German rule, in Hungary the HCP began to "gain strength and
move ahead." In mid-April Rákosi claimed that the international environment was changing, "Communist influence was growing in the Romanian
government." Referring to the coalition arrangement of 27 March, he pointed
out that in Czechoslovakia seven out of twenty-one ministers were Communists. He revealed that the Hungarian party's moderation was only a tactical
measure: "Among such neighbors Hungarian democracy cannot be satisfied
with the situation of four months ago, when we had to justify to the world
that the government was not Communist. We overdid it a little. The persons
we needed then can now be gotten rid of and the international situation is
forcing us to do this as well."[94] Rákosi illustrated his policy in connection
with the workers' committees. He considered them too radical for the present, which did not understand that "Moscow does not want to step on the
road towards socialism immediately." Nonetheless the party was devoting a
lot of attention to these committees since "when the situation is right we
can go one step further and then these committees will be able to provide
enormous help."[95]

The HCP resented some members of the Dálnoki Miklós cabinet from
the outset. The time was ripe for removing "reactionary ministers," even
certain "reactionary social democrats" from the government. Révai, who
had wanted to reshuffle the government by firing the "reactionaries" since
February thought that Miklós was a weakling, and dishonest, even though
Gerő had commended him as someone the Communists could work with.
Rákosi contacted Marshal Voroshilov and the ACC's political advisor,
Pushkin. The Russians recommended the dismissal of only two ministers;
the Smallholder finance minister István Vásáry, a former member of the
revolutionary socialist party in 1919, and General Gábor Faragho, who had
led the Hungarian armistice talks in Moscow. Rákosi informed Georgii
Dimitrov that reactionaries would be fired from the cabinet as soon as the
government moved from its original seat in Debrecen to the capital city,
which he believed was under "the control of the radical masses."[96] But caution was needed. First the public had to be prepared, through a press campaign designed to disgrace the reactionary elements. They could count on
an influential left wing Social Democrat, Árpád Szakasits, who was dissatisfied with both Miklós and Faragho. Most SDP leaders agreed with the
Communists concerning the future of the government: to withhold their

most influential men while they would gradually get rid of its undesirable members.[97]

The first step in this process was the government reshuffle in May: Gerő entered as minister of trade and finance and the left-wing deputy secretary general of the SDP, Antal Bán came in as minister of industry replacing an allegedly less talented representative of the "right wing." The SHP was compensated with a new portfolio of national reconstruction for Ferenc Nagy. The Communists received four state secretary positions. Rákosi was satisfied: "democratization of the government in such a manner is good because it makes little noise outside."[98] This embodied the philosophy of gaining ground without attracting Western attention.

The opportunity to cleanse the cabinet further presented itself when the allegedly right-wing Minister of Justice Ágoston Valentiny, who had been a Social Democrat since 1918 and actively supported the Communist dictatorship of 1919, introduced a decree that was directed at curbing the power of the Communist-dominated political police. With the support of the SHP Valentiny wanted to establish a separate organ to investigate war crimes, which would be under the jurisdiction of his own portfolio instead of the Communist-controlled Interior Ministry. At the cabinet meeting the Communists and their allies, the recently appointed Bán and the putatively independent, but clandestine Communist Erik Molnár, voted against the decree, but it passed nonetheless. At Rákosi's instigation the Soviet minister in Budapest, Pushkin, intervened. Pushkin was a tough, emotionless, imposing figure, who played an instrumental role in helping the HCP to power. Schoenfeld recalled that "his eyes and expression are remarkably hard. He is completely successful in preventing an indication of emotion or reaction appearing while listening [...] his eyes never lose their coldness," and had "a determined ruthlessness verging on the fanatical."[99]

Pushkin summoned foreign minister János Gyöngyösi, who held a school teacher's diploma in Hungarian and Latin, and called him to account for supporting the bill of which the ACC had not been consulted, and which would make it more difficult to try war criminals and fascist elements. He then saw Dálnoki Miklós and condemned his government for not supporting efforts to persecute fascist elements. Pushkin complained that Miklós was giving the ACC a hard time by opposing the measures proposed by the "democratic parties." Cowed by Pushkin's verbal onslaught Miklós, who had had abstained from voting, promised not to sign the decree.[100]

For the Soviets this episode highlighted the need to strengthen the left wing within the government. In order to do so they assumed a role that they would play on many more occasions to come: that of the arbiter between competing political forces. They intervened behind the scenes when the Communists were unable to prevail on their own. In such a way the Kremlin was able to tip the scale in favor of its political protégés without a high political cost. This is one of the reasons why the situation in Hungary was misleading to some observers, for example the U.S. representative in Hungary. It looked as though the Hungarian political parties made compromises of their own accord. In reality the Soviets prudently extracted the concessions behind the scenes.

In the meantime the Communists were strengthening their rank and file. Although it was Hungary's international obligation to persecute the remnants of Nazi radicalism, they were willing to make exceptions when it came to their own interests. Rákosi, who was of Jewish descent, held a highly dubious stance on anti-Semitism and extreme right-wing radicalism. While in public he posed as the champion "anti-fascist struggle," in smaller circles he lectured on the dangers of an incursion of formerly persecuted Jews into the Communist movement. He was ready to give the fight against fascism a distinctly Communist perspective by declaring that "fascists who have a working class background" should receive a favorable treatment, while "non-working class fascists should be handled more harshly." Révai interpreted the question in terms of class struggle: Nazi exploiters should be persecuted, while "little Nazis" would be allowed to rectify their sins. In June 1945 he told an audience of party members:

"We shall differentiate in our struggle against the Arrow Cross and fascists. We shall differentiate between the small Arrow Cross and the Arrow Cross that came from the ruling classes. We must direct our struggle at the leaders. Gradually we shall change to a policy, which will allow the small Arrow Cross men to repent, to expiate themselves, to return to Hungarian democracy, the Hungarian working class movement."[101] "Petty" Nazis were treated similarly in Austria: there the Soviets turned denazification into class warfare, hoping to find converts to communism among the "good" Nazis and severely punishing the "bourgeois" war criminals.[102] Rákosi claimed that the SPD was admitting workers who had been members of "fascist parties," while the Communists were sending them to work into trade unions to see how they worked before they can join them.[103] In July he authorized the recruitment into the HCP of Arrow Cross "small fry."[104] The Szeged organization of the party issued membership forms to enlist them as a way to rectify their sins: "I undersigned declare herewith that I have been a member of the Arrow Cross Party. [...] I want to make good my fault and I [...] solemnly promise to be from now on a faithful, fighting member of the [...] Hungarian Communist Party."[105] These people would be loyal since it was easy to blackmail them because of their shady past. They could be disposed of when they were no longer needed. Ironically it was such a convert, Judge Vilmos Olti, who sentenced the architect of the Communist police state, László Rajk to death in 1949.

Simultaneously, the Communists launched an offensive against the "bourgeois right wing." In order to strengthen their control of the administration they replaced the state secretary responsible for the police with a Muscovite, Mihály Farkas. The Communists extracted an agreement from the SPD that they would replace Justice Minister Valentiny and convinced the SHP to remove finance minister Vásáry. Valentiny, who opposed unconditional collaboration with the Communist Party resigned on 9 July. Vásáry, who had strong support within his party, was harder to get rid of. Eventually his own party leader ousted him. Inadvertently or not, through such actions, Tildy helped pave the way towards the elimination of the political opposition. Perhaps he wanted to convince the Soviets that beside the Communists they could rely on pro-Soviet elements in other parties. Tildy was convinced that Hungary was left out of the western sphere of influence and "the Soviet troops would not leave Hungary for another fifty years."[106]

After Valentiny and Vásáry it was Faragho's turn. This was understandable, since Faragho had been the commander of the gendarmerie, which played a crucial role in the deportation of Hungarian Jews. His portfolio was offered to the SPD, which supported the Communist effort to remove him.[107] Valentiny's position went to István Ries, whose unswerving readiness to collaborate made him acceptable to both the Communists and the Soviets. Ries's life ended tragically: arrested under false charges in 1950 he was beaten to death during interrogation. Faragho's succession was a different story, since the Social Democrats nominated a veteran of their movement, while the Communists wanted a clandestine member of their party, Sándor Rónai. Soviet support was needed again to resolve the stalemate. This time Pushkin summoned Árpád Szakasits, and declared that the SPD's candidate for the Ministry of Public Supply was unsuitable for the job and recommended the Communists' choice, Rónai. The Prime Minister attempted to counter this recommendation by suggesting an independent candidate, but Pushkin remained adamant and Rónai was accepted. There were two candidates for the vacant Ministry of Finance: the Communist choice was the Smallholder president of the National Bank, Artúr Kárász, and Dezső Sulyok, who enjoyed the support of the Smallholders themselves. Sulyok, who supported neutrality for Hungary, made no secret of his anti-Communism and attraction to political Catholicism. Low key Soviet diplomacy came into play once more: Pushkin convinced Tildy to drop Sulyok and accept the professionally more competent (and from the leftist perspective politically more reliable) candidate of the HCP.[108] Tildy gave in and the crisis subsided for the time being.

Moscow's Hungarian allies had every reason to be satisfied. The vote on the Valentiny bill had showed that the Communists could be voted down on sensitive issues and fundamental interests such as control of the police could be challenged. Now they had a majority within the cabinet, which could guarantee that such mishaps would not recur. Communist control of the police was secured and the new ministers were willing to collaborate. All this happened with minimal attention from abroad.[109] The Soviet foreign ministry expressed satisfaction as well, since "reactionaries and right wingers" were out of the government, and in their place sat a majority of Communists, Social Democrats and National Peasants, who were "close to the Communists".[110]

The American appraisal of the Dálnoki Miklós government before it was reshuffled was relatively favorable. Ambassador Harriman reported that it had a wide and respectable membership.[111] Despite anxieties concerning the extent of Soviet and Communist influence in the country, Hungary was allowed to send a diplomatic representative to the United States, albeit without diplomatic recognition. Stalin proposed diplomatic recognition for the former German satellites, but Washington was unwilling to do so with regard to Hungary, Romania and Bulgaria in disapproval of the way those governments exercised their authority. At the Potsdam conference the Western powers accepted Soviet predominance in Eastern Europe. Soviet deputy foreign minister Vishinskii noted with satisfaction that the "U.S. delegation left Potsdam realizing Eastern Europe has been permanently lost to Russia by the Anglo-Americans."[112] Nevertheless, Washington wished to postpone Hungary's diplomatic recognition until the reorganization of the government—obviously not along the lines presented above—took place. After Potsdam the U.S. stance towards Eastern Europe hardened and in August Washington reasserted its interest in Romania's future. This prompted the Romanian king to attempt a repetition of the anti-Antonescu coup of 1944 and dismiss Groza but he failed dismally. At the London Council of Foreign Ministers meeting in September the U.S. offered diplomatic recognition to Hungary after Molotov's complaint that the West did not recognize any government friendly to the Soviet Union. Perhaps Byrnes meant to emphasize the difference between the Hungarian government on one hand and the administrations in Bucharest and Sofia on the other. It may also have been a demonstration of interest in Hungarian affairs in order to strengthen pro-American political forces. Diplomatic recognition might have been meant to further the cause of free elections, since the policy of non-recognition failed to work in Bulgaria and Romania.[113] Or, in the light of Byrnes' new approach to cooperation with the Soviet Union, it may have been a conciliatory gesture. Subsequent U.S. actions suggest that Hungary may not have been on the list of countries unconditionally relinquished to Moscow. But signs of U.S. discontent with Sovietization in Hungary were vague and were inadequate in strengthening the wavering resolve of democratic elements.

Being aware of Russian predominance, the Hungarian government was wary of accepting the American offer. Before responding, Miklós decided to sound out Voroshilov's view and to declare that his government wished to establish diplomatic relations first of all with the Soviet Union. Marshal Voroshilov opined that the reference to free elections in the U.S. note was "offending," but emphasized that he expressed his views on the matter only because the premier himself wanted to hear them. Miklós assured Voroshilov that Budapest's response would reflect the spirit of the Soviet comments. Eager to please the Marshal, the former army commander confided that the important thing for the Hungarians was to reestablish diplomatic relations with the Soviet Union. Voroshilov must have been either unprepared or unauthorized to respond to an initiative of such magnitude and gave no immediate answer. This meant that Moscow was not considering the establishment of diplomatic relations with the former enemy, hence, had the Hungarian premier been bolder the pro-Western political forces might have scored a significant diplomatic victory. Voroshilov seized the opportunity and recommended the immediate and unconditional establishment of diplomatic relations with Hungary.[114] This episode is of interest for two reasons. First, for a moment the Soviet Union lost the initiative in its own sphere but no advantage was taken of this. The second concerns domestic attitudes in Hungary. Many of those who deplored Communists designs failed to oppose them actively because of their resignation to Soviet preponderance: notwithstanding lack of popular support, most believed that the HCP would prevail. This fatalistic but understandable attitude helped the Communists seize power with relative ease.

The Communist appraisal of the political situation in the second part of 1945 vindicated the tactic of gradualism that had been used successfully during the summer crisis. The struggle against "leftist, sectarian" elements clamoring for an immediate proletarian dictatorship would continue, and there would be no change in relations with the SDP either. Cooperation with their pro-Communist left wing would be pursued and so would the "isolation" (i.e. elimination) of the right, those who would cooperate, but refused to *collaborate* with the Communists. The same was true for the SHP, which contained "democratic elements," but was the focal point of reactionaries at the same time. Still, there was reason to be satisfied because of the success in forcing the Smallholder left wing to turn against the right. But this was only the beginning, since the greater part of the SHP still favored the British and the Americans.[115] The central question was therefore whether the U.S. was willing and able to capitalize on this sentiment. If liberal internationalism prevailed, Washington would try to save democracy in Hungary. If *realpolitik* mingled with the doctrine of non-intervention gained the upper hand, the Soviets would be able to further impose their control.

Prior to the national elections scheduled for November the American mission in Budapest began to view Hungarian prospects with greater optimism. Non-Communist elements regained their confidence in the light of Western statements and were resolved to resisting Communist expansion. If the Western democracies were willing to take firm measures on Hungary's behalf, they would be sending a signal that Hungary's "full and final Bolshevization" could be avoided and the Communist efforts to achieve unlimited control would be partially, although not fully blocked.[116] The proof of the pudding would be in the eating—in this case the forthcoming municipal elections in Budapest. The prevailing American approach was one of non-intervention. In an "unofficial message" to the Hungarian government Byrnes expressed that his "Government is ready, if requested by the Hungarian government, or if it should have adequate reason to believe that free elections will not be held, to consult with the British and Soviet Governments on such measures as may be taken to ensure the discharge of obligation undertaken at Yalta."[117] Exactly what these measures would be remained just as unclear as the meaning of the Yalta Declaration; moreover, the provisional government was in no position to request U.S. intervention.

Nevertheless, the Smallholders did unofficially request U.S. assistance. State Secretary István Balogh, and the managing director of the Hungarian General Credit Bank, Baron Ullmann approached Schoenfeld to request U.S. financial support for the upcoming elections. Schoenfeld was a tactful, amiable, and exceptionally hardworking officer, who shared the prejudices prevalent in the Foreign Service. A fellow diplomat, Joseph Grew, felt that he was "a very keen and brilliant man," and did not observe any of the "unfavorable Jewish attitudes" in his behavior. From 1931 Schoenfeld served as minister in Santo Domingo, which he found a most "primitive" capital. In 1936 Schoenfeld took up a new position in Finland, where he was delighted with the Nordic climate and among such a "sturdy, upstanding race" as the Finns. Appalled by Stalin's aggression in Finland Schoenfeld appealed to Secretary of State Hull for diplomatic action under the leadership of the U.S.[118] If he was satisfied with the Finns, the same could not be said of his impression of the Hungarians. Schoenfeld rejected any U.S. assistance on behalf of his government: his response encapsulated U.S. attitudes towards Eastern Europe.

"I explained that Americans thought of democratic processes as involving effort to overcome obstacle by necessary personal sacrifice. Since [the] time of the Magna Charta freedom had been won by vigorous assertion of popular rights and willingness to fight for them when necessary [...] Democracy in this country would have to be secured by similar qualities of character on the part of the Hungarians."[119] Schoenfeld's self-righteous sermon reflected the position expounded by liberal philosopher John Stewart

Mill. In a treatise published in 1859 Mill argued that each nation should fight to deserve the privilege of good government and freedom. Hence Hungarians had to acquire freedom through their own efforts and Schoenfeld clearly felt that they did not merit American aid. His attitude did not solely derive from Mill's Social Darwinist stance, but more fundamentally from preconceptions towards East Europeans shared by the east-coast elite. In the first two decades of the 20th century laws were enacted to restrict immigration from Eastern Europe, whose people were widely thought to be culturally and racially inferior to the Anglo-Saxon stock and therefore a threat to American democracy. Prejudices were "verified" by such pseudo sciences as craniology.[120] Images of Eastern Europe were arranged to fit these prejudices. "U.S. diplomats' cultural image of Soviet Russia and the Slavic lands of Eastern Europe," Hugh DeSantis wrote, "mirrored ethnocentric and racial prejudices that permeated American society in the early years of the 20th century, particularly urban, nativist, upper middle-class American society, reared in this social milieu, career diplomats carried with them a stereotype of southern and eastern immigrants as dirty and unruly, inferior and uncivilized who had vulgarized American social, political and moral life [...] Appalled by the amoral conduct of her people (State Department official) Durbrow considered Romania a profession, not a country."[121] Schoenfeld tended to select from Hungarian political attitudes phenomena that reaffirmed collectively held prejudices. "Partly because of disrespect for the Magyar people, who unlike the sturdy Finns, displayed 'rabbit-like squeaks of pain and terror' with each sudden movement of Russian interlopers, Schoenfeld avoided involvement in the nation's political affairs."[122] Schoenfeld bemoaned the corrupt and self-serving attitude of some SHP leaders, but tended to ignore manifestations of courage and self-sacrifice demonstrated by such politicians as Dezső Sulyok or Margit Schlachta.

The election in Budapest belied pessimists who doubted Hungary's democratic future. Although the Communists and the Social Democrats ran on a common list, the Smallholders beat them by 50,000 votes. Mutual recriminations ensued. The Soviets deplored Communist performance and were frustrated with the HCP's "unhelpful" attitude. On the other hand, the Hungarian Communists bemoaned Moscow's failure to return Hungarian POWs, the unbridled Soviet quest for reparations which was causing runaway inflation, as well as the obligation to feed the Red Army that created food shortages. Therefore the HCP wanted Moscow to release the POWs, to be less demanding in reparations, to suspend the delivery of foodstuffs to the Soviet armed forces and to take more effective measures to harness excesses by Red Army personnel.[123] Voroshilov agreed that Hungarian inmates in Soviet camps who had not served in the German SS or SA and did not participate in brutalities against the Soviet Union should be repatri-

ated because of the forthcoming elections. This gesture was expected to offset the disadvantage caused by the fact that the British and the Americans
had already released their own Hungarian prisoners. Although Beria supported this measure as well,[124] nothing came of it.

Voroshilov believed that the party's half a million members were far
from being real Communists. The leadership had few trained cadres, left
wing tendencies were strong, and all kinds of "adventurists," or "criminal
elements" who had been members of fascist organizations had infiltrated
the party. These had to be eliminated in case their activities weakened the
party's position. The Communist leadership and Rákosi in particular failed
to put forward "one single practical proposal" to fight the rampant inflation
prevalent in the country. Mistakes were made in the campaign: instead of
organizing mass rallies the Communists should have followed the Smallholder example by campaigning at a grass roots level, among the churches
and individual people, especially women. Women, according to the ACC
Chairman, were the keys to victory. Furthermore, the Communists were
over-confident and were unable to estimate realistically the "correlation of
forces" in the country. After the election in Budapest the HCP made a political mistake by launching an "inadmissible campaign" against the SHP,
lumping together both left and right wing members. Voroshilov warned that
Rákosi's political authority was diminishing. He was concerned about the
party leadership's domination by Jews, which gave rise to anti-Semitic
propaganda.[125]

Enraged by his party's poor showing, Rákosi contemplated more violent means to seize power. "I explained to Szakasits that with the proletarian fist we demonstrated at the election we are not scared of the reactionaries and we know that in class struggle we have other weapons beside elections; if needed we shall take the proletariat of greater Budapest to the
streets and we shall see where the SHP and the reaction will be."[126] Rákosi
could not afford another mistake. As part of the electoral campaign the HCP
accused the Smallholders of being the "most responsible for the country's
difficult [economic] situation." At the same time they envisioned closer
cooperation with the NPP and the SDP. In practice this meant that the Communists hoped to eliminate their rivals by running on a common list. In
view of the events it is hardly surprising that Moscow preferred this "Bulgarian type" arrangement. Voroshilov tried to persuade Tildy and Ferenc
Nagy to accept the idea. They rejected it, claiming that they would lose
votes to the "bourgeois parties." Insisting that he had no desire to coerce
anyone, Voroshilov also tried to gain Social Democratic support for the
idea but with equal failure. Tildy recommended a joint declaration of the
four major parties, which would state that irrespective of the election's
result they would form a coalition government. This benefited the Commu-

nists since even Voroshilov expected the SHP to win by a large margin. Voroshilov, especially in view of the fact that the Smallholders rejected the electoral bloc, supported the declaration. The Marshal received Tildy's unsolicited assurance that he would strengthen cooperation with the workers' parties because he was "frightened by his party's unexpected victory at the municipal election which was due to the votes of right wing elements."[127] But the Kremlin was upset by Voroshilov's failure to secure the Bulgarian model and reprimanded him for "acting incorrectly" in accepting Tildy's face saving formula for the declaration.[128] Molotov also blamed Rákosi for making a great mistake of taking part in the election separately and not in an electoral bloc.[129] In reality the Russians themselves shied away from it because of Anglo-American diplomatic pressure.

The elections were conducted without fraud and with this backdrop it brought a sweeping victory for the SHP, which received 59 percent of the votes as opposed to 17 percent for the Communists, an almost equal percentage for the Social Democrats and five percent for the NPP. This was in stark contrast with the Bulgarian situation where single list elections were held in November in which the Communist-dominated government coalition received 86 percent of the votes. Since Tildy had committed his party to forming a coalition the SHP did not insist on asserting its absolute majority in the newly elected cabinet. On 9 November the four major parties shared out the portfolios. Accordingly the SHP received the Ministry of the Interior while the Communists obtained that of finance. For the Interior Ministry the SHP nominated their general secretary, Béla Kovács and Gerő received the Ministry of Finance. However, this agreement was rejected by Molotov, who instructed Voroshilov to renegotiate the government positions for the HCP to get the Interior Ministry, as well as two deputy prime minister posts for the HCP and the SDP. Voroshilov gave the appropriate instruction to Rákosi who declared that the previous arrangement was unsatisfactory after all much to the confusion of the coalition partners. Although Voroshilov was ready to accept Kovács as minister of the interior in case the Smallholders mounted a tough resistance, Molotov was not. Hence, when the renewed talks broke down, Voroshilov and Pushkin took the matter into their own hands. They had an unexpectedly easy time in convincing the Smallholder leaders of the need to accept the Communist proposal. Finally the Communist Imre Nagy took the Interior Ministry; while Szakasits, whose allegiance to Moscow was easily as strong as Rákosi's, was appointed deputy prime minister. Although the SHP was compensated with one position of deputy prime minister, it made little difference, since its own candidate was turned down and the position went to István Dobi, a card carrying secret member of the HCP.[130]

Rákosi had predicted that the general elections would "not play an important role in Communist plans."[131] He turned out to be right. Molotov's intervention reduced the positive effect of the election to a considerable extent. Furthermore, low key Soviet diplomacy was also effective in the sense that it remained unnoticed, hence there was no chance for domestic or Western reaction. Although Voroshilov was flexible, he was not the source of power. The new cabinet won Soviet approval. An evaluation made by Soviet military organs in Hungary asserted that Tildy "favored cooperation with the Soviet Union," just like Szakasits, Bán, Rónai, Ries and Gyöngyösi. Only two were unsatisfactory: Béla Kovács was "an ardent enemy of the Communists" and Minister of Defense Vörös was thought to be anti-Soviet.[132]

While the Communists were rectifying their electoral defeat with Soviet assistance, the U.S. continued to stay aloof of the events. Hungary's politically conservative and staunchly anti-Communist primate, Archbishop József Mindszenty asked for U.S. intervention. Schoenfeld reiterated that the United States insisted on the principle of non-involvement, which excluded all measures that could be conceived as interference in Hungary's domestic affairs or which were not part of the normal function of diplomatic missions.[133] State Department analysts predicted that Moscow would now want to install a "friendly government," meaning that the coalition would be placed under Communist control. The Red Army would remain in Hungary and politics would be cleansed of anti-Soviet elements.[134] Although Soviet takeover was clearly unfolding, other matters occupied the Truman administration.

1946: Green light for Socialism

In 1946 a fundamental shift occurred in U.S. foreign policy. Truman reinterpreted events in Eastern Europe and the U.S. administration changed its policy on Germany. Byrnes' approach of realistic cooperation was abandoned meaning that Washington wanted to handle Germany on an all-German basis, a transformation that played a role in setting the great powers against each other. The Soviets would not be allowed to collect reparations the same way as agreed at Potsdam. This halt on reparation payments paved the way for the "organization" of the Western zone, while allowing the U.S. to place the blame on the Soviets.[135]

Germany was by far the most significant question in U.S.–Soviet relations, and the U.S. administration was divided over the course to take.[136] Some, like George Kennan, wanted to see the integration of the Western zone into Western Europe. Kennan warned that the ultimate aim of the Soviets was a Communist Germany, and the pursuit by the United States of a unified Germany played into their hands. Acting Secretary of State Acheson on the other hand was not ready to rupture Soviet–American relations or to abandon the eastern part of Germany and the continent. Nor did Acheson want to yield raw materials and foodstuffs in the Soviet sphere, or assume responsibility for the division of Europe and Germany. Byrnes was wary of a showdown over Germany while the peace treaties for the former satellites were still being framed, and therefore floated the idea of a treaty guaranteeing the disarmament and demilitarization of Germany. Molotov rejected the proposal and requested Russian participation in the international control of the Ruhr. The U.S. suspected that the Russians wanted a revived, united and peaceful Germany in order to gain direct control of the Ruhr. Byrnes, who now read an expansionist pattern into Moscow's policy, feared the political appeal of the Soviet position and dreaded the prospect of an eventual Soviet–German coalition. Therefore he instructed subordinates to fuse the British and American zones into an economic unit called Bizonia. Germany had to retain sovereignty over the Rhine and the Ruhr regions and have a unified finance and economic policy. The Truman administration was willing to finance Bizonia, retain troops in Germany, guarantee a demilitarization treaty and divide Germany. Bizonia meant that Americans envisaged a Western economic and geopolitical entity as their preeminent concern. Reconstructing Western Europe superceded Soviet reparations and allaying Moscow's security concerns.

A further divisive issue in the Soviet–American relationship were Moscow's ambitions in Turkey. In fact the Turkish standoff (and the Iranian crisis) were two of the central factors that led to the reappraisal of U.S. policy towards the USSR. As the historian Eduard Mark argues, when the year 1946 began, the two great powers were still allies; by the time it ended, American war plans for a Soviet attack on Western Europe had been prepared.[137] The Truman administration perceived a Soviet effort to gain control of the Near East. Moscow aimed to revise the 1936 Montreux convention on the status of the Straits—something that Molotov had already suggested to Hitler in 1940—and possibly at Beria's instigation wanted Turkey to cede the regions of Kars and Ardagan. Reports on the Soviets' aggressive intentions convinced the American political and military leadership to prepare for the use force to preserve Turkish sovereignty. Eventually Stalin backed down, but a lasting impression was made that Moscow was on a quest for European expansion.[138]

George Kennan's Long Telegram of February 1946 provided a theoretical framework for the interpretation of Soviet foreign policy and convinced many in the Truman administration of the expansionist motives of the Soviet Union. Interpreting Soviet actions in the framework of liberal internationalism Kennan argued that the Soviets did not believe in peaceful coexistence between socialism and the capitalist states and were determined to export the proletarian revolution. Thus, in Kennan's view, which gained immediate acceptance in government circles, cooperation with the former ally would be problematic, if not impossible. [139]

In July 1946 President Truman requested an inter-departmental assessment of Soviet motivations. The result, the Clifford–Elsey report, repeated many of the themes of the Long Telegram and presented an ominous picture.[140] Moscow was making military preparations "to weaken the position and to destroy the prestige of the United States" and ultimately sought nothing less than world domination. To stop the preponderant resources and human capital of Eurasia from falling under the Kremlin's control, America had to revitalize its military capabilities and assist democracies that were endangered by the USSR. Western Europe and the Middle East had to stay outside of the Russian sphere of influence. Tacitly therefore, the Clifford–Elsey report recognized the Kremlin's claim on Eastern Europe.

Domestic relaxation in the Soviet Union turned out to be short-lived. In February 1946 Stalin called for rapid industrialization combined with massive rearmament. This called for new sacrifices from the part of the Soviet people since Stalin's program would rely on domestic resources— plus industrial dismantling in the occupied areas. Foreign policy would steer back to its anti-Western pre-1942 course. The Soviet equivalent of Kennan's Long Telegram was a report prepared by the Soviet ambassador in Washington possibly at Molotov's instruction. William Taubman has pointed out that it was written to confirm a set of *a priori* ideas held by the Soviet leadership about the aims of the United States.[141]

Arguing that the United States was "striving for world supremacy," and that "preparation by the United States for a future war is being conducted with the prospect of war against the Soviet Union," the document ruled out any possibility of future cooperation with the Western world. Reflecting little nostalgia for the Soviet–American alliance Ambassador Novikov claimed that the United States hoped for the Soviet Union to be "exhausted" or perhaps "completely destroyed" in the war against the Nazis. This was not a new theme: already in 1943 Litvinov had argued that the military calculations of the U.S. and British governments were intended to wear down the USSR's strength to the maximum extent possible to diminish its role in the solution of postwar problems.[142] According to Novikov American hostility towards Russia survived: the United States was allegedly reviving an "imperialist Germany" in order to use it in a future war against the Soviet Union. American capital would "infiltrate" national economies and would be a "stage on the road for world domination by the United States." Logically Novikov's reasoning meant that the USSR no longer had an interest in economic cooperation with the U.S. otherwise they would facilitate their opponents' quest for world mastery. In fact the allusion that the Soviet Union continued "to remain economically independent of the outside world and is rebuilding its national economy with its own forces" indicated that the alliance was dead. All the more so since the United States was encircling the Soviet Union with aggressive intent—the "offensive nature of the strategic concepts" of the American armed forces was emphasized—and threatened the Soviet Union.

There is some indication that Stalin did not wholly agree with this analysis. In a speech given on 24 September he claimed that the danger of war "at present does not exist," and doubted whether "the governing circles of Great Britain and the United States could create a capitalist encirclement of the Soviet Union even if they wished to, which, I cannot assert."[143] If public statements are indicative of real intentions Stalin and Molotov may have differed although it must be said that publicly Molotov supported the continuation of the Grand Alliance.[144] However, there is little doubt that Stalin agreed with the Novikov telegram on at least one point: the position of Eastern Europe.

Washington, according to Novikov, was out to "limit" or "dislodge" Soviet influence from the neighboring countries. The U.S. supported "reactionary forces with the purpose of creating obstacles to the process of democratization of these countries." It "penetrated their economies" so as to weaken the pro-Soviet governments there, in order to replace them with ones that would "obediently carry out policy dictated from the United States." The Soviet Union's influence in the countries of South Eastern Europe was "an obstacle in the path of the expansionist policy of the United States." It followed from the analysis that Moscow would be opposed to any arrangement that fell short of unquestioned Soviet domination in adjacent areas, such as an "open sphere" advocated by Byrnes. As a consequence of this analysis, Sovietization in Eastern Europe was speeded up. The initiative may have come from Stalin.

The year 1946 brought momentous changes in Hungary. Rákosi announced the "liberation of the proletariat," Hungarian–Soviet joint companies extended Moscow's control to important sectors of the Hungarian economy, and the HCP launched its offensive to liquidate the non-collaborationist faction of the Smallholder Party. In theory there was a duality of power: a Smallholder majority in parliament, while the political left dominated the government. In practice, however, parliament was a fig leaf that concealed the true scope of Communist influence. Its powers were severely limited and the nation was governed by decrees discussed at inter-party meetings *a posteriori* sanctioned by a select legislative body, the Political Committee. The composition of the latter was determined by the arithmetic of political power and had little to do with the electoral will expressed at the ballot.

Communist preponderance in the "organs of power" was apparent. Control of the police was of utmost importance for all the Communist parties from Poland to Bulgaria. Rákosi made it clear that no matter what the opposition did, the police would remain democratic (meaning Communist), and no compromises would be made. The nation's largest party was willing to accept this state of affairs with the proviso that the police would "not beat the peasants."[145] Even before the election Rákosi boasted to Dimitrov that the police was basically in Communist hands;[146] an assessment that was largely accurate. Sixty-four percent of its officers belonged to the parties of the so-called left wing bloc (out of which 31 percent were Communist) and only the remaining minority to the SHP and the Citizen Democratic Party. In terms of power positions the situation was even more one-sided. Thus officers of Communist affiliation led 46 percent of the county police stations and 66 percent of the political departments of the police. The political police, which was organized under NKVD instructions and was entitled to intern "reactionaries," was under Communist control, as was the counter intelligence department of the Ministry of Defense. General Pálffy-Österreicher, a clandestine Communist in the SHP was in charge of the counter-intelligence department and was also in command of the border guards, the only combat-ready force in the country at the time. Although the Smallholders promised to curb its authority, this remained a promise they were never able to deliver. The Ministry of Defense and the Hungarian army were under the direct operational control of the Soviet occupation forces.[147]

On the government level the Social Democrats and the Communists controlled 203 "key positions" in the ministries as opposed to the 74 held by the SHP. The situation in the local governments was only a little better, with only three Smallholder mayors governing in 57 towns there were only three Smallholder mayors in comparison with twenty-two Communist mayors. President Tildy had reason to complain that "the largest democratic party had no role in leading the country."[148]

Soviet minister Pushkin and Acting ACC Chairman Sviridov explained Soviet intentions concerning the immediate future of Hungarian politics to Ferenc Nagy and Tildy on 6 January 1946. They reprimanded the Hungarians for harboring "anti-democrats and open monarchists in the (Smallholder) party." Tildy and Nagy explained that "a lot of opportunistic elements attached themselves to the party and they have not yet put things in order." Turning to Soviet–Hungarian relations the Soviets remarked that the Smallholders' policy of procrastination in cleansing the anti-democratic elements was leading to non-cooperation with the Soviet Union in economic affairs, non-compliance with the reparation clauses, in sum, to "playing

around with the Soviet Union instead of establishing friendly relations."
They warned that "the domestic situation in Hungary for the liberation of
which the Soviet Union paid a very high price was by no means neutral to
them."[149]

In the light of this exchange Révai's prediction that "struggle against
reaction" would increase is not surprising. Instead of a "chatting" democracy he called for an "active" one. In late January, the Communist leadership decided to launch a "popular" campaign so as to cleanse public administration from "reactionary elements." Mass demonstrations were organized
and as part of "popular verdicts" coordinated by local Communist elements
in conjunction with "fraternal parties," non-leftist leaders of the county or
municipal administrations were driven away. Lynching occurred in several
places. In the town of Békéscsaba Communists murdered two Smallholders
and seriously wounded a third on Labor Day.[150] The Communist leadership
declared war on "black marketers" and "speculators" whom Rákosi threatened to hang. Such careless remarks were pouring oil on the smoldering
ashes of anti-Semitism since in popular parlance the black marketers and
speculators were identified with Jews. Thus only two years after Hungarian
Jews had been all but exterminated, the Communist Party used anti-Semitic
slogans for political ends, for the creation of a chaotic situation in which the
opposition could be destroyed under the guise of restoring order. Révai
explained "We cannot of course renounce applying pressure at inter-party
meetings from above; but this in itself is insufficient, it has to be coupled
with pressure from below. The question arises whether we will use the
methods we did in March, namely mass demonstrations and popular verdicts if need be. We are not bashful comrades [...] the truce is over."[151] As
in Poland and Slovakia, pogroms resulting in deaths occurred in several
locations, notably in Kunmadaras, Makó and the working class city of
Miskolc. Local Communist leaders—some of them former members of the
Arrow Cross Party—took the lead in organizing and carrying them out.
When they were over, the Interior Ministry ensured the perpetrators were
not punished.[152]

The center and right wing of the SHP were dissatisfied with the deficiencies of democratic governance. They took exception to the fact that
national issues were decided behind closed doors at inter-party meetings
and wanted the state administration to determine political affairs. Moreover,
they wanted the separation of the branches of power and wished to curb
nationalization in the economy. Vásáry's faction was dissatisfied with their
party's 50 percent representation in the cabinet, and being oblivious of
Russian intervention, attacked Tildy for having yielded the Interior Ministry
to the Communists. Their most important demands were to receive proportionate representation in the police and the administration and local elec-

tions all over the country. At the same time the party had a small, but all the more outspoken left wing, which identified itself with the idea of a people's democracy and used the Communist press to promulgate their ideas.[153]

In the midst of political struggle in Hungary and elsewhere, notably Bulgaria, where fruitless efforts were made to include democratic elements in the government, Soviet leaders were making public announcements on the future of East–West relations in February 1946. Lazar Kaganovich warned of the danger of capitalist encirclement and the need to be strong in the future. Lavrentii Beria and Georgii Malenkov advocated the strengthening of Soviet industrial and military power. Molotov emphasized that the danger of new war on the Soviet Union stemmed from "war mongers" in the U.S. and Britain, and emphasized Soviet opposition to blocs. Andrei Zhdanov, an ideological revivalist on the other hand declared that the USSR was more secure than ever, therefore consumer industry could be developed. In a major speech on 9 February 1946 Stalin called for rearmament. Contemporary observers interpreted Stalin's speech as a definite break with the West, and East European prospects appeared bleak. Malenkov declared that the "fruits of victory" must be secured. "If we have the chestnuts, let us have them for the benefit of our own glorious Soviet people."[154] Moscow was keeping Eastern Europe no matter how the Grand Alliance would fare.

In May 1946 the prospects of Hungarian democracy changed for the worse. Referring to changing international conditions, Rákosi announced the dictatorship of the proletariat and in March and April economic Sovietization was in full swing with the establishment of Hungarian–Soviet joint companies. While the SHP were struggling for proportionate representation and to preserve their internal unity, their opponents set up a "Left Wing Bloc" to concert their policies against the political which launched a "counter-attack" on the "reactionary" majority of the Smallholders "from above and below." Two months before, on 1 March the new Prime Minister, Ferenc Nagy had received the Communist demands, which included purging public administration of reactionary elements, the nationalization of mining, state control of the nation's largest heavy industrial concerns and attaching the Hungarian National Bank to the government.[155] The Communists blamed the SHP for the sorry state of the country—hyperinflation in particular—and launched a press campaign to this effect. Without even waiting for Nagy's response Rákosi sent an ultimatum: his party would quit the coalition unless the SHP eliminated its right wing.[156] He rejected Nagy's proposal for resolving outstanding issues with a consensus of the political forces involved, and proceeded to organize a mass rally, but failed to consult Voroshilov. Placing a call at midnight, Voroshilov, who feared that mass mobilization could lead to undesirable international repercussions, demanded that Rákosi cancel the demonstration. Although the Marshal threatened to inform Stalin of the HCP's insubordination, Rákosi decided to go ahead with the rally. Before long the Smallholders gave in. On 5 March, while Churchill was announcing the descent of the iron curtain, the parliament passed a law on the "protection of the republic," which was to provide the legal basis for the liquidation of the Hungarian political opposition.

Before long, Nagy agreed to get rid of those who were "conspiring" against the coalition.[157] The question was who these should be. The HCP had its own list, which included Sulyok and Vásáry. Though the SHP took exception to Communists interference, as a compromise Tildy recommended the removal of 36 members of parliament and eight members of the Budapest municipal assembly. Eventually, on 12 March Nagy accepted almost every Communist demand, though only 20 deputies were expelled. Most of them continued their political careers; as an example, Sulyok formed a political party of his own. The SHP thereby accepted self-mutilation for the sake of maintaining the coalition. If they had any illusion that this would satisfy their political foes, it was rapidly dispelled. The very same day Nagy announced capitulation, the Communists decided to "cleanse" the SHP on the local level as well. They decided to subvert their enemy from inside: a three-member committee was set up "to organize the left wing" of the SHP.[158] Rákosi's celebrated "salami tactic" was unfolding, each concession led to an even more radical attack. Why did the nation's most popular political force give in so easily, especially in view of the fact that this time there seems to have been no direct Soviet involvement? Why was it unnecessary for Moscow to enter the political arena? In sum, because the Communists had an easy time getting what they wanted. There may have been several reasons for this.

From the perspective of the non-Communist elements, the dangers inherent in resistance could have outweighed the potential setbacks of conceding. Tildy and Nagy may have figured that the men the Communists wanted to oust were ballast on the coalition. In addition the party's left wing openly supported the acceptance of their rivals' demands in the Communist newspaper, *Szabad Nép*.[159] Western assistance was not forthcoming either, and foreign financial aid was minimal. Prime Minister Nagy wanted to preserve the coalition at all costs, but Washington disagreed. In mid-March Byrnes warned that "continual concessions to minority groups cannot but in the end lead to the negation of the People's mandate given to the Prime Minister's majority party in the recent free elections."[160] But the secretary of state reiterated his reluctance to interfere in Hungary's internal affairs. He indicated that the "problem is one for solution by the Hungarians and the opinion of this government is given merely in an effort to be helpful." Schoenfeld conveyed the message to Nagy, but omitted the part relating to the Hungarians having to solve their problem on their own.[161] Besides the

general principle of non-intervention in the Soviet zone there were two specific motives behind this attitude. First of all, the Americans were dissatisfied with SHP resistance to Communist pressure. Schoenfeld claimed that
"supply minister Bárányos is the only exception in resisting Soviet penetration and is politically ineffective, [while] Prime Minister Nagy's frequent
expression of devotion to Soviet–Hungarian collaboration [...] cannot be
explained by Soviet pressure alone, but suggests that he also had deemed
expedient at least tactical surrender to pro-Russian elements which surround
him." Second, it was thought that financial assistance would make little
contribution to Hungary's economic rehabilitation and may even end up
aiding Soviets.[162] This may have been true, but the fact remains that the
U.S. offered little support to defy the Communist onslaught in Hungary.

The chance to negotiate with the Soviet leadership was a significant
    Finally, there is evidence that Nagy was the victim of a ploy contrived
by Rákosi and the Kremlin. During his secret visit Moscow in March
Rákosi explored the possibility whether the Soviet leaders would be willing
to support Budapest's territorial claims at the forthcoming peace talks, or
at least to receive a Hungarian delegation to discuss this issue. Rákosi was
promised that if the Communists were able to achieve the disintegration of
the SHP and secure the establishment of Soviet–Hungarian joint companies,
Moscow would support Hungary's limited territorial claim in Transylvania.
Rákosi then convinced Nagy to accept the Communist demands and in return
Nagy would be invited for an official visit to Moscow where he would
receive territorial concessions. This was a highly appealing arrangement
since nothing would have strengthened the SHP's public standing more than
a slice of territory from the ancient Hungarian land of Transylvania. As a
matter of fact the very day Nagy announced his surrender to Communist
wishes on 12 March, the Communist leadership passed a resolution that a
government delegation headed by Nagy would travel to the Soviet capital to
discuss outstanding issues.[163] In addition Hungary signed the agreement
on joint Soviet–Hungarian bauxite and oil companies the same day Nagy
departed for Moscow. Moscow used the classic carrot and stick policy with
success: Pushkin and Voroshilov warned the SHP to get rid of the most
"intransigent" elements of the party. Non-compliance would invite negative
political repercussions, whilst compliance would bring territorial gain in
Transylvania.

    The chance to negotiate with the Soviet leadership was a significant
breakthrough for Hungarian foreign policy and the general feeling was that
there would be a chance to get certain concessions in reparations and the
maintenance of the Red Army, which were driving the economy into bankruptcy. Perhaps Moscow would also show some understanding for mod-
est Hungarian territorial claims against the other former German satellite,
Romania, and in the question of the forced removal of ethnic Hungarians

from Slovakia. On the other hand a careful observer may have wondered why the visitors were "advised" not to take any experts, allegedly so as to avoid the impression that Hungary was preparing for a separate deal.[164]

Molotov received the Premier and his entourage at the airport. The "pomp and parade" of their reception overawed the Hungarians. A whole palace and automobiles were placed at Nagy's disposal while his ministers were put up in the best Moscow hotel. The Hungarians were permitted to see whatever they wanted obviously to disprove the allegation that visitors were prevented from seeing the "true" Soviet Union. In contrast to the lavish treatment of his guests, Stalin made a point of living up to his image as a ruler who led a frugal life. He received his apprehensive guests in "simple circumstances." This struck a chord with Ferenc Nagy, whose humble origin made him sensitive to such things.[165] Molotov saw foreign minister Gyöngyösi the night he arrived. Gyöngyösi raised the two central issues: the plight of the Hungarian minority in Slovakia, which was being threatened by mass expulsion, and a minor territorial rectification for Hungary at Romania's expense.

The Soviet and Hungarian records of the meeting differ significantly. While the Hungarian version indicates that Molotov was favorably disposed towards Hungary on the forced population transfer from Czechoslovakia as well as its territorial claim against Romania, the Soviet records suggest quite the opposite. Thus the Hungarians negotiated under the false assumption of Soviet good faith.[166] It was a special favor that Generalissimo Stalin received the Hungarians. No such high-level meeting had ever taken place before between the two countries. The meeting, which took place at nine o'clock at night was scheduled to fit the dictator's nocturnal life-style. On behalf of his nation Nagy expressed his gratitude to the "Red Army and Generalissimo Stalin for the liberation of Hungary, for the freedom of Hungarian political life and the independence of the Hungarian homeland." Then Nagy offered to "brief" his host on the domestic situation, but Stalin interjected that as the leader of an independent state he need not give a briefing, his account would be taken "as information." Stalin was told that "reactionary forces were continually attacking Hungarian democracy," but the government was doing everything in its power against them. The economic bases of reaction—that is large enterprises—were being "liquidated." Most importantly the Premier declared that gratitude, as well as Hungary's geographical and nationality situation, dictated *Realpolitik*, which "leads to the Soviet Union." Hungary turned to the Soviet Union with "full confidence" and Nagy announced the signing of the agreement on Hungarian–Soviet joint companies in the bauxite and oil industries.

After a discussion of the Czechoslovak–Hungarian population transfer they turned to the question of Transylvania, which was a main reason for

the Hungarian visit to Moscow. There was no way of knowing that the
Kremlin had already decided in Romania's favor shortly before Nagy's
visit, and the Soviet delegation in London was instructed to propose that the
whole of Transylvania should be returned to Romania.[167] In this light it is
clear that the question was used as a deception to convince the Hungarians
to pursue a pro-Soviet line especially since the Soviets thought that the
Anglo-Saxons supported the Hungarians.[168]

When Gyöngyösi presented the minimal Hungarian claim, Stalin asked
Molotov about the wording of the Romanian armistice. He was reminded
that the "whole or greater part thereof" was designated to the Romanians.
Stalin opined that this formula allowed the Hungarians to obtain a part of
Transylvania, but "it remained to be seen how much." Hinting at his real
intentions, the Generalissimo remarked that in his view the Romanians
would not agree to a territorial concession, in which case King Michael
would be forced to resign. At least Romania would become a republic, like
Hungary, Nagy replied jokingly. Stalin hinted that the Romanians could not
accept territorial changes without risking the fall of the government, but
none of the guests grasped what this meant: the Soviets would never allow
that to happen. They swallowed the bait and went home with some hope of
Russian support of territorial rectification.[169] Gyöngyösi was overwhelmed.
"The whole conversation bore the captivating effect of [Stalin's] extraordinary historical personality and at the same time the relaxing, encouraging
character of the intimacy of a human being, who is every inch a human."
Gyöngyösi was not the only one who painted such a rosy picture of the dictator. Truman grew to respect Stalin at Potsdam and even Churchill with all
his experience in handling domestic and foreign opponents of great stature
was captivated by the tyrant's personality and grew "fond" of Stalin after
their meeting in Moscow. It is no wonder that Stalin, for whom mendacity
was a tool of diplomacy, outsmarted the inexperienced Hungarians.

Hungary was misled on another crucial issue, namely the stationing of
the Red Army in Hungary. Many at home and abroad hoped that its withdrawal would restore Hungarian sovereignty. Therefore, any hint that
Moscow would pull out its troops would reinforce the illusion that the SHP
was doing the right thing in giving in to Soviet demands. According to the
Hungarian notes of the meeting "Stalin made the important announcement
that the occupying troops would be withdrawn from Hungary soon and only
small units would remain." In contrast, the verbatim Russian minutes quote
Stalin as saying that "of the Soviet army will be gradually withdrawn from
Hungary," the "whole army cannot be withdrawn at once."[170] The context
in which this was said is also relevant. Nagy was complaining about economic hardships and the burden of supplying the occupation forces in particular. It was in reflection to this complaint that Stalin announced that not

many troops would stay "and as a result the Hungarian economy will be relieved of a part of the burden." That is, partial troop withdrawal was an economic and not a political concession. When the visit ended Stalin toasted the Hungarians: he affirmed that the Soviet Union would respect the sovereignty and independence of small nations like Hungary. This, he said, would make it possible for "such a great power as the Soviet Union and such a small state like Hungary" to live in true friendship.[171] He neglected to mention the condition of friendship.

The Hungarians had little insight into Kremlin politics. They had no experienced negotiator; in fact they had virtually no practical experience in, or any knowledge of international affairs. Moreover, they lacked sound advice on the nature of Soviet foreign policy. Gyula Szekfű, the Hungarian minister in Moscow, was an outstanding historian of great intellectual influence, but nevertheless had little expertise in Soviet affairs and had no access to Soviet leaders. An assessment prepared by the chargé d'affaires in June 1946 was no help either. After a mostly positive appraisal of the Soviet political and social system he claimed that "The Soviet Union's present [...] situation inspires a peaceful foreign policy and there are also external signs that the government opted for such a course." Thus there was "no need to doubt the Soviet Union's goodwill" especially since the Anglo-Americans were largely to blame for the international tension.[172] The lack of expertise or intellectual courage is only underscored by the fact that the Hungarian records of the negotiations were imprecise on the most crucial points. Thus the "results"of the Moscow talks[173] served to strengthen the hand of those who advocated a *"Realpolitik* that led toward the Kremlin."

After the talks the parties resumed their struggle for power. The Smallholders made a desperate attempt to change the correlation of forces by demanding proportionate representation in local governments and the police, while the Communists incited street demonstrations to hasten the cleansing of their enemies. Unbeknownst to his opponents Rákosi gave the clarion call for the establishment of a proletarian dictatorship, even though the party's liaison in Moscow, Rezső Szántó, had just concluded that the internal conditions in Hungary were not yet ripe for the construction of socialism.[174] In a lengthy address at the session of the HCP Central Committee on 17 May the party leader revealed the result of his secret discussion with Stalin. Rákosi announced the time had come to "raise the question of socialism," which had been "concealed for tactical reasons."

"We must tell the comrades that the situation changed as compared to last year [...] Before the elections [of 1945] we deliberately downplayed our socialist line. The reason was in part that the workers and even more a significant part of the bourgeoisie thought [...] the Communists would doubtless want a proletarian dictatorship, or a socialist republic. In order to calm them down, we deliberately down played our socialist face. In the meantime we managed to convince them, that we are not aiming for socialism. [...] But in any case, since they know that we do not want a proletarian dictatorship or socialist republic immediately, it is time to remind our own party and the working class once more that we are socialists."[175]

Rákosi revealed that the creation of a new Communist International was under consideration in the Kremlin and that the local Communist Parties had a free hand to "liberate the proletariat." This resuscitated version of the Comintern would not be centralized like its predecessor, to avoid "hinder[ing] the progress of the individual parties." Instead, it would provide a means for them "to execute the tasks leading to the liberation of the proletariat, bearing local circumstances in mind." With regards to the "conditions for revolution," one no longer had to wait until they appeared "in at least a bunch of countries," "Stalinist reasoning would say something totally different." The Communist parties no longer had to be concerned with the inner or international situation in their fight for socialism. "Whenever a country achieves the conditions for the liberation of the proletariat or for socialism, this will be carried out, with no regard for whether the respective country is in a capitalist environment or not. This is also a new perspective, which simply means that in a country where as a result of the work of the Communist party these conditions are present, it has to be realized. This is fresh encouragement for all Communist parties, because now it will be dependent on their work whether or not the conditions for the liberation of the proletariat are created in their own country."[176]

In public Rákosi was more cautious, but only for tactical reasons. Yet he left no doubt that the eventual aim was a Hungarian version of socialism even at the cost of blood and sacrifice. At the Third Congress of the HCP in September Rákosi announced the construction of socialism. But there were "several roads to socialism, which shall take into account the particular conditions in each country." People's Democracy, which was a political formation preceding the socialist stage, would include elements of socialism, and the more elements of which were present in the people's democracy, "the quicker the transition to socialism will be with less sacrifice, less blood." Utilizing the experience of the Soviet Union would enable Hungary "to spare a great part of the suffering incurred by the Soviet people." Hungary was constructing Hungarian democracy not because of "tactic but out of deep Communist conviction, and we shall see to it that it shall include as many elements of socialism as possible, which in turn will accelerate the development that takes mankind to socialism...This socialism can be established as a result of Hungarian historical development, Hungarian economic, political and social forces. As such it will be a socialism produced on Hungarian soil fitted to Hungarian conditions."[177]

Rákosi remembered that "even at the party Congress we talked about the socialist nature of people's democracy in generalities, without sharp definitions. This generality, lack of clear definitions was not because we ourselves were unclear which way we were heading, what our aims were, ...but because tactically this was correct at the time. We agreed to avoid the term dictatorship of the proletariat, which would have made it only harder for us domestically and internationally... But for the politically literate what we said at the Congress was enough."[178]

If Rákosi's view reflected Stalin's—and there is a clear indication in his presentation in May that it did—the Sovietization of Eastern Europe received Soviet sanction. The consolidation of Soviet power in the region was seen as a bulwark against American imperialist expansion.[179] There was no longer caution about the Soviet Union's relations with its former allies, let alone any limitation as to when the conditions for the Communist takeover would be ripe. As Stalin had said in 1944, the Communists were allowed to go ahead with full speed. Perhaps it is not a coincidence that almost simultaneously with Rákosi's revelation on Hungary's path to Socialism, the Greek Communist leader Nikos Zachariades expounded the policies prescribed by the Prague meeting of the Communist parties that had been held in March. The purpose of that meeting was to determine the strategy of "consistent and uncompromising struggle against Anglo-Saxon Imperialism." "The peoples of Europe," Zachariades declared, "with the USSR as their beacon, will march forward towards their complete liberation, and no power, including the Anglo-Saxons, can stop this advance."[180] Rákosi's account suggests that the consolidation of Soviet power in Eastern Europe took precedence over continuing cooperation with the West. Isolationism from the West, a recurrent phenomenon in the Russian political tradition, seemed to take the upper hand not only in Beria's, Malenkov's or Molotov's thinking, but also in Stalin's far earlier than previously suggested.[181]

Shortly after Rákosi's secret speech, on 21 May Nagy announced the SHP's demand of proportionate representation in local administrations and elections, and in the police. The Left offered an unacceptable compromise and Révai called for a counter offensive from "above and below." Neither side yielded, and Nagy threatened to resign. A political impasse ensued that threatened the coalition, and with it political stability. In Soviet eyes the crisis was provoked by the Western missions, particularly the British, who allegedly advised the SHP to break with the Communists and even to set up a one party government. Pushkin summoned the Prime Minister declaring that "the government could not afford the luxury of a grave crisis at this time when Hungary was having to fight for a satisfactory peace treaty." Pushkin warned against forcing a showdown with the Left, and threatened that "the dissolution of the coalition would necessarily result in the Soviets taking a hand in the political crisis." Nagy's resistance seemed to stiffen, he refused to yield and threatened to resign again.[182] It was now Rákosi's turn to visit Pushkin, and the Communist leader was instructed to compromise. Pushkin's intervention was not without avail. The parties accepted a trade-off after Tildy defused a potential crisis by convincing Nagy not to resign. Although local elections were envisioned at the "earliest moment," no fixed date was given. The Smallholders were to receive one hundred important police posts, including the positions of those Communists and Social Democrats who would be dropped as a result of "B listing" (the campaign to downsize the civil service).[183]

In the absence of external support and as a result of Soviet pressure the SHP backed down and accepted a settlement that benefited their political opponents. President Tildy seems to have played a crucial role in his party's surrender, since he was convinced that the crisis was potentially disastrous for the country. He assured the Soviets of his sympathy and pledged to "reorient" the Hungarian people toward the USSR.[184] Local elections were never held. Under the pretext of downsizing public administration the Communist-dominated Interior Ministry held a witch-hunt to "cleanse reaction." In order to save the coalition Schoenfeld recommended that the U.S. support a modification of the Hungarian–Romanian boundary, since such a rectification, no matter how small, "will greatly strengthen the Hungarian government's position." He thought that the State Department should do all it could in this respect, since it would be likely "to strengthen Nagy's hand in trying to redress internal balance of power." Byrnes was skeptical as to whether a boundary modification would enhance the Smallholders' position. He thought that a minor concession would have no impact on the Hungarian domestic scene and would only make it worse for the Hungarians in Transylvania. Furthermore, Byrnes was aware that Moscow supported the Romanian claim on the whole of Transylvania and had no wish to confront the Kremlin on such an insignificant issue.[185]

Prime Minister Nagy's planned visit to the United States and Great Britain was an opportunity for the West to strengthen his political standing. Nagy pressed for the visit, but Washington was only moderately enthusiastic about the idea: an official in the State Department hoped that Byrnes would be able to devote "a few minutes" to the Hungarians. Nagy was cautious about setting the agenda for the talks for good reasons. First of all he was constrained by Rákosi's presence. Second, Pushkin warned him of the "realities" of Hungary's geographical position, the international conditions and the pitfalls of duplicity.[186] In order to calm Soviet anxiety Hungarian diplomatic figures assured the Soviet foreign ministry that Hungary was guided by the desire "to win the Soviet government's friendship and goodwill, which continued to be the cornerstone" of Budapest's policy. No political questions would be raised in Washington, and Hungary pledged to "rely on the Soviet Union in foreign policy. If political questions should arise in Washington the Hungarian delegation would limit itself to provide information, which will be in harmony with the spirit of the talks between the Hungarian and the Soviet governments in Moscow." Moscow received a list of the topics Hungary wanted to discuss.

Unlike the more fortunate Austria, which with strong American backing skillfully maneuvered between the Schylla of appearing to be too pro-Soviet and the Charybdes of raising Soviet eyebrows by rubbing too closely with the West, the Hungarians were drifting towards a unilateral Soviet orientation. They informed the Soviets of their aim to secure American assistance in the restitution of Hungarian property and of the Hungarian gold reserve for the sake of financial stabilization; the increase of surplus property credit and UNRRA aid.[187] In reality Hungary raised two other issues as well: territorial claims in Transylvania and the fate of the Hungarian minority in Czechoslovakia. On the other hand, the Hungarians avoided any mention of domestic politics and the hosts remained silent as well. On the whole the trip to Washington was worth making, especially in view of the very limited objectives in mind. Nagy and his entourage met acting Secretary of State Byrnes, and albeit briefly, President Truman. They were taken to the TVA, no doubt to impress them with America's version of economic centralization. In order to demonstrate U.S. interest in Hungarian affairs, Washington agreed to return the gold reserve immediately, which had been taken to Germany in the last days of the war, without delay as well as to restitute the property removed from Hungary after the signing of the armistice. The U.S. agreed to grant more surplus property credit. American generosity was not unlimited. Byrnes recommended a loan but the Eximbank rejected it on the grounds that loans could not be granted on the basis of political considerations alone. A few million dollars could be easily lost in such a politically unstable country.

Although the Americans were reluctant to commit themselves on territorial revision, they were more forthcoming about the fate of the Hungarian minority in Slovakia. Prague intended to expel most ethnic Hungarians on the spurious grounds that they had all collaborated with the Nazis. In Potsdam the Czechoslovak government was granted a free hand to expatriate the German minority but this did not extend to the Hungarian minority. Nevertheless, with Soviet backing Prague insisted on expelling them. The United States sided with the former enemy on this count. As a result, the Czechoslovak attempt to insert this point into the peace treaty with Hungary failed. President Truman asked Nagy for landing rights in Hungary not knowing that the prime minister was not in a position to oblige. All issues

related to air traffic were solely within the competence of the Soviet authorities.[188] Pushkin regarded the American request for landing rights as a question of military bases and declared that "it would be easier for the U.S. to
get an airport in the Soviet Union itself."[189]

Rákosi later ridiculed his experience in the U.S. describing most people he met as fools or warmongers, but at the time he gave a relatively positive evaluation of the visit to Stalin. He was satisfied with the economic
concessions, and with the fact that American "official circles did not try to
turn them against the Soviet Union." On the other hand he remarked that
American economic strength—which he attributed to the fact that it was not
damaged by the war—made a good impression on the Smallholder members of the delegation.[190] If this was so, it was not unreserved. Nagy was
critical of what he saw. He recounted that they were taken to a farm, where
the animals were kept under awful conditions, limited in their ability to
move around. A Hungarian would never treat his livestock that way. It was
clear to him that the only motive was to make a profit and the livelihood of
the animals did not matter to the American farmers he saw.[191] For Nagy,
who had been a farmer himself, such things were important, the way one
treated livestock expressed one's view of the world. In Hungary a well-kept
animal was the source of pride; a farmer was judged by the conditions of
his animals. Nagy's critique expressed the great psychological distance that
separated rural Hungary from the mercantile culture of the United States.
This cultural distance may in part explain why Nagy never made a serious
effort to solicit America's aid to save his country from communization. It is
an irony of history that Nagy ended up in emigration in the U.S., where he
took up farming.

After a brief respite the struggle for power resumed. In July Interior
Minister László Rajk dealt a severe blow to civil society by banning as
many as 1,000—1,500 organizations,[192] 744 of them in Greater Budapest
alone.[193] The pretext for the measure, which Rajk had already recommended
in mid-June, was cited as the attacks against Soviet military personnel
including the shooting of a Soviet officer and a private (as well as a young
Hungarian woman) in Budapest in broad daylight. Initially the political
police established that the perpetrator, whose body was found burnt to ashes
on the crime scene, acted alone. Later the police claimed that the perpetrator had accomplices who burned the body proving that the crime was part
of a conspiracy, which the Communist press blamed on the Catholic youth
organization (KALOT). A Communist weekly called for revenge and wanted
to exploit the opportunity to finish off reactionaries: "The outrage, which
spread across the nation should grow into an onslaught to finish off the enemies of the country and democracy [...]. The public demands reprisal, strict
reprisal, and a deterring example [...] Enough of the policy of softness!"

The HCP informed Moscow that the assassination was a premeditated plot schemed by fascist organizations.[194]

On 2 July Voroshilov's replacement, Acting Chairman of the ACC Sviridov, who was far less sympathetic to the Hungarians than his predecessor, demanded the dissolution of reactionary youth movements, including KALOT, and recommended proceedings against certain politicians. Sviridov's unilateral action enraged the British and American representatives of the ACC, but they raised the issue only three weeks after Sviridov's order. Edgcumbe and Weems protested that the Soviets had not consulted them. Weems pointed out that the Hungarians had already carried out Article XV of the Armistice Agreement, which mandated the dissolution of fascist and pro-fascist organizations. He reminded that Svridov himself had confirmed this at the 23 April meeting of the ACC,[195] and asked him to rescind his order. Sviridov claimed that although the Hungarian government desired to fulfill Article XV, there were still fascist organizations left.[196] It was too late anyway: the government had already moved to carry out the Soviet ultimatum. Weems opined that if Nagy had refused to comply "the Russians would undoubtedly have incited the Communists to cause strife and bring about the dissolution of the Parliament," which in turn might have lead to their seizure of the government.[197] The Interior Ministry proceeded to disband the designated organizations, including over 600 local KALOT organizations. With the exception of the Prime Minister everyone, including Tildy, argued in favor of accepting the Sviridov note and banning KALOT, "the hotbed of reaction," which was the only serious rival of the leftist youth organizations.[198]

Although the SHP yielded on the Sviridov note, the campaign against it was pursued relentlessly. The agreement on proportional representation was not carried out; instead both the SDP and the Communists accused the SHP of not going fast and far enough in cleansing the reactionaries. Tildy agreed to get rid of the right wing elements and announced further measures against them. Nagy also vowed to pursue the struggle against reactionary political forces and pledged allegiance to the coalition. In a spurious show of harmony the four parties publicly branded all those who disagreed with the official policies the "enemies of the nation, the Hungarian people."[199] Even so Rákosi indicated that the next target would be the SHP's recalcitrant general secretary, Béla Kovács.

On one occasion, the Communist leader mused that people were longing for peace and quiet after a war, which was understandable but "dangerous," since the "work" had not been finished yet.[200] Rákosi saw to it that no domestic tranquility would ensue. In August the HCP Central Committee resolved to "break into the ranks of the SHP from above and below."[201] The showdown started in December 1946 when the Defense Ministry's Military Intelligence Department "exposed" a conspiracy against the republic. György Pálffy Österreicher, who was soon to be disposed of himself, led the investigation. The alleged conspirators were charged with having been in touch with a "secret racist organization" named Magyar Közösség (Hungarian Community). Six Smallholder functionaries were among the suspects and their party's Political Committee agreed to waive their parliamentary immunity. Nagy doubted whether the conspiracy existed and launched an investigation against Pálffy-Österreicher. But the investigation was never concluded. As on other occasions when Communist plans were about to be disrupted, the Soviet factor came into play. Sviridov demanded that the investigation against Pálffy be discontinued otherwise the case would be taken over by the Soviet military police. The case against the "conspirators" went ahead and over a hundred people were arrested. Events took a similar turn elsewhere in Soviet-controlled Europe. In November mass political trials were held in Romania to discredit the opposition. In Czechoslovakia the leaders of the Slovak Democratic Party—which had defeated the Communists in the Slovak election—were implicated in a spurious "anti-state conspiracy."

If Sovietization was to be halted by the Western powers, this was the time. But State Department officials like the Director of the Office of European Affairs Freeman Matthews thought that the conspiracy was real, the Communists were only exaggerating it. Matthews believed that the campaign against the plotters was motivated by the Soviets' desire to consolidate their power before they would be compelled to withdraw by the peace treaty. By blaming the conspiracy on the largest coalition party, he argued, they would force it to dissolve and in such a way the results of the 1945 national election would be nullified and the HCP would erect a new "front" government. Since the danger of a Communist seizure of power was apparent, Secretary of State George C. Marshall considered financial assistance to the democratic elements, but added that the resources would be hard to find.[202] The proceedings against the anti-republic plotters was only the prelude to the final offensive against the remnants of the independent wing of the SHP that was to reach its conclusion in the first part of 1947.

NOTES

1 Eduard Mark, "Revolution by Degrees: Stalin's National-Front Strategy for Europe, 1941–1947, p. 6.

2 Yalta Briefing Book Paper, Subject: The Necessity of the Three Principal Allies Arriving at a Common Political Program for Liberated Countries, *FRUS, 1945, The Conferences of Malta and Yalta*, pp. 102–103.

3 See on this Willie Thompson, *The Communist Movement since 1945* (Oxford: Blackwell, 1945), pp. 20–22.

4 Ibid., pp. 22–23.

5 Walter Laqueur, *Europe in Our Time, A History, 1945–1992* (New York: Penguin Books, 1992), p. 140.

6 Ibid., pp. 31–32.

7 Ibid., pp. 126–127.

8 David Holloway, *Stalin and the Bomb—The Soviet Union and Atomic Energy, 1939–1956* (New Haven and London: Yale University Press, 1994), pp. 132–133.

9 See Levening et al., *Debating the Origins of the Cold War* (New York, Oxford: Rowman and Littlefield Publishers Inc., 2002), p. 104

10 Hugh DeSantis, *The Diplomacy of Silence—The American Foreign Service, the Soviet Union and the Cold War* (Chicago, London: The University of Chicago Press, 1979), pp. 114–130. In late 1944 Charles Bohlen wrote that American policy "remains unchanged in its objective of working out the fullest cooperation with the Soviet Union," both politically and militarily "without making any concessions which would compromise our basic principles." Ibid. p. 129.

11 For the Soviet part in the Iranian crisis see Natalia Yegorova, *The "Iranian Crisis" of 1945–1946—A View from the Russian Archives,* CWIHP Working Paper no. 15 (Washington D.C.: Woodrow Wilson center, 1996); for the evolution of American policy toward Iran see Bruce Robellet Kuniholm, *The Origins of the Cold War in the Near East—Great Power Conflict and Diplomacy in Iran, Turkey and Greece* (Princeton, New Jersey: Princeton University Press), pp. 271–282 and pp. 304–350.

12 Wilson D. Miscamble, *George F. Kennan and the Making of American Foreign Policy, 1947–1950* (Princeton, New Jersey: Princeton University Press, 1992), p. 141.

13 Leffler, *A Preponderance of Power*, pp. 65–67.

14 Adomeit, *Imperial Overstrech,* pp. 57–71. Adomeit stresses that the division occurred by default rather than design, but the default was less than accidental or coincidental, the exigencies of ideology and empire played a significant part. For the parallel Soviet policies in eastern Germany see Norman Naimark, *The Russians in Germany: A History of the Soviet Zone of Occupation, 1945–1949* (Cambridge, Mass.: Belknap Press of Harvard University Press, 1995), pp. 351–352.

15 Marc Trachtenberg, *A Constructed Peace - The Making of the European Settle-*

ment 1945-1963, (Princeton, New Jersey: Princeton University Press, 1999), pp. 6–30.

16 Levering et al., *Debating the Origins of the Cold War*, pp. 92–93.

17 Ibid., pp. 88–96.

18 Ibid., p. 88.

19 McCagg, *Stalin Embattled*, p. 14, p. 50, p. 70.

20 Hugh Seton-Watson, *From Lenin to Malenkov*, pp. 248–249. Others have adopted this approach, drawing a clear line between Hungary and Czechoslovakia on the one hand and the rest of the people's democracies on the other. See e.g. Charles Gati, *Hungary and the Soviet Bloc*.

21 Minutes of a formal ACC meeting, 3 August 1945, in *Documents of the Meetings of the Allied Control Commission in Hungary*. Documents collected, selected, edited and the footnotes and introduction written by Bendegúz Gergő Cseh (Budapest: MTA Jelenkor-kutató Bizottság, 2000), pp. 65–66. Marshal Voroshilov stated that the entrance of correspondents to Hungary "cannot be decided at this time." About Western trade representatives he declared that "At the present time it is not possible to permit representatives of industry to enter Hungary."

22 Throughout the war the Russian authorities refused to allow foreign aircraft to enter Russia except for the transport of the highest foreign dignitaries like Churchill, De Gaulle and others. See John R. Deane, *The Strange Alliance—The Story of Our Efforts at Wartime Cooperation with Russia* (Bloomington, London: Indiana University Press, 1973), p. 55.

23 Minutes of a normal meeting of the ACC, 6 September 1945, in *Documents of the meetings of the Allied Control Commission for Hungary*, p. 78.

24 I will use the term Communist domination to denote both Hungarian Communist and Soviet rule.

25 Levering et al., *Debating the Origins of the Cold War*, p. 91. Eduard Mark argued that Stalin's policy combined collaboration with aggrandizement; both were intertwined. His imperial ambitions and his desire to preserve the alliance were different aspects of the same policy. "Wartime cooperation was not an impediment to his ambitions, to be lightly discarded when he no longer needed Western cooperation against Germany. On the contrary, continued alliance with the Anglo-Americans was an essential condition for achieving his expansionist ends in full measure." Mark, *Revolution by Degrees*, p. 13.

26 Soviet losses were staggering. The Red Army lost 80 thousand dead and 240 thousand wounded in the siege of Budapest alone. The combined German and Hungarian losses may have reached around 60 percent of this figure.

27 Iván Berend T., *A szocialista gazdaság fejlődése Magyarországon* [The development of socialist economy in Hungary] (Budapest: Akadémia Kiadó, 1974), pp. 10–11.

28 Tamás Stark, *Magyarország második világháborús embervesztesége* [Hungary's human hosses in World War II] (Budapest: MTA Történettudományi Intézete, 1989), p. 60.

29 Levering et al., *Debating the Origins of the Cold War*, p. 96.

30 For a treatment of the first months under Soviet occupation see László Szűcs,

ed., *Dálnoki Miklós Béla Kormányának minisztertanácsi jegyzőkönyvei* vol. A, pp. 9–79.

31 As cited by Raack, *Stalin's Drive to the West*, p. 50.

32 Norman Davies, *God's Playground, A History of Poland* (New York: Columbia University Press, 1982), p. 447.

33 On the German experience see Naimark, *The Russians in Germany*.

34 "Rákosi levele Dimitrovnak," [Rákosi's letter to Dimitrov] in Feitl István, ed., "Dokumentumok Rákositól—Rákosiról," [Documents from Rákosi - on Rákosi], *Múltunk*, 1991, no. 1–2, p. 247

35 Pola-Tódorhegy község lakóinak panasza az orosz és bolgár katonák túlkapásai miatt, jegyzőkönyv, [Complaint of the inhabitants of Pola-Tódorhegy village about the excesses of Soviet and Bulgarian troops], 25 May 1945 in *Dokumentumok Zala megye történetéből 1944–1947* [Documents on the history of Zala County] (Zalaegerszeg, 1995), p. 88.

36 "Postanovlenie GKO ob internirovanii trudnosposobnogo nemetskogo naseleniia na territorii Bolgarii, Vengrii, Ruminii, Chekhoslovakii i Yugoslavii i otpravke ego na rabotu v SSSR," [Report of the GKO on the internment of the able bodied German population on the territory of Bulgaria, Hungary, Romania, Czechoslovakia and Yugoslavia and sending them to work to the USSR] 16 December 1944, in T. V. Volokitina et al. eds., *Sovietskii faktor in Vostochnoi Evrope 1944–1953* (The Soviet factor in eastern Europe 1944–1953, herafter cited as SVE) Tom 1 (Moscow: Rosspen, 1999), Document 27, pp. 116–118.

37 "Donesenie L. P. Berii I.V. Stalinu i V. M. Molotovu ob otpravke na rabotu v SSSR nemtsev internirovannikh na territorii Vengrii, Ruminii Chehoslovakii i Yugoslavii," [L. P. Beria's report to I.V. Stalin and V. M. Molotov on sending to the territory of the USSR Germans interned on the territory of Hungary, Romania, Czechoslovakia and Yugoslavia] 20 January 1945, ibid., Document 33, p. 132. Of the 27,707 people 8,609 were women.

38 György Zielbauer, "Magyar polgári lakosok deportálása és hadifogsága, 1945–1948" [The Deportation and War Captivity of Hungarian civilians, 1945–1948], *Történelmi Szemle*, 1989/3–4, p. 289.

39 A Külügyminisztérium jegyzéke a Szovjetunió kormányához [The Foreign Ministry's note to the government of the Soviet Union] 7 February 1945, Mol, Küm, Szovjetunió (Szu) tük, XIX-J-1-j, IV-482, 29. doboz, 25044-45; "A külügyminiszter szóbeli jegyzéke a Szovjetunió kormányának," [The foreign minister's verbal note to the government of the Soviet Union] 5 February 1945, ibid. 25044/45.

40 Quoted in Péter Sipos, "A szovjetek és Magyarország, 1945" [The Soviets and Hungary, 1945], *História*, 1995. no. 2.

41 Jelentés a Muraköz területén, magyar községek ellen elkövetett atrocitásokról [Report on atrocities carried out in Hungarian villages in the Muraköz region], 11 July 1945, in *Dokumentumok Zala megye történetéből*, p. 107.

42 Révai József levele Rákosi Mátyásnak [József Révai's letter to Mátyás Rákosi] 7 January 1945, in Lajos Izsák and Miklós Kun eds., *Moszkvának jelentjük: Titkos dokumentumok, 1944-1948* [Reporting to Moscow: secret documents, 1944–1948] (Budapest: Századvég, 1994), pp. 33–36.

43 Stefan Karner and Barbara Marx, "World War II Prisoners of War in the Soviet Economy," in *1945: The Consequences and Sequels of the Second World War.* Bulletin du Comité international de la deuxième guerre mondiale (Montreal, 1995), pp. 194–195.
44 According to the census of the Hungarian Statistical Bureau 600,000 people were taken to the Soviet Union; the Soviet armed forces gave the figure 425,000, while the NKVD branch dealing with POWs in GUPVI camps 526,000. According to contemporary Hungarian estimates 322–377,000 have been sent back to Hungary; NKVD mentioned 419,000. See Tamás Stark, "Hungarian Prisoners in the Soviet Union, 1941–1945" *Ibid.*, pp. 203–213.
45 See Norman Naimark, *The Russians in Germany.*
46 Andrea Pető, "Átvonuló hadsereg, maradandó trauma—Az 1945-os budapesti nemi erőszak esetek emlékezete" [Passing army, lasting trauma—The memory of Soviet rape cases in Budapest], *Történelmi Szemle*, 1999, vol. XLI, no. 1–2, pp. 86–89.
47 Ibid., pp. 100–102.
48 As cited by Ungváry, *Budapest ostroma*, p. 276.
49 A keszthelyi járás főjegyzőjének jelentése orosz katonák által elkövetett atrocitásokról [Report by the chief notary of Keszthely district on atrocities committed by Soviet troops], 2 July 1945 in *Dokumentumok Zala megye történetéből*, p. 102.
50 Feljegyzés a Vörös Hadsereg által elvitt értékekről [Memorandum on the valuables taken by the Red Army], undated, MOL, KÜM, XIX-J-1-j, Szu tük, IV-482, 23. doboz, 441 sz.n. 1945.
51 László Mravik, *The "Sacco di Budapest" and the Depredation of Hungary, 1938–1949* (Budapest: The Hungarian National Gallery, 1998).
52 See above, Feljegyzés a Vörös Hadsereg által elvitt értékekről.
53 Mravik, *The "Sacco di Budapest,"* document 43, pp. 109–111.
54 Kelemen Ferenc nagykanizsai bankigazgató feljegyzése a Takarékpénztár arany- és ezüstkészletének oroszok általi elhurcolásáról [Bank director Ferenc Kelemen's report on the looting of the Savings Bank's gold and silver reserve by the Russians], 9 August 1945 in *Dokumentumok Zala megye történetéből*, p. 115.
55 A keszthelyi járás főjegyzőjének jelentése, op. cit.
56 Márai, *Memoir of Hungary 1944–1948*, pp. 42–44.
57 Ibid., p. 86.
58 Gróf Erdődy Ferenc panasza a vépi kastélyból műemlékszámba menő értékeinek az oroszok által történt elrablása miatt [Complaint by Count Ferenc Erdődy about the robbery by the Russians of his art treasures from his castle in Vép] 18 October 1945, MOL, Küm, Szu tük, XIX-J-1-j, IV-536, 30. doboz, 1489/45.
59 See Günter Bischof, *Austria in the First Cold War, 1945–1955—The Leverage of the Weak* (London: Macmillan, 1999), p. 38
60 As cited by Ungváry, *Budapest ostroma*, p. 275.
61 A mezőgazdasági miniszter feljegyzése a Külügyminisztérium Fegyverszüneti Bizottságának, 2 November 1945 [Memorandum by the minister of agriculture] MOL vegyes admin, XIX-J-1-k, 4/fh, 165. doboz.
62 Vorosilov feljegyzése a külügyminiszternek [Memorandum by Voroshilov to the

foreign minister] MOL, Küm, Szu tük, XIX-J-1-j, IV-483.1, 23. doboz, 1288-FO-1945

63 A közellátásügyi miniszter (Faragho) jelentése a miniszterelnöknek [Memorandum by the minister of supply to the prime minister] 10 January 1945, MOL, XIX-A-1-j, 12. doboz, 1945-VIII-42.

64 Révai József levele Rákosi Mátyásnak [József Révai's letter to Mátyás Rákosi] 7 January 1945, Moszkvának jelentjük, p. 35.

65 A Magyarországi Szövetséges Ellenőrző Bizottság emlékirata [Memorandum by the Allied Control Commission in Hungary] July 1945, MOL, vegyes admin, XIX-J-1-k 4-fh, 165. doboz, 174 F.B.

66 Department of State Interim Research and Intelligence Service, microfilm no. 3467, 31 December 1945.

67 The American and Soviet Drafts of the Statute of the ACC in Hungary in *Documents of the Meetings of the Allied Control Commission*, pp. 436–439.

68 See Mark, *Revolution by Degrees*, pp. 22–32.

69 Rákosi beszámolója a politikai helyzetről [Rákosi's report on the political situation], 14 April 1945, Rossisikii Tsentr Hraneniya i Izucheniia Dokumentov Noveishei Istorii (RTsHIDNI), fond 17, op. 128, ed. hr. no. 37.

70 On Révai see Károly Urbán, "Révai József, (1898–1959)" *Párttörténeti Szemle,* 1978, vol. 24, no. 3, pp. 162–223.

71 Révai József levele Rákosi Mátyásnak [József Révai's letter to Mátyás Rákosi] 7 December 1944, RTsHIDNI, fond 17, op. 128, ed. hr. no. 7.

72 József Révai, *Az ország újjáépítésének politikai előfeltételei* [The political preconditions of national reconstruction] 12 June 1945 (Budapest, Szikra, a publication of the Propaganda Division of the Central Committee of the HCP, 1945], pp. 5–6.

73 Nicholas Nyárádi, *My Ringside Seat in Moscow*, (New York: Crowell, 1952) p. 57.

74 On Gerő's life see Magdolna Baráth, *Gerő Ernő politikai pályája, 1944–1946* [A political biography of Ernő Gerő. 1944–1946]. Ph. D. dissertation (Budapest, 2002).

75 Gerő Ernő levele Rákosi Mátyásnak [Ernő Gerő's letter to Mátyás Rákosi] 28 December 1944. ibid. ed. Hr. no. 7.

76 Iz stenogrammi vistupleniia M. Rákosi v OMI TsK VKP(b) o polozhenii v Vengrii i deiatelnosti vengerskoi kompartii [Shorthand of M. Rákosi's speech at the Central Committee of the Hungarian Communist Party on the situation in Hungary and the activity of the Communist Party] 23 June 1945, in *SFVE*, vol. I, p. 199.

77 See Éva Standeiszky, *A magyar kommunista párt irodalompolitikája, 1944–1948* [The literary politics of the Hungarian Communist Party, 1944–1948] (Budapest: Kossuth Könyvkiadó, 1987); Mihály Szegedy-Maszák, "The Rise and Fall of Bourgeois Literature in Hungary (1945–1949)" *Hungarian Studies*, vol. 13, no. 2, 1998/99, pp. 199–214.

78 Iz stenogrammi vistuplenia M. Rákosi, 23 June 1945, *SFVE,* op. cit, p. 198.

79 A magyar kommunista párt és a szociáldemokrata párt határozata a fasizmus elleni közös harcról és a munkásosztály egységének megteremtéséről [Resolu-

tion of the Hungarian Communist Party and the Social Democratic Party on the joint struggle against fascism and the unity of the working class] 5 January 1945, Politika Történeti Intézet Leváltára (Archive of the Political History Institute hereafter cited as PIL) 253 F., 677, 1–12.

80 PIL, 274 F, 253, 1–270.
81 Farkas Mihály levele Rákosi Mátyásnak [Mihály Farkas's letter to Mátyás Rákosi] 7 January 1945, RTsHIDNI fond 17 op. 128. ed. hr. no. 37.
82 A magyar kommunista párt és a szociáldemokrata párt nyílt levele valamennyi szervezetéhez és tagjához [Open letter by the Hungarian Communist Party and the Social Democratic Party to all their organizations and members]. Published in *Népszava* and *Szabad Nép*, 27 April 1945. p. 3.
83 See Károly Vigh, *Tildy Zoltán életútja* [The life of Zoltán Tildy] (Békéscsaba: Tevan Kiadó, 1991).
84 Mátyás Rákosi, *Visszaemlékezések 1940–1956* [Memoires 1940–1956], edited by István Feitl, et al., vol. I, (Budapest: Napvilág Kiadó, 1997), p. 218.
85 Iz stenogrammi vistuplenia M. Rákosi, 23 June 1945, in *SFVE*, op. cit., pp. 198–199.
86 Szegedy-Maszák, *The Rise and Fall of Bourgeois Literature in Hungary*.
87 Postanovlenie GKO o pervoocherednikh ekonomicheskikh meropriiatiiakh vengerskogo pravitelstva i ob udovletvorenii ego prosbi ob okazanii pomoshchi [Resolution of the High Command on the most important economic measures of the Hungarian government and the satisfaction of its request for assistance] 7 March 1945, in *SFVE*, vol. 1, Document 43, pp. 162–164.
88 See János M. Rainer, *Nagy Imre—Politikai életrajz* [Imre Nagy—A political biography] vol. I (Budapest: Századvég, 1996), pp. 267–273.
89 A kommunista párt szegedi szervezetének jegyzőkönyve, 19 November 1944, RTsHIDNI fond 17 op. 128 ed. hr. no. 7 [Protocol of the Szeged organization of the Communist Party]. The proceedings are discussed by Kovrig, *Communism in Hungary from Kun to Kádár*, p. 169.
90 Rákosi, *Visszaemlékezések*, vol. II, p. 708.
91 The Representative in Hungary (Schoenfeld) to the Secretary of State, 17 August 1945 *FRUS, 1945*, IV, p. 849.
92 Ibid.
93 Nyárádi, *My Ringside Seat in Moscow*, pp. 51–63.
94 Rákosi beszámolója az MKP központi vezetőségének a politikai helyzetről [Rákosi's report to the Central Commitee of the HCP on the political situation], 13 April 1945, RTsHIDNI, fond 17. op. 128 ed. hr. no. 37; and PIL, 274. F., KV 63.
95 Iz stenogramma vistuplenia M. Rákosi, 23 June 1945, *SFVA*, op. cit., p. 197.
96 See István Vida, "Az Ideiglenes Nemzeti Kormány átalakítása 1945 júliusában és a szovjet diplomácia" [The Reconstruction of the Provisional National Government in July 1945 and Soviet Diplomacy] in Lajos Izsák, Gyula Stemler eds., *Vissza a történelemhez. Emlékkönyv Balogh Sándor 70. születésnapjára* [Back to History. Festschrift in honor of Sándor Balogh's 70th birthday] (Budapest: Napvilág, 1996), pp. 389–417.

97 Jegyzőkönyv a szociáldemokrata párt és a magyar kommunista párt összekötő bizottsági üléséről [Record of meeting of the liason committee of the Social Democratic Party and the Communist Party], 16 April 1945. PIL, 283 F.

98 Rákosi beszámolója a politikai helyzetről az MKP PB ülésén [Rákosi's briefing of the political situation], 7 June 1945. PIL, 274 F., 3. cs., 2 őe.

99 The Representative in Hungary (Schoenfeld) to the Secretary of State, 19 May 1945, *FRUS*, vol. IV, 1945.

100 Vida, *Az Ideiglenes Nemzeti Kormány átalakítása*, pp. 389-419.

101 Révai, *Az ország újjáépítésének politikai feltételei*, p. 23.

102 Rákosi beszámolója az MKP PB ülésén, 7 June 1945, op. cit.; Günter Bischof, *Austria in the First Cold War*, p. 58.

103 Iz stenogrammi vistupleniia M. Rákosi, 23 June 1945, *SFVE*, op. cit., p. 199.

104 Az MKP KV ülése, 7 July 1945. RTsHIDNI, fond 17, op. 128 ed. hr. no. 37.

105 The form was sent to the State Department by Schoenfeld. Byrnes sent a personal response—exactly a year later. American diplomacy failed to exploit this unique opportunity to put the Communists on the defensive. Schoenfeld to the Secretary of State, 5 October 1945, USNA, RG 59, 864.00/10-545.

106 Vígh, *Tildy Zoltán életútja*, pp. 140–141.

107 Vida, *Az Ideiglenes Nemzeti Kormány átalakítása*, pp. 389-419.

108 The discussion between Pushkin and Miklós is published in *VEDRA*, vol I, document 79, pp. 234–236.

109 Gerő Ernő tájékoztatója a magyarországi helyzetről [Ernő Gerő's briefing on the situation in Hungary], 6 August 1945, *Moszkvának jelentjük*, pp. 57–74.

110 Dokladnaia zapiska zaveduiushchego III EO NKID SSSR A. A. Smirnova V.G. Dekanozovu v sviazi s reorganizatsiei pravitelstva Vengrii [Report by the head of the IIIrd European Department of the Foreign Ministry of the USSR A. A. Smirnov to V. G. Dekanozov in connection with the reorganization of the Hungarian Government] 27 June 1945, *VEDRA* vol. I, document 82, pp. 242–243.

111 *FRUS*, The Conferences of Malta and Yalta, pp. 244–253.

112 Vishinskii's conversation with the Bulgarian Representative in Moscow. Cited in The U.S. Representative in Moscow (Barnes) to the Secretary of State, 18 August 1945 *FRUS*, 1945, vol. IV, pp. 295–296.

113 Lundestad, *American Non-Policy Towards Eastern Europe, 1943–1947*, pp. 121–128.

114 Informatsia po VTs predsedatelia SKK v Vengrii K. E. Voroshilova I. V. Stalinu o pisme politicheskogo predstavitelia SShA v Vengrii H. F. Schoenefelda ob usloviah ustanovlenia diplomaticheskikh otnoshenii mezhdu SShA I Vengriei [Information on VTs line by the Chairman of the ACC in Hungary Voroshilov to I. V. Stalin on the letter by the political representative in Hungary of the U.S. Schoenfeld on the conditions of the establishment of diplomatic relations between the U.S. and Hungary] *VEDRA*, vol. I, document 94, pp. 263–264.

115 Gerő Ernő tájékoztatója a nemzetközi helyzetről [Briefing by Ernő Gerő on the international situation], 6 August 1945, op. cit.

116 Memorandum by the Secretary of the American Mission in Hungary (Squires) to the Secretary of State, 15 September 1945. *FRUS*, 1945, vol. IV, pp. 869–873.

117 The Secretary of State to the Representative in Hungary (Schoenfeld), 23 August 1945, *FRUS*, 1945, vol. IV, p. 854. See also Lundestad, *The American Non-Policy Toward Eastern Europe*, p. 126.

118 See De Santis, *Diplomacy of Silence*, p. 23, p. 48, pp. 59–60.

119 The Representative in Hungary (Schoenfeld) to the Secretary of State, 21 August 1945, *FRUS*, 1945, vol. IV, pp. 852–853; Lundestad, *The American Non-Policy Toward Eastern Europe*, p. 126.

120 See Tibor Frank, "Franz Boas and the Anthropology of U.S. Immigration from the Austro-Hungarian Monarchy," in Frank, *Ethnicity, Propaganda, Mythmaking*, pp. 35–72.

121 Hugh DeSantis, *Diplomacy of Silence*, p. 21, p. 77.

122 Ibid., p. 144.

123 Jegyzőkönyv az MKP PB üléséről [Record of meeting of the HCP Political Committee], 8 October 1945 and 15 October 1945, PIL, 274. F., 3. cs., 11. őe.

124 Soobshchenie L. I. Berii I. V. Stalinu o predlozhenii predsedatelia SKK v Vengrii K. E. Voroshilova ob osvobozhdenii vengerskikh voennoplennikh v sviazi s viborami v Vengrii [Communication by L. I. Beria to I. V. Stalin on the recommendation by the Chaiman of the ACC in Hungary K. E. Voroshilov on the liberation of Hungarian POWs in connection with the elections in Hungary] 21 October 1945, *VEDRA*, vol. I, document 98, pp. 270–271.

125 Telefonogramma po VTs. K. E. Voroshilova I. V. Stalinu i V. M. Molotovu o hode predvibornoi kampanii v Vengrii [Telephone message by VTs line from K. E. Voroshilov to I. V. Stalin and V. M. Molotov on the staus of the election campaign in Hungary] *VEDRA*, vol. I, pp. 271–274, document 98.

126 Rákosi, *Visszaemlékezések*, vol. I, p. 218.

127 Ibid.

128 Soobshchenie V. M. Molotova, L. I. Berii, G. M. Malenkova, A. I. Mikoyana I. V. Stalinu na vipusk predvibornogo manifesta chetirekh partii Vengrii [Communication by V. M. Molotov, L. I. Beria, G. M. Malenkov, A. I. Mikoyan to I. V. Stalin in the issuance of a pre-election four-party manifesto in Hungary] *VEDRA*, vol. I, pp. 276–277, document 100.

129 Iz zapis besedi V. M. Molotova s M. Rákosi o politicheskoi situatsii v Vengrii, 29 April 1947 [From the record of conversation between V. M. Molotov and M. Rákosi on the political situation in Hungary] *VEDRA* vol. I, Document 209, pp. 613–623; *Moszkvának jelentjük*, pp. 195–206.

130 For Voroshilov's reports on the events and his exchange with the CPSU PB see K. J. Vorosilov marsall jelentései a Tildy-kormány megalakulásáról [Marshall K. J. Voroshilov's Reports on the formation of the Tildy Government]. Published and the introductory essay written by István Vida, *Társadalmi Szemle*, 1996, no. 2. pp. 80–94; some of these documents were published in *VEDRA* vol. I, document 107, pp. 293–294; document 111, pp. 299–301; document 113, pp. 303–305.

131 Rákosi beszámolója a politikai helyzetről [Rákosi's briefing on the political situation] 7 June 1945, PIL, 274 F., 3 cs., 2 őe.

132 A Tildy-kormány tagjainak jellemzése [Characterization of the members of the Tildy government], 14 December 1945, *Moszkvának jelentjük*, pp. 87–90.

133 Kertesz, *Hungary between Russia and the West*, pp. 50–51.
134 Paper prepared by the Department of State Research and Intelligence Service, op. cit.
135 Trachtenberg, *Constructed Peace*, pp. 33–50.
136 The account is based on Leffler, *The Preponderance of Power*; pp. 116–121; and Miscamble, *George F. Kennan and the Making of American Foreign Policy*, pp. 141–177.
137 Eduard Mark, "The War Scare of 1946 and its Consequences," *Diplomatic History*, vol. 2, no. 3, (Summer 1997), pp. 383–416. The account of the crisis is based on Mark's study.
138 The impression that Moscow intended to alter the European balance and the power structure of the Balkans was enhanced by the publication of the German records of Molotov's talks in Berlin in November 1940.
139 For an analysis of Stalin's speech and the Kennan paper see Albert Resis, *Stalin, the Politburo and the Onset of the Cold War 1945–1946* (Pittsburgh: Pittsburgh Center for Russian and East European Studies, 1988), pp. 18–19.
140 Leffler, *The Preponderance of Power*, pp. 130–138.
141 The Novikov Telegram Washington, September 27, 1946. *Diplomatic History* no. 3, 1996 (Summer). See also the comment by William Taubman.
142 Levering et. al., *Debating the Origin of the Cold War*, p. 93.
143 McCagg, *Stalin Embattled*, p. 166.
144 Ibid., p. 163.
145 Jegyzőkönyv az MKP PB üléséről [Record of meeting of the HCP Political Committee], 7 July 1945, RTsHIDNI fond 17 op. 128 ed. hr. no. 315.
146 Iz stenogrammi vistuplenia M. Rákosi [Shorthand of Rákosi's speech] 23 June 1945, *SFVE*, op. cit. pp. 200–201.
147 Minutes of a former ACC meeting, 18 June 1946, General Sviridov's statement, *Documents of the Meetings of the Allied Control Commission for Hungary*, p. 173.
148 For the figures and the quote see György Gyarmati, "Harc a közigazgatás birtoklásáért – 1946" [Struggle for power in public administration – 1946], *Századok*, 1996, vol. 130, no. 3. pp. 497–570.
149 Informatsia po VTs poslannika SSSR v Vengrii G. M. Pushkina i zamestitelia predsedatelia SKK V. P. Sviridova K. E. Voroshilovu o besede s premer-ministrom Z. Tildy i s predsedatelem Natsionalnogo Sobraniia F. Nagy po voprosu o viborakh prezidenta strani, 6 January 1946 [Information by Vts line from the representative of the USSR in Hungary G. M. Pushkin and the deputy Chairman of the ACC V. P. Sviridov to K. E. Voroshilov of discussion with Prime Minister Z. Tildy and Speaker of the National Assembly F. Nagy on the question of the election of the country's President], *VEDRA* vol. I, document 124, pp. 346–349.
150 Gyarmati, "Harc a közigazgatás birtoklásáért," p. 506.
151 Ibid., p. 507.
152 On the anti-semitic pogroms see Pelle János, *Az utolsó vérvádak—Az etnikai és a politikai manipuláció kelet-európai történetéből* [The last accusations of ritual murder—From the east ruropean history of political manipulation] (Budapest: Pelikán kiadó, 1995); Standeiszky Éva, "Antiszemita megmozdulások a koaliciós időszakban," *Századok*, 1992, vol. 126, no. 2.

153 See István Vida, *A Független Kisgazdapárt Politikája, 1944–1947* [The policy of the Independent Smallholder Party, 1944–1947] (Budapest: Akadémiai Kiadó, 1976), pp. 162–192.

154 See Resis, *Stalin, the Politburo and the Onset of the Cold War*, pp. 10–19; McCagg, *Stalin Embattled*, pp. 159–167.

155 PIL, 274. F. 3. cs., 26. őe; and Vida, *A Független Kisgazdapárt Politikája*, p. 155.

156 István Vida, *Koalició es Pártharcok* [Coalition and Party Struggle] (Budapest: Európa, 1986), p. 171.

157 Vida, *A Független Kisgazdapárt politikája*, pp. 158–159.

158 Jegyzőkönyv a magyar kommunista párt Politikai Bizottságának üléséről [Record of meetings of the Political Committee of the HCP] 4 March 1946 and 6 March 1946, PIL, 274. F., 3. cs., 29. and 30. őe.

159 For their manifesto see Vida, *A Független Kisgazdapárt politikája*, p. 159.

160 Quoted in Lundestad, *The American Non-Policy Toward Eastern Europe*, p. 133.

161 The Secretary of State to the Minister in Hungary, 19 March 1945, *FRUS*, 1946, vol. VI, pp. 273–274; Schoenfeld to the Secretary of State, 3 April 1946. Ibid., pp. 275–276.

162 Schoenfeld to the Secretary of State 2 May 1946. *FRUS*, 1946, vol. VI, pp. 293–294.

163 See Csaba Békés, "Dokumentumok a magyar kormánydelegáció 1946. áprilisi moszkvai tárgyalásairól" [Documents on the April 1946 Moscow talks of the Hungarian government delegation], *Régió—Kisebbségi Szemle*, vol. 3, no. 2, 1992, pp. 161–194.

164 Record of the meeting of the Council of Ministers, 8 April 1946, Békés, "Dokumentumok a magyar kormánydelegáció 1946 áprilisi moszkvai tárgyalásairól," pp. 172–177.

165 Ferenc Nagy gave a highly enthusiastic, and on many counts imprecise account of the visit to the Council of Ministers. Minisztertanácsi jegyzőkönyv [Meeting of the Council of Ministers] MOL, XIX-A-83-a 102 sz. jkv.

166 For the Gyöngyösi notes see Békés, "A magyar kormánydelegáció 1946 áprilisi tárgyalásairól," pp. 177–182; for the Soviet record: Iz dnevnika V. M. Molotova. Priem ministra inostrannikh del Vengrii J. Gyöngyösi po voprosam sviazannim s podgotovkoi mirnikh dogovorov [From the diary of V. M. Molotov. Reception of Foreign Minister J. Gyöngyösi in questions related to the preparation of the peace treaty] *VEDRA* vol. I, pp. document 141, 402–406.

167 Reshenie Politburo TsK VKP(b) ob utverzhdenii proektov direktiv o mirnikh dogovorah s Bolgariei i Vengriei na soveshanii zamestitelei v SMID v Londone [Resolution of the Politburo Central Committee SCP on the ratification of the draft directive on the peace treaties with Bulgaria and Hungary] *VEDRA,* vol I, document 138, pp. 388–393. Published also in T. V. Volokitina, T. M. Islamov, T. A. Pokivailova, eds., *Transilvanskii vopros: vengero–ruminskikh territorialnikh spor i SSSR, 1940–1946, dokumenti* [The Transylvanian Question: The Hungarian-Romanian territorial dispute and the USSR] (Moscow: Rosspen, 2000), document 101, pp. 369–372.

168 See e.g. Andrei Vishinskii's conversation with the Romanian ambassador in Moscow, *VEDRA*, vol. I, document 114, pp. 305–307.

169 The foreign minister informed the parliament's foreign relations committee of the Moscow talks in which he claimed that the conditions of realizing some measure of territorial revision in Transylvania were favorable. Nagy publicly claimed that Hungary could count on great Soviet understanding on all issues related to the peace treaty. See Sándor Balogh, *Magyarország külpolitikája, 1945–1950* [Hungary's foreign policy, 1945–1950] (Budapest: Kossuth Könyvkiadó, 1988), pp. 162–169.

170 Ferenc Nagy's account was misleading as well: he informed his fellow ministers that the whole Russian army would be withdrawn, but only gradually. MOL, XIX-A-83-a, 102 sz. jkv.

171 For the Hungarian records see Békés, "Dokumentumok a magyar kormánydelegáció 1946. áprilisi moszkvai tárgyalásairól," pp. 179–182. For the Russian minutes on the talk with Stalin: *VEDRA*, vol. I, document 142, pp. 407–419.

172 Kemény Ferenc ideiglenes ügyvivő jelentése a Szovjetunió biztonsági politikájáról [Report by chargé d'affairs ad interim Ferenc Kemény on the security policy of the USSR] 8 June 1946, György Lázár, ed., *Szekfű Gyula követ és a moszkvai követség jelentései* [The reports of Minister Gyula Szekfű and the delegation in Moscow] (Budapest: Magyar Országos Levéltár, 1998), pp. 81–85.

173 The Hungarian minister, who had no access to higher political circles, reported that the Soviet government "trusts" the Hungarian one and according to diplomatic rumors Moscow would support Hungary in the minority question *vis-à-vis* Romania, Czechoslovakia and Yugoslavia. The question of the Hungarian minority in Yugoslavia was not even raised. Szekfű Gyula követ jelentése a magyar kormánydelegáció moszkvai látogatásáról, Lázár, *Szekfű Gyula követ és a moszkvai követség jelentései*, pp. 39–40.

174 Zamechania o brosiurakh dlia kompartii Vengrii [Remarks on the brochures for the Hungarian Communist Party] April 1946, PIL, 274 F., 10 cs., 116. őe.

175 Rákosi beszámolója az MKP Politikai Bizottságának ülésén [Rákosi's report at the meeting of the Political Committee of the HCP], 17 May 1946, PIL, 274. F., 2 cs., 34 őe. p. 18.

176 The document was in part published by Csaba Békés, "Soviet Plans to Establish the COMINFORM in Early 1946: New Evidence from the Hungarian Archives," *CWIHP Bulletin*, no. 10. pp. 135–136.

177 A Magyar Kommunista Párt Budapesten 1946. szeptember 28., 29., 30., és október 1. napján megtartott III. Kongresszusának jegyzőkönyve [Protocol of the Third Congress of the HCP held on 28, 29, 30 September, 1 October] (Budapest: Szikra, 1946), pp. 55–90.

178 Rákosi, *Visszaemlékezések,* vol. I, p. 325.

179 See the Novikov telegram.

180 As quoted by Mark, "The War Scare of 1946 and Its Consequences," p. 395.

181 According to McCagg Stalin decided to adopt "a blocist definition of his policies [...] throughout Europe" after December 1947. McCagg, *Stalin Embattled*, p. 291. More recent works have also emphasized that the Marshall Plan was the dividing line in Stalin's concept of Eastern Europe.

182 Schoenfeld to the Secretary of State, 11 June 1946, *FRUS*, 1946, vol. VI, pp. 304–306.

183 Ibid; see also Vida, *Koalíció és pártharcok*, pp. 190–191; Vida, *A Független Kisgazdapárt politikája*, pp. 183–184.

184 Informatsia po Vch G. M. Pushkina V. M. Molotovu o besede s prezidentom Vengrii Z. Tildy v sviazi s pravitelstvennim krizisom v strane, *VEDRA*, vol. I, document 153, pp. 464–465. Apparently Pushkin and Sviridov had had a private conversation with the President the previous night in which they spelled out their position regarding the crisis, but we have not found a written record of this event.

185 The Minister in Hungary to the Secretary of State, 6 June 1946, *FRUS*, 1946, vol. VI, pp. 302–304; The Secretary of State to the Minister in Bucharest, *FRUS*, 1946, vol. VI. pp. 586–588.

186 István Vida, "Iratok a magyar kormányküldöttség 1946. évi washingtoni látogatásához," [Documents on the 1946 Washington visit of the Hungarian government delegation], *Levéltári Szemle*, 1987, vol. 48–49, p. 253.

187 Szekfű Gyula követ jelentése a magyar kormányküldöttség washingtoni útjáról a szovjet vezetőkhöz eljuttatott emlékiratról és a látogatás visszhangjáról [Report by minister Gyula Szekfű on the memorandum to the Soviet leadership on the Washington visit of the government delegation and the on the repercussions of the visit], 21 June 1946, Lázár, *Szekfű Gyula követ és a moszkvai magyar követség jelentései*, pp. 86–90.

188 See the next chapter for details.

189 "Questions Pertaining to the Economic Situation in Hungary. Congressional hearing of Ferenc Nagy, 1947," Szegedy-Maszák collection, Országos Széchenyi Könyvtár Kézirattár.

190 Rákosi Sztálinhoz továbbított levele [Rákosi's letter to Stalin] 2 July 1946, *Moszkvának jelentjük*, pp. 95–97.

191 Minisztertanácsi jegyzőkönyv [Record of meeting of the Council of Ministers] July 1946, MOL, XIX-A-83-a, MT jkv.

192 Vida, *Koalíció és pártharcok*, p. 201.

193 See Tibor Zinner, "Az egyesületek és pártok feloszlatása Budapesten 1945 és 1948 között" [The Dissolution of Associations and Parties in Budapest, 1945–1948] *Politikatudomány*, 1988, vol. VI., no. 1, pp. 76–88.

194 For the details see Margit Balogh, *A KALOT és a katolikus társadalompolitika, 1935–1946* [KALOT and Catholic social policy] (Budapest: MTA Történettudományi Intézete, 1998), pp. 198–202. For the Soviet report see *Moszkvának jelentjük*, pp. 98–102.

195 Sviridov said on Article XV that "All organizations mentioned have been dissolved by the decree" [no. 529/1945 ME]. *Documents of the Meetings of the Allied Control Commission*, p. 141. At the July 24 meeting Sviridov claimed that he had said that "the Hungarian government was in the process of fulfilling the Article." Ibid., p. 167.

196 Ibid., p. 168.

197 For the Weems protest see The letter of the US representative in the ACC to the Acting Chairman of the ACC, USNA, RG 59, 864.00/7-1646. For Weems's view of the situation: *FRUS*, 1946, vol. VI, pp. 318–320. In the same report Weems reported the arrest of two prominent personalities, including Lajos Iván, who had predicted Nazi Germany's defeat in 1938, and reported on Germany's preparations for a military alliance with Moscow.

198 Ibid; for the Rajk quote see Jegyzőkönyv Tildy Zoltán köztársasági elnök lakásán tartott értekezletről [Record of meeting held at the apartment of President of the Republic Zoltán Tildy], 8 July 1946, PIL, 274. F. 7. cs., 152. őe.

199 For the exchange between the left wing and the Smallholders see Jegyzőkönyv Tildy Zoltán lakásán megtartott értekezletről, 15 July 1945. PIL, 283. F., 10. cs, 124. őe. A public announcement of the meeting was made, which promised "the sharpest struggle" against the part of the opposition which had been pushed out of the Smallholder Party as well as against "reactionary elements who wormed their way into the Smallholder Party." Anyone, who came out against the official economic policy, which was "against the foreign policy of the democracy," who disseminated anti-Semitism or incited conflict among the workers or between the town and the village were declared "enemies of the nation, the Hungarian people."

200 Rákosi beszámolója az MKP Politikai Bizottságának [Rákosi's report to the Political Committee of the HCP] 17 May 1946, op. cit. p. 8.

201 Feljegyzés az MKP Központi Vezetőségének üléséről [Record of meeting of the HCP Central Committee], 14 August 1946, RTsHIDNI, fond 17, op. 128, hr. ed. no. 121.

202 "Memorandum of the Office of European Affairs to the Undersecretary of State," 23 January 1947, *FRUS*, 1947, vol. IV, pp. 260–261; "The Secretary of State to the Legation in Hungary," 24 January 1947, *Ibid.*, pp. 263.

CHAPTER III

THE COMMUNISTS TAKE OVER

International politics in 1947 revolved around the German question. The Soviets understood that a shift had taken place in U.S. policy on Germany and feared that Germany was being organized against them. Although it was clear that a settlement based on each power having a free hand in their own zone was an impossibility, the splitting of Germany was not implemented immediately. The new Secretary of State George C. Marshall, was reluctant to break with the Soviets being afraid that the Germans would play the U.S. off against the Soviets. When the Soviets offered to unify Germany on the western model in return for reparations from current West German production, Marshall was ready to accept limited deliveries. Eventually Stalin's offer was rejected because for the United States, a unified Germany was no longer an attractive alternative. Western Europe would be unified behind a common policy of defending Western civilization, and West Germany would be a central partner in this arrangement. In late 1947 settlement on a unified basis was no longer an alternative, as this would involve bringing the Russians into the Ruhr region and giving them control of the western zones. By 1948, historian Marc Trachtenberg argues, the need for an integrated Western Europe, of which West Germany was a part, had become a dogma of U.S. policy.[1] The Russians themselves kept two stakes in the fire: on the diplomatic front they tried to keep the options open for a unified Germany, while at the same time worked toward the Sovietization of their own zone of occupation.[2] The rift between the great powers over the fate of Germany was not the only development that pointed toward continental division. Secretary of State Marshall's July 1947 speech offered American assistance to freedom loving nations, but there was an implicit indication that the parts of Europe already occupied by the Soviet Union would not benefit from it. Although some architects of the Marshall Plan originally conceived it to promote European economic and in consequence political unity, in reality it contributed to the opposite. Initially Stalin seems to have considered Soviet and limited East European participation. But when it turned out that the terms were at odds with the Soviet Union's exclusive domination of the region and involved foreign meddling in its domestic economy, the Soviets walked out and ordered their satellites to follow suit.[3] They went ahead with the new Communist International and Zhdanov—echoing Churchill's Fulton speech a year earlier— declared that the world had split into two hostile camps. The Americans in turn prepared an economic embargo of the Soviet-dominated part of Europe. Stalin's rejection of the Marshall Plan had profound and long lasting consequences for Eastern Europe, which lost a unique opportunity for economic modernization from (non-Soviet) external resources.

Communist penetration in Hungary had come a long way since 1945. Rákosi put the construction of socialism on the HCP's agenda irrespectively of international circumstances; his opposition still put its faith in a policy of appeasement. The Smallholders' seeming equanimity in facing the Soviet threat dampened what little enthusiasm the U.S. had in opposing Hungary's Sovietization. In the hope of retaining 'realistic' cooperation with the Soviets, by 1947 Washington was reluctant to oppose Soviet designs in Eastern Europe; in return for U.S. compliance the Kremlin was expected to stop short of introducing the Soviet model of Socialism in the eastern countries. But this also meant that Washington was sending mixed signals: its half-hearted actions in support of democracy convinced anti-Communist Hungarian forces that Washington relinquished them to the Soviet Union, therefore appeasement was the only appropriate policy facing the Communists, who enjoyed full-fledged Soviet support. But such "dual appeasement" failed to satisfy the Soviets, who gradually took control of the economy and with adroit application of pressure assisted their Communist patrons in seizing positions of power and ousting their political opponents.

In January 1947 the Communist Party launched a new, decisive campaign to destroy the Smallholders. Rákosi was skeptical whether the Smallholders would continue to "cleanse" itself of its own accord; therefore the Communists had to "start the cleaning" itself.[4] Béla Kovács, the Smallholder General Secretary was the first target. There was no love lost between Rákosi and Kovács. Rákosi sensed a rival in the Smallholders' strong man and knew that Kovács, who had a great influence on Ferenc Nagy, opposed the concessions the Smallholder Party made to the Communists in the course of 1946. Kovács, on the other hand felt that Rákosi was a cunning intellectual who "abused his intellectual superiority against the simple child of the people."[5] Honest, frugal, selfless and endowed with a robust physique, Kovács was known to be a man of boundless energy. Voroshilov respected Kovács for being able to work with him, the Communist Zoltán Vas described him as "clever, well-read; a real democrat, who sticks to his principles."[6] Kovács was born in a Roman Catholic family of poor peasants. Trained as a waiter, he cultivated land and educated himself. Kovács entered the Smallholder Party in 1933, and became the party's general secretary in 1945. A year later he took charge of the party's administrative apparatus and was the editor-in-chief of the party's daily, *Kisújság*. With his elimination, the Smallholders would be deprived of their most influential politician who was willing to resist Soviet pressure. To successfully withstand this pressure, therefore, the Smallholders needed political allies.

They were unlikely to find such an ally in the Social Democratic Party. The Social Democrats were split on the issue of collaboration. Their right wing, which deplored collaboration, thought that Ferenc Nagy had "deferred to the Russians completely," allowing Sviridov to push for more and more concessions. Officially, however, the Communists and the Social Democrats expressed their desire to cooperate closely in the joint struggle for power. In fact some of the Social Democrats wanted an even more leftist policy and closer cooperation with the Soviet Union. Justice Minister Ries thought that it was no longer possible to work with the Smallholders and advocated a minority government with the Communist Party, but Szakasits and Bán rejected the idea.[7]

On 9 January the Communists proceeded with the plan to "cleanse" the Smallholder Party in connection with the alleged right wing conspiracy. Interior Minister Rajk and Ries were put in charge of the carefully planned procedure. Rajk was to inform Tildy of the investigation. A press campaign was launched, which implicated SHP politicians—members of the party center's young generation—of being involved in the conspiracy. After one of the suspects managed to flee the country, the Communists decided to have Tildy convene an inter-party meeting, which would "propose" to the council of ministers that the seven Smallholder suspects be taken into custody and held under house arrest.[8] This episode demonstrated beyond doubt who wielded ultimate power. *Szabad Nép* reassured its readers that the culprits would receive their well-deserved punishment. On 20 January Rákosi and Szakasits demanded that Béla Kovács, who had been involved in the conspiracy, should resign or take a vacation. Kovács opted for the latter. He was now the focus of attack. Two Communists potentates, Farkas and Révai joined Rajk in an effort to bring the case to fruition. They were to make sure that the "right audience" for the trial would be invited, that the state attorney and the presiding judge should receive the appropriate instructions and that the "people's attorneys would be carefully selected." On the "political front" the Smallholders would be told that they would have to alter their political course once Kovács was out of the way. The Communist MP-s had to mollify their political adversaries by "paying attention to the smallholder deputies on the parliament corridor and by making an attempt to influence them."[9] Next Kovács's parliamentary immunity would be waived and he would be taken over by the political police. In order to do so, Rákosi put pressure on the Social Democratic Minister of Justice, István Ries.[10]

In desperation, Nagy met with Pushkin and complained that the Communists were inflating the conspiracy and were using it as a pretext to hunt down certain members of his party without any grounds. Pushkin indicated that no help could be expected from his quarters, reminding Nagy that the Soviets had recommended a purge of the reactionaries on several occasions, but to no avail.[11] Although the Smallholders refused to waive Kovács's immunity, Prime Minister Nagy did agree to have Kovács interrogated at the notorious headquarters of the political police at 60 Andrássy út. Although he showed at the headquarters of the political police for interrogation on 25 February, later that day Soviet authorities seized him. After a psychologically shattering interrogation by the head of the political police, Gábor Péter high-ranking NKVD officials escorted Kovács to his home, where two Soviet officers were already searching his apartment. Kovács's spouse was told that her husband would be home in a couple of days. Kovács would not come home for nine years; until 1953 his family did not even know whether he was dead or alive.[12]

Kovács's arrest prompted Washington's protest and aid. A package of economic assistance was compiled and announced in three steps in order to increase the political effect. Hungary was to receive a $15 million increase in surplus property credit followed by a $10 million cotton credit and finally post-UNRRA aid.[13] The Department of Commerce lifted the export restriction that applied to Hungary as a former enemy state and made her eligible to receive goods of limited availability.[14] John Hickerson of the State Department Office of European Affairs urged effective measures for a tripartite examination of Kovács's arrest, or in case this could not be carried out, a UN investigation. Secretary of State Marshall protested that the Soviets had failed to consult with the British and the American authorities. Marshall charged that the accusations against Kovács were groundless, were designed to substitute democracy with dictatorship and accused the Soviet High Command of direct and unjustified intervention, thus bringing the situation in Hungary to a crisis. The secretary of state declared that the United States would oppose the Soviet aspirations, and demanded a tripartite investigation with the participation of the members of the Hungarian government and the speaker of the National Assembly. Marshall's note, which was delivered to Molotov by Ambassador Walter Bedell Smith made no mention of a United Nations investigation. The U.S. representative in the ACC gave a similarly worded note to Sviridov on 5 March, in order to demonstrate American support of Nagy and hence avert his resignation.[15] As could be expected, Moscow would not hear of any tripartite investigation, which "would appear to be an open intervention into the internal affairs of the Hungarian Republic" and refuted the charges against the USSR.[16] Nevertheless the unusually rapid response suggested that the Soviets were on the defensive.

At the same time the State Department expressed dissatisfaction with the performance of the Smallholders. With some justification Hickerson wrote that Nagy was not strong enough to withstand pressure, and would therefore not be able to provide adequate support if the Hungarian question was put on the UN agenda. Schoenfeld complained bitterly that "the Hungarian government as presently composed is unable, and in many cases unwilling to cooperate effectively at this time in resisting minority pressure."[17] The *New York Times* accused Nagy and Tildy of leaning over backward to cooperate with the Communists and appease the Soviets[18]—a charge that was more appropriate for the latter than the former. However, the article failed to mention that the two men were subjected to slander and relentless Soviet-backed Communist pressure with no external support to count on. Nevertheless, Nagy was grateful for the American note, which he said made a compromise possible. A part of the compromise, which was not made public, provided for the termination of terror against non-left wingers, prohibited the intimidation of civil servants, curbed press attacks on party leaders and repeated the commitment for the proportionate redistribution of positions in public administration. The radical left benefited from the purge carried out in the ranks of the Smallholders as a result of the alleged conspiracy. According to a Soviet assessment out of the five new Smallholder cabinet members three belonged to the party's left wing. These included the new minister of defense, Lajos Dinnyés, an unprincipled opportunist whose financial problems enabled the Communists to manipulate him. Since another newcomer in the cabinet, Péter Veres of the National Peasant Party was more or less reliable from Moscow's perspective,[19] two thirds of the government were either Communists or more or less identified with their aims. Still, the HCP accused its helpless opponents of not proceeding with their self-mutilation "quickly and honestly enough."

Kovács's arrest put the Sovietization of Hungary in the international limelight. The *New York Times* compared the Hungarian events to the Greek civil war and speculated that the protest against Soviet intervention in Hungary's internal affairs and its willingness to act rapidly in Greece indicated that the U.S. would not accept the division of Europe into spheres of influence. State Department officials hinted at linking Hungary's case to Greek and Turkish independence. Acting Secretary of State Acheson's memorandum to the British ambassador in Washington stated that "the maintenance of Greek and Turkish independence and territorial integrity is closely related to problems of common concern involving other countries in Europe and Asia." In a conversation with the same diplomat on 8 March, Acheson mentioned Hungary as one of the countries in question.[20] But London had little enthusiasm for the "energetic steps" Washington was taking on Budapest's behalf. Britain's reluctance may have been one of the reasons why Hungary was not mentioned among the states where Communism ought to have been contained, but not the only one. Bedell Smith opined that the conspiracy was real and thought that there was some measure of Smallholder complicity in it.[21] Furthermore Schoenefeld's devastating and consequently disheartening view of the Hungarian opposition, which stated that they had neither the resources of character nor the political will to enable them to oppose Communist encroachments[22] reinforced U.S. acceptance of the gradual loss of Hungary.

While there was a crisis on the domestic front, Hungary's future on the political map of Europe was decided by the Peace Treaty signed on 10 February 1947. In certain questions of lesser international significance, such as the forced transfer of Hungarians from Slovakia, the United States actually supported Hungary against the position taken by the Soviet Union. Nevertheless, the treaty confirmed the hegemonic position Moscow enjoyed in Hungary, as did the ones signed with Romania and Bulgaria.[23] Although the Western powers supported minimal Hungarian territorial claims against Romania, the Soviet position prevailed, and Hungary returned to its pre-1938 boundaries with the exception of three villages around the city of Bratislava, which were ceded to Czechoslovakia.[24] What concerned the Soviets' position in Hungary most was the stationing of their troops. With the conclusion of the Peace Treaty the Soviet Union theoretically lost its right to station troops on Hungarian (and Romanian) territory. Yet on the basis of a *British* proposal the former allies inserted a clause whereby the Soviet Union would be allowed to retain troops in Hungary and Romania in order to maintain the logistical line to its occupation forces in Austria. Hence Soviet troop withdrawal was tied to the conclusion of peace with Austria and thus postponed indefinitely, particularly in view of the fact that there was little prospect for an agreement on that issue.[25] Thus the Soviets were entitled to maintain the occupation of Romania and Hungary on a perfectly legal basis. Although the U.S. wanted to compensate the adverse effect of the British proposal by adding a clause similar to the one in the Italian treaty, which would explicitly restore Hungarian (and Romanian) sovereignty after the treaty was concluded,[26] the Soviets rejected it.[27] The Treaty therefore enabled the Russians to keep their troops in Hungary for an unspecified period of time, infringing on Hungarian sovereignty. Translated into domestic politics, this situation greatly enhanced the HCP's position. The ink on the compromise with the Smallholders was hardly dry when the Communist Party launched its next phase of the campaign to liquidate its political opponents. Falsified evidence extracted from Kovács by his NKVD interrogators was put to use to eliminate Prime Minister Ferenc Nagy. Kovács's confession gave Rákosi what he needed: the former General Secretary of the SHP stated that Nagy knew about the conspiracy. As he wrote to Stalin, the Communists were out for a breach with the strongest party.[28]

Kovács's interrogations "revealed" that the Smallholder Party was organizing armed units in order to seize power. Kovács and Nagy were also said to be responsible for their party having become the "focal point of reactionary forces and the nest of conspiracy." When the interrogations were concluded, Rákosi informed the Soviet leadership that it was now Nagy's turn to be arrested. He declared that the liquidation of the "fascist conspiracy continued to be the central issue." Since it was now a "proven fact" that Nagy had been a part of the sinister intrigue, the only remaining question, Rákosi wrote to Moscow, was how to get him. He repeatedly tried to persuade the Soviets to allow Kovács to testify before a Hungarian court, but Molotov was understandably skeptical about what the suspect would say in court, not to mention the political risks of trying such a popular figure publicly. The Hungarians would have to settle with his written confessions, which were to be provided by the Soviet authorities.[29] As the confrontation with the Smallholder Party was entering its final phase, the impatient Rákosi and his fervent Interior Minister outlined their future plans to the Soviet leadership. This was to attack the Social Democrats, many of which, they claimed, were "British agents."[30] The accusation was probably prompted by Szakasits's recent talks with representatives of the Labour Party in London, although Szakasits expressed his unquestioned loyalty to the Soviet Union and to collaboration with the Communists.[31] But before they could turn against their allies, Nagy had to be out of the way. On 14 May the prime minister went to Switzerland for a vacation unaware that he would never see his country again. While he was away, Stalin instructed Rákosi to seize the opportunity and clamp down on the Smallholders. "The Soviet ambassador in Budapest," Rákosi recalled, "asked me to travel to Arad, Romania to an important and urgent meeting. The matter seemed so urgent, that half an hour after the communication I was already sitting in a car accompanied by a high-ranking Soviet official, which was necessary because at the time Soviet guards manned most Hungarian–Romanian border stations. [Romanian ACC Chairman] Susaikov gave me an unsigned hand written letter saying that this is Stalin's personal message. It stated that according to Soviet information Ferenc Nagy is not resting in Switzerland, but is negotiating with the enemy of the plans designed to oust the Communists from the government. We should exploit his absence and launch an attack, because if we miss the chance we shall be in a difficult situation (Vam budet ochen tugo)."[32]

Rákosi wanted to "unmask" Nagy before June and to present the revealing documents to the justice minister before Nagy returned from vacation. He admitted that the party was out to get State Secretary Balogh as well.

The political offensive would be accompanied by a public campaign against the "wealthy" coupled with a demand to nationalize the banks.[33] On 25 May Rákosi publicly hinted that there were still people in office who had participated in the conspiracy. The Smallholders tried find a way out of the crisis. They agreed to have Nagy announce his resignation. Nagy agreed, but in return he demanded that his five-year-old son should be allowed to join him and wanted money to ensure his livelihood. Rákosi immediately agreed to the first condition, stating that the child was not a political tool, but rejected the second: "traitors are not entitled to money." He insisted that Nagy should announce his resignation not later than by three p.m. May 30. When this did not happen the Communists announced his resignation themselves. Nagy finally announced his resignation himself when his son reached Swiss soil, on 2 June.[34]

A few days later, to the Communists' great relief, speaker of parliament Béla Varga, a priest who had saved the lives of tens of thousands of Polish refugees in the war, left the country. Nikola Petkov, the peasant leader of the Bulgarian opposition was arrested on 4 June, which was hardly a coincidence, given Nagy's resignation just two days before. Rákosi hastened to call Moscow's attention to his merits in getting rid of his chief opponent. "We speeded up the crisis," he boasted, "because we had cause to worry that procrastination will enable our opponents to launch their attack."[35] At Sviridov's advice, Lajos Dinnyés was appointed as the new prime minister.

On the last day of May the *New York Times* commented that "the Reds have come to power," arguing that the abdication of the Premier meant the beginning of a "Communist police state." It also reported panic in the business world in Hungary, where not a single deal was transacted on the stock market.[36] The Hungarian minister in Washington, Aladár Szegedy-Maszák, who had taken a leading part in Hungary's diplomatic effort to jump out of the war, requested that the Truman administration take the necessary measures through the ACC and by tabling of the Hungarian issue in the UN Security Council. Szegedy-Maszák's initiative was supported by Senator Eastland, who urged the Head of the State Department's Office of Special Political Affairs, Robert McClintock to examine the possibility of Security Council action. McClintock agreed, believing that such an action would be worthwhile even though the Soviets would undoubtedly veto a resolution. Acting Director of the Office of European Affairs John Hickerson was thinking along similar lines. He suspected that the Russians were behind the prime minister's sudden resignation and thought that the ruthless intervention was a "clear cut act of political aggression." Therefore Hickerson drafted a note that underlined the USSR's responsibility and recommended that a fact-finding mission, made up of the three powers represented in the ACC, be sent to Hungary. If the Soviets refused to comply, the matter would be raised in the UN Security Council and would be pursued with the "utmost persistence by this government [...] until it may be possible to raise the matter in the General Assembly and press for action by that body, possibly on the basis of a general indictment of Soviet political actions in the entire Eastern European area."[37] Before any remonstrations would be made— Washington was planning a strongly worded note—the Americans consulted with London on the possibility of a concerted action. The Foreign Office was hostile to the idea of forceful action and disagreed with emphasizing the Soviet Union's responsibility. It would be hard to prove Moscow's complicity in the events and therefore London failed to support the American protest to the ACC. But behind this formal excuse there was a more profound cause for the British reluctance to oppose the Soviets on Hungary.

The Labour government was sympathetic to Russia, and Foreign Secretary Ernest Bevin harbored a secret hope that the "Left would be able to speak to the Left." Few people were prepared for confrontation with Communism. When troops were used against Communist partisans in Greece the public and most of the press protested. Many within the Labour government thought that communism suited countries that lacked democratic traditions of long standing. Reports on forced labor camps were dismissed as slanderous fabrications, people blamed Western statesmen for not getting along with Stalin.[38] In addition British strategy concentrated on retaining a dominant position in the Middle East in the framework of Britain's role as a world power. In 1944 the Foreign Office was thinking in terms of an Anglo-Soviet alliance to contain Germany; Britain's concern was not Soviet domination of East-Central Europe, but this domination extending westward and southward. The Post Hostilities Planning Staff defined British strategic interest as the security of the Commonwealth and the protection of Middle Eastern oil. It was assumed that the Soviets would have "predominant" influence in Hungary. In 1945 a new approach gained prominence in the Foreign Office, which was adopted by the Labour government. This repudiated Churchill's spheres of influence arrangement, which amounted to a cynical abandoning of small nations, and at the same time abdicated Britain's role as a great power to be carried with the affairs of Europe as a whole not just where London had a special interest. In spite of this, the architect of the new course, Sir Orme Sargent believed that Romania and Hungary were the two countries where decisive Soviet influence could be permitted, even if this meant Communization. These were the two countries which had no bearing on British position in the eastern Mediterranean.[39] Hence, in 1947 Sargent saw no justification for a public dispute with the Soviet Union over Hungary. Another official of the Foreign Office thought that the Americans were only "making fools of themselves." Although Foreign Secretary Bevin publicly denounced the Soviet Union for introducing one party dictatorships, and declared that the policy of "appeasement" was over, he saw no reason to protest either. London was satisfied with requesting Molotov's assurance that his government would not impede normal Anglo-Hungarian relations and signaled that Britain would join a tripartite commission called for by the Americans to investigate the situation in Hungary.[40] Taking into account the British reservations, the American representative in the ACC, General Weems, was instructed to present a milder note than previously envisioned, which toned down the reference to Soviet intervention and more importantly, made no mention of the United Nations Security Council. Washington limited itself to calling for a tripartite committee and reserved the right for further action.[41] Moscow rejected even this milder proposal, on the grounds that it would be an inadmissible interference in Hungarian matters.

Although President Truman was outraged at the Hungarian situation and made a public pledge not to sit idly by, Washington did not push for a UN investigation. The State Department feared that the smaller European nations would not support Hungary, or any other ex-German satellite against a former ally. Moreover, it seemed unlikely that in a dispute between the Soviet Union and the West, the new Communist-dominated government in Budapest would side with the latter. Thus it hardly seemed advisable to put the world organization to such a hard test over a former enemy. Finally and perhaps most importantly, the U.S. administration did not want the Hungarian question to divert attention from Greece, which was being threatened by armed Communist insurgence. For the time being then, the *putsch* in Budapest would not be discussed in the UN forum, although its inscription in the General Assembly was left open for the Fall session.[42] Senator Vandenberg summed up the U.S. position, which "cannot deal with Hungary, a former enemy as it deals with Greece. Hungary had been an enemy, while Greece was an 'eternal, permanent ally.' Hungary is under armed occupation by Soviet troops [...] Greece is an independent state. Hungary cannot, therefore ask or receive our aid in the Greek manner. They are parallel tragedies, but cannot have parallel treatment."[43]

Clearly, for the Western powers the dividing line was between Hungary and Austria. London concluded that Soviet domination of Austria would have disastrous effects on Czechoslovakia, Germany and Italy. The British Defense Department agreed that Austria—the history of which was being doctored to make it out as Hitler's victim—was of vital strategic interest to Great Britain because of its crucial Central European location on the Danube.[44] The Truman Administration was coming round to the British perspective that Austria was becoming a test case of Anglo-American resolve *vis-à-vis* Soviet intimidation and was listed on top of the American list of priorities along with Greece, Turkey, Italy and France where Communist takeover seemed imminent. Hence the United States decided to shore up the ailing Austrian economy, reoriented its trade toward the West and assumed responsibility for the Austrian trade deficits.[45] Austria was partly under Western occupation. Soviet control of it would have jeopardized the Western position in Germany. Russian possession of Austria as a satellite would have placed the USSR in a position to outflank Central Europe and Italy in a military offensive.[46] Although the geographical distance between Budapest and Vienna is a mere 200 miles, the space between the two capitals in terms of Western policies could be measured in light years.

Washington took no positive steps on behalf of the non-Communist political forces in Hungary. Instead Washington suspended Hungary's surplus property credit and canceled the cotton credit that had been approved in March. Thus the Hungarians were penalized for something for which they were only partly responsible, while Moscow received nothing more than a diplomatic warning. This was clearly not the right time and Hungary was not the right place for a showdown with the Soviets. A group of officials from the State, War and Navy Departments ranked the order of urgency as follows: Greece, Turkey, Iran, Italy, Korea, France, Austria and finally, Hungary.[47]

Although the Senate recommended severing diplomatic relations with Hungary, the State Department did not think that this, or the idea of setting up of an émigré government, would be expedient.[48] The idea of rupturing diplomatic relations was advocated by Szegedy-Maszák as well, who seemed to be the only Hungarian official going to any lengths in trying to raise American support. Senator Vandenberg erred on one point: the Hungarians *could* not receive U.S. assistance, but they *would* not ask for any either. Perhaps this was just as well, since the State Department would not make the slightest move that might have put the newly installed Hungarian government in jeopardy. Szegedy-Maszák, like some of his colleagues, refused to recognize, and therefore to represent the newly appointed Dinnyés government. In a dramatic, but quite futile show of defiance, the Hungarian diplomatic representatives in Paris, London and Rome resigned alongside Szegedy-Maszák. This was the only way left for the remnant of what was left of the well-educated, Western-oriented portion of Hungary's diplomatic corps. Their like-minded predecessors took the same step when another predatory dictatorship, Germany, occupied the country only three years before. While they could do little for their country, at least they spared themselves from the humiliation of having to serve a foreign power. Szegedy-Maszák hoped that at least Washington would continue to treat him as his *country's* representative and that it would refrain from dispatching Schoenfeld's designated successor, Selden Chapin to Budapest. But to his disappointment the State Department terminated his mission and Chapin

proceeded to the Hungarian capital "as planned."[49] State Department officials argued that in the absence of diplomatic contact America would be
unable to do anything for Hungary. In contrast, the former minister was
probably right in saying that the new government's immediate recognition
was unnecessary for the preservation of American presence, since the Legation kept on working even in the absence of a head of mission. Furthermore,
the United States was still represented in the ACC.[50] The U.S. authorities
granted the agreement to Szegedy-Maszák's successor, the Social Democrat
Rusztem Vámbéry without delay.

Perhaps it was a historical coincidence that the Communist putsch
against the democratically elected government in Hungary and the announcement of the Marshall Plan, Eastern Europe's last chance for economic integration with the Western world, all but coincided in the summer of 1947.
But instead of uniting the continent, the Marshall Plan helped divide it.
George F. Kennan, an intellectual who cherished Russian culture, was an
avid reader of Spengler, and deplored the triumph of America's technical
civilization over European culture, hoped that in the interest of preserving
a European identity the European Reconstruction Plan would hasten European reunification and would allow the U.S. to go home. Even though
Kennan anticipated that the Soviet Union may reject the Marshall Plan, he
insisted that the offer of participation should be extended to the Soviet
Union and Eastern Europe and in doing so the U.S. would be implementing
a policy designed to prevent the consolidation of the Soviet power in Eastern Europe. Most of his fellow policy makers, however, did not seriously
question the inevitability of a Soviet sphere of influence in the East. For
them the invitation to the eastern countries was a device to place the onus of
dividing Europe on Moscow, not as a tool of overcoming the continental
division.[51]

The initial Hungarian reaction to the Marshall Plan was cautious, but
on the whole positive. Economists had calculated that without external assistance it would take up to four decades to rebuild Hungary's economy. The
Social Democrats welcomed the forthcoming meeting in Paris as "the real
peace conference," even the party's left-wingers emphasized that Hungary
was interested in participation. After Moscow made public its own participation at the conference, the Communists announced their intention to take
part, but emphasized that national independence would have to be safe-
guarded. The NPP hoped that the Marshall Plan would draw the world
closer together.[52] All this depended on the Russian attitude. The British and
the French wanted to invite them to disarm domestic criticism, but hoped
that they would refuse to cooperate.[53] The Soviets were skeptical from the
beginning, but hoped to use the plan to their advantage and receive reconstruction credits. Novikov cabled that it was directed against the Soviet

Union, but the economist of Hungarian birth, Jenő Varga, did not advocate rejection.[54]

Although *Pravda* denounced the plan on the 15th, Molotov favored exploring the possibilities. On the 21st he went to Paris in order to collect data about the "character and conditions" of the aid.[55] The next day Yugoslavia, Poland and Czechoslovakia got permission from the Kremlin for participation at the conference,[56] but on the same day Molotov announced that Moscow would "protest against the inclusion of the former satellites, including Austria, as well as the former neutrals."[57] He warned that the Americans were hoping to hinder European democratization and Washington did not desire Soviet participation. Soviet intelligence reported that Washington's intent was to deprive Moscow of influence in Germany and Central Europe, the British and the French were plotting to bring the Germans in, and keep the Russians out. Molotov suspected their collusion with Washington.[58] The Soviets objected to multilateral committees that were being planned to examine aid requests and the revitalization of East–West trade. Hoping to create tension among the Western representatives, Molotov decided to reject the plan. This was the death sentence for East European participation and hence its hope for economic rehabilitation from foreign resources. With one stroke East European nations lost their best chance for economic modernization and growth. Austria, a country of Hungary's size received almost 1,5 billion dollars in aid from the U.S. in one decade. For Hungary frantic heavy industrialization from meager domestic resources, shortage, low quality of goods, and constant austerity would be the order of the day for the years to come.

Hungary was invited to attend the Paris conference on 4 July but in view of Molotov's declaration the response was cautious. The Communist Party went through a complete change of heart. Révai declared that "Hungary cannot and will not pursue an anti-Soviet policy and therefore cannot accept an invitation to participate in an anti-Soviet bloc."[59] Tildy shared this view and with Communist assistance persuaded Prime Minister Dinnyés, who had been ready to accept a loan without political strings attached, to change his mind. The right and the center of the SHP decided to send Hungarian representatives to the conference and even its left wing intellectuals favored this position. Their resolution, however, was never made public nor was it discussed in Parliament. On 8 July Molotov advised the fraternal parties not to attend. The very same day the Poles announced that they would not be participating. Embarrassingly, Moscow Radio had announced Polish non-participation before the Polish government announced its decision. On 9 July Stalin received a Czechoslovakian delegation and accused Prague of assisting the West in the Soviet Union's isolation by wishing to attend the Paris conference. The faster the Czechs announced their with-

drawal, the better. Stalin advised his stunned guests to put more emphasis
on trade with the Soviet Union, which desired a number of the Czechoslovakian products which had been hitherto sold to the West.[60]

No such drastic intervention was needed in Hungary. An inter-party
meeting was convened on 10 July, which adopted the Soviet position in a
matter of ten minutes. The next day less than an hour was enough for the
government to affirm the decision to reject the plan at one most important
junctures of modern Hungarian history. Dinnyés did not even bother to take
a vote. A "polite" formula was drafted, expressing the government's "greatest sorrow" for not being able to attend, the reason being the lack of consensus among the great powers. It did not mean that Hungary had no desire
to participate in European reconstruction and "nothing was further from it
than to discount mutual aid." The wording reflected a forlorn hope that the
window of opportunity would somehow be left open. [61]

The Communists were poised to consolidate and extend their power in
an election on the Bulgarian model. Rákosi and the whole party leadership
were optimistic after having scored a "decisive victory over the Smallholders. In such a way Hungary, that is the Communist Party, was the first to
foil the aspirations of American imperialism."[62] In fact they were already
in a dominant position. Rákosi told Molotov that the Communists managed
to establish a "kind of economic dictatorship in the country." Without their
approval "the banks would not lend to anyone." They also held the key
positions in the army.[63] In addition 80 percent of the political police was
made up of party members. Training in the political police was assisted by
a Soviet NKVD general, Fedor Belkin. Its leader, Gábor Péter had a wide
web of informers and planted his men in every political party. They were
able to blackmail "activists" of other political parties thanks to the compromising materials they held on them. Communist informers infiltrated the
ministries and even the churches, and were able to provide a full picture of
political developments. In such a way the Communists enjoyed a significant
advantage over their political foes, in their ability to find out about their
intentions in advance. Telephone conversations were tapped and the most
important conversations were reported to Rákosi. By 1947 the political
police were recording the telephone conversations of the Prime Minister as
well as the party leaders.[64] The Communists, with memories of the Soviet
criticism of their performance in the first national election uppermost in
their minds, wanted to ensure a strong victory.[65]

Rákosi presented a list of desiderata to the Kremlin during his April
visit in Moscow. He queried whether the Red Army would stay in Hungary.
Molotov reassured him that a part of it would remain until the Austrian
Peace Treaty, which would definitely not be signed that year. He even promised that the Soviet government would soon pay for its own army in Hun-

gary (a promise that was not kept). Rákosi asked for two or three hundred German or preferably Soviet made machine guns to arm the Communist-dominated police and the workers since the "fascists," he claimed, were well armed. Sviridov had already offered looted German weapons from the Soviet stocks, but expected Moscow's approval first.[66] Now Molotov gave it.

Rákosi complained that "the Czechoslovak comrades seem to have gone berserk." They were persecuting ethnic Hungarians, which was diminishing the Communist party's popularity. The fate of the Hungarian national minorities had domestic ramifications since the Communists were building on the support of the left wing populists, for whom this issue was of utmost significance. For this reason Rákosi asked for Soviet assistance to relieve the lot of the Hungarian minority in Slovakia. Molotov, however, refused to commit himself. Neither did he promise to speed up the repatriation of prisoners of war, a further request of the Hungarian party leader aimed at raising the HCP's popularity.[67]

In most areas Soviet support for the forthcoming struggle was reassuring. The Communists wanted to organize the left wing along the Bulgarian model[68] and to disenfranchise as many of their political enemies as possible. Although the SPD tried to veto this, the pro-Soviet György Marosán, armed with Pushkin's verbal support, managed to repeal the veto.[69] Rákosi hoped to disenfranchise half a million "fascists and reactionaries" with the full support of Communist sympathizers in the Social Democratic Party. Immediately before the elections he managed to get the Soviets to suspend the repatriation of POWs, presumably because he feared that they would vote for his opponents.[70] The Communists made no secret of the fact that they intended to rig the election. Interior Minister Rajk declared that his party would win even if the Social Democrats and the Smallholders "stood on the top of their heads." He instructed the Communist organizers of the election not to worry about legality. The Social Democrats were to be treated with hostility, their candidates had to be discredited. Whispering propaganda was to be conducted in order to imply that the Social Democratic Party would merge with the Communists.[71]

The electoral campaign showed how deeply entrenched the Communist power was in Hungary. An illustration of this was their capacity to manipulate prices and the supply of consumer goods to increase their popularity before the election.[72] This example also reveals the Communists' notion of democracy. They did not view the election as a political contest, but as a "struggle" which would decide who was to rule not for a temporary period of time, but for the rest of history. It was one more opportunity to annihilate their opposition with quasi-parliamentary methods as silently as possible. Where it was necessary to bend the laws they did so without compunction.

In the summer of 1947 the new American minister prepared a lengthy analysis of the situation. Selden Chapin had few illusions about Soviet methods. Like Schoenfeld before him, he was somewhat biased and had a low opinion of the Smallholder leaders, which inevitably affected his views. He thought that the situation in Hungary was deteriorating and the Kremlin was resolved to integrate Hungary into its sphere, but did not think that this would necessarily involve the total and immediate Sovietization of the nation's social and economic structure. It seemed to Chapin that in the absence of democratic traditions, the country was lacking the moral strength to resist. Chapin was also critical of the United States, which failed to exploit every opportunity to save Hungary's independence, although it seemed to him that the Hungarians overestimated American capabilities. There was still time, he thought, for Washington to pursue a more constructive policy. He preferred to see Hungary's case taken to the UN Security Council and hoped for the rapid ratification of the peace treaty, which he erroneously believed would eliminate the legal basis for Soviet intervention in internal affairs. Chapin advocated economic assistance as well as a cultural and information program to influence the people. Expecting the worst, he recommended that the State Department help escape those opposition politicians whose lives were endangered.[73]

There was no positive change in U.S. policy. Smallholder deputies sought financial support and two Social Democrats asked for help in forming an "opposition" SDP as the original one had come under the influence of fellow travelers. But the response remained the same as in 1945: the American government would not interfere in other countries' domestic affairs.[74] Under these circumstances recurring American criticism of the Smallholders seems too harsh. No doubt, there were many who "did not resist" because they were closet Communists, opportunistic or because of personal expediency and weakness of character. There were also political forces, which could and would have resisted had they received support. But they had to count with political realities. Given the lack of outside assistance, was it not the only viable alternative for them to give concessions, even if in retrospect it is clear that this was the wrong tactic? Had not the Mongols spared those cities, which opened their gates to them and annihilated the ones that resisted?

Mihály Farkas's statement expressed the mood of the day and the Communist belief in the law of history, the agent of which was the Communist Party: "We live in times when all roads lead to Communism [...] there is no point in exerting ourselves because if a serious opposition party should emerge, the Communist Party will destroy it. [...] The things the Communist Party desires are the only things that will happen and that are good for the Hungarian people."[75] In the election of 31 August an estimated 466,000 people were disenfranchised, and 50,000 fraudulent votes were cast for the Hungarian Communist Party.[76] The coalition bloc received 67 percent of the votes, but the Communists managed to poll only 22 percent, that is only five more than two years before. Nonetheless, they defeated the rump and emasculated SHP. The strength of popular commitment to pluralism was shown by the fact that a real opposition party, Demokrata Néppárt (Democratic People's Party) emerged as the second largest party.

A few weeks later the Allied Control Commission terminated its activities. In his final communication General Weems told Sviridov that his country would not recognize those measures which the Soviet Union took without the concurrence of his mission. The American government reserved the right to reopen pertinent questions,[77] but this threat hardly bothered the Communists, who were preparing to further entrench themselves in power. They had to make a strong effort, since the CPSU's international department was dissatisfied with their performance at the election and accused them of committing serious mistakes.[78] Révai declared that it was up to Communis tactic, energy and expertise to determine whether Hungary would be a "people's or a bourgeois democracy."[79] This declaration came only two days after a Soviet invitation to attend a meeting of the world's Communist Parties at the Polish town of Sklarska Poreba had been delivered. There, they received a reminder to be even more energetic than they had been before. The preparatory papers of the conference noted the obsolescence of national roads to Communism and emphasized the necessity of unity in waging anti-American struggle with all means at their disposal.[80]

Back in Budapest Révai and Farkas told their colleagues that the newly established Information Bureau had created the conditions for the cooperation of the Communist parties and for the struggle against American imperialism. Concrete directives were given as to how the Communist parties should exploit the coalition governments to acquire positions of power. They were advised to control the army and the police and to destroy the economic power of the bourgeoisie. The Communist leaders decided to speed up the process of working out the political guidelines for a new coalition and to liquidate the Hungarian Independence Party.[81] In reality there was nothing new in these set of instructions; the Communists had been carrying them out for over two years. They had been occupying positions of power in the armed forces, the police, the government and the economy, liquidating political and economic pluralism as they went along.[82]

There were to be no constraints by the rules of formal democracy,[83] and preparations were made to unite the workers parties. In this process the right wing Social Democrats were to be eliminated from the party leadership.[84] Under the pretext of electoral fraud, the Hungarian Independence

Party's forty-nine mandates were declared null and void, and finally Rajk dissolved the party. Its leader, Zoltán Pfeiffer fled to the United States. In the Soviet view the "majority of the Hungarian people were on the new, democratic road of development."[85]

Adopting the Stalinist model

By the end of 1948 the division of Germany and of the continent was irreversible. In London the Western powers proposed the creation of a West German state. In order to implement the Potsdam and Yalta agreements, that is to assert the four-power administration of Germany, Stalin decided to blockade Berlin and squeeze out the Allies.[86] The immediate cause of the blockade was the imposition of a new currency in the Western zone. Historians differ as to Soviet aims. Perhaps the Berlin blockade was meant to be a lever with which to prevent the formation of a West German state. An alternative explanation is that Berlin was the prize of the blockade and the Soviets were aiming to merge it into their occupation zone in an effort to consolidate the Soviet portion of Germany. The Soviet leaders may have pursued several goals simultaneously, or were simply testing what could be achieved, but evidence definitely suggests that they were yearning for an undivided Germany that would be at their disposal.[87] Be that as it may, Stalin failed on both counts, which meant that his apparent bid for mastery in the western part of the continent ended disastrously, especially as it added to western cohesion and prodded the United States to guarantee Western Europe's security.

Possibly the most unexpected turn of the year was the schism between Belgrade and Moscow. The underlying cause of this, as Vojtech Mastny explained, was Moscow's desire to discipline the satellites facing the conclusion of the Brussels pact. The Yugoslavs were ostracized from the Cominform even though Tito's loyalty to Stalin was unquestionable. The problem was its spontaneity. Stalin demanded deference that stemmed from fear, in order to shore up his empire against the alleged Western threat.[88] In American eyes the "break" with Moscow came to serve as the model for the other satellites and Washington's policy toward Eastern Europe was tailored to hasten another schism within the bloc. This policy was founded on a misunderstanding. The Americans assumed that Tito broke with Stalin. In reality it was the other way round. The remainder of the Soviet bloc was gradually isolated from the rest of Europe. A significant move in this direction was the Belgrade convention on navigation on the river Danube, the most significant waterway in Eastern Europe. This replaced the international regime with Soviet control on the river from Bratislava to the mouth on the Black Sea.

It is hard to disagree with Vojtech Mastny in that the Cominform was neither so urgent nor so consequential for the Eastern as for the Western powers, since the Soviets did not cast doubt on the viability of national roads to socialism. In Czechoslovakia Rudolf Slansky thought the time was ripe to prepare for a showdown during a crisis that would enable the Communists to come to power, but in the summer of 1948 he still believed in marching to Communism on a special road.[89] As a remnant of the party's pact with the populists, the party program of the Hungarian Workers Party pledged to employ the teachings of Marx, Lenin and Stalin and to develop them "according to the Hungarian conditions." The passage remained in the program in spite of the criticism of it by the deputy-head of the CPSU Foreign Relations Department.[90] By the end of 1948 however, even this illusion of independence was gone.

The Hungarian Communists were making the final preparations for one party rule. From January 1948 there was a mass exodus from the Social Democratic party. Unification with the Communists became possible after the party "purged" itself of the "remnants of reactionary influence." Some of the Social Democrats hoped that their party would be able to retain some of its identity after the unification, but this was self-delusion. Only one ideology would exist in the new party "without compromise," and that was Marxism–Leninism[91]; Social Democratic views and interests would not be represented.[92] The Hungarians' proposal for the new unified party was unacceptable to Moscow. Rákosi recommended "Hungarian Workers–Peasant Party," but this proposal failed to reflect the "hegemony of the proletariat" and "disguised the proletariat's leading role over the peasantry." Gerő's idea of a "Socialist Party" failed to emphasize the party's national character and could be evaluated as a concession to social democracy. In contrast, the name had to emphasize that it was the vanguard of the working class, which united and guided the proletariat's class struggle.[93] Hence the Soviet version was chosen and the party was named Magyar Dolgozók Pártja (Hungarian Workers Party). Its foreign policy program prescribed alliance with the Soviet Union and close cooperation and friendship with the people's democracies, even though the serious conflict with Czechoslovakia on the fate of the Hungarian minority was still pending. No mention was made of the West, which was now the enemy.

Bloc solidarity was becoming increasingly important in a situation when the West was pulling its ranks together as manifested by the Brussels pact signed on 12 March. Hungary concluded a Treaty of Cooperation and Friendship in Moscow on 18 February. There the Hungarian delegation, which was led by Tildy, obtained the Soviet draft of the agreement. After a chance to "study it," they were received by Stalin at a meeting which lasted thirty minutes. The Hungarians accepted the document and announced that minor—unspecified—changes would have to be made in it for parliamentary ratification. Thereafter they asked for the repatriation of POWs to commence in April and the upgrading of the mutual diplomatic missions. Stalin agreed and offered to mediate between Hungary and Czechoslovakia for a good neighborly relationship. Alluding to the Soviet Union's interest in a strong Hungarian army he also agreed to send weapons. The treaty contained a clause on Soviet–Hungarian mutual assistance in the case of war and aggression from *any quarters*.[94]

Five days later, on 25 February the Finnish president received a letter from Stalin, which contained an invitation for a pact of mutual friendship, cooperation and mutual assistance with the Soviet Union. But Finland, where Soviet penetration was not nearly as deep as it was in Hungary, got a much better deal. The agreement that Helsinki signed in April entitled Finland to stay out of disputes between the superpowers and did not force her to sign a military pact with the USSR. According to one interpretation Stalin kept his options open in Finland: if Helsinki delivered the reparations the existing regime would be allowed to survive, but Communist takeover would occur in the event of Finnish non-compliance. Alternatively, the Russians perhaps shied away from Sovietization because they expected the Finns to resist and because they were ready to guarantee Soviet security. Helsinki was able to exploit the Finnish ACC's reluctance to intervene in domestic affairs directly—this was not the case with the ACC in Hungary—to keep the Communists from infiltrating power positions. President Paasikivi in fact fired the Communist minister of defense and head of the secret police, and was able to count on the support of the army. As a result, Moscow had to contend with the potential of armed resistance in Finland. Hence Moscow offered a deal: Finnish sovereignty for Soviet security.[95] While the Finns were anxiously waiting for the outcome of the Stalin–Paasikivi exchange, the Communist party in Czechoslovakia, which had rapidly been losing popularity since 1947, executed a putsch in February in recognition of the fact that the parliamentary road to power would not work. Beneš, badly outmaneuvered by the Communists, resigned on 25 February, two days after Paasikivi received Stalin's invitation.

In Hungary the liquidation of the multi-party system was officially announced after the unification of the Communist and the Social Democratic parties. Former Social Democrat Árpád Szakasits, the newly appointed President of the Hungarian Workers Party, rejected the special road to Communism: "Our party must follow the example and guidance of the Soviet Union faithfully, for comrade Rákosi is right: there is no separate Hungarian road, the same way as there is no licensed Yugoslavian road or any other special road. There is only one road: the Soviet Union's triumphant road consecrated with blood, the road of Marxism–Leninism."[96] The announcement was in harmony with the Soviet doctrine enunciated in response to the Yugoslav threat to Moscow's undisputed role as the leader and protector of the Communist movement in Eastern Europe. People's democracy was no longer a transitional stage to socialism but a system undistinguishable from the dictatorship of the proletariat practiced in the Soviet Union.[97] Szakasits ignored another law of Stalinism: that, which says that revolutions gobble up their own children. He soon fell victim to this rule.

Rákosi, who first announced that the Soviet form of proletarian dictatorship would be adopted, denounced leftist Social Democrats as police informers. In the light of the Moscow–Belgrade schism it was essential for him to make the Russians forget his previously pro-Tito stance. The remaining opposition parties were liquidated simultaneously with the trial of Hungary's Roman Catholic Primate, Cardinal Mindszenty. Mindszenty had been a consistent opponent of the Communists' gradual seizure of power and had thus become a prime target of their attacks. With Mindszenty under arrest, this spiritual bulwark to Communism was gone. Hungary was effectively written off in Washington, although it offered the opportunity to create a network of intelligence of high importance.[98] Minister Chapin recommended an active policy against Russian expansion using all means, which would not lead to a direct clash with the Soviet Union. But the only concrete measure he was able to propose was the setting up of an intelligence network with a few trained men of high quality and sufficient funds which might later prove of inestimable value. The response was sobering. Hungary would not be the focal point of U.S. policy. Neither would the "issues which are taking shape in U.S.–Soviet relations [...] assume most acute form in connection with Hungarian developments."[99]

By this point the faint prospect that the United States might be able to preserve an economic foothold was gone. Lacking potent external support, Hungarian democratic forces which suffered from the lack of internal cohesion sufficient courage and devotion to liberal democratic ideals, were helpless against a well-disciplined, single-minded political force that enjoyed full-fledged Soviet backing. American aims and means were limited. Washington accepted complete Soviet domination of Hungarian defense and foreign policy in the vain hope that the Soviets would accept a coalition government friendly to the Kremlin together with an open door arrangement for the Hungarian economy. In practice, however, the U.S. was unwilling to expend effort on halting the Soviet domination of Hungary. The Hungarian opposition also adopted a policy of appeasement, in part because there was no clear sign of Western backing for a policy of defiance. As a result not even the minimal aim was achieved: Soviet economic penetration drove out all Western presence in Hungary. It is to the description of this process that we now turn. All the more so, since economic expansion as a source of Soviet domination in Eastern Europe has hitherto received scant attention and this was the sphere where the expansionist nature of Soviet politics became the most apparent.

NOTES

1 Trachtenberg, *Constructed Peace*, pp. 55–78.
2 Adomeit, *Imperial Overstretch*, pp. 71–80.
3 For an analysis of the ideological origins and the idea behind the Marshall Plan see Michael Hogan, *The Marshall Plan—America, Britain and the Reconstruction of Western Europe, 1947–1952* (Cambridge University Press, 1987); for the Soviet response Zubok and Pleshakov, *Inside the Kremlin's Cold War*, pp. 103–109; Parrish, *The Marshall Plan, Soviet-American Relations and the Division of Europe*.
4 Mária Palasik, *Kovács Béla 1908–1959* (Budapest: Occidental Press, 2002), p. 47.
5 Ibid., p. 52, p. 34.
6 Ibid., p. 27.
7 Beszámoló a szociáldemokrata pártról, July–December 1946 [Report on the Social Democratic Party.] RTsHIDNI, fond 17, op 128, ed. hr. no. 124.
8 Feljegyzés az MKP Politikai Bizottságának üléséről [Record of meeting of the Political Committee of the HCP] 16 January 1947, PIL, 274. F, 3. cs., 66. and 67. őe; RTsHIDNI, fond 17, op 128, ed. hr. no. 308; See also Sándor Szakács – Tibor Zinner, *A háború "megváltozott természete"—Adatok és adalékok, tények és összefüggések—1944–1948* [The "changed nature of war"—Data, addenda, facts and relationships] (Budapest, 1998), pp. 292–293.
9 Feljegyzés az MKP Politikai Bizottságának üléséről [Record of meeting of the HCP Political Committee] 23 January and 6 February 1947, PIL, 274. F., 3. cs., 68. and 71. őe; RTsHIDNI, fond 17, op. 128, ed. hr. no. 308; Szakács and Zinner, *A háború megváltozott természete,* pp. 295–296.
10 Feljegyzés az MKP Politikai Bizottságának üléséről [Record of meeting of the HCP Political Committee] 13 February 1947, PIL, 276. F., 3. cs., 68. and 71. őe; RTsHIDNI, fond 17, op. 128, ed. hr. no. 308.
11 "Iz zapis besedi G. M. Pushkina s premer-ministrom Vengrii F. Nagy o vnutropoliticheskoi situatsii v sviazi s razoblacheniem antirepublikanskogo zagovora," [From the record of conversation of G. M. Pushkin with Hungarian Prime Minister F. Nagy on the domestic political situation in connection with the uncovering of the anti-republic conspiracy] 24 January 1947, *VEDRA*, vol. I, Document 189, pp. 561–562.
12 For the details of the HCP–Smallholder struggle for the fate of Béla Kovács see Palasik, *Kovács Béla,* pp. 51–67.
13 The Secretary of State to the Legation in Hungary, 22 February 1947, *FRUS,* 1947, vol. IV, pp. 269–271; On the American response to the Kovács affair see Lundestad, *The American Non-Policy Towards Eastern Europe,* pp. 137–140.

14 MOL, Küm, USA admin, XIX-J-1-k, 25c, 55. doboz, 40.934/47.

15 The Deputy Director of the Office of European Affairs to the Secretary of State, 1 March 1947, USNA, RG 59, 864.00/3-147; The Secretary of State to the Legation in Hungary, 3 March 1947, *FRUS*, 1947, vol. IV, pp. 272–275. The two telegrams were sent the same day.

16 The Acting Chairman of the ACC to the Chief of the United States Representation on the ACC, 8 March 1947, *FRUS*, 1947, vol. IV, p. 277.

17 Schoenfeld to the Secretary of State, 21 March 1947, *FRUS*, 1947, vol. IV, pp. 288–289.

18 Memorandum by Hickerson to Acting Secretary of State Acheson, 12 March 1947, USNA, RG 59, 864.00/3-1247; The Minister in Hungary (Schoenfeld) to the Secretary of State, 21 March 1947, *FRUS*, 1947, vol. IV, pp. 288–289; New York Times, 8 March 1947.

19 Változások a magyar kormány összetételében [Changes in the makeup of the Hungarian government] 3 April 1947, *Moszkvának jelentjük*, pp. 154–157. Only the new Finance Minister, Miklós Nyárádi was identified as belonging to his party's right wing with "close contacts to Anglo-American financial circles." According to the evaluation the government saw a shift toward the left.

20 Memorandum of Conversation by Barbour, *FRUS*, 1947, vol. IV, p. 292.

21 The Ambassador in the Soviet Union to the Acting Secretary of State, 5 March 1947, *FRUS*, 1947, vol. IV, p. 276.

22 The Minister in Hungary (Schoenfeld) to the Secretary of State, 27 January 1947, *FRUS*, 1947, vol. IV, pp. 264–265.

23 See Mihály Fülöp, *A befejezetlen béke—A Külügyminiszterek Tanácsa és a magyar békeszerződés, 1947* [The unfinished peace—The Council of Foreign Ministers and the Hungarian peace treaty, 1947] (Published in Budapest, undated) and Kertesz, *Between Russia and the West*.

24 At the Paris meeting of the CFM the U.S. accepted the Russian position about restoring the whole of Transylvania to Romania.

25 Fülöp, *A befejezetlen béke*, p. 47.

26 Ibid., p. 50.

27 The Russians argued that the signing of the treaty itself restores sovereignty. "Reshenie Politburo TsK VKP(b) ob utverzhdenii proekta direktiv o mirnom dogovore s Vengriei na soveshchanii zamestitelei v SMID v Londone," op cit 21 March 1946 in *TV*, Document 102, p. 371.

28 Rákosi Mátyás levele Sztálinnak [Mátyás Rákosi's letter to Stalin] 5 April 1947, *Moszkvának jelentjük*, pp. 159–162.

29 Rákosi Mátyás levele Sztálinnak, 5 April 1947, op. cit.; Rákosi Mátyás levele Zsdanovnak [Rákosi's letter to Zhdanov] 28 April 1947, *Moszkvának jelentjük*, pp. 193–195; V. M. Molotov és Rákosi M. elvtársak 1947. április 29-i megbeszéléseinek lejegyzett szövege [Record of conversation between comrades V. M. Molotov and M. Rákosi] 29 April 1947, Ibid., pp. 199–206 and Iz zapisi besedi V. M. Molotova s M. Rakosi o politicheskoi situatsii v Vengrii [From the record of conversation of V. M. Molotov with M. Rákosi on the political situation in Hungary] *VEDRA*, vol. I, Document 209, pp. 613–623.

30 G. J. Korotkevich, the head of the Hungarian desk of the CPSU Foreign Information Bureau paid a visit to Budapest in early April. He took part at the sessions of the HCP Politburo and held discussions with leading members of the party, including Gerő, Rákosi, Rajk, Kádár, Kossa and the head of the political police, Gábor Péter, who gave detailed information on political and economic matters, as well as their future strategy. Korotkevich summarized these for his superiors. See "Megbeszélések a magyar kommunista pártok vezetőivel" [Discussions with the leaders of the HCP] April 1947, *Moszkvának jelentjük*, pp. 208–210.

31 Iz zapisi besedi G.M. Pushkina s liderom vengerskikh social-demokratov Á. Szakasitsem ob otnoshenii k SSSR [From the record of conversation between G. M. Pushkin and Hungarian social democratic leader Á. Szakasits on relations with the USSR] *SFVE*, vol. I., document 144, pp. 407–408. Szakasits recounted that Labour Party leaders recommended more independence in the Social Democrats' foreign policy and less reliance on the USSR, but Szakasits rejected the advice.

32 Rákosi, *Visszaemlékezések*, vol. I, p. 377.

33 Megbeszélések a magyar kommunista párt vezetőivel, May 1947, *Moszkvának jelentjük*, op. cit. pp. 208–210.

34 Szakács and Zinner, *A háború "megváltozott természete,"* pp. 329–341.

35 Pismo generalnogo sekretaria kompartii Vengrii M. Rakosi v TsK VKP(b) o pravitelstvennom krizise i otstavke F. Nagy [Letter by the General Secretary of the HCP M. Rákosi on the government crisis and the resignation of F. Nagy] 12 June 1947, *VEDRA* vol. I, document 216, pp. 641–647.

36 New York Times, 31 May 1947.

37 Record of Conversation between Szegedy-Maszák and Walwourth Barbor, 2 June 1947, NA, RG 59, 864.00/6-247; Mclintock to Rusk, 2 June 1947, NA, RG 59, 864.00/6-247; The Acting Director of the Office of European Affairs to the Secretary of State, 3 June 1947, *FRUS*, 1947, vol. IV, pp. 308–309.

38 Laqueur, *Europe in Our Time*, pp. 36–38.

39 See Kent, "British Planning for Post War Europe," pp. 44–46.

40 See Ignác Romsics, "A brit külpolitika és a 'magyar kérdés', 1914–1946," [British Foreign Policy and the "Hungarian Question"] *Századok*, 1996, vol. 130, no. 2; The Second Secretary of the British Embassy to the Acting Head of the Division of European Affairs, 9 June 1947, *FRUS*, 1947, vol. IV, pp. 315–316; Max, *The Anglo-American Response to the Sovietization of Hungary*, p. 128.

41 The Secretary of State to the Legation in Budapest, 10 June 1947, *FRUS*, 1947, vol. IV, pp. 317–319.

42 Memorandum by the Director of the Office of European Affairs, 1 July 1947, *FRUS*, 1947, vol. IV, pp. 329–332.

43 Congressional Record, 80th Congress, vol. 93, Part 5, pp. 6306–6307. The speech was published in the 4 June issue of the *New York Times*.

44 Bischof, *Austria in the First Cold War*, p. 94.

45 Ibid., p. 94; p. 98.

46 Bischof, *Between Responsibility and Rehabilitation*, part II, pp. 838–839.

47 Lundestad, *American Non-Policy Towards Eastern Europe*, p. 143.
48 The Secretary of State to the Legation in Hungary, 6 June 1947, *FRUS*, 1947, vol. IV, p. 314; Marshall to the Legation in Prague, 6 June 1947, NA, RG 59, 864.00/6-397.
49 Memorandum of conversation by the Acting Chief of Division of Southern European Affairs, 6 June 1947, *FRUS*, 1947, vol. IV, pp. 311–313. Szegedy-Maszák was called home, but refused to come. This probably saved him from a very uncertain future. Tildy's son-in-law, who worked at the Legation for some time, was tried, sentenced and executed, a year later.
50 Szegedy-Maszák's letter to Freeman Matthews, 6 June 1947, NA, RG 59, 864.00/6-647.
51 Lamberton Harper, *American Visions of Europe*, pp. 199–200.
52 See László Szűcs, "Magyarország és a Marshall Terv," *Levéltári Szemle*, 1998, vol. 50, no. 1.
53 Parrish, *The Marshall Plan, Soviet–American Relations and the Division of Europe*, p. 274.
54 Ibid., p. 278.
55 Zubok and Pleshakov, *Inside the Kremlin's Cold War*, p. 104.
56 Parrish, *The Marshall Plan, Soviet–American Relations and the Division of Europe*, p. 275.
57 Galina Takhnienko, "Anatomiia odnogo politicheskogo resheniia," *Mezhdunarodnaya Zhizn*, 1992, no. 5. pp. 119–120.
58 Parrish, *The Marshall Plan, Soviet–American Relations and the Division of Europe*, p. 283; Zubok–Pleshakov, *Inside the Kremlin's Cold War*, p. 105.
59 Szűcs, "Magyarország és a Marshall Terv."
60 Zapis besedi sotrudnika MID SSSR A. M. Aleksandrova s sovetnikom polskogo posolstva A. Iushkevichem po povodu otkaza Polshi ot uchastie v konferantsii po planu Marshalla [Record of conversation between A. M. Aleksandrov of the Foreign Ministry of the USSR and the counselor of the Polish Embassy A. Yushkevich in the matter of Poland's rejection of participation at the Marshall Plan conference] 8 July 1947, *VEDRA*, vol. I, document 126, pp. 671–672; Zapis besedi I.V. Stalina s chekhoslovatskoi pravitelstvennoi delegatsii po voprosu ob otnoshenii k planu Marshalla i perspektivakh ekonomicheskogo sotrudnichestva s SSSR [Record of conversation between I. V. Stalin and the Czechoslovak government delegation in the question of the relationship with the Marshall Plan and the perspective of economic cooperation with the USSR] Ibid., document 227, pp. 672–675.
61 A minisztertanács ülése [Record of meeting of the Council of Ministers], 10 July 1947, MOL, XIX-A-83-a MT, jkv.
62 Quoted by György Gyarmati, "'Itt az fog történni, amit a kommunista párt akar'—Adalékok az 1947. évi országgyűlési választások történetéhez,"["The Communist Party will dictate—Addenda to the history of the 1947 national elections] *Társadalmi Szemle*, 1997, vol. 52, no. 8–9. p. 146.
63 V. M. Molotov és Rákosi M. elvtársak 1947. április 29.-i megbeszélésének lejegyzett szövege, 29 April 1947, op. cit.

64 Feljegyzés a Péter Gábor elvtárssal, a magyar rendőrség vezetőjével folytatott beszélgetésről [Record of conversation with comrade Gábor Péter, head of the Hungarian police] early April 1947, *Moszkvának jelentjük*, pp. 170–171; *VEDRA*, vol. I, document 205, pp. 605–606.

65 According to a Soviet assessment of the elections, the Hungarian party overestimated its influence in Hungary and therefore made the mistake of entering the election in one bloc with the other parties. They failed to comprehend the "objective reality," which was evident to the Soviets that in those countries which "came under Soviet influence" the Communists were able to consolidate their position "in coalition with other parties only." Iz politicheskogo otcheta diplomaticheskoi missii SSSR v Vengrii za 1945 g. Analiz itogov munitsipalnikh viborov v Bolshom Budapeste [From the political report on the year 1945 of the diplomatic mission of the USSR in Hungary. Analysis of the results of the municipal elections in Greater Budapest] 17 April, 1947, *VEDRA*, vol. I, document 208, pp. 609–613. The very fact that this document was forwarded to Moscow after almost two years shows that it was deemed relevant in the present situation. Incidentally Molotov reprimanded Rákosi for making this mistake and Rákosi had to concede that he was right.

66 Zapis besedi sotrudnika OVP VKP (b) G. Ya. Korotkevicha s zamestitelem predsedatelia TsKK V. P. Sviridovim o politicheskoi situatsii v Vengrii [Record of conversation between G. Ia. Korotkevich of the division of foreign affairs of the CPSU with the deputy Chairman of the ACC V. P. Sviridov on the political situation in Hungary] early April 1947, *VEDRA*, vol. I, document 204, pp. 601–605.

67 V. M. Molotov és Rákosi M. elvtársak 1947. április 29.-én lezajlott megbeszélésének lejegyzett szövege, 29 April 1947, op. cit.

68 See Az MKP PB határozata [Resolution of the Political Committee of the HCP] 6 June 1947, RTsHIDNI, fond 17, op 128, ed. hr. no. 308

69 Iz zapisi besedi G. M. Pushkina s zamestitelem generalnogo sekretaria SDP Maroshanom o pozitsii sotsial-demokratov v sviazi s viborom [From the record of conversation between G. M. Pushkin and deputy general secretary of the SPD Marosán on the position of the social democrats in connection with the elections] 27 June 1947, *VEDRA* vol. I, document 221, pp. 660–661.

70 Iz dnevnika G. M. Pushkina. Zapis besedi s Szakasitsom o situatsii v rukovodstve SPD i predstoyashchikh parlamentskikh viborakh [From the diary of G. M. Pushkin. Record of conversation with Szakasits on the situation in the leadership of the SPD on the imminent parliamentary elections] 6 February 1947, *VEDRA*, vol. I, document 193, pp. 570–571; Pismo generalnogo sekretaria kompartii Vengrii M. Rákosi v TsK VKP (b) o pravitelstvennom krizise i otstavke Nagy, op. cit.; Soobshchenie zamestitelia ministra vnutrennikh del SSSR I. A. Serova V. M. Molotovu o priostanovke repatriatsii voennoplennikh vengerskikh ofitserov po khodataistvu Rákosi [Communication by deputy Minister of Internal Affairs I. A. Serov to V. M. Molotov on the suspension of the repatriation of the Hungarian POW officers at Rákosi's request] 28 June 1947, *VEDRA*, Document 231, p. 684.

71 For the quotes see Gyarmati, "Itt csak az fog történni, amit a Kommunista Párt akar," pp. 145–147.

72 Record of the June 6 meeting of the HCP Politburo, op. cit.

73 The Minister in Hungary (Chapin) to the Secretary of State, 22 July 1947, *FRUS, 1947*, vol. IV, pp. 340–348.

74 The Minister in Hungary (Chapin) to the Secretary of State, 29 July 1947, *FRUS, 1947*, vol. IV, pp. 351–352.

75 Quoted by Gyarmati, "Itt csak az fog történni, amit a Kommunista Párt akar," p. 161.

76 Ibid. The figure given by historian, György Gyarmati for the number of disenfranchised voters is almost exactly the same as the number given by Dinnyés to the American minister prior to the election. *FRUS, 1947*, vol. IV, p. 360. The Communist party cheated also by supplying its voters with "blue cards" that could be used to vote in several different locations. Hence many of them cast more than one vote. See on this Károly Szerencsés, *A kékcédulás hadművelet—Választások Magyarországon, 1947* [Operation Blue Card—Elections in Hungary, 1947] (Budapest, 1992).

77 The Chief of the United States Representation on the Allied Control Commission to the Acting Chairman of the Commission, 15 September 1947, *FRUS, 1947*, vol. IV, pp. 367–368.

78 Tájékoztató jelentés az MKP tevékenységéről Sztálin számára [Briefing report for Stalin on the activity of the HCP] 9 December 1947, *Moszkvának jelentjük*, p. 241.

79 Zsdanov feljegyzése Sztálinnak Révai előadásáról [Zhdanov's memorandum for Stalin on Révai's presentation] 24 September 1947, *Moszkvának jelentjük*, pp. 229–230.

80 Mastny, *The Cold War and Soviet Insecurity*, pp. 30–31.

81 See on this Lajos Izsák, *Rendszerváltástól rendszerváltásig, 1944–1989* [From transition to transition, 1944–1989] (Budapest: Kulturtrade, 1998), p. 93.

82 The Sovietization of the economy will be discussed in the next chapter.

83 Pismo M. Rákosi k pravitelstvu SSSR o formiroianii pravitelstva Vengrii posle viborov [Rákosi's letter to the government of the USSR on the formation of the Hungarian government after the elections] 2 October 1947, *VEDRA*, vol. I, document 241 pp. 710–714.

84 Feljegyzés az MKP szervező bizottságának üléséről [Record of meeting of the HCP organization committee] 21 October 1947, RTsHIDNI, fond 17, op. 128, ed. hr. no. 310.

85 Tájékoztató jelentés az MKP tevékenységéről Sztálin számára, 9 December 1947, op. cit.

86 Zubok and Pleshakov, *Inside the Kremlin's Cold War*, p. 51.

87 For a presentation of the arguments see Adomeit, *Imperial Overstretch*, pp. 80–84; for the Soviet position on a divided Germany, Mastny, *The Cold War and Soviet Insecurity*, p. 50.

88 For this passage I used Mastny, *The Cold War and Soviet Insecurity*, pp. 30–46.

89 Ibid., p. 33; p. 53.

90 Észrevételek az MKP programnyilatkozatához, Baranov Szuszlovnak [Baranov to Suslov, Remarks on the HCP program declaration] *Moszkvának jelentjük*, p. 267.

91 Megbeszélés Horváth Mártonnal [Discussion with Márton Horváth], 19 April 1948, *Moszkvának jelentjük*, p. 258.

92 Iz dnevnika G. M. Pushkina. Zapis besedi s Marosanom o zavershenii podgotovki obedinitelnogo sezda i perspektivakh sotrudnichestia Marosana s sovietskim poslom, [From the diary of G. M. Pushkin. Record of conversation with Marosán on the conclusion of preparations of the unification session and the perspectives of Marosán's cooperation with the Soviet ambassador] 11 June 1948, *VEDRA*, vol. I, document 292, pp. 902–903.

93 Zapiska L. S. Baranova M. A. Suslovu o nazvanii budushchei obedinennoi rabochei partii Vengrii [Baranov's memoandum to Suslov on the name of the future unified workers party of Hungary] *VEDRA*, vol. I, document 271, pp. 812–813, *Moszkvának jelentjük*, pp. 255–256.

94 Zapis besedi I. V. Stalina s prezidentom Vengrii Z. Tildy [Record of conversation between I. V. Stalin and Hungarian President Z. Tildy] 17 February 1948, *VEDRA*, vol. I, document 258, pp. 757–760. The CPSU PB instructed the Soviet Foreign Ministry to have the East Europeans conclude agreements with one another and Moscow such treaties of mutual assistance, which provide mutual assistance against aggression from the part of all nations, not only Germany and its former satellites. Direktiva Politburo TsK VKP (b) Ministerstvu inostrannikh del SSSR o zakliuchenii dogovorov o vzaimopomoshchi so stranami Vostochnoi Evropi [Directive of the CPSU Politburo to the Foreign Minister of the USSR on the conclusion of the treaties of mutual assistance among the countries of Eastern Europe] Ibid., document 245, pp. 727–728.

95 See Jussi Hanhimaki, *Containing Coexistence—America, Russia and the "Finnish Solution," 1945–1956* (Ohio: The Kent State University Press, 1997); Zubok–Pleshakov, *Inside the Kremlin's Cold War*, pp. 118–119; Jukka Nevakivi, "A Decisive Armistice 1944–1947: Why was Finland not Sovietized?" *Scandinavian Journal of History*, 1994, No. 19, pp. 91–115; Pekka Visuri, "Finland in the Cold War – Why did Finland Remain outside the Soviet Bloc?" *Paper given at the Finnish–Hungarian Conference in Helsinki*, May 1998.

96 Quoted in Izsák, *Rendszerváltástól rendszerváltásig*, p. 101.

97 The interpretation was formulated by Zhdanov's assistant, Pavel Yudin. See Mastny, *The Cold War and Soviet Insecurity*, pp. 53–54.

98 In a contradictory manner the United States purchased a large number of valuable real estate in Budapest in 1947 and 1948. This paradox is yet to be explained.

99 The Minister in Hungary (Chapin) to the Secretary of State, 2 October 1947, *FRUS*, 1947, vol. IV, pp. 384–392; The Acting Secretary of State to the Legation in Hungary, 6 October 1947, Ibid., pp. 393–394.

CHAPTER IV

THE MERCHANTS OF THE KREMLIN

Historical literature—even the recent works—emphasizes the security and ideological aspects of post war Soviet conduct and their relation to the beginning of the Cold War conflict. Economic expansionism as the tool of, and perhaps, the aim of Soviet foreign policy is, by and large, neglected even in works that emphasize that the Soviet takeover was premeditated or, even worse, knew no limits.[1] This is surprising in view of the intense focus of the New Left and also of the so-called post-revisionist literature on the perceived economic motives of American foreign policy.[2] Such an economic aspect is missing from the specialized literature dealing with the Sovietization of Hungary.[3] Its absence is all the more conspicuous in the light of the fact that historical and theoretical works generally acknowledge the role economic factors play in expansionism, even though Marxist-inspired theories of economic imperialism are no longer widely accepted.[4] Through the act of omission, then, historians perhaps unintentionally lend credence to the Marxist view that economic imperialism is the vice of capitalist powers only. Yet, even at first sight the economic motive seems to have been present in the Soviet policy of expansion. The Soviet Union extracted $23.2 billion from the East European countries (including East Germany) between 1945 and 1960; a figure significantly greater than the amount the U.S. handed out in the framework of the Marshall Plan.[5] Furthermore, this amount does not contain the cost of the Red Army's maintenance in Soviet-occupied countries, the value of uranium shipments, the profit from unequal trade agreements and a host of other payments received by the Soviets in the decade after the war. As a strange coincidence Austria paid a reparation of 1,433 billion dollars to the USSR and received a roughly equal amount of Marshall aid.[6]

The role of economics in expansionism is widely disputed. According to Martin Wight, political, cultural and economic expansion is sometimes summed up in territorial expansion. Edward Luttwak argues that states expand because it is in their power to do so and the motive of profit is only a side issue. He argues that in the case of the Kremlin there were no merchants, that is to say economic issues did not play a role in Soviet foreign policy. Hans Morgenthau in his classic work *Politics among Nations*, lists

economic penetration as a tool and rarely an end for conquest. He argues
that the common characteristics of economic imperialism are "on one hand
to overthrow the status-quo by changing the power relations between the
imperialist nation and the other, and on the other hand to do so not through
the conquest of territory but by way of economic control." Kenneth Waltz,
by contrast, expressed that "states use economic means for military and
political ends and military and political means for economic ends."[7] For
Waltz, therefore, economic imperialism is both a means and an end. In fact
some states, like Germany in the 1930s, used economic penetration to create virtual colonies or economic satellites.[8]

Through an examination of evidence from Hungarian archives, it is
clear that that the Soviet Union used drastic and rapid economic penetration
during its occupation of Hungary to destroy the economic pillars of Hungarian independence and consequently, further Hungary's political subjugation. The Soviets implemented this penetration in several ways: first,
by gaining control of the key sectors of Hungarian economy using newly
founded Soviet companies and joint Soviet–Hungarian companies operating
in Hungary; second, by exploiting its rights to Hungarian reparations, and
finally by reorienting Hungarian foreign trade. These measures, coupled
with the steady introduction of elements of centrally planned economy
through the Communist-controlled Economic High Council, furthered Hungary's political subjugation. Using these methods Moscow extracted machinery, foodstuffs, finished goods, strategic and non-strategic raw materials and
a continuous flow of monetary payments, that far exceeded the amount set
by the Hungarian Armistice Agreement and Peace Treaty. In fact, as early as
the beginning of the Cold War, the Hungarian economy was rigged to serve
the needs of the Soviet economy.

While Stalin was busy reassuring American businessmen that Eastern
Europe would be allowed to trade with the Western world,[9] the Soviets
were rapidly consolidating their economic empire. Western business representatives needed Soviet permission to enter Hungary, which the Russian
authorities often arbitrarily denied or delayed until the persons in question
canceled their trip of their own accord.[10] The Soviet attitude stemmed from
a mixture of distrust and the desire for exclusiveness. The following episode
illustrates this point. Alarmed by the decline of the Hungarian economy, the
U.S. representative in the ACC asked the Hungarian authorities to supply
data on the state of the Hungarian economy. When the president of the Hungarian National Bank sent his report to the American representative of the
ACC, Chairman Sviridov found a pretext—the continued circulation of
Soviet rubles in Hungary—to have him and other pro-Western leaders of
the National bank dismissed.[11]

This chapter will follow the stages of the Sovietization of the Hungarian economy and the simultaneous elimination of Western economic presence. There will be a discussion of the role of reparations in economic centralization and how reparation payments set the pattern of the economic exploitation of Hungary by the Soviets. As part and parcel of the punitive measures against the former German satellites the Soviet Union was entitled to acquire former German properties. This in turn enabled the Soviets to control the most important parts of Hungarian economy. Having reviewed this process the chapter will investigate the consequences of the 1945 Soviet–Hungarian economic agreement. As part of this agreement, joint companies were established that strengthened Soviet control of key parts of the economy and Hungary's foreign trade was reoriented towards the Soviet Union. Simultaneously the American efforts to create an economically open sphere in Hungary will be examined and it will be argued that that this attempt failed mainly because the Soviet Union preferred a closed sphere of influence to economic cooperation with the West; secondly, for the United States' continued cooperation with the Soviets gained precedence over keeping Eastern Europe an economically open sphere. Finally the last phase of economic Sovietization, nationalization and the concomitant elimination of Western investments will be investigated through the fate of American business interest in Hungary.

Economic centralization

Economic centralization was the order of the day in postwar Europe. Whereas in the West this meant state intervention in the creation of jobs, fiscal policies, welfare and some measure of nationalization, in Eastern Europe it was a process that led to central command, and politicized economies. In Hungary, conditions for a highly centralized, politically controlled economy were created soon after Soviet occupation. Many elements of centralization had been introduced in response to the Great Depression and subsequently the war. The Communist program was outlined by Stalin's Hungarian-born advisor, Jenő Varga in October 1945, who explained that for the time being Hungarian economic policy "must resemble NEP, we must adopt half solutions because it is impossible to establish a closed system *yet*" (emphasis mine).[12] Rapid centralizing steps were taken nonetheless, to revive the country's economy and to promote the payment of reparations. In April 1947 Rákosi announced that a "kind of Communist economic dictatorship" existed in Hungary, where banks "give no loans" without the consent of the Communist Party.[13]

In July 1945 the government empowered the minister of industry to requisition raw materials, fuel and semi-finished goods in order to assist industrial production. By December the minister of industry controlled 550 materials and semi-finished products. The allocation of textiles, wood, paper, metals, coal and leather became a government prerogative and the Anyag- és Árhivatal (Material and Price Office) was set up to control allocations and prices. Although Stalin had at one point insisted that the provisional government's program should emphasize the need for private initiative and the protection of private property to make it sound more attractive,[14] government decrees passed in 1945 made it theoretically possible to nationalize the whole economy.[15] However, the defeat of the Communist Party in the 1945 national election endangered Communist control over the economy and the Smallholder majority in parliament threatened to impede the nationalization of the industry and the Soviet Union's acquisition of Hungarian firms. Thus, in order to ensure the unhindered accomplishment of Communist economic objectives, the Soviet chairman of the ACC "recommended" the establishment of an organ called the Supreme Economic Council (SEC). Prime Minister Tildy accepted this proposal and the SEC were set up by a government decree. This was theoretically unconstitutional, because such a measure would have formally required parliamentary action.

Prime Minister Ferenc Nagy remembered that the SEC became "a state within the state, to which later so many complaints and curses came to be attached and through which the Communists exercised their irreversible influence."[16] Indeed, it was authorized to issue decrees without consulting the government except in cases when the decree in question belonged to the jurisdiction of the Council of Ministers. Even then in "special" cases it was enough to "circulate," that is to merely show the decree to the members of the government.[17] The council was directed by the General Secretary, Zoltán Vas, the Communist Party's economic expert. Its decrees were legally binding and the ministers whose jurisdiction they involved were required to carry them out. A report from the Soviet political mission in 1947 appraised the SEC's significance from Moscow's perspective: "It is not mistaken to state that without the SEC we could not have received even half the former German properties we now have in Hungary [...] the SEC substituted the Hungarian government and ensured that each fundamental question related to the country's reconstruction on democratic principles could be resolved successfully."[18] SEC played a crucial role in the formulation of financial and credit policies, the allocation of raw materials and the regulation of prices and wages. Furthermore, the legislative branch of government—where the non-Communists were in a majority—all but lost its power to formulate the budget. Foreign trade, one of the most important sectors of the Hungarian economy was controlled by a state organ called Külkereskedelmi Igazgatóság (Foreign Trade Directorate), which in turn was subordinated to the SEC. Private enterprises were allowed to survive until their production was needed for reparations.

Reparations

The Hungarian economy was severely damaged during the heavy fighting in the last few months of the war. As a result the GNP plummeted to only half of the 1938 level. In such circumstances the oversized reparations caused hyperinflation. The Communist Party seized the opportunity to usher in its own economic program that envisioned the transformation of the economy according to the Soviet model. Furthermore, reparation payments established a pattern of economic exploitation by the Soviet Union that lasted throughout the early Cold War.

Due to the outcome of the World War I reparation settlement, Washington recommended that reparations should be extracted only to the extent it was possible without ruining the economies of the defeated powers. In other words, reparation payments should not be fixed in advance, but ought to be calculated in relation to the given economy's capacity to pay. This principle was to be asserted in Hungary. In fact, the British Foreign Office accused the State Department of attaching more importance to maintaining the standard of living in Hungary than to the justifiable exigencies of the Allies. Nonetheless, the British also supported the principle. Since the Soviet view prevailed, however, Hungary's reparations were fixed in advance in one sum, which turned out to be significantly lower than the amount originally envisioned by Soviet plans. The Maisky commission had suggested for the Soviet Union to demand an amount of $75 billion in order to take everything possible from Germany and its allies "short of starvation." Stalin must have found this sum exorbitant, since at Yalta he was willing to settle for $10 billion. Molotov later claimed that what they received under this heading was "a pittance." Recent research suggests that his statement was wide of the mark. In Germany, trophy battalions were charged with removing military machinery, science labs, communication equipment and the like. Until the period up to August 1945, the Soviets took almost 1.3 million tons of "materials" and 3.6 million tons of equipment from Germany. It is estimated that one third of the East German productive capacity was removed for reparations. By the early 1950s the Soviet Union may have extracted $10–19 billion from Germany. Moreover, Austria paid 1,325 billion dollars, which included industrial equipment, the seizure of former German property and the payments to repurchase them, as well as the occupation costs.[19]

Due to American pressure the Soviets agreed to reduce Hungary's payments from $400 to $300 million, of which $200 million were allocated to the Soviet Union, and the rest was divided between Czechoslovakia and Yugoslavia. This was to be paid over six years by deliveries in kind. This sum was acceptable to the U.S. However, the Soviet Union, without consulting its Allies, decided to determine the value of the reparation goods according to 1938 world prices plus a 10–15 percent bonus. Incidentally, the same rule was applied in Romania. As a result payments far exceeded the $300 million originally agreed upon. According to an Office of Strategic Services (OSS) report of October 1944 Hungary would be able to pay $50 million annually for a protracted period without hurting the economy.[20] Of course, at the time the report was written, it could not be known that the Hungarian economy was to suffer far more from October 1944 until the end of the war than it had prior to that time. Nonetheless, the OSS estimate coincided with the Soviet position as outlined to the Western Allies by Molotov on 30 December 1944.[21] After the reparation payments were agreed upon, however, the Germans and later the Soviets dismantled and carried off a significant portion of Hungarian productive capacity. Moreover, the labor force decreased drastically between 1944 and 1945 due to war losses as well as German and Soviet deportations. Finally, Hungary's capacity to pay $300 million over six years was undercut by the arbitrary way in which the Soviets determined the price for the goods delivered to them. Averell Harriman, the U.S. Ambassador in Moscow, who negotiated Hungary's armistice terms with the Soviets, had "sympathy for the Soviet view that $50 million a year of goods as reparation payments from Hungary over six-year period is not in fact excessive." He correctly asserted "that the manner in which reparations are completed, the character of goods demanded, and the value placed on them, are all matters which would vitally affect the recovery and stability of the economy of Hungary and Central Europe. Whoever controls reparation deliveries could practically control Hungarian economy and exercise an important economic influence in other directions."

Harriman could not accept the Soviet position that only countries with a vested interest in reparations could decide "the way in which they are collected [...] The British and we have an equal interest in the stability of Europe even though neither of us are demanding reparations from Hungary." He thought that the reparation clause of the armistice agreement was unacceptable, since it contained no provision for the Anglo-Saxon members of the ACC to influence reparation issues. Therefore he wanted the secretary of state to put pressure on the Soviets to allow Anglo-American participation in those problems. Harriman received instructions to "dissociate from the reparation clause" from the last day of 1944, but the ambassador did not think that this would be "effective in changing the Soviet position." He recommended that Soviet non-cooperation in economic matters "such as in the case of Hungary" should have a negative bearing on issues of Soviet interests, such as lend-lease shipments.[22]

Artúr Kárász, the chairman of the Hungarian National Bank in 1945, commented in his memoirs that "the Communists wished to realize the country's conquest with indirect means. The chief method of this new type of colonization was the transformation of the economy."[23] The Soviets used reparations to facilitate such a transformation. Yet, even before the first reparation shipments were sent, the war-torn country's economic burdens were significantly increased when the Soviet Union placed on Hungary the responsibility of supplying the Soviet army with food, fodder and coal. This was done despite the fact that Article 11 of the Armistice Agreement only obligated Hungary to supply the Allied (Soviet) *High Command* and the Allied missions of the ACC. In a memorandum to the ACC Foreign Minister János Gyöngyösi wrote that supplying the Red Army had "nearly exhausted Hungary's food reserve. The value of foodstuffs given to the Soviet Army in the months of April, May and June [1945] alone amounted to 1.5 billion pengős."[24] In the last nine months of 1945 the Soviet army ordered 64,500 tons of flour, 23,000 tons of beef, 91,000 tons of oats and 175,000 tons of hay, which would have stretched public supply even if the Soviets had been willing to pay for the shipments, which was not the case. Not to mention the 52 tons of sweets for "non-smokers," 25,000 buckets with zinc coating, soured cream, cottage cheese, milk, tea, sugar, matches, tobacco, ground pepper, etc. For the last quarter of 1945, the Red Army requisitioned 40,000 tons of coal and 25,000 cubic meters of wood as well, although there was a serious shortage of both products.[25]

Although in April 1946 Stalin promised to reduce the Soviet army presence in Hungary in order to alleviate the burden on the Hungarian economy, nothing changed. In the months of June and July 1946 alone, the Soviet forces demanded 3000 tons of meat, 800,000 eggs, 645 tons of milk, 23 tons of spices, 15,000 tons of hay, 10,000 tons of fresh fruit and vegetables and 203 tons of butter. A contemporary report indicated what this meant for the Hungarian economy, although considering that this report was intended for Stalin, the figures may have been exaggerated. There were roughly 6.6 million cows in Hungary, but only 1.2 tons of milk were delivered to Budapest daily as compared to the 300 tons a day in 1938.[26] Even if one takes into account the informal trade channels, the Red Army consumed more milk than a city of well over a million. The minister of public supply estimated that aside from maize, the amount of foodstuffs ordered by the Soviet armed forces for the last quarter of the year exceeded the quantity the whole population would be able to consume in the same period. Sviridov admitted that the Soviets were exporting to the West much of the foodstuffs they were getting, since they regarded them as war trophy.[27]

All in all, Hungary was forced to cater for 1–1.5 million men in 1945,[28] a significant additional burden, which was not taken into account when reparations were calculated. Even though the maintenance of the Soviet army seriously hindered economic rehabilitation and indirectly American efforts directed at all-European economic recovery, the Western members of the ACC did not address the issue. In fact the U.S. representative, General Key claimed that "the expenses caused by the Red Army was the same as the upkeep of the Hungarian Civil Service." In 1946, at a time of food shortage in Hungary the Western representatives accepted Sviridov's untruthful claim that the Soviet High Command made no request for food.[29]

Reparations to be paid to the Soviet Union were spelled out by the agreement signed on 15 June 1945. In the course of the preparatory talks the Hungarians argued that the armistice agreement made no mention of world market prices. Moreover, for many of the goods the Soviets wanted no such prices had existed, making "1938 world market prices" impossible to calculate. To accept 1938 prices—which were lower than current ones—would seriously strain the economy and may cause inflation. These observations were conveyed to Voroshilov's deputy, Major-General Stahurskii and Pushkin. To make things even more difficult, the Russians wished to remove factories that were producing goods for reparations and for the Red Army. But General L. U. Zorin, who was responsible for reparations, pointed out that reparation talks were not commercial negotiations and thus different principles would prevail.[30]

Deliveries under the reparation agreement were listed under three major headings. Firstly, Hungary was to deliver "existing equipment," which meant that specified machinery in certain power stations and industrial plants had to be dismantled and transported to the Soviet Union.[31] Secondly, Hungary was obligated to deliver new machines, railway equipment, ships and metals to be manufactured according to technical specifications prescribed by the Soviet Union. Finally the agreement provided for agricultural products —grain, seeds, livestock, horticultural products.[32] Hungary was responsible for the cost of packing and shipping.

The composition of the reparation shipments, mostly industrial products and equipment, was in itself a great setback for the Hungarian economy. It was no coincidence that the Hungarian government's original proposal had primarily offered agricultural goods as reparations. In spite of the food shortage in the Soviet Union, Moscow preferred machines to agricultural products. More than half of Hungarian industry and practically all of Hungarian heavy industry—which was under Soviet supervision—was working for reparations.[33] According to the figures given by historians Pető and Szakács, international obligations flowing from reparation payments amounted to 30 percent of the total budget until 1948. A major part of this went to the Soviet Union.[34] Other data, however, suggest that this was only an average. The figure may have been much higher in 1945 and 1946, which were key years for Hungarian economic recovery and political–economic independence. Artúr Kárász thought that reparations made up 50 percent of the 1945 budget;[35] István Kertész, who was in charge peace preparation in the Hungarian Foreign Ministry estimated it to be 60 percent in the last four months of 1945 and 40 percent in the first half of 1946.[36] Rákosi remembered that reparations "meant a very serious burden at the time of the inflation [i.e. in 1945–1946], but its significance diminished as production went up and the economy was stabilized."[37]

Although reparations were fixed at 1938 "world market prices," in actuality the prices of goods were set by the Soviets. In the course of negotiations, they determined which products they wanted and what their 1938 values were. In order to squeeze the largest possible amount of the $200 million, they made up prices, which were both unrealistic and fictitious. One example of this practice was the case of floating cranes and ships made by the Ganz Company. The prices for the floating cranes were determined by the Hungarians according to 1938 prices (that is in accordance with the letter of the Armistice Agreement, which made no mention of "world market"), while those for the ships were calculated according to the costs of the vessel "Tisza" built in 1939. Lieutenant-Colonel Riabchenko protested that these prices were far higher than they would be in America. Hungarian experts countered that the Americans were making larger ships and more importantly, in mass production. This made their prices much lower than Hungary could offer. Riabchenko was not moved; he insisted on world market prices, disregarding the fact that in many cases Hungarian products had no world market prices since they had been previously produced only for domestic consumption.[38] In 1947 the Hungarian government charged that due to underpricing $145 million worth of goods already delivered were in actual fact worth $225 million. Disregarding actual 1938 prices, 270 vertical drilling machines and 550 radial drilling machines were shipped at one-third of the "real price," 525 locomotives for 50 percent and 15,000 electric engines for only 15 percent. When the Soviets dismantled factories they also demanded newly made equipment to go with them. Oftentimes the production of the new equipment alone cost more than the reparation agreement envisioned for the whole factory.[39]

Given that the exchange rate of the Hungarian currency (pengő) to the dollar was 5.16 to 1, and adding the bonus of 10–15 percent, 933 million pengős worth of goods should have been shipped to the Soviet Union. Research undertaken by the Hungarian National Bank in 1945, however, concluded that a "reparation dollar" cost the Hungarian economy 10.2 pengős to produce,[40] i.e. nearly double the official exchange rate. According to Rákosi's estimate one "reparation" dollar equaled three dollars.[41] In turn, this meant that 200 million dollars worth of goods cost 2,000–3,000 million 1938 pengős to produce; in other words, twice to three times the original amount. In 1947 a Hungarian government committee concluded that world market prices were 188 percent higher in 1946 and 1947 than the ones in 1938, furthermore Hungarian production costs were 22 percent higher than the contemporary world average.[42] This underscores Rákosi's view that reparation deliveries cost the Hungarian economy three times more than the amount fixed by the armistice.

The cost of shipping added 15–20 percent, and the penalty for late shipment another 5 percent to the original costs, for a grand total to approximately 2,500–3,600 million 1938 pengős. Per capita national income dropped dramatically between 1938 and 1945, from 543 pengős to 177, principally as a result of war damages, reparations and reconstruction burdens. Payments amounted to 19–22 percent of the national income. The maintenance of the Red Army and the ACC came to 262 million pengős, that is 10 percent of the national income, adding up to a total of 29–32 percent of the national income. The most unfortunate consequence of this situation was the worst inflation in history: eventually money had to be weighed on a scale because it lost all its value. Nevertheless, we will never know precisely how much was paid. In 1946 the Soviet Union cancelled the accrued penalty for late shipments, agreed to write off the value of a formerly Hungarian owned coal mine in Transylvania, raised the deadline for payment from six to eight years and cancelled fifty percent of the remaining obligations in June 1948. Nevertheless, it is clear that in the crucial first year following the end of the war, reparations were a huge burden. Moreover, Moscow found pretexts to collect the amount it waived under other auspices, which will be discussed later.

While industrial production in 1945 was only 35 percent of that in 1938, and production of reparation goods required significant expenditures for imports, industrial equipment removed by the Soviet Union for reparations in 1945 amounted to roughly $50 million.[43] The National Bank wanted reparations not to exceed a third of the national income, since a 50 percent decrease of the latter put a large strain on the economy, but the government approved the list of shipments. As a result, the quantity of goods shrank drastically. This combined with newly acquired purchasing power—trade unions successfully battled for higher wages, and until June 1946 the Soviet army issued Hungarian currency—also contributed to the runaway inflation. An opportunity was in turn presented to eliminate the market economy under the pretext of "stabilization" and to adopt a Soviet-type economy under the heading of state intervention. Currency stabilization in August 1946 succeeded in curbing hyperinflation. As a contemporary economist observed, it was "one of the most daring experiments of planned economy in the world."[44]

Financial data from this period illustrates the relationship between hyperinflation and reparations. Between June 1945 and July 1946 the price index sky-rocketed to 400 quadrillion pengős. The black market value of the dollar was 1320 pengős in July 1945, rose to 290 thousand in December 1945 and by mid-1946 it soared to 4.6 quadrillion pengős.[45] Although there was inflation in the aftermath of the war, the turn toward hyperinflation occurred when the shipment of goods to the Soviet Union began. The number of banknotes in circulation was 4,312 million in late 1943, 11,312 million at the end of 1944 and 355 billion in November 1945. There was a similar trend in the growth of the state budget: this was eleven billion pengős in March 1945, 42 billion in September and 181 trillion in April 1946. This increased the demand for money, which was coupled with a diminishing availability of goods. The scarcity of goods was increased also by the consumption of the Red Army.[46] The Communist Party capitalized on Hungarian hyperinflation. As one historian put it, reparations "became a basic factor in restricting and driving out capitalist economy."[47] The Communists exploited the problems caused by reparations in a more direct manner as well. They launched a political attack on the Smallholders for not doing enough to arrest the inflation.

As in Germany and Austria, the dismantling of industrial plants in Hungary caused great damage to the economy and impeded production for reparations. This practice was started by the Germans but was increased significantly by the Soviet Union. Sometimes Soviet authorities took factories as war trophy even when that plant was producing goods for the Soviet Union. A case in point was the dismantling of the Magyar Állami Vas-, Acél- és Gépgyárak (Hungarian State Iron-, Steel- and Machine Works) of Miskolc. The plant was making locomotives and other machinery for the Soviet Union. Neither this, nor the Hungarian diplomatic efforts, nor the fact that many of the factory workers were Communist Party members was enough for the Soviet trophy brigade to spare it. As a result its 5,000 workers were left without work.[48] Some one hundred factories were taken in a similar way, under the pretext of war booty. Perhaps the best-known example was the dismantling of the pride of Hungarian industry, Tungsram, which produced lighting equipment. Tungsram was partly American-owned and represented contemporary high technology. The Soviets began dismembering it in March 1945, while German and Soviet troops were still fighting in western Hungary. It took eight weeks and 600–700 wagons to dismantle and carry Tungsram's machinery and most of its inventory. The material taken from Tungsram was valued at $12 million, which amounted to 6 percent of Hungary's obligations to the Soviet Union. Despite the government's repeated request, Moscow refused to include it as part of the reparation payments.[49] The United States sent four notes to the Soviet Union on the Tungsram issue, all of which were left unanswered. At the personal intervention of the American representative in the ACC, the Soviets gave an elusive answer.[50] Later, they acknowledged that Tungsram was not on the list of reparations, and was taken as war trophy because it possessed war material, which the Soviet High Command badly needed. Tungsram was not an isolated case, and in June 1945 the Hungarian government requested ACC intervention to act to halt the looting of industrial plants.[51]

The Hungarian Ministry of Foreign Affairs pointed out that the dismantling of industrial objects was a heavy burden on the Hungarian economy, and therefore the government requested that the Soviet army should put a stop "without delay" to the requisitioning of industrial equipment, finished products, raw materials and other goods not included on the list of reparations. Furthermore, Hungary wanted the Russians to return, or include as reparations, all the goods the Soviet army had already taken, but which under international law could not be regarded as war booty.[52] Since no answer was forthcoming, Prime Minister Nagy visited Voroshilov in order to repeat this message, but to no avail.

The list of machines and equipment taken by the Russians as war trophy is a long one. It included Felten and Guillaume Cable and Wire Ltd. valued at six million dollars, the dismantling of which seriously hindered the flow of reparation shipments. Other fully or partially requisitioned factories include those involved in the aircraft, optical, machine, food and the textile industries. These included some of the cream of Hungarian industry: Magyar Optikai Művek (Hungarian Optical Works), Goldberger és Fia Textilgyár (Goldberger and Son Textile Works), Dunai Repülőgépgyár (Danube Aircraft Works) and Ganz és Társa (Ganz and Associate), an important representative of the Hungarian machine industry. In one instance the Russians took a canning plant (Weiss Manfréd Konzervgyár) that the Germans had dismantled but had no time to remove. They stored the valuable equipment at railway stations without protection, letting the machines rust under the open sky.[53] Fifty workers and three hundred Russian soldiers packed up the 1200-ton equipment of the country's largest paper mill.[54] Sometimes the Soviets took the inventory only. On many occasions the Hungarian government did not learn about the removals until they were already over and was too late to do anything about them. Soviet trophy hunters took much railway equipment, for example in 1950 there were two hundred and twenty Russian-removed Hungarian locomotives in Czechoslovakia.[55]

The Armistice Agreement obligated the Hungarian government to preserve German property in the same condition as it was at the time the Agreement was signed, on 20 January 1945. This was quite absurd, since the war in Hungary was in full swing and beside the operations of the Wehrmacht and the Red Army, Hungary was the target of Allied strategic bombing. Nevertheless, Hungary was financially responsible for the damage that occurred after the armistice. Since the Soviet Union was entitled to all German property in the former Axis states under the Potsdam agreement, it had to be compensated. According to the figure given by the Communist Daily, *Népszabadság* in 1957, Hungary paid $150–180 million under this pretext.[56] This means that this heading alone added 50–60 percent to the amount of reparations envisioned by the armistice.

The Potsdam Declaration

While trophy brigades and reparations enriched the Soviet treasury and contributed to the accomplishment of the Communist economic program, the Sovietization of certain sectors of the Hungarian economy helped the Soviet Union in deepening its economic, and indirectly, political control. The Potsdam Declaration entitled the Russians to seize German property in Bulgaria, Hungary, Romania and the Soviet zones of Germany and Austria as a form of reparations. All in all four hundred factories, several hundred immovables[57] like houses, land estates, stores and cinemas went into Soviet ownership in Hungary alone. As previously noted, Soviet authorities often exploited this provision to seize property that had little or nothing to do with German ownership. For this reason, few Allied agreements contributed more to the Sovietization of Eastern Europe than the Potsdam Declaration. This seemingly careless provision—formulated by Secretary of State Byrnes—concealed a conscious strategy to appease the Soviets. The idea was to preserve a measure of cooperation with the Soviet Union on the basis of allowing the Soviets to economically exploit their own sphere of influence without limit. The way to get along was to pull apart.[58] Byrnes intended the agreement to ease tension in Germany and to relieve Western economies from having to finance the economy of the Soviet zone in Germany, but the Potsdam declaration on German assets greatly facilitated the Soviet economic penetration in Eastern Europe.

There are numerous examples of how the Soviets were able to take advantage of the loopholes of the Potsdam agreement. In Austria, only 10 percent of all property was German-owned before the Anschluss, but many more were converted to German ownership after it. It was a question whether one regarded these transactions as having been made under duress, or on a voluntary basis. The Soviets took the latter position despite Anglo-

American opposition. Thus in July 1945 they seized 280 allegedly German assets.[59] This affected Hungary adversely because quite a few Hungarian companies had been Austrian-owned. If an Austrian-owned company was Germanized, the Soviets automatically considered its subsidiary German-owned as well.

Potsdam enabled the Soviet Union to acquire non-German financial institutions as the Hungarian government was forced to hand over property that belonged to Austria, France, the United States, England or other states. One such example was Creditanstalt Bankverein, the Hungarian subsidiary of which was handed over to the Soviet Union on the basis of a ruling by the ACC in Hungary and the Supreme Economic Council, even though the Austrian ACC in Vienna ruled that the bank was Austrian property. The basis for the Soviet Union's seizure of these assets was that the Austrian government had been forced to transfer the shares of Creditanstalt Bankverein to the German Goering group after the 1938 Anschluss. The U.S. view, however, was that assets owned by nationals of Austria or other areas which did not constitute part of Das Deutsche Reich on 31 December 1937, should not be regarded German and were not to be included in reparations to the Soviet Union. Moreover, according to the 3 January 1943 London Declaration of the United Nations, assets seized by the Third Reich through coercion following the annexation of a country were not to be considered German assets.[60] Although the Soviet Union had signed the declaration, it ruled that all properties in Hungary that were German-owned at the end of the war were to be regarded as German assets irrespectively of how they had been acquired. This interpretation entitled the Soviet Union to seize them.

Besides Crediatanstalt the Soviets acquired the greater or lesser part of forty other Austrian companies. The Austrians laid the blame on the Hungarians and wanted compensation for them as part of a general settlement of financial issues between the two countries in 1955. By then the Soviets had resold their companies to the Hungarian state, but the Austrians wanted Hungary to compensate them nonetheless.[61] A similar controversy developed over the partially French-owned Magyar Általános Hitelbank (General Credit Bank of Hungary), which controlled 40 percent of Hungarian industry. The Office of Reparations handed over 23 percent of its registered capital to the Soviet Union. These shares were the property of the German Dresdner Bank, yet in 1941 the Germans acquired them through coercion from a French group under Banque de l'Union Parisienne and Union Européenne, which had owned them since 1920. This was obviously a situation in which the London Declaration should have been applied, but Moscow thought otherwise. France protested under the London Declaration, and was joined by Great Britain and the United States. The Acting Chairman of the ACC responded by saying that the Germans had acquired the shares legally, since according to his information Germany had paid for them. The Soviet division of the Soviet–Hungarian committee rejected a repeated French protest sent in May 1947.[62] The Hungarian government then informed France that they were not in a position to represent the French claim towards the Soviet Union, therefore they should turn directly to Moscow.[63]

In January 1946 the U.S. minister in Budapest warned that Potsdam contributed significantly to the realization of Soviet objectives in Hungary by giving Moscow an Anglo-American license for an attack on the independence of Hungarian economy, which the Soviets were exploiting.[64] Moscow's offensive on the economic front clearly alarmed Washington. By the end of 1945, it was evident that if economic collapse could not be halted, the free elections had been held in vain. Schoenfeld claimed that "one time economically independent Hungary has in the space of little more than a year gone far towards becoming a Soviet economic colony [...] In one year, the USSR has acquired more far reaching control over Hungarian commerce and industry than the Germans."[65] Clearly, the Soviet Union was striving for a similar role in Hungary's economy as its predatory predecessor—that is to become Hungary's predominant investor and trading partner. In November 1945, Hungarian minister of finance Ferenc Gordon and minister of public supply Károly Bárányos demanded a review of Hungary's economic situation and Anglo-American intervention on the country's behalf. U.S. minister Schoenfeld feared that public dissatisfaction due to the economic chaos would bring down the government and lessen enthusiasm for "democratic development." To prevent this from happening he proposed that the U.S. representative in the ACC initiate negotiations with Voroshilov on economic rehabilitation, and he also recommended the expansion and acceleration of economic assistance.[66] But acting Secretary of State Dean Acheson only agreed to the implementation of the first recommendation, a tripartite approach to Hungarian economic problems.[67] Nevertheless, Schoenfeld continued to urge aid to Hungary partly in order to deny the Communist claim that because the Western powers were disinterested in the country's well-being Hungary had to depend on Soviet goodwill, and partly to counterbalance Moscow's economic monopoly.[68]

The U.S. Congress, in an effort to support democratic regimes in Eastern Europe, approved a $50 million EximBank loan for Czechoslovakia in July 1946. Earlier Hungary had received $10 million from the same source. Many interpreted this as a sign that the U.S. would not desert Hungary.[69] Byrnes, whose strategy was to appease the Soviets in Eastern Europe, did not hesitate to sober the optimists; $10 million was not a "loan," and the U.S. government would not guarantee that the amount's worth of surplus property would in fact be available. He repudiated Premier Ferenc Nagy's statement that a fuller understanding of Hungary's economic plight would result in further American loans.[70] The United States drew the line on the Austro-Hungarian border: Washington supplied Austria with food and in late 1947 Congress approved an intermediate aid of 597 million dollars for Austria, Italy and France, of which the Danubian state received $57 million.[71]

Although the Hungarian minister in Washington proposed an Exim-Bank loan for Hungary, in mid-May Schoenfeld changed his mind and no longer supported the idea in view of Soviet economic penetration. The minister's change of heart was probably caused by the ongoing Soviet–Hungarian talks on the establishment of joint-venture companies. In contrast to his February memorandum, he now thought that a limited American assistance would not suffice to secure Hungary's economic independence until a Soviet–American accord was made on Eastern Europe. He bitterly stated that only Minister of Supply Károly Bárányos opposed Soviet actions but had no political influence, while Finance Minister Ferenc Gordon "cared only about momentary expedience and his personal safety." Schoenfeld also thought that the Prime Minister, upon his return from Moscow had deemed it tactically expedient not to oppose his pro-Soviet entourage, which was reflected by his frequent allusions to his attachment to Hungarian–Soviet cooperation. Schoenfeld failed to note that the passive U.S. attitude towards Soviet penetration in Hungary offered the Hungarian leadership no alternative but to pursue a pro-Soviet course. Schoenfeld claimed that an Exim-Bank loan to Hungary would not have any important political effect. "The situation had altered since February when assistance could have helped Hungary's ability to remain economically independent of the USSR. Unilateral American assistance now would make little contribution to its recovery because the Soviets would neutralize its beneficial effects." Furthermore, "key Hungarian officials would divert American aid to the USSR."[72] Although Byrnes actually recommended a $10 million loan to Hungary, Acheson replied that the chairman and the chief economist of EximBank declined this possibility based on Schoenfeld's aforementioned telegram. When Gordon raised the question of an EximBank loan during the Hungarian delegation's official visit to Washington in June, his request was denied. State Department experts pointed out that the Bank did not want to make loans, which the Department desired for broad political reasons but were contrary to good banking standards. The Bank had stated that the likelihood of Hungary getting a loan was nil and told the Department to stop pressuring them. It was concluded that, "given the present state of the Hungarian economy, the credit policy of EximBank and other Federal agencies, the State Department has no available means of extending economic assistance to Hungary and thereby implementing its political objectives" there.[73]

Clearly there was no financial incentive to keep Hungary out of the Soviet zone.

The most important effort by the United States to halt economic Sovietization came on 2 March 1946, when the U.S. chargé in Moscow intervened with Molotov about the status of Hungary's economy, linking its rehabilitation with that of Europe as a whole. Kennan's note suggested that Byrnes' two Europes policy had not gained full currency in government circles. On the other hand, the Soviet response revealed that Moscow would preserve its exclusive position in Hungary even if it meant rejecting economic cooperation with and aid from the U.S.

Kennan argued that his government was particularly interested in Hungary's economic stability, primarily in order for it to be able to contribute to "European recovery in general." He reminded Molotov that when signing the armistice, Harriman had reserved the right to return to the question of reparations unless American interests were observed. He referred also to the Yalta Declaration, according to which the three Allies were to coordinate their policies in order to seek democratic solutions to the economic problems of the former Axis states. Kennan objected to the Soviet Union's refusal of the American offer to cooperate, and criticized the Soviet government for not informing Washington of its intentions about the future of the Hungarian economy. Kennan stated that Hungary's economic situation was deteriorating drastically, which not only made it impossible for the country to contribute to Europe's economic recovery, but threatened it with internal economic and financial collapse as well.

In the U.S.'s view "It is clear that this situation is due in a very considerable degree to the overburdening of the country with reparations, to requisitions, to the maintenance of very large occupying forces, to the interference of occupying authorities in economic matters and to the failure of those authorities to take energetic steps to combat inflation and other undesirable tendencies." In Kennan's view this situation was unacceptable to his government on two counts. First, if a nation was unable to take part in Europe's restoration, then America's burden in supplying Europe increased. Second, it was incompatible with the UN's objectives to let the living standard of a nation sink below the poverty level. In the spirit of liberal internationalism Kennan declared that the United States wanted to assure the UN Charter related to cooperation among the nations for better labor conditions, economic adaptation and social security. Finally, he warned that unless the Soviet Union cooperated with Washington on the issue of Hungary, the former would be excluded from American sponsored international economic cooperation.

"The United States is at present engaged in the promulgation of a broad economic program of economic cooperation, designed to lead to the greatest possible freedom of international exchanges for all nations, great and small. It believes that this program will be mutually beneficial to all that participate in it, and wishes to see no nation deprived of those benefits. But it is self-evident that no nation can claim the benefits of broad international collaboration in the economic field unless it is willing to recognize corresponding obligations in its own international dealings: to refrain from seeking special privilege in particular areas and to use its best efforts, in collaboration with those of other countries, for the general promotion of world prosperity [...] The U.S. will necessarily have to be guided by this fact in formulating its economic policies."

Setting a deadline of 15 March, Kennan demanded that within the framework of the ACC the Soviet Union cooperate with the other two allies in "devising a program which will not only put a stop to the present disintegration of Hungary, but will also provide a framework within which the rehabilitation of that country and its earliest reintegration with the general economy of Europe will be possible."[74]

Soviet policies undoubtedly affected U.S. economic interests. Washington complained that American citizens were in a worse legal position than other UN nationals, meaning of course the nationals of the Soviet Union. Kennan's warnings notwithstanding, Soviet reparation claims continued to receive priority over the demands of either the western Allies or Hungary's own rehabilitation. The Soviets put forth their demands without consulting the British or the U.S. representatives in the ACC, and London and Washington's position was not taken into account when the Potsdam Declaration was implemented. Because the burden of reparations and exports to the Soviet Union was so high, Hungary was unable to earn foreign currency and thus unable to keep its payment obligations to the United States. Hungary, after all, still owed Washington $10 million, borrowed prior to the war. Damages caused to American property in Hungary during the war were estimated at another $35 million, but the American government postponed the collection of its claims.

Molotov was no doubt worried and perplexed by the contents of the Kennan note. He did not believe that the "imperialistic" United States had altruistic motives; rather it was out to exploit other countries. In this light, American participation in the rehabilitation of the Hungarian economy must have sounded like a challenge to Soviet hegemony. Hence the Kremlin was in no hurry to respond to Kennan's démarche. Deputy Foreign Minister Andrei Ia. Vishinskii's reply did not arrive until 21 April, in which he refuted

American charges and ignored the threats. The failure by the American note to alter Soviet behavior was significant enough that Kennan still remembered it 50 years later.[75] After Kennan's note the Soviets speeded up talks on the joint Soviet–Hungarian companies, which were finally established in late March and early April. Simultaneously the Soviets granted some concessions to the Hungarian government; they agreed to the reduction of reparation payments by canceling $6 million worth of penalties for the tardy shipment of goods; the payment period for reparations was extended from six to eight years and Hungary was relieved of paying for the costs of a railway line built by the Red Army.[76] Furthermore, the Soviet leadership agreed to deduct the value of Hungarian investment in two Soviet-owned mines on former Hungarian territory in Romania.

At the April/July 1946 Paris meeting of the Council of Foreign Ministers, the Soviet Union proposed that Hungary be compensated for one-third of its material losses suffered in the fight against Germany, while Secretary of State Byrnes advocated the reduction of reparations. Both proposals were rejected. In order to halt the further deterioration of the Hungarian economy, the United States made a renewed attempt to modify Soviet conduct on 23 July. A note, which was made public to enhance its effect, alleged that payments to the Soviet Union tied down 80 to 90 percent of the Hungarian heavy industry and proposed the renegotiation of reparations. It was also claimed that out of $345 million worth of damages inflicted on Hungarian industry, (according to "reliable estimates") $124 million was caused by the Soviet Union. Moscow was again called upon to work with the United States and Great Britain in order to formulate an economic program of stabilization. To help with stabilization the American government returned Hungary's gold reserve.[77] This time it was Deputy Minister of Foreign Affairs Vladimir G. Dekanozov who replied within 4 days, by refuting the allegations.[78] Washington never made another attempt to force the Soviets to cooperate in solving Hungary's economic problems, even when it was requested to do so by the Hungarian government.

By late 1946, therefore, the United States had given up its efforts to combat Soviet expansion in Eastern Europe with economic means, with the only exception being Austria. The U.S. minister in Prague for example advised against a large reconstruction loan until the Czechoslovak people "rid themselves of the very real threat of Communist domination or [...] until American properties which have been nationalized will be paid for". In September it was decided that no new credit would be given to Czechoslovakia since Prague supported Vishinskii's view that the U.S. was trying to enslave Europe by a policy of handouts.[79] Although the EximBank approved a $50 million loan, Byrnes instructed Acheson to determine whether the unused portion of the credit ($41 million) could be prevented from being used up. He wanted to see that no new contracts were made which would subsidize the Communists in Czechoslovakia. "I am convinced that the time has come [...] to assist our friends in Western Europe [...] rather than continue to extend material aid to those countries in East Europe at present engaged in the campaign of vilification of the U.S. and distortion of our motives and policies."[80] Eventually the remainder of the loan was not transferred to Czechoslovakia partly because its economic situation did not justify it anyway.[81] Soviet economic expansion continued unhindered.

According to the first, provisional list compiled by the Soviet authorities fifty German-owned companies within Hungary were to become Soviet property under the Potsdam Declaration. The list was compiled from a list prepared by the Hungarian National Bank for Dresdner Bank in 1942 of those firms, which according to a German–Hungarian agreement of the same year were allowed to transfer dividends to Germany.

The Hungarian government wanted to apply the Potsdam Declaration to companies that had been German owned even *before* the Anschluss. The Soviets clung to their "liberal" interpretation of "German assets." Their argument that it did not matter when and in what way Germany acquired the assets made it possible for the Soviet Union to broaden its economic expansion. At the same time, Hungary was forced to assume responsibility for liabilities towards third countries on property taken over by the Soviets. Yet, the Hungarian government shared some of the responsibility for the arbitrary way the Soviets were able to seize the nation's assets because the government had allowed the Communist controlled Supreme Economic Council to determine which companies were to be transferred to the Soviet Union.[82] Implementation of the Potsdam Declaration indicated the government's inability to influence issues that affected the fate of the nation.

In Germany for instance the Russians established Soviet stock companies (Sowjetische Aktiongesellschaften) which would operate under German law and make it possible for Soviet organizations to own them. The Soviet Military Administration formally transferred German factories to Soviet ownership "as part of the satisfaction of reparation claims to the USSR." By the end of 1946 Moscow owned close to 30 percent of all production in East Germany, including virtually all synthetic fuel and mineral oil production and the chemical industry.[83] The Soviet government's list for Hungary bore witness to the fact that Moscow was intent on controlling strategic branches of industry. Among the companies to be taken over were the country's largest manganese mine as well as the bauxite-aluminum industry—Hungary was one of the world's largest producer of bauxite.[84] Since coal was in short supply in the USSR,[85] the Soviets took over most of the coal mining industry as well. Hungary was forced to give up its only aircraft factory and some of its most important and prestigious industrial concerns: Orenstein és Koppel Iparvasutak Általános Gépgyár Rt. (Orenstein and Koppel Industrial Railways General Machine Works), and Ganz és Társa Villamos Gép- Waggon- és Hajógyár Rt. (Ganz and Co. Electric, Machine Wagon and Ship Works Ltd.), as well as a significant textile plant. In short, the Soviets took the most meaningful parts of what remained of Hungarian light and heavy industry.

The Hungarians maintained that only a minor part of the shares of the listed companies were in German hands, and that rightful German ownership was questionable under the London Declaration. The government produced documentary evidence to support its position. Thus, for example, Bakonyi Bauxit Rt (Bakony Bauxite Co.) had been Swiss-owned, the German shares of Salgótarjáni Kőszénbánya (Salgótarján Coal Ltd.) had been repurchased from Germany during the war, as had those of two other major coal mines. The shares of Dunai Repülőgépgyár Rt. (Duna Aircraft Works) had been in Hungarian hands all along, while less than five percent of the shares of Ganz és Társai were actually German-owned. Over 76 percent of Telefongyár Rt.'s (Telephone Works Ltd.) shares were American-owned and other companies had Austrian proprietors or the Germans acquired their ownership by coercion.[86] In fact in 1943 there had been a general trend for Hungary to purchase German-held shares. Beside German assets, the Soviet Union acquired the majority of Italian property in Hungary due to the Italian peace treaty. Although this was not too significant, it allowed the Soviet Union to make further inroads in the Hungarian economy, particularly in the field of banking and insurance.[87] Companies acquired by the Soviet Union under the Potsdam Declaration became Soviet companies operating extraterritorially and produced for the Soviet Union until 1952, when they were sold back to the Hungarian state at a hefty price.[88]

One of the most significant Soviet claims on the basis of the Potsdam Declaration was the collection on a valorized basis of German claims against Hungary. These included Hungary's wartime debt to Germany, which the Soviets estimated at cca. $230 million, as well as the liabilities of German assets in Hungary estimated at $40 million.[89] At the same time the Hungarian claim of 750 million Reichmarks resulting from Hungary's trade surplus with Germany was waived by Article 30 of the Peace Treaty. On the latter count the Soviet Union sided with Hungary and wanted the Germans to settle their debt to Hungary. Byrnes was opposed to it because he feared that American taxpayers would have to pick up the cheque.[90] Although the American position seldom prevailed when it came to the Soviet zone, it did in this case, and the waiver, which was tantamount to a punitive measure, was included in the Peace Treaty. The Hungarians thought that the amount the Soviets demanded was unreasonably high and payment of the exuberant sum threatened the economy. On the other hand non-payment would entail political crisis. Ferenc Nagy appreciated the gravity of the crisis and persuaded his reluctant finance minister, Miklós Nyárádi, to accept the Soviet invitation for talks in Moscow. Nagy told Nyárádi that Hungary was "in great danger. […] Russian pressure to bring about a Communist dictatorship in our country is increasing. If you refuse to go the Russians can enforce their demands and throw us into complete economic chaos. This might be the pretext Rákosi needs to seize government."

Nyárádi traveled to Moscow in May 1947 not knowing that it would take seven months to negotiate an agreement. He was put up in Moscow's most exclusive hotel, usually reserved for Communist dignitaries. His negotiating partner was a high-ranking official of the Soviet Ministry of the Interior, General Vsevolod Merkulov, who oversaw the agency for Soviet property abroad. Merkulov impressed Nyárádi as a man who "looked and acted like an aging schoolmaster. He was well built with a broad Slavic face that radiated good will and behind rimless spectacles a pair of intelligent blue eyes looked upon me benignly." Since Merkulov had the reputation of having overseen the deportation and killing of millions of Balts "with heartless efficiency," whenever they were together Nyárádi "always felt that uneasy cordiality which one might display while locked in the same cell with a suave homicidal maniac." Nevertheless they got along. The first two meetings were staged with elaborate pageantry and began with a drinking bout. Then followed months of horse-trading that ended with Merkulov dropping the larger part of the Soviet claim. According to the agreement of 9 December 1947 $45 million had to be paid, which covered all outstanding Hungarian debts to the Soviet Union under the Potsdam Declaration. At first Merkulov wanted to take Hungary's largest heavy industrial complex, the Weiss Manfred Works, but Nyárádi refused and the Communist dominated Hungarian government backed him. Eventually it was agreed that the Soviets would receive $30 million in Hungarian currency to be spent in Hungary. Because the Hungarian currency was overvalued, the actual payment was $6 million. The rest, $15 million, was paid in kind over five years in the form of locomotives, tobacco, pulp and marmalade.[91] In this instance tough negotiation paid off, but Nyárádi was one of the few Hungarians who dared stand up against the Soviet economic offensive.

Trade and joint companies

According to a *New York Times* report on 23 September 1945 the Soviet Union had signed a treaty of economic cooperation with Hungary, which would allow Moscow to exploit Hungary's major industries, natural resources, agriculture and transport. In fact, Minister of Commerce Ernő Gerő and Minister of Industry Antal Bán had concluded such a treaty on 27 August without clear authorization by their government. Upon his return to Budapest, Gerő commented that "the foundations of a lasting economic and commercial cooperation between Hungary and the Soviet Union had been laid."[92] The President of the Smallholder Party, Ferenc Nagy, was against the treaty's ratification on the grounds that "it could involve the monopolization of the whole Hungarian economy, which in turn could facilitate the growth of the Soviet Union's political influence." While the commercial part of the treaty was widely accepted, several other prominent politicians rejected the section on economic cooperation. The trade agreement provided raw materials and a market for the Hungarian textile industry, but the agreement on economic cooperation effectively secured broad Soviet participation in the Hungarian economy. Undeniably the trade agreement benefited the economy by replacing the German and Austrian markets with the Soviet Union, but in the longer run it would undoubtedly strengthen Hungary's political subjugation to the hegemonic power. Economic cooperation meant that the contracting parties would participate in equal parts in existing or future companies in the iron, steel, aluminum, oil, electricity, chemical and machine industry, the banking sphere, water, air and road transport. Joint venture companies were to be established for industrial and agricultural development as well. The Soviet Union was to receive a 50 percent share in the joint venture companies, the functioning capital of which was to be supplied by the Soviet Union.[93] In contrast to the opposition expressed by many within the Hungarian government to the treaty, János Erős, the head of the Office of Reparations, argued that "Hungarian–Soviet trade of $30 million will make it possible for Hungarian industry to make a huge leap in the field of reconstruction." As part of the agreement, the Soviet Union was obliged to furnish raw materials for the textile and chemical industries, iron and other metals, tractors, fertilizers, lorries and even sugar.[94]

The significance of the treaty was not lost on the U.S. representative in Budapest; Schoenfeld thought that the ratification of the treaty "remains a critical Hungarian political issue. Non-Marxist ministers have thus far resisted but admit that in absence of outside assistance ratification is inevitable."[95] In the meantime Voroshilov and the Soviet diplomatic representative in Budapest, Pushkin, threatened to take all German assets to the Soviet Union if the treaty was not ratified. Although Schoenfeld tried to persuade the State Department that a lack of Western assistance made the position of those resisting Soviet pressure hopeless, the State Department did not directly support the refusal to ratify. It was well aware that the West would be unable to counter Soviet reprisals. Crucially, for example, the Soviet Union could deny Hungary important raw materials which Britain and the United States would be unwilling or unable to provide.[96]

While the British encouraged the Hungarian government to turn to the ACC regarding the treaty,[97] Byrnes instructed the Budapest mission not to support those who wanted to turn down the treaty since the United States could neither compensate for the economic losses which a possible Soviet retorsion could inflict on the country, nor provide those goods, capital and technical aid which Hungary would obtain in the framework of the accord.[98] At the same time, the Truman administration informed Moscow that the U.S. government was seriously concerned about the treaty; in particular about the clauses which gave the Soviet Union exclusive positions in trade, market and raw materials. It therefore requested that the treaty's implementation be postponed until the peace treaty was signed.[99] Since no Soviet reply was forthcoming, the State Department decided to publicize the affair, declaring that the treaty violated the spirit of Yalta.[100] Simultaneously the Western representatives in the ACC called on Voroshilov "not to press the Hungarian government on behalf of the ACC to ratify the proposed agreement."[101] Washington wanted to have the agreement modified so that in the fields of industry, agriculture, investment, transport, banking, and Danubian shipping it was made compatible with the most favored nation clause of the 1925 U.S.–Hungarian Treaty.[102] The agreement envisioned in Washington would have provided equal opportunities for each country in the economy and commerce, in effect an "Open Door" type arrangement. Washington stated it would be "concerned" if the treaty were not modified in such a manner, especially since the case of Romania showed that a similar agreement provided dominant, even monopolistic status for the joint venture companies.[103]

Because the United States was opposed to the monopolization of Hungarian trade by the Soviets, it refused to negotiate its own commercial agreement with Hungary until after the signing of the peace treaty.[104] In fact, the Americans repeated what England had done in the face of Germany's economic Drang nach Osten during the late 1930s: recognized its dangers, but refused to alter its trade policies to counter it.[105] Thus for instance Hungarian meat products—the country's main export item to the United States—were kept out of the U.S. because allegedly they did not meet American animal health standards.[106] Hungary's other important prewar export item, paprika, was barred from the American market because of quality problems, but Russia purchased a large quantity of it. In the absence of Hungary's traditional markets like Germany or Italy, Moscow easily became its most important trading partner under the guise of helping its economy. The U.S. government did indicate, though, that it would validate the 1925 U.S.–Hungarian Treaty even before the conclusion of the peace treaty, would help restore the economy and would support the activity of the American private companies in Hungary. Furthermore, Washington made an implicit pledge that Hungary would be involved in the new liberal economic order. In return, the Hungarian government was called upon to make sure that the treaty with the Soviet Union did not impinge on American economic interests, that it did not to restrict American access to Hungarian markets and raw materials and that Hungary would extend to other nations commercial and investment opportunities offered to the Soviet Union. Finally, Budapest was told that the peace treaty would need to guarantee the most favored nation status and equal treatment of American citizens.[107]

This position was in line with traditional American economic diplomacy and the recognition in American government circles that the division of the continent would hinder the triumph of the new liberal political and economic order. Acting Secretary of State Dean Acheson summed up Washington's goals in terms of Hungary's future economic treaties: "We deem it essential that the satellites do not conclude treaties, agreements or arrangements which deny to Allied nationals access on equal terms to their trade, raw materials and industry" and appropriate modification would have to be made of "any existing arrangements which may have that effect."[108] Washington's passive stance in Hungary stood in stark contrast with the U.S. role in Austria, where the United States undertook to finance Vienna's trade deficit and reoriented Austrian trade.[109] This was a clear sign that the Ostmark was the eastern limit of American involvement, i.e. it was far more important to keep the strategically located Austria in the Western sphere of influence than its less fortunate neighbor. Austria's significance compared to Hungary's was demonstrated also by the fact that the Americans insisted on Austrian economic unity even when they had already given up the idea of an economically united Germany.[110]

Pressed from all sides, the Hungarian government was in dire straits. Prime Minister Dálnoki Miklós convened a special meeting of the council of ministers in order to discuss ratification. Several ministers thought that Gerő and Bán had only had authorization to conclude a treaty on trade, and that the agreement they had initialed went well beyond their mandate. Miklós believed that the Provisional National Government's scope of authority did not extend to determining the nation's economic future for five years or more. Therefore Gerő was forced to allow his fellow ministers and the leaders of the political parties to have a look at the text. In his presentation at the Council of Ministers' meeting, State Secretary István Balogh, a Smallholder who was willing to cooperate with the Communists, proposed the treaty's ratification. He argued that concerns about the growth of Soviet political influence were unjustified. He believed that the treaty was "beneficial for reparations" and to turn it down would signal "the lack of confidence vis-à-vis the Soviet Union." Hungary would not receive the benefits it desired and "a revolution would have to be counted with in the spring."[111] In order to reassure world opinion, Balogh proposed that a *lettre d'envoi* be attached to the agreement to the effect that it did not discriminate against other nations and involved *primarily* those German assets which went to the Soviet Union as a result of the Potsdam Declaration. Balogh's attitude reflected the perceived hopelessness of the domestic and international scene. It was typical of the attitude of many Smallholders, in that he thought that concessions would appease the Soviets and their Hungarian Communist allies. Almost every one agreed with Gerő that the treaty would safeguard the economy against a crisis. Bán and Foreign Minister Gyöngyösi supported Balogh's notion that the treaty was not discriminatory. The only exceptions were the Minister of Defense, General János Vörös, who left the meeting half way through, and the Minister of Religion and Education, Count Géza Teleki. They wanted to sound out the views of the British and American members of the ACC after having been informed that they objected to the treaty. At this point Gerő reminded the participants of Hungary's political reality: "we have only one ACC and it is headed by Voroshilov and being aware of this fact there is nothing more to talk about." Thereafter, the Council of Ministers forwarded the treaty for ratification to the Political Committee of the National Assembly and a select body of the latter, Nemzeti Főtanács (Supreme National Council) with some modifications. Unexpectedly, the Soviets agreed to modify the treaty, guaranteeing equal rights for all nations. The Supreme National Council ratified the treaty in December 1945 with the stipulation that it "by no means impedes the Hungarian state to conclude economic or commercial agreements of any kind with other states."[112]

In view of Hungary's economic plight and Soviet economic penetration, Schoenfeld proposed the rescheduling of reparations—to which the Soviet Union agreed—and the reduction of the burdens deriving from supplying the occupation army.[113] Schoenfeld thought that the Soviet Union was refusing to assist Hungary's economic recovery in order to promote economic collapse, since that was believed to be a necessary part of Moscow's strategy of penetration.[114] The Soviets, he believed, would be interested in reviving the Hungarian economy only when the program of economic penetration ended. The Soviet Union would then have a stake in increasing the productivity of its newly acquired property, and would want to attract American capital. Schoenfeld believed that the economic treaty would place Hungary firmly in the Soviet sphere of influence, and in January 1946 he therefore urged rapid and decisive American assistance before Hungary became "the Soviet Union's economic colony."[115] The minister also knew that it might be too late. Nearly all sectors of the economy were already under Soviet control, with only a small segment remaining free. He complained that factories involved in reparations were supervised by Soviets on the spot, ready-made goods and raw materials could be transported from one place to the other only with Soviet "assistance". Ministers of the government were allowed to leave Hungary to negotiate loans and economic benefits only with Soviet authorization. Danube shipping, air traffic, oil, bauxite, aluminum production was under Soviet control, and the Soviets did their best to divert foreign trade towards their own sphere. Communist sympathizers held key positions in the ministries of industry and transport and the Supreme Economic Council.[116]

As part of the Soviet economic offensive Hungary's foreign trade was in effect reoriented towards the USSR. In 1946 the Soviet Union was already Hungary's most important trading partner, which was quite a feat considering that before the war Hungarian–Soviet trade remained below one percent of the Hungarian turnover. By 1947, the Soviet Union accounted for $30 million of Hungary's $70 million trade. Anastas Mikoyan remarked that "the aim of Soviet trade was not just to defend the Soviet economy from 'imperialist' penetration, but to bind others to it."[117]

Certain transactions of Soviet–Hungarian trade were financed by the Hungarian treasury. In 1946 Hungary sold fruit pulp to the Soviet Union, for a price of 6,935 forints per ton, but the Soviets paid 3,100 forints only, meaning that the fruit pulp exported to the Soviet Union cost the Hungarian treasury 3,815 forints per ton. In the first 8 months of the 1946–1947 budget year similar costs reached 142 million forints, slightly more than the monthly foreign trade turnover. Another example was coke. Hungary bought coke from the Soviet Union, which actually originated from Poland. The Poles received raw cotton in exchange from the Soviets. The coke was supplied to Hungary for steel products. In 1948 the world market price of coke was $14, which the Poles sold for cotton, which cost only $12 a ton. Hungary paid with steel products worth $17 a ton for the $14 coke. Thus Moscow made a profit of $5 on each ton of cotton sold in the triangular deal.[118]

Beside reparations and the seizure of "German assets," Soviet–Hungarian joint venture companies were the third major means of Soviet economic penetration, even if the Russians and their sympathizers tried to portray these ventures as economic assistance rendered to Hungary. Joint venture companies were established in the industries of transportation, oil, and

bauxite. The Soviet contribution consisted of assets seized under the Potsdam Declaration. Hungary's share was made up of remaining Hungarian
property such as equipment, installations, and raw materials to be discovered by bauxite and oil companies. As a result of an overvaluation of the
Soviet and an underestimation of the Hungarian contribution, Moscow
acquired a larger share of the economy than the value of earlier German
assets justified. Moreover, the companies had Hungarian presidents, but real
power was vested in the Soviet directors.[119]

The joint companies were not unique to Hungary. They were set up in
East Germany, Romania, Bulgaria, Czechoslovakia, Yugoslavia and in
countries that were only partially under Soviet control, such as Austria and
Iran, China and North Korea. As an example a joint company was established to exploit Czechoslovakian uranium for Soviet use. The agreements
for the Soviet–Hungarian companies were not discussed in the Hungarian
National Assembly, against the wishes of both the president and the prime
minister. The pro-Communist ministers convinced them that this would take
too long and was not legally mandatory for such agreements anyway.[120]
Some, like the minister of defense, were not allowed to see the agreements
until the day they were signed. Although a number of reservations were
raised, such as the fact that the companies were not bound to any time limit,
Prime Minister Nagy insisted that they should be signed so as not to hurt
the Soviet Union's prestige. Gerő claimed that the agreements were dictated
by the "political circumstances."

The joint firms were set up for an indefinite time, which suggested that
the Soviet Union was making long-term arrangements. It is interesting to
note that the Russians wanted to establish a joint oil company in Austria
called "Sanaphta," but this was envisioned for fifty years only. Nothing
came of it because the Americans were strongly against it. They questioned
the Austrian government's competence to sign such an agreement prior to
the restoration of Austrian sovereignty. With American backing the Renner
government was able to foil the project.[121] The fact that the Sanaphta was
planned for a definite period suggests that Austria was less important for the
Soviets than Hungary.

On 29 March 1946 the two governments signed a navigation agreement, which established MESZHART (Hungarian–Soviet Navigation Ltd.).
The company controlled navigation on the river Danube and its tributaries,
and on the seas, as well as the operation of ports, stations, ship factories,
maintenance installations and the management of companies involved in the
production and procurement of fuel. The Hungarian government leased to
the company all ports on the rivers Danube and Tisza, including the country's only free port on the Danube Island of Csepel. Its vessels were to

enjoy most favored nation treatment and the company was made exempt from all taxes and duties.[122] MESZHART's potential was significantly raised by Soviet contribution. An agreement signed in 1947 improved Hungary's maritime navigation by giving the contracting parties the right to use each other's ports and port services on the most favored nation basis—an arrangement that obviously benefited land-locked Hungary.[123]

A similar accord was concluded a few days later, when MASZOVLET (Hungarian–Soviet Airlines) was set up, which was in charge of organizing and controlling Hungarian air traffic, and participating in the international airline network. MASZOVLET was given the right to use all civil airports and their installations for 30 years and was given territory to construct new ones. The Hungarian government renounced its rights concerning the airfields allocated to MASZOVLET's use. Until the Peace Treaty Hungarian airspace was under Soviet military control, thus landing and transit rights could be granted only by the Soviet High Command seated in Wiesbaden.[124] The Hungarian government was not allowed to negotiate air agreements with foreign states, even though the U.S. and Great Britain requested landing rights. In 1947 these privileges to the Soviet Union were extended when, in violation of the Peace Treaty, the Soviet and the Hungarian governments attached a protocol to the agreement on MASZOVLET which provided the Soviet civilian air fleet transit and landing rights, while other foreign airlines needed Soviet permission for the same. The Peace Treaty should have restored Hungary's sovereignty over its airspace, but in signing this protocol, the Hungarian government renounced any such independence.

On 8 April 1946, the day before the Hungarian delegation departed for the talks in Moscow, Deputy Prime Minister Árpád Szakasits signed the Hungarian–Soviet Bauxite Agreement, which provided for the establishment of three joint venture companies. Interestingly enough, the signing of the bilateral agreement on the bauxite companies roughly coincided with a report in late April 1946 that Junkers began to produce jet aircraft for the Soviet Union on a large scale and that for this reason the Soviet authorities had banned the use of aluminum for any other form of manufacturing in the Soviet zone of Germany.[125] The Hungarian government discussed the agreement in great haste, since the Soviets wanted it signed before the Hungarian delegation's departure to Moscow. Prime Minister Nagy's revealing remark that the Soviet Union had to be won over to support Hungary at the peace talks[126] seems to underline the assumption that there existed a phony "deal" between Rákosi and Stalin on Soviet support for territorial concessions in return for the rapid conclusion of the economic agreements.[127] Reservations, such as the Soviet monopoly of the companies' exports and the fact that the companies would be established for an indefinite period of time, were brushed aside. The ongoing negotiations between experts were immediately suspended and the agreement was signed before the special committees could come to a mutually acceptable agreement.

Thus the Soviets did not allow the Hungarian government to retain their own bauxite mines, and refused to make a commitment to satisfy Hungary's own demand for bauxite. They did agree for the Hungarians to have their own aluminum-oxide plant as well as two bauxite furnaces, and theoretically the companies were to operate under Hungarian law.[128] Under the agreement the USSR gained a 50 percent interest in Alumíniumérc Bánya és Ipar Rt. (Aluminum Ore Mine and Industry Ltd.) and its subsidiaries, which controlled 90 percent of Hungary's bauxite resources, and obtained another 50 percent share in the second largest company in the industry. The Soviets contributed German assets acquired under the Potsdam Declaration and the equipment they obtained for reparations.[129]

Special provision was made for raising bauxite production for domestic consumption and export with the stipulation that the Soviet Union's needs would enjoy priority. The companies were granted their predecessors' rights to explore new bauxite deposits for an indefinite time and were given the "privilege" to explore new deposits in the whole country. This provision was modified in March 1947 to the effect that the Soviet–Hungarian companies obtained an *exclusive right* to search for bauxite in Hungary.[130] The agreement prescribed the amount of the ore to be produced in the following three years, which would rise from 400 thousand tons in 1946 to 700 thousand in 1948. In 1953, the year before the joint firms were sold to Hungary, 500,000 tons of bauxite and 350,000 tons of aluminum oxide were exported to the Soviet Union.[131] The three bauxite-aluminum joint companies were established without time limit and the Hungarian authorities provided them with foreign currency to cover their expenses abroad. This provision applied to all Soviet–Hungarian firms and put them in an exclusive position. No other Hungarian or foreign companies were allowed to keep their income or receive foreign currency, and the joint companies were also exempted from all taxes and duties.

A board of directors, a managing-director and his deputy, plus an Assembly of Shareholders managed the joint companies. The president of the Board of Directors was Hungarian, while the managing director, who was responsible for administration, was Soviet. The latter was the one who wielded power, with the capacity "to act in all matters relating to the company"; he was empowered to sign agreements, issue bonds, was responsible for the acquisition, encumbrance and lease of assets and for raising loans of cash. The managing director was also responsible for the companies' banking and credit operations, and had the right to hire and fire the firm's employees and to determine their wages and salaries. When the Hungarian–

Soviet Bauxite Company's managing director decided to appoint new directors he failed to consult with the Hungarian management, which was expected to accept the appointment without knowing who the company hired. Therefore the Hungarian board of directors requested the Soviet managing director to postpone his decision and to inform the Board of such intentions in the future. The reply revealed that Soviet control was unlimited: "Personal matters belong to my competence and therefore I can decide the issue without convening the Board of Directors."[132] Although the companies were supposed to operate under Hungarian law, the managing directors often disregarded it and acted arbitrarily.

Only four days after the Iranian government agreed to set up a joint Soviet–Iranian oil company to exploit crude oil in Northern Iran,[133] a similar agreement was concluded with the Hungarian oil industry as well. Signed on 8 April (the same day as the bauxite agreement) it created two companies: MASZOVOL (Hungarian–Soviet Oil Company) and MOLAJ (Hungarian Oil). It was stipulated that MASZOVOL inherited the concessions that had previously belonged to the Hungarian–German Oil Company (MANAT) to explore, drill and exploit crude oil and gas, and to process and sell oil and gas products. MASZOVOL acquired the Hungarian government's 15 percent share of all the crude oil produced in Hungary, and it had the right to export to those countries with which Hungary had a commercial treaty.[134] As for MOLAJ, the Soviet Union was given 50 percent of the Hungarian government's shares of the state-owned company (Magyar Olajművek) and the Hungarian government was compensated for them by the Soviets. MOLAJ, which largely produced refined oil, was allocated 15 percent of all crude oil refined in Hungary, plus a share of the remaining 85 percent of the remaining oil refinery business.[135] All the rights and assets of the former German–Hungarian oil company were vested on MASZOVOL, thus all the concessions and obligations included in MANAT's 1940 Concession Treaty.

The treaties were amended by a protocol on the operation of Hungarian–Soviet companies signed on 9 December 1947. The protocol provided that Hungary give an advance payment of 33.5 million forints (cca. $3 million) on profits and dividends to the Soviet Union in the form of commodities, out of which 3 million had to be invested by the latter in Hungary. The advance payment on profit and dividends was established even *before* the annual financial balance was known.[136] That is, the profit had to be advanced by the Hungarian treasury to the Soviets, while other Hungarian or foreign companies in Hungary were not allowed to pay dividends to their shareholders or dispose of their profits. Such privileges, extended to Soviet companies from 1946, violated Article 33/C of the Hungarian Peace Treaty according to which United Nations nationals "shall be granted national and

most favored nations treatment" in "commerce, industry and shipping."
The agreement also provided for the joint companies' right to explore bauxite. If an applicant sought a concession for a territory also requested by the
Soviet–Hungarian Bauxite Company, the latter automatically enjoyed priority, but was obliged to offer the same conditions promised by the other
applicant.

Soviet influence extended to the insurance business as well—the
Soviets acquired ten insurance companies, five of which had been previously Austrian-owned. In the banking sphere the Soviets acquired the formerly Austrian-owned Merkur Bank and put it in charge of the financial
affairs of all companies with a Soviet interest in Hungary. Moscow got hold
of 80 percent of the Budapest branch of Creditanstalt Bankverein and an
18 percent interest in Általános Magyar Hitelbank (General Hungarian
Credit Bank). As provided by the Italian Peace Treaty, the Soviets acquired
Magyar–Olasz Bank (Hungarian–Italian Bank), which had been one of the
five most important financial institutes in Hungary prior to World War II.
Soviet presence in the most important branches of Hungarian economy was
established even before the Russians were in full control of the political
sphere. Even so, to a certain extent these Soviet companies were designed
to work in a politically and economically pluralistic system. Since pluralistic conditions ceased to exist in 1948 and extreme measures of centralization were introduced in the economy, the rules governing the operation of
the joint firms had to be changed. As it turned out, in some respects the new
centralistic regulations were detrimental to the Soviet owners.

The new rules were worked out in 1949, in the course of Soviet–Hungarian talks held in Moscow. The negotiations focused on the fusion of joint
companies operating in the oil and bauxite industry and the problem of fit-
ting these companies into the new economic system. Soviet–Hungarian
conflicts resulting from the operation of the joint companies now surfaced.
The Hungarians endeavored to protect their economic sovereignty within
the limits set by previous agreements and political relations. On the other
hand, Moscow wished to preserve its privileges and to put even more favorable conditions into the new treaty. The head of the Soviet delegation,
Vladimir Dekanozov, Merkulov's deputy in Gusimz, who had previously
served as deputy minister of foreign affairs and in the NKVD as Beria's
confident, remarked that "the victorious country demands to assert its rights
for the reason that the defeated nation started war against her."[137] When it
came to economics, proletarian fraternity did not matter.

The Hungarian delegation, headed by István Vásárhelyi, argued that
"the Soviet companies in Hungary and the Hungarian–Soviet joint venture
companies should be fitted into the country's external and domestic trade
relations." Dekanozov retorted that it was "unjust that in the companies

where the [Soviet Union] is an owner, and which produce strategically and economically important materials like bauxite and oil, the Soviet Union should have no say."[138] The Soviet functionary was twisting the truth: it was Hungary that was trying to gain influence in controlling and directing the companies. The Hungarians stated that "the institution of the managing director lends the companies a Soviet character and certain Soviet organs in Hungary instruct those companies as if they were Soviet ones. The managing directors should be a part of the uniform system of control, and the Hungarian side would like to secure full influence on the functioning of the companies [...] the institution of the managing director means that the companies are looked upon as Soviet ones."

Thus, for example the managing directors did not comply with a decree stipulating that insurance had to be made with a native insurance company, nor with the law that all companies operating in Hungary were supposed to use a Hungarian bank for their financial transactions.[139]

With regards to the question of prices, an ambiguous situation existed. As co-owner, the Soviet Union had a legitimate claim in formulating bauxite and oil prices, but in the recently established economic system, theoretically only the Hungarian Office of Prices had such a right. The Soviets as *owners* were interested in high prices, but as *buyers* they wanted to keep prices as low as possible. Since it hardly mattered how much they would pay for the companies' products in a centralized price system insensitive to production costs, they wanted to pay as little as possible. Moscow was able to refer to the fact that it was the number one purchaser of the commodities, and used this as an excuse to involve the Soviet state authorities in fixing the prices. By contrast the Hungarians thought that this demand was tantamount to an infringement of Hungarian sovereignty and made a counter-proposal to the effect that the Office of Prices would *consult* with the Soviet managing directors, but the Hungarian authorities would have the final word.[140]

One of the biggest disputes concerned the profits and dividends of the oil companies. These had to be renegotiated, since the Soviets decided on the fusion of the two joint oil companies. Both sides agreed on the absurd provision that the profit should be determined in advance for several years in a fixed sum, including a rate of growth: what they could not agree upon was the sum. The Soviets demanded an unrealistically high figure, which did not follow from earlier results. While the Hungarians wanted to calculate the profit by taking into account earlier profits—which were themselves arrived at fictitiously—the Soviets wanted profits calculated according to a fictive multiplier, in proportion to the capital of the two companies added together. Hungary was reluctant to do this, since MASZOVOL, one of the companies involved, was in actual fact showing a deficit.[141] Additionally the Soviets demanded that the 15 percent royalty going to the Hungarian government under the earlier concession treaty be reduced to 5 percent. Finally, the Soviet Union wanted to change the mining law in effect since 1911 in order to abolish the institution of mining concessions. This proposal aimed at vesting exploration, drilling and production rights directly on the joint companies.

According to the 1946 agreement the companies were allowed to dispose of their own products, but the nationalization of domestic and foreign trade required that they renounce this right in the new 1949 agreement. State foreign trading companies would henceforth take over. The Hungarians, however, insisted that the joint firms should be obliged to produce the amount fixed by the Planning Office (a state organ responsible for formulating plans for the national economy's production). This, of course, violated the Soviet owners' right to have a say in the production of their own companies. The Soviet delegation wished to set this right and demanded that the production plans of the two countries be harmonized with those of the joint companies. This issue, in a similar way to the prices dispute, raised the problem of national sovereignty.[142] In their finances, the joint companies did not participate in the single-account system of the Hungarian National Bank but had their accounts kept by the Soviet-owned Kereskedelmi és Iparbank. The Hungarians wanted to put an end to this and bring the Soviet companies under the jurisdiction of the National Bank.

The talks ended in compromise, in part due to skilful negotiation by the Hungarians, and in part because Moscow made concessions on questions of lesser significance. At Hungary's request Moscow thus dropped its proposal to acquire 50 percent of Ajkai Erőmű és Trust (Ajka Power Station) and thereby acquire a significant portion of the Hungarian electricity industry. The negotiators almost concluded an agreement on a joint Hungarian–Soviet manganese company. The idea was not realized because the Soviets wanted a share in the full Hungarian production of manganese, which the Budapest government found unacceptable.

The Hungarians also wanted a revision of the properties it believed had been erroneously seized by the Soviet Union under the Potsdam Declaration, but Moscow refused to give in on this point. All the Soviet government was willing to agree to was a deal, whereby the Potsdam issue was pronounced closed, and in return, the Soviet authorities terminated their search for German properties in Hungary. The Soviet Union assumed responsibility for dealing with foreign governments that filed claims against Hungary as a result of the Potsdam Declaration's implementation. This was important because several governments, including the British and the French, had put forward claims against Hungary.

The Hungarian–Soviet airline was instructed to take into account the

Hungarian government's financial wishes "as far as possible," but the Hungarian treasury continued to finance its losses. But at least the Hungarians were able to gain influence on the company's schedule for foreign flights. As a compromise on finances, however, three of the joint companies' accounts were transferred to the Hungarian National Bank. The several Hungarian–Soviet bauxite companies were restructured into one such firm (MASZOBAL), just as it happened in the oil industry (MASZOLAJ).[143] Compromise was reached concerning the price question of the bauxite-aluminum commodities. According to the agreement signed in Moscow on 31 December 1949, when fixing the prices, the Hungarian price authorities were to "make preliminary consultations with the Soviet representative in the company, and to take into account his observations as far as possible."

Hungarian state organs were to sell the products of the joint companies, and the Hungarian government obliged itself to purchase the amount of products fixed by the state economic plan. This meant that the joint companies were forced to produce the amount envisioned by the Hungarian authorities. The Soviet Union withdrew its claim to participate in the formulation of the Hungarian plan. The question of oil profits was left unresolved by the treaty—the only reference to the issue was a sentence providing that profit would be paid only in case production exceeded the 50,000-ton annual minimal limit. Hungary preserved the right of concession but would receive its 15 percent royalty only if production exceeded the 50,000-ton annual limit.[144]

The leadership of the joint companies was left to the Soviets with slight modifications. A member of the Hungarian delegation, László Bauer, who was an expert from the Hungarian Workers' Party, declared that "as far as the role of the deputy managing-director is concerned, we do not want them to be limited to secondary roles, for them to become puppets, which in certain cases did in fact occur."[145] As a compromise Moscow agreed to instruct the company managers to adhere strictly to Hungarian laws and decrees, but reserved the right to turn to the Hungarian government if any legislation seemed to violate the companies' contractual rights.[146]

Finally, the 1949 agreement provided for an exchange of shares. The Soviet Union handed over to Hungary those properties, which it acquired as German assets, but in which its share was lower than 50 percent, and Hungary likewise turned over to the Soviets those companies in which the Soviet share was *more than* 50 percent. The balance was $14 million in favor of the Soviet Union. Hungary settled this claim by paying half the amount in forints, which the Soviets were obligated to use in Hungary, the other half by payment in kind over a period of four years.[147] A final agreement on joint companies was signed in 1952, according to which MASZOBAL and MASZOLAJ integrated new companies. The Hungarian government received fifty percent of their value in compensation. The new treaty secured the right to explore oil on the *whole* of Hungarian territory, including the concession previously enjoyed by the Hungarian–American Oil Company (MAORT), which was fused into MASZOVOL in June 1952. As a result MASZOVOL came to control 99 percent of Hungarian oil production.[148]

Throughout the period under discussion Hungarian leaders offered little resistance against Soviet economic penetration. This not only had to do with the lack of foreign support, Soviet pressure and the lack of personal character, but also with the nature of economic penetration, which was a less obvious method of undermining independence than the Sovietization of politics. Perhaps concessions in the economy may have been given so as to appease the Soviets and thereby avoid Hungary's total Sovietization. It is ironic that Hungary first resisted Soviet demands of economic nature when Sovietization had already taken place. Even though Soviet economic presence in Hungary was further strengthened resulting from the 1949 agreement, Soviet encroachments to partially integrate the Hungarian economy into the Soviet one were successfully resisted.

The Elimination of Western investments

All over Eastern Europe Soviet economic penetration meant the elimination of foreign investments. This was the fate of American companies in Hungary, the most significant of which operated in the oil industry. Simultaneously, practically all private enterprises were nationalized, ensuring the virtual disappearance of private ownership in Hungary.

The largest Hungarian oil company, Magyar–Amerikai Olaj Rt.— Hungarian–American Oil Ltd. (MAORT)—was founded in July 1938 as the subsidiary of Standard Oil of New Jersey, with 94 percent of the shares being held by Standard Oil. In 1943 the company was valued at over $58 million.[149] This occurred within a general drive from the part of U.S. companies to exploit East European oil reserves in competition with Germany: both countries had large investments in Hungary and Romania. On 13 December 1941 Hungary declared war on the U.S. and MAORT was sequestered by the Ministry of Industry without, however, changing the ownership. The American director, Paul Ruedemann handed over management to his Hungarian deputy, the geologist Simon Papp. Sequestration prevented Germany from taking over the company. Between April and August 1945 the Soviets took over the operation of all oil fields and oil refineries in Hungary, including those of MAORT. On 12 July 1945 MAORT's sequester was terminated and Ruedemann resumed the company's management in November. In 1943 MAORT fields had yielded a peak production of 837,710 tons of oil, and produced 3.1 million tons during eight years of operation. The company's war damages were estimated at 5.8 million pengős (cca. $1 million). The Hungarian Armistice Agreement provided that United Nations property had to be returned in good condition after Hungary's military administration was terminated, but because of the heavy fighting in Hungary this was an impossible requirement. Hungary delivered refined oil to the Soviet Union as reparations, but the oil refineries often refused to pay MAORT for the crude oil. This was a violation of the concession treaty and meant that the American owners paid for the oil deliveries to the Soviet Union.[150]

The Soviets were interested in the Central European oil and gas situation and in December 1944 the Soviet Military Oil Commission asked MAORT's chief geologist, Simon Papp, to give his assessment on the prospects of finding new deposits in Hungary and Romania.[151] The Hungarian Communists took an early interest in oil as well, and proceeded to work out the most convenient way to seize it without a diplomatic crisis. The best way seemed to be to prove that MAORT was sabotaging production. For Colonel István Timár of the political police, whose task it was to find such evidence, it was no secret that the aim was to nationalize the company.[152]

In April 1945, a government plenipotentiary was assigned to MAORT to supervise production, since the company was involved in reparations. The plenipotentiary, Zoltán Gombosi instructed MAORT to maintain an unrealistically high level of production, which, according to expert opinion, led to the loss of a significant amount of gas, and consequently, of oil. Gombosi was fueled by personal ambitions that included his desire to control oil production in Hungary as well as political hostility towards the U.S.[153] In 1945, 54.5 percent (148 million cubic meters) of MAORT's gas production were lost and oil production diminished from 810,000 tons to 655,000 tons as a result of an excessive exploitation of the oil fields.[154] As a response, the representative of the American shareholders gave instructions for a 10 percent reduction of production in January 1946, but this was not carried out. Moreover, on 17 January the Soviets resumed management of the oil fields. In addition, the Hungarian government paid so little for the oil that it was not even sufficient to cover the costs of production.

Hungary's other U.S.-owned oil company, Vacuum Oil, a subsidiary of Socony Vacuum Oil Co. had similar experiences. Vacuum Oil was involved in oil refining, storage and marketing; its refinery in Almásfüzitő was one of the largest in the country. Like MAORT, it was sequestered in 1941, but its former director continued to manage it. The Germans were kept from seizing it, and until their invasion of Hungary in 1944, when the Vacuum's refinery was put under military control, the Germans had not been allowed to take part in its operation. After 20 January 1945 the Soviets seized Vacuum's products stored in Almásfüzitő as war trophy. No payment was made to the company for the oil products delivered to the Soviet Union until August, therefore the company was forced to apply for a government loan. Vacuum Oil was at a disadvantage as compared to the Hungarian–Soviet-owned MOLAJ, since the Hungarian government allocated oil so that Vacuum operated at 60 percent of its capacity, while MOLAJ at 80 percent.

The question of American interests became one of the chief issues of conflict between the United States on the one hand, and the Soviet Union and Hungary on the other. Washington had the following aims concerning the protection of U.S. investments. First, that American companies, or those with significant American investment in them, should be able to operate free from discrimination and under equal conditions to their Soviet counterparts; and second, that the shareholders receive dividends and compensation for war damages, or nationalization. Finally, Washington wanted to avoid the Soviet Union receiving American property as reparations. In order to secure these objectives, the American ACC representative was empowered to act in defense of U.S. interests.[155]

U.S. officials charged that oil fields were wastefully exploited with no regard for the correct method of utilizing an oil field; that Americans were kept away from production; and that the equipment of MAORT were taken away. Moreover, the Americans were afraid that the Soviet-dictated unbridled pace of oil production would cause serious, irreparable damage to the oil fields. For this reason, the U.S. government insisted that Soviet personnel be withdrawn from MAORT and that the company regain full control over its activities. Yet, in spite of the State Department's protests, the Soviets retained control of the oil fields, and furthermore, the Soviets and Commissioner Gombosi put pressure on the company to increase production. Seeing the future of oil production in danger, the Supreme Economic Council recommended a 10 percent reduction of the company's oil production. The Ministry of Industry proposed a more significant, 16 percent cut and was of the opinion that unless this was done, the following consequences could occur: half of the country's 7 million-ton known oil deposit would be lost, resulting in a budgetary loss of 1.7 billion forints in the forthcoming 10–15 years. Furthermore, 3.5 million tons of oil represented six years' production and covered 12 years of internal consumption; MAORT would be able to demand $50 million for compensation and finally, without the 16 percent cut, the rate of decline in production could reach 25–30 percent.[156]

In January 1946 ACC representative General Key told Voroshilov that the company had no objection to the presence of Red Army personnel to provide security for its installations and stated that the reasons given for the curtailment of production were sound. He recommended a long-range view to prevent the oil industry from being "killed off entirely." Finally he asked the Marshal to allow the company to operate without interference by Soviet authorities. Voroshilov denied that the Soviets were in control of the company.[157] The Hungarian–American Oil Company was unable to pay dividends, since state prices for its products were too low.[158]

Voroshilov refused to allow the production cut demanded by the Americans. Deputy foreign minister Vishinskii explained that Soviet intervention was justified by Soviet expenditures and German investment in MAORT and the importance of a high rate of production.[159] Washington found it especially painful that American companies received no payment for reparation deliveries. The Hungarian Office of Reparations was of the opinion that Hungary's reparations could be fulfilled only in case "we increase our exports [...] in these exports companies with foreign relations will be in the vanguard [...] the American foreign service must be made to understand that American firms cannot receive special treatment."[160] Since the American companies were not paid for their shipments, new equipment could be bought. MAORT, after the victory of the Smallholder party in the 1945 elections, ordered $340,000 worth of equipment, out of which only $70,000 worth was known to have arrived in Hungary.[161]

On 2 April 1946, while the Soviet–Hungarian joint companies were in the process of being set up, the U.S. Legation turned to the Hungarian Ministry of Foreign Affairs to complain that reparation orders to Standard Electric Co. Ltd. were consuming the American firm's total production and in several areas even exceeded its productive capacity. Since the firm was paid in local currency and had no access to foreign currency, it was unable to purchase raw materials and equipment required for efficient operation and was unable to pay dividends to its shareholders, which meant that American citizens were bearing reparation burdens. For this reason the U.S. Legation requested that American firms involved in reparations be remunerated either in foreign exchange or in goods that could be sold for foreign currency.[162]

Prime Minister Ferenc Nagy responded that although the Hungarian government would "take into consideration the financial interests of the United States,"[163] all ministries and government organs involved agreed that no foreign currency should be placed at the company's disposal for the purpose of paying dividends. The Hungarian National Bank thought it desirable to increase Standard Electric's export possibilities, so that its South-East European markets could be preserved in Hungary. Thus, it was recommended that "no more than 30 percent" of the payments for its deliveries should be allocated to cover the company's imports, but "at present time there is no possibility to transfer dividends owed to its shareholders." The Ministry of Industry stated that the government "will not take responsibility for the profitability of that capital, capital will always have to count with certain risks."[164]

The Foreign Ministry did promise to attempt to reschedule reparation shipments and thus reduce export obligations, which was a precondition of increasing "free" exports. An increase of "free" exports in turn allowed income in foreign currency, a part of which was to be used to acquire new equipment. In response to Standard Electric's complaint, it was promised that the company would be allowed to have 30 percent of its foreign currency earnings—hitherto all earnings had been available in Hungarian currency. Foreign exchange could be used to purchase necessary machinery and raw materials. Nevertheless reparation shipments continued to go uncompensated, allegedly in order to curb rampant inflation. Furthermore, it was pledged that blocked accounts would be unfrozen after the stabilization of the Hungarian currency. Finally, Standard Electric was informed that no currency was available for the payment of dividends.[165] In contrast, Soviet and Soviet–Hungarian companies enjoyed important advantages. They were guaranteed exemption from taxes and duties under the 1945–1946 agreements and were allowed to transfer their profits, which were guaranteed in advance, to the Soviet Union without limitations, as foreign currency restrictions did not apply to them.

Yet, even after the "stabilization" of the Hungarian currency, the government decided that, in protection of the new currency, no claims of financial nature could be asserted against the Hungarian state. No doubt, "with stabilization a tendency that had prevailed since 1945 was institutionalized and finalized, which, as a result of a now conscious economic policy made it impossible to accumulate private capital."[166] This policy was a prelude to the final elimination of foreign (and Hungarian private) investments. The U.S. government outlined its official position on nationalization of American property in May 1947. Nationalization was regarded as the domestic affair of the given country. On the other hand, Washington insisted on prompt, adequate and efficient compensation of the owners, stating that nationalization did not change obligations of foreign governments or their citizens towards the U.S. government and its citizens. Finally, the U.S. expected all companies to be treated on the same terms.[167]

In order to solve outstanding problems between Hungary and the United States, several rounds of negotiations were held in Budapest during July 1947 with the participation of the Minister of Foreign Affairs, Gyöngyösi. Gyöngyösi, however, whose days in that position were numbered, was not empowered to make a statement on his government's political position. He was enabled only to sound out American complaints and investigate them.[168] Among the questions to be resolved were the compensation of American citizens, the restitution of Hungarian goods from the American zones of

Germany and Austria, and compensation for the Ajka power station which had been a subsidiary of the partially American-owned, but nationalized Tungsram Ltd.

Hungary unilaterally declared that it would recognize as U.S. citizens Hungarians who had been naturalized prior to 1931 only, meaning that the properties of Hungarians naturalized after that date would be taken as Hungarian. Washington would hear nothing of the idea, even though the Hungarians held out compensation for nationalized property. The Truman administration clearly felt that it was in its competence to decide who was an American citizen and who was not. Eventually, the Hungarians acknowledged that the Soviet-owned companies were being given special treatment, and that these provisions violated the Peace Treaty's most favored nation clause, which provided equal rights for all foreign companies.[169]

By late August the Hungarian–American talks had broken down. One U.S. negotiator remarked that if things went on as they had been, the Hungarian government would get everything without having to give anything. After twelve sessions, every issue remained unresolved; there was no agreement on war claims, the Hungarians paid no compensation, and the Americans froze the restitution of property from their zone. No meeting of minds occurred about American claims deriving from the land reform either. As far as nationalized property was concerned, an agreement was made on compensation, but neither the timeframe nor the means were defined. Since the question of compensation remained unsettled the United States suspended the execution of Article 26 of the Peace Treaty while Budapest did the same with Article 30.[170] The Nationalization Act of 1948 theoretically did not apply to property which was over 50 percent foreign-owned, but this provision was left ignored if the proprietor gained U.S. citizenship after 1931.

In May 1948, Zoltán Vas, the head of the Supreme Economic Council, declared that American interests would not be nationalized and the state managers would be recalled. He said that a Communist supervisor (Pál Székely) had been appointed to MAORT because of "overemployment" and the "lack of discipline" and, that a quarter of the company's 4,000 workers would be laid off.[171] The U.S. Legation reiterated that Hungarian prices did not cover production costs. Additionally, they argued that the government's insistence on overproduction, which was harming both the company and the oil fields, was being done partly because it would reduce the profitability of the investment so that the *Hungarian government could then accuse them of sabotage*. If proper prices were given for shipments and the company was to be granted an export-quota, revenues could be used for new drilling and construction of pipelines thereby increasing investment.

In regard to Ford Motor Co., the Legation complained that it had not obtained an import license, while the Hungarian state-owned company specializing in motor vehicles was free to import cars. The Hungarian government was held responsible for the transfer of American property to the USSR under the Potsdam Declaration. The Hungarian argument that the Soviet officials of the ACC, Marshal Voroshilov and General Sviridov gave orders for the transfer of these properties, was refuted with the statement that the United States had repeatedly informed Hungary that until the signing of the Peace Treaty it did not regard the implementation of the Potsdam Declaration either legal or necessary.[172]

By 1946, the production of crude oil had already been placed under state supervision and in July 1947 the Supreme Economic Council took direct control of MAORT's investments. The Council had already been granted the competence to determine the price of crude oil. In late spring 1948 a state supervisor was appointed to MAORT, who accused the Hungarian–American Oil Company of having experts that were "Hungarian agents of imperialism who intentionally installed 25 exploratory wells in the wrong place." Then MAORT was sued for procrastinating the acquisition of new equipment, for trial boring where there was no hope to find oil, for consciously deploying oil drills in such a way that would decrease potential production and for reducing production in order to sabotage the three-year plan.[173] This motion would prepare the company's nationalization and merger into the Soviet–Hungarian oil interests. A similar fate awaited the other companies as well.

Vacuum Oil was allocated far less oil for refinement in proportion to its capacity than its Hungarian–Soviet rival. Although the company's income was insufficient to purchase new equipment, instruction to do so was given by the Hungarian government. The American Legation protested and demanded that Vacuum Oil be treated on the most favored nation basis, but the authorities refused to alter the pattern of oil allocation. Ford Motor Co., which had barely escaped being handed over to the Soviet Union, already faced bankruptcy in 1947 because the company had neither the permit, nor the financial means to import automobiles, therefore it was reduced to repairing them. As a result of U.S. intervention the payment of Ford's debts to the government was temporarily suspended. Ford's indebtedness was later used as a pretext for nationalization.

On 25 September 1948 the government took over MAORT's management, confiscated its assets and deprived it of its rights. The measure was based on a decree to "prevent intentional sabotage of the production of crude oil [...] and [...] to secure undisturbed production."[174] Soon Vacuum Oil Co. also lost its independence: its financial control was taken over by the authorities and was obliged to pay a tax equal to the net value of the company.[175] In September 1949 the American-owned Union Textilművek

Rt. (Union Textile Works Ltd.) was liquidated, its machines and equipment were taken away.[176] A similar fate awaited Ford Motor Co.: the Hungarian state-owned company, MOGÜRT took possession of its buildings and immovables. Borsodvidéki Bányaipari Rt. (Borsodvidéki Mining Ltd.) was also nationalized, its owners were promised compensation—(they failed to receive any) and in return agreed to renounce their ownership.[177] Nationalization of foreign property without compensation was not limited to Hungary; for example it can be seen in the fate of the Romanian subsidiary of Standard Oil, Romano-Americana, which was nationalized in 1948. Since American citizens were unable to protect their interests under the prevailing legal system in Hungary, the United States sought to intervene diplomatically so that its citizens might obtain compensation for their lost properties. Washington initiated negotiations to that effect, but no response was forthcoming: Budapest resented that restitution of Hungarian property was halted from the American zone.

Eventually the construction of a Communist state took precedence over the interests of the national economy. In late 1948 the so-called sabotage trials against "bourgeois experts" were launched, which involved American citizens as well. In September 1948, the two American leaders of MAORT, Paul Ruedemann and George Bannantine were taken into custody by the Hungarian political police (ÁVH). The actual arrest was made by the head of the secret police, Gábor Péter himself, but not without difficulty. According to the official account, an American of "huge size" appeared on the scene, who "threw a detective to a distance of three meters." The American version of the same story recounted that a pistol was aimed at a Legation employee and the two individuals were taken away in handcuffs.[178] Minister of Foreign Affairs László Rajk informed the American Legation that the two had been taken into custody because several Hungarians had confessed against them to the effect that at Ruedemann and Bannantine's instructions, and with their active participation, "MAORT's oil production was sabotaged, so that the Hungarian state should obtain less oil." Rajk pointed out that the two Americans confessed that they had acted on the orders of Standard Oil New Jersey. He gave no information on where they were held and violating diplomatic norms he rejected the U.S. consul's request to contact them.[179]

MAORT's former president and director, Simon Papp had been arrested the previous month, on 18 August 1948, along with other Hungarian officials and experts of the company. One person committed suicide so as to avoid arrest. During interrogation Papp confessed that he was out to minimize MAORT's oil production from the first moment, partly because of technical reasons and partly because he did not want to produce oil for the Russians. He claimed that in Ruedemann's view "oil production had to be reduced in Hungary because this is the United States' political and economic interest."[180] In his own confession, Bannantine stated that he received instructions from the Standard Oil management "to reduce Hungarian oil production because of political reasons," since "in the future, Hungary might participate in a new war." He also admitted to having caused "greater harm to the Hungarian economy than what natural occurrences in oil production would have caused." Ruedemann in turn confessed that his intention was to influence production negatively, but denied giving specific instructions to this effect. He also denied an allegation in Papp's confession that they purposefully designated test-drilling spots in places where no oil deposits could be expected.[181]

As a response to the arrests, the U.S. threatened to close the Hungarian consulates in Cleveland and New York, suspended the restitution talks and considered banning American citizens from Hungary. These measures proved to be needless, since the two Americans were soon expelled from the country. Immediately after they left Hungary Ruedemann and Bannantine renounced their confessions claiming that their confessions had been extracted under duress. The Hungarian participants were sentenced in a political show trial—Simon Papp was sentenced to death, which was then changed to life imprisonment. His services were used while he was in prison to help the Soviets discover new deposits and he was released in 1955 with an amnesty. MAORT's former head of the production, Bódog Ábel, died in prison.

The proceedings lacked all elements of truth or legality. Firstly, MAORT's concession treaty, which was not introduced at the trial as evidence, did not oblige the company to satisfy foreign demands and protected the company from measures that were injurious to its own interests. As previously mentioned, it was the Communist-led Supreme Economic Council which recommended a 10 percent cut in production in 1947 as "an unavoidable necessity"—otherwise the "drop in production would reach 25–30 percent." The Council also thought that domestic and international needs could be met even if the 10 percent cut were implemented. This report was sent to the Communist leadership.[182] Furthermore, not even MAORT's Communist party members noticed that any sabotage was going on. Rákosi admitted this much at a meeting of the HWP Political Committee: "the party organs not only did not signal the machinations of the American leaders and their accomplices, not only did they not draw the attention of the party leaders to the possibility of sabotage, but party members working for MAORT kept repeating to leading comrades [...] that there was no sabotage and that the constant plummeting of production was justified from the national economy's perspective."[183] An arrested geologist, György Kertay, who was

MAORT's Communist party secretary, admitted that he had denied the possibility of sabotage.[184]

The point is that production *was* being maintained. Sabotage did not have to be proven—it was taken for granted from the very beginning, just like American participation in it. On 26 August 1948, even before Ruedemann and Bannantine were arrested, Papp's interrogating officer reported to party leader Rákosi that after sabotage was proven there would be no legal obstacle to the annulment of the MAORT treaty, meaning that all of MAORT's properties could be immediately sequestered by the Hungarian Treasury.[185] The officer knew exactly what outcome the interrogation had to deliver. Beside MAORT's nationalization, the objective was to extract information on where to find oil, which the Hungarian–Soviet oil companies were unable to do. Colonel Timár reported that the political police were "occupying" Simon Papp for him to give information on "how to increase production on known oil fields and how new fields could be found with fruitful research."[186] The government also coveted MAORT's concession. Even before the trial was held, the charge of sabotage was found proven. This was used to justify nationalization to be effected by a special decree. The Hungarian Workers Party's Political Committee resolved that "judicial proceedings in the MAORT affairs must take place within a month and as a result of this proceeding the confiscation of all MAORT's assets and the termination of the MAORT concession must be ruled to cover the Hungarian state's losses which it suffered as a result of the sabotage."[187] In keeping with the Stalinist practice, the verdict was ready even before the trial could begin.

Similar practices prevailed in the case of Robert Vogeler, the deputy director of Standard Electric and IT&T who was arrested on 18 November 1949 alongside with the Director of Standard Electric, Imre Geiger and its Deputy Director, Edgar Sanders, a British citizen. As a result, American–Hungarian relations sank to a nadir. According to the Hungarian Ministry of Foreign Affairs, "Within the general growth of tension between the United States and Hungary, the concrete reason for this was the Vogeler affair."[188] Vogeler did not get away with it as lightly as Rudemann and Bannantine, he along with Sanders, received a prison sentence. Imre Geiger was sentenced to death. It was in Vogeler's case that the United States' inability to defend the interests of its investments and citizens became the most obvious. The Hungarian authorities barred the U.S. consul from visiting him and refused to allow his attorney to enter the country. It is an ironical twist of history that the notes sent by the American minister on Vogeler's behalf, all of which were rejected by Minister of the Interior László Rajk, and the notes the Americans sent on Rajk's behalf in order to save him a year later, are now found side by side in the files of the Hungarian National Archives.

Although Secretary of State Acheson warned Rákosi that he could be a "tough" man, and the Hungarian consulates were closed, Rákosi refused to yield. Instead, he demanded political concessions in return for the American's release, such as to changing of the wave length of the VOA broadcasts and the return of the Hungarian Holy Crown, which, after having been taken to Germany in 1944 had ended up in the United States. No agreement was reached until 1951, when Vogeler was released in return for the reopening of the consulates, and a minor concession was given on the Voice of America. By then all American and other foreign economic presence—except that of the Soviet Union's—was a thing of the past.

The Soviet Union's economic stranglehold on Hungary had grave *political* consequences. First of all it contributed to the violation of Hungarian sovereignty and worked toward the country's transformation into a Soviet client state. Secondly, the Soviet economic dictates put a severe strain on Hungary's relationship with the Western world and ultimately these strains led to the breakdown of Hungary's relations with the U.S. In 1948 the "sabotage" trials involving American citizens led to outright hostility between Washington and Budapest. Again, these trials were related to the Sovietization of the economy, namely to the ideological imperative that no capitalist investment should be allowed to survive. It would be a mistake to find only ideology behind it. There was in the words of George Lichtheim[189] an interplay of "practical" and "ideological" factors. There was the motive of profit: large investments could be seized free of change.

The Soviets found many pretexts to receive payment from the Hungarians. Perhaps we shall never know the real sum extracted by the Soviets in the first ten years of Hungary's occupation. It is safe to say that reparation payments reached $450 million even though Molotov canceled the remaining $65 million in 1948. Hungary paid $150 to $180 million to compensate for damaged German property, $45 million for the Weiss Manfréd debt, over $160 million to repurchase Soviet companies, and the maintenance of the Red Army may have cost $60 million. To these amounts we must add the value of war trophy (Tungsram alone was worth $12 million), the Soviet companies' fictitious profits, and the value of oil, bauxite, manganese, coal and other commodities the Soviets "purchased" well below the market price, not to mention Soviet profit from unequal trade. To all this we must add the value of the labors of 600 thousand Hungarian slave laborers that toiled in Soviet labor camps. Perhaps it is not far from the truth that the Soviet Union extracted from Hungary the same amount as Austria received from the Marshall Plan, well above $1 billion. The more serious economic consequences of Sovietization cannot be quantified. Hungary, as the other countries of Eastern Europe were excluded from European integration, their economies were deprived from the benefits of advanced Western technology. Instead Eastern Europe embarked on a path of economic development dictated by Stalinist ideology and Soviet military needs. The merchants of the Kremlin had every reason to be satisfied. Economic expansion provided a continuous flow of wealth from Hungary to the Soviet Union; contributed to the Soviets' unchallenged control and Sovietization of Hungary; and last but not least provided a relatively safe way to decouple it from its Western links, to destroy the only kind of presence the Americans hoped to maintain.

NOTES

1 Notable exceptions are Naimark, *The Russians in Germany*; and Bischof, *Austria in the First Cold War*. Bischof wrote that in Austria the Soviets were driven by the "maximum exploitation of their zone."

2 See e.g. Williams, *The Tragedy of American Diplomacy*. The economic aspect of American conduct was emphasized also by John Lewis Gaddis, "The Emerging Post Revisionist Synthesis on the Origins of the Cold War," *Diplomatic History*, vol. 7, no. 3, (Summer, 1983).

3 Max, *The Anglo-American Response to the Sovietization of Hungary*; Kertesz, *Between Russia and the West*; Gati, *Hungary and the Soviet Bloc*; Kovrig, *Communism in Hungary*. One paper, however, did call attention to the significance of the economic sector in Hungary's Sovietization: András B. Göllner, "Foundations of Soviet Domination and Communist Political Power in Hungary," *Canadian–American Review of Hungarian Studies*, vol. III, no. 2, (Fall 1976), pp. 73–105.

4 According to the liberal thinker Hobson "the economic root of imperialism is the device of strong organized industrial and financial interest to secure and develop [...] private markets for their surplus goods and their surplus capital. Rudolf Hilferding established a connection between imperialism and finance capital. V. I. Lenin thought that uneven development and falling rates of profit made capitalism into a world system of colonial oppression. Lenin's theory of uneven development locates the source of conflict in the advanced capitalist economies' need to export surplus goods and capital and to engage in imperialistic conquest." See George Lichtheim, *Imperialism* (New York – Washington: Praeger, 1971), pp. 105–122; Robert Gilpin, *The Political Economy of International Relations* (Princeton, New Jersey: Princeton University Press, 1987), pp. 25–64.

5 Paul Marer, "Soviet economic Policy in Eastern Europe," in "Reorientation and Commercial Relations of the Economies of East-Central Europe," *A Compendium of Papers Submitted to the Joint Economic Committee, U. S. Congress*, 1972. p. 145; Paul Marer, "The 'Soviet Bloc' as an Integration Model—Economic, Political and Cultural Aspects," in *Competing in One World* (Indiana University School of Business, n. d.) p. 40.

6 Bischof, *Austria in the First Cold War*, p. 101.

7 Martin Wight, *Power Politics* (London: Royal Institute of International Affairs, 1946), p. 40; Edward Luttwak, *The Grand Strategy of the Soviet Union* (London: St. Martin's Press, 1983) pp. 73–74; Hans Morgenthau, *Politics among Nations —The Struggle for Power and Peace* (Revised by Kenneth W. Thompson) (New York: Knopf, 1985); Kenneth Waltz, *Theory of International Politics* (New York: Random House, 1979). p. 94.

8 K. J. Holsti, *International Politics—A Framework for Analysis* (Englewood Cliffs, New Jersey: Prentice Hall, 1967), p. 292.

9 See Resis, *Stalin, the Politburo and the Onset of the Cold War*, p. 3; Gaddis, *The United States and the Origins of the Cold War*, pp. 182–189.

10 Hence for example between 10 July 1946 and October 1946 29 British business-men were cleared and 23 were refused without explanation. Minutes of a formal meeting of the ACC where matters concerning Article 11 and 13 concerning the Armistice, clearances, formation and regulation of new political parties were dis-cussed, 17 October 1946, Cseh ed., *Documents of the Meetings of the Allied Control Commission in Hungary*, p. 232.

11 Artúr Kárász, *80 év alatt a föld körül* [80 Years around the world] (Buda-pest–Paris, 1990); for the Sviridov letter: Meeting of the Council of Ministers, 14 June 1946, MOL, XIX-A-83-a, MT jkv.

12 Varga Jenő előadása az MKP Politikai Bizottságának [Jenő Varga's presentation to the Politburo of the HCP], 1 October 1945, PIL, 274 F., 3 cs., 10 őe.

13 Iz zapisi besedi V. M. Molotova s M. Rákosi o politicheskoi situatsii v Vengrii [From record of conversation between V. M. Molotov and M. Rákosi on the political situation in Hungary] *VEDRA* tom I, p. 616; *Moszkvának jelentjük*, p. 198.

14 See McCagg, *Stalin Embattled, 1943–1948*, pp. 315–316; Korom, *Az Ideiglenes Nemzeti Kormány és a Fegyverszünet*, pp. 112–115.

15 See Pető and Szakács, *A hazai gazdaság négy évtizedének története*, vol. I [The history of four decades of the Hungarian economy] (Budapest: Közgazdasági Kiadó, 1986).

16 Ferenc Nagy, *Küzdelem a vasfüggöny mögött* (Budapest: Európa-História, 1990), vol. I. p. 221. Originally published as *Struggle behind the Iron Curtain*, by Ferenc Nagy, former prime minister of Hungary (New York: MacMillan, 1948). The Hungarian version was published on the basis of the author's original Hun-garian manuscript.

17 Jegyzőkönyv a minisztertanácsról [Record of meeting of the Council of Minis-ters] 22 December, 1945, MOL, XIX-A-83-a, MT jkv, no. 22. In the first month of its existence from the end of November the SEC functioned without any legal limitations whatsoever.

18 Iz politicheskogo otcheta diplomaticheskoi missii SSSR v Vengrii za 1946 g. O sozdanii Visshego Ekonomicheskogo Sovieta [From the political report of the diplomatic mission of the USSR in Hungary for the year 1946. On the establish-ment of the Supreme Economic Council] 16 April 1947, *VEDRA*, tom I, docu-ment 207, pp. 608–609.

19 Beside the factories taken by trophy groups, dismantling groups operated as well, which were organized by various Soviet ministries and took production

facilities. Another form of payment were deliveries in kind. See Naimark, *The Russians in Germany*; Bischof, *Austria in the First Cold War*, p. 101; Paul Marer, "The 'Soviet Bloc' as an Integration Model," p. 33.

20 OSS Research and Analysis Branch, op. cit.

21 The Ambassador in the Soviet Union (Harriman) to the Secretary of State, 30 December 1944, *FRUS*, 1944, vol. III, pp. 948–950.

22 Harriman to the Secretary of State, 31 December 1944, USNA, RG 59, 740.00/119 Control (Hungary) 12-3144.

23 Kárász, *80 év alatt a föld körül*, p. 75.

24 A külügyminiszter szóbeli feljegyzése, 1945, undated, MOL, Küm, vegyes admin, XIX-J-1-k, 165. doboz, 4fh, 174/FB, 1945.

25 MOL, KÜM, Szu tük, XIX-J-1-j, IV-483.1, 24. doboz, 1912 11062/1945 M.E.

26 The Hungarian government drafted a letter to Stalin on 5 June in which the dramatic food shortage was described. It is not known whether the letter was ever sent. Szviridov levele a miniszterelnöknek [Sviridov's letter tto the prime minister] 31 May 1946, in Sándor Balogh, Margit Földesi, eds., *A magyar jóvátétel és ami mögötte van... 1945–1949* [Hungarian Reparations and What Is Behind It, 1945–1949] (Budapest: Napvilág kiadó, 1998).

27 A közellátásügyi miniszter jelentése a minisztertanácsnak [Report by the minister of public pupply to the Council of Ministers] 12 June 1946, MOL, XIX-A-83-a, MT jkv.

28 Péter Sipos, "Two Armies—Two Occupations in Hungary in 1944–1945," in *Bulletin du Comité international d'histoire de la Deuxième Guerre Mondial*, p.138.

29 See General Edgecumbe's notes of an ACC meeting concerning the freedom of movement of the ACC staff in Hungary, the Hungarian National Bank, Article 11 of the Armistice, etc., 25 January 1946 and Minutes of the formal meeting of the ACC where matters concerning the Statutes of the Armistice, Navigation on the Danube, transfer of German assets to the Soviet government, etc. were discussed, 23 April 1946, Cseh ed., *Documents of the Meetings of the Allied Control Commission in Hungary*, p. 123; p. 137.

30 Feljegyzés a fegyverszüneti ellenőrző bizottság kártérítési osztályán megtartott megbeszélésről [Record of meeting held at the indemnification department of the armistice control commission] 24 April 1945, MOL, Küm, Szu tük, XIX-J-1-j, IV-536, 29. doboz, ikt. sz. n.

31 The stipulation involved nearly all the significant industrial plants, thus the power stations at Ajka and Hatvan, certain units of the most significant and developed Hungarian industrial complexes such as Weiss Manfréd Művek (Weiss Manfred Works), units of Lampart, Rimamurányi–Salgótarjáni Vasmű (Rimamurány–Salgótarján Iron Works), Almásfüzitői Timföldgyár (Almásfüzitő Aluminium Oxide Works), etc.

32 The text of the agreement is published in Balogh–Földesi eds., *A magyar jóvátétel és ami mögötte van*, pp. 28–31.

33 Pető and Szakács, *A hazai gazdaság négy évtizedének története*, p. 21.

34 Ibid., pp. 90–91.

35 Kárász, *80 év alatt a föld körül*, pp. 81–86.

36 Kertesz, *Between Russia and the West*, p. 43.
37 Rákosi, *Visszaemlékezések*, vol. II, p. 659.
38 Jegyzőkönyv a fegyverszüneti ellenőrző bizottság kártérítési osztályán megtartott tárgyalásról [Record of negotiation held at the indemnification division of the reparation control committee] 30 April 1945, MOL, Küm, Szu tük, XIX-J-1-j, IV-480.1, 23. doboz, ikt. sz. n. 1945.
39 A külügyminiszter szóbeli feljegyzése [The foreign minister's verbal memorandum] 21 October 1947, MOL, Küm, Szu tük, XIX-J-1-j, IV-536.2, 30. doboz, 452/Pol./res-1947.
40 Feljegyzés Magyarország jóvátételi kötelezettsége tárgyában [Memorandum on Hungary's reparations] 15 November 1945, MOL, Küm, Szu tük, XIX-J-1-j, IV-526.5, 28. doboz, ikt. sz. n. 1945; Feljegyzés az ipari miniszter számára [Memorandum for the minister of industry] 8 January 1947, MOL, XIX-F-1-b, 44. doboz, ikt. sz. n.
41 Rákosi, *Visszaemlékezések*, Vol. II, p. 659.
42 Feljegyzés az ipari miniszter számára [Memorandum for the minister of industry] 30 November 1947, MOL, XIX-F-1-b, 44. doboz, 11-025-1947.
43 Feljegyzés Magyarország jóvátételi kötelezettségéről [Memorandum on Hungary's reparations] 15 November 1945, MOL, Küm, Szu tuk, XIX-J-1-j, IV-526.5, 28. doboz, ikt. sz. n. 1945.
44 István Varga, *A magyar valutacsoda* [The Hungarian currency miracle] (Magyar Gazdaságkutató Intézet Közleményei: 1. Füzet, October 1946).
45 Ibid.
46 For the budget see A pénzügyi államtitkár jelentése [Report by the state secretary of financial affairs] 30 April 1946, MOL, XIX-A-83-a, MT jkv, 10. doboz; for the circulation figures and the statement on the link between the consumption of the Red Army: A pénzügyminiszter jelentése [Report by the minister of finance] 5 December 1945, Ibid., 5. doboz.
47 Berend, *A szocialista gazdaság fejlődése Magyarországon, 1945–1968*, pp. 49–50.
48 Jelentés a Magyar Állami Vas-, Acél- és Gépgyárak leszerelési tervéről [Report on plans to dismantle the Hungarian State Iron, Steel and Machine Works] Balogh–Földesi eds., *A magyar jóvátétel és ami mögötte van*, pp. 24–26.
49 Az Egyesült Izzó Feljegyzése Pokorni Hemann altábornagy jóvátételi kormánybiztosnak [Memorandum by Egyesült Izzó to reparations commissioner General Hermann Pokorni] 22 June 1945, MOL, Küm, Szu tük, XIX-J-1-j, IV-536, 30. doboz, ikt. sz. n.
50 Report by the Chief of the United States Military Representation on the Allied Control Commission for Hungary (Key), 6 June 1945, *FRUS*, 1945, vol. IV, p. 825.
51 A külügyminiszter feljegyzése [Memorandum by the foreign minister] 1945, undated, MOL, Küm, vegyes admin, XIX-J-1-k, 4/fh, 165. doboz, ikt. sz. n.
52 Aide Memoire,1945, undated, MOL, Küm, vegyes admin, XIX-J-1-k, 4/fh, 165. doboz 174/F.B. 1945.
53 Azon vállalatok jegyzéke, amelyeket a szovjet hatóságok teljesen vagy részben leszereltek és gépi berendezésüket elszállították, amelyek nem szerepelnek a

jóvátételi listán [List of companies partially or fully dismantled and taken by the Soviet authorities which do not appear on the list of reparations] 1945, undated, MOL, Küm, Szu tük, XIX-J-1-j, 31. doboz, IV-536/5, 116/45.

54 Feljegyzés az ipari miniszternek leszerelt gyárakról [Memorandum to the minister of industry on dismantled factories] 27 June 1945, MOL, XIX-F-1-b 44. doboz, ikt. sz. n.

55 Feljegyzés a Külügyminisztériumnak [Memorandum for the Foreign Ministry] 1950, undated, MOL, Küm, NDK tük, XIX-J-1-j, 20. doboz, ikt. sz. n.

56 The figure is quoted in Balogh–Földesi eds., *A magyar jóvátétel és ami mögötte van*, p. 10.

57 Ibid.

58 See Trachtenberg, *Constructed Peace*, pp. 15–33.

59 Bischof, *Austria in the First Cold War*, pp. 39–41; pp. 85–86.

60 Memorandum by the United States to the Hungarian Ministry of Foreign Affairs, 20 December 1945, MOL, Küm, Szu tük, XIX-J-1-j, IV-536/4, sz. n. 1945.

61 Otchet MID Vengrii posoltsvu SSSR v Vengrii [The Hungarian Foreign Ministry's note to the Soviet Embassy in Hungary] 21 July 1955, Arkhiv Vneshnei Politiki Rossiskoi Federatsii (hereafter cited as AVPRF) Fond 77 opis (op) 35 por 4 papka (pap) 45 delo (d) 14. According to the note the list of Austrian property in Hungary obtained by the Russians included 60 percent of Steyer–Austro–Daimler–Putsch, 78 percent of Hofherr and Schrantz, Hungary's most important maker of agricultural machinery, 100 percent of Julius Meinl (a delicacy chain), 100 percent of Wiener Allianz (insurance), 100 percent of Fellten és Guillaume (cable works), etc.

62 This article obliged Hungary to restore assets that were seized on United States territory by force or coercion, irrespectively of any later transaction, through which the present owner of those assets got hold of them.

63 A Szovjetuniónak átadott Magyar Általános Hitelbank részvényekkel kapcsolatos külföldről bejelentett igények [Foreign claims concerning the Hungarian General Credit Bank shares handed over to the Soviet Union]1947, undated, MOL, Küm, SZU tük, XIX-J-1-j, IV-510/c, 26. doboz ikt. sz. n.

64 The Minister in Hungary (Schoenfeld) to the Secretary of State, 31 January 1946, USNA, RG 59, 864.00/3146.

65 The Minister in Hungary (Schoenfeld) to the Secretary of State, 2 May 1946, *FRUS*, 1946, vol. VI, 1946. p. 293.

66 The Minister in Hungary (Schoenfeld) to the Secretary of State, 5 December 1945, *FRUS*, 1945, vol. IV, pp. 918–921.

67 The Representative in Hungary (Schoenfeld) to the Secretary of State, *FRUS*, 1945, vol. IV, p. 921.

68 The Minister in Hungary (Schoenfeld) to the Secretary of State, 2 February 1946, *FRUS*, 1946, vol, VI. pp. 256–257.

69 The Minister in Hungary (Schoenfeld) to the Secretary of State, 27 February 1946, *FRUS*, 1946, vol. VI, p. 263.

70 The Secretary of State to the Minister in Hungary (Schoenfeld), 2 March 1946, *FRUS*, 1946, vol. VI, p. 264.

71 Bischof, *Austria in the First Cold War*, p. 101.

72 The Minister in Hungary (Schoenfeld) to the Secretary of State, 2 May 1946, *FRUS*, 1946, vol. VI, pp. 293–294.

73 Memorandum of Conversation by Mr. Robert McKisson of the Division of South-East European Affairs, *FRUS*, 1946, vol. VI, pp. 347–348.

74 The Chargé in the Soviet Union (Kennan) to the People's Commissar of Foreign Affairs (Molotov), 2 March 1946, *FRUS*, 1946, vol. VI, pp. 265–267.

75 Kennan referred to the episode in his comments on the Novikov telegram. *Diplomatic History*, (Summer 1996), pp. 527–536.

76 István Vida, "Iratok a magyar kormányküldöttség 1946. évi amerikai látogatásának történetéhez," pp. 245–279.

77 Department of State Bulletin, 1946. pp. 229–232. The Hungarian gold reserve was taken out of Hungary in the last days of the war allegedly to save it from being captured by the Soviet army.

78 Ibid., pp. 263–265.

79 The Ambassador in Czechoslovakia (Steinhardt) to the Secretary of State, 26 February 1946, *FRUS*, 1946, vol. VI, pp. 185–188.

80 The Secretary of State to the Acting Secretary of State, 30 August 1946, *FRUS*, 1946, vol. VI, pp. 216–217.

81 The Acting Secretary of State to the Secretary of State, 21 September 1946, *FRUS*, 1946, vol. VI, p. 224.

82 A minisztertanács határozata [Resolution by the Council of Ministers] 18 December 1945, MOL, XIX-A-83-a, MT jkv.

83 Norman Naimark, *The Russians in Germany*, pp. 187–190.

84 The companies in question included Gróf Zichy Béla Urkuti Bányaművek (Count Béla Zichy Mines of Urkut), Hungary's main source of manganese; Dunavölgyi Timföldgyár Rt. (Dunavölgyi Aluminium Oxide Ltd.), Transdanubia Bauxit Rt. (Transdanubia Bauxite Ltd.), Alumínium Ércbánya Ipari Rt. (Aluminium Ore Industry Ltd.).

85 For example Poland was forced to deliver coal to the USSR at one tenth of the world market price. See Marer, "The 'Soviet Bloc' as an Integration Model," pp. 33–34. Of the Hungarian coal industry the Soviets took Urikány Zsilvölgy Magyar Szén Rt. (Urikány Zsilvölgy Hungarian Coal Ltd.), Felsőmagyarországi Bánya és Kohómű Rt. (Felsőmagyarországi Mine and Foundry Ltd.), Magyar Általános Kőszénbánya Rt. (General Hungarian Coal Ltd.), Salgótarjáni Szén Rt. (Salgótarján Coal Ltd.).

86 A miniszterelnök (Tildy) jegyzéke a SZEB elnökének (Vorosilov) [The Prime Minister's note to the Chairman of the ACC] 1945, undated, MOL, Küm, Szu tük, XIX-J-1-j, IV-536.4, 31. doboz, 96-615/II-1945.

87 The Representative in Hungary (Schoenfeld) to the Secretary of State (Marshall), 7 May 1947, USNA, RG 59, 864-50-15-749.

88 See chapter 3.

89 A Szovjetunió követelései Magyarország ellen [Soviet claims against Hungary], 23 May 1947, MOL, Küm, XIX-J-1-j, Szu tük, 30. doboz, IV-536/2. See also Nicholas Nyaradi, *My Ringside Seat in Moscow* (New York: Crowell, 1952), pp. 49–50.

90 See on this Fülöp, *Befejezetlen béke*, pp. 152–153.

91 See Nyaradi, *My Ringside Seat in Moscow*, p. 3, pp. 55–57, pp. 238–239. For the agreement see Jegyzőkönyv a magyar kormány által a Szovjetunió kormánya számára a magyar természetes és jogi személyeknek német jogi és természetes személyek iránti adósságának kifizetéséről [Protocol on payment by the Hungarian government to the Soviet government of the debt owed by Hungarian natural and legal persons to German natural and legal persons] 9 December 1947, MOL, Küm, XIX-J-1-j, Szu tük, IV-526.5, 28. doboz, ikt. sz. n.

92 Quoted in Péter Sipos and István Vida, "Az 1945. augusztus 27-én megkötött szovjet–magyar gazdasági egyezmény és a nyugati diplomácia," [The Soviet–Hungarian economic agreement of 27 August 1945 and Western Diplomacy] *Külpolitika*, 1985, No. 4., p. 102.

93 Ibid., p. 102.

94 MOL, Küm, Szu tük, XIX-J-1-j, IV-571/a, 37. doboz, ad 10 respol 1945.

95 The Representative in Hungary (Schoenfeld) to the Secretary of State, 6 October 1945, *FRUS*, 1945, vol. IV, p. 882.

96 Department of State Research and Analysis Branch, microfilm no. 3467.

97 Sipos and Vida, *Az 1945. augusztus 27-én megkötött szovjet-magyar gazdasági egyezmény*, p. 107.

98 The Secretary of State to the Representative in Hungary (Schoenfeld), *FRUS*, 1945, vol. IV, p. 887.

99 The Secretary of State to the Ambassador in the Soviet Union (Harriman), *FRUS*, 1945, vol. IV, pp. 888–889.

100 New York Times, 23 October 1945, p. 1.

101 The Representative in Hungary (Schoenfeld) to the Secretary of State, 25 October 1945, *FRUS*, 1945, vol. IV, p. 898.

102 The Secretary of State to the Representative in Hungary (Schoenfeld), 26 October 1945, *FRUS*, 1945, vol. IV, p. 899.

103 The Secretary of State to the Representative in Hungary (Schoenfeld), 16 November 1945, *FRUS*, 1945, vol. IV, pp. 908–909.

104 The Secretary of State to the Representative in Hungary (Schoenfeld), 26 November 1945, *FRUS*, 1945, vol. IV, p. 912.

105 For instance the Foreign Office failed in its effort to have the duty lowered on Hungarian turkey imported to Britain.

106 When meat is a nation's important export item, trade restriction imposed on it for animal health reasons often conceal more deep seated political disputes. The U.S. had such a dispute with Germany in the 19th century, Hungary also with Germany in the first half of the 1930s.

107 The Acting Secretary of State to the Ambassador in the Soviet Union (Harriman), 18 December 1945, *FRUS*, 1945, vol. IV, pp. 922–925.

108 Ibid.

109 Bischof, *Austria in the First Cold War*, p. 98.

110 Ibid., 97.

111 Feljegyzés a minisztertanácsról [Record of meeting of the Council of Ministers] 12 October 1945, in László Szűcs, ed., *Dálnoki Miklós Béla kormányának minisztertanácsi jegyzőkönyvei*, pp. 335–343.

112 The Representative in Hungary (Schoenfeld) to the Secretary of State, 21 December 1945, *FRUS*, 1945, vol. IV, p. 926.

113 The Minister in Hungary (Schoenfeld) to the Secretary of State, 15 February 1946, *FRUS*, 1946, vol. VI, pp. 258–260.

114 Ibid.

115 The Minister in Hungary (Schoenfeld) to the Secretary of State, 31 January 1946, USNA, RG 59, 864.00/1-3146.

116 Report on events in Hungary, 31 January 1946, USNA, RG 59, 864.00/1-3146.

117 As cited in Holsti, *International Politics*, pp. 282–283.

118 Nyaradi, *My Ringside Seat in Moscow*, p. 254.

119 Memorandum on Soviet economic penetration, 7 May 1947, USNA, RG 59, 864.50/5-747.

120 Jegyzőkönyv a minisztertanácsról [Record of meeting of the Council of Ministers] 12 October 1945, in Szűcs ed., *Dálnoki Miklós Béla kormányának minisztertanácsi jegyzőkönyvei*, p. 342.

121 See Bischof, *Austria in the First Cold War*, pp. 41–42.

122 Egyezmény a Magyar Kormány és a Szocialista Szovjet Köztársaságok Szövetségének Kormánya között Magyar–Szovjet Hajózási Társaság létesítéséről [Agreement between the Hungarian Government and the Government of the USSR on the establishment of Hungarian–Soviet Navigation Company] 29 March 1946, MOL, XIX-A-83-a, 9. doboz.

123 Interestingly enough this act is still in force. Törvényjavaslat a Magyar Köztársaság és a Szocialista Szovjetköztársaságok között Moszkvában az 1947. évi július hónap 15-én aláírt kereskedelmi és tengerhajózási szerződés becikkelyezéséről [Bill on the enactment of the 15 July 1947 commercial and maritime navigation agreement of Mosocw signed between the Republic of Hungary and the Soviet Socialist Republics] 17 July 1947, MOL, Küm, XIX-J-1-j, IV-571/b, 37. doboz, ikt. sz. n.

124 Memorandum on Soviet Economic Penetration, op. cit., and Minutes of a formal meeting of the ACC, 20 May 1947, in Cseh ed., *Documents of the Meetings of the Allied Control Commission in Hungary*, pp. 351–353.

125 See Eduard Mark, "The War Scare of 1946 and its Consequences," p. 395.

126 Feljegyzés a minisztertanácsról [Record of meeting of the Council of Ministers] 8 April 1946, MOL, XIX-A-83-a, MT jkv.

127 See Békés, *Dokumentumok a magyar kormánydelegáció 1946. áprilisi moszkvai tárgyalásairól*, pp. 161–194

128 Összefoglaló jelentés a vegyes magyar–orosz bauxit-aluminium társaságok alapítására vonatkozó tárgyalásokról [Summary of reports on talks concerning the establishment of joint Hungarian–Russian bauxite-aluminum companies] 10 April 1946, MOL, XIX-F-1-ll, 2. doboz, ikt. sz. n.

129 Egyezmény a Magyar Köztársaság Kormánya és a Szocialista Szovjet Köztársaságok Szövetségének Kormánya közötti Magyar–Szovjet Bauxit-Aluminium Társaságok létesítése tárgyában [Agreement between the Government of the Republic of Hungary and the Government of the Soviet Socialist Republics on the establishment of Hungarian–Soviet Bauxite-Aluminum Companies] 8 April 1946, MOL, Küm, Szu tük, XIX-J-1-j, IV-548, 34. doboz, 97 res/h 1946.

130 For the 1947 modification of the 1946 agreement see Jegyzőkönyv a Magyar-ország és a SZ. SZ. K. SZ. közötti gazdasági együttműködésről szóló az 1945. évi augusztus hónap 27. napján kelt egyezménynek megfelelően alakított Szovjet–Magyar társaságok, valamint a berlini egyezménynek megfelelően alakított Magyar–Szovjet vegyes társaságok, valamint a berlini háromhatalami értekezlet határozata alapján a Sz. Sz. Sz. K. tulajdonába átment vállalatok működésével kapcsolatban egyes kérdések rendezése tárgyában [Protocol on the settlement of certain questions concerning the operation of Soviet–Hungarian companies established according to the agreement of 27 August 1945, of the Hungarian–Soviet joint companies established in accordance with the tripartite Berlin agreement and of the companies that went into the ownership of the USSR on the basis of the resolution of the tripartite conference in Berlin] 9 December 1947, MOL, Küm, Szu tük, XIX-J-1-j, IV. 526-5, 28. doboz, ikt. sz. n.

131 In the first nine months of 1952 420, 000 tons went to the USSR. See: Bauxit export a Szovjetunióba [The export of bauxite to the Soviet Union] 1954, undated, MOL, XXIX-F-35, Maszobal, 240. doboz, ikt. sz. n.

132 Feljegyzés a MASZOBAL igazgatótanácsának üléséről [Record of meeting of the Board of Directors of Maszobal] 31 July 1948, MOL, XIX-F-1-s, 1. doboz, 3. tétel.

133 See Yegorova, *The "Iran Crisis" of 1945–1946*, p. 20.

134 Egyezmény a Magyar Köztársaság Kormánya és a Szocialista Szovjet Köztársaságok Szövetségének Kormánya között Magyar–Szovjet Nyersolaj Részvénytársaságok létesítése tárgyában [Agreement between the Government of the Republic of Hungary and the Government of the USSR on the establishment of Hungarian–Soviet Crude Oil Joint Stock Companies] 8 April 1946, MOL, Küm, Szu tuk, XIX-J-1-j, IV-548, 34. doboz, ikt. sz. n.

135 Ibid.

136 Jegyzőkönyv a Magyarország és a SZ. SZ K. SZ. közötti gazdasági együttműködésről szóló, az 1945. évi augusztus hónap 27. napján kelt egyezménynek megfelelően alakított Magyar–Szovjet Vegyestársaságok, valamint a Berlini Háromhatalmi Értekezlet határozatai alapján a SZ. SZ. K. SZ. tulajdonába átment vállalatok működésével kapcsolatos egyes kérdések rendezése tárgyában [Protocol on the Settlement of Certain Questions Concerning the Operation of Hungarian–Soviet Joint Companies Established in Accordance with the Agreement of 27 August 1945 between Hungary and the USSR and of the Companies transferred into the ownership of the USSR according to the Resolutions of the Tripartite Conference in Berlin] 9 December 1947, op. cit.

137 A magyar-szovjet gazdasági bizottság második, moszkvai ülésszaka. Az Állandó Bizottság második ülése [The Second, Moscow session of the Hungarian–Soviet economic committee. The second session of the Permanent Committee] 11 April 1949, MOL, Küm, Szu tük, XIX-J-1-j, IV-510/b, 26. doboz, ikt. sz. n..

138 Ibid.

139 Ibid.

140 Ibid.

141 Ibid.

142 Ibid.

143 The founders of the new Hungarian–Soviet Bauxite-Aluminium Joint Stock Company were the Hungarian Ministry of Heavy Industry and the Glavnoe Upravlenie Sovetskim Imuschestvo za Granitsei (Gusimz) operating under the Soviet Council of Ministers. The shares of the Hungarian–Soviet Oil Joint Stock Company were held by the same organs.

144 Egyezmény a Magyar Népköztársaság kormánya és a Szovjet Szocialista Köztársaságok Szövetségének kormánya között az Aluminiumércbánya és Ipar és a Magyar Bauxitbánya magyar-szovjet bauxit-aluminium részvénytársaságok egyesülése és egységes magyar-szovjet bauxit-aluminium részvénytársaság alapítása tárgyában [Agreement between the Government of the Hungarian People's Republic and the Government of the Union of Soviet Socialist Republics on the merger of the Hungarian–Soviet bauxite-aluminum joint stock companies Aluminiumércbánya és Ipar and Magyar Bauxitbánya and the establishment of a unified Hungarian–Soviet bauxite-aluminum joint stock company] 31 December 1949, MOL, Küm, Szu tük, XIX-J-1-j, IV-548.1, 35. doboz, ikt. sz. n.

145 A Magyar–Szovjet Gazdasági Vegyesbizottság Első Albizottságának 17. Ülése, Moszkva [The 17th session of the first subcommittee of the Hungarian–Soviet Mixed Economic Committee, Moscow] 13 July 1949, MOL, Küm, Szu tük, XIX-J-1-j, IV-510/b, 26. doboz, ikt. sz. n.

146 Melléklet, A Magyar Népköztársaság Kormánya és a Szovjet Szocialista Köztársaságok Szövetségének Kormánya között az Aluminium Ércbánya és Ipar és a Magyar Bauxitbánya magyar–szovjet bauxit-aluminium részvénytársaságok egyesülése és egységes magyar–szovjet bauxit-aluminium részvénytársaság alapítása tárgyában [Appendix, in the matter of the establishment between the Government of the People's Republic of Hungary and the Government of the Union of Soviet Socialist Republics of a unified Hungarian–Soviet bauxite-aluminum joint stock company and the merger of Aluminium Ércbánya és Ipar and Magyar Bauxitbánya] 31 December 1949, op. cit.

147 Jegyzőkönyv A Magyar Népköztársaság Kormánya és a Szovjet Szocialista Köztársaságok Szövetségének kormánya között az Aluminium Ércbánya és Ipar és a Magyar Bauxitbánya magyar–szovjet bauxit-aluminium részvénytársaságok egyesülése és egységes magyar–szovjet bauxit-aluminium társaság alapítása tárgyában [Protocol between the Government of the People's Republic of Hungary and the Government of the Union of Soviet Socialist Republics in the matter of the merger of Aluminium Ércbánya és Ipar and Magyar Bauxitbánya and the establishment of a unified Hungarian–Soviet bauxite-aluminum company] 31 December 1949, op. cit.

148 MOL, Küm, Szu tük, XIX-J-1-j, IV-548/3, 35. doboz, 1717 sz; and USNA, RG 59, 864. 053/7-1052 and 764.00/10-2152.

149 Department of State Research and Analysis Branch, microfilm no. 3467. See also: Géza Szurovy, *A kőolaj regénye* [The novel of oil] (Budapest, 1993).

150 Article 10 of the concession treaty provided that MAORT was obliged to satisfy Hungary's domestic demands only and to take into account Hungary's interests, but only if it can do so without causing harm to the company. See

Klára Katona, "A MAORT-per előtörténete" in György Gyarmati ed., *A Történeti Hivatal Évkönyve 2002* (Budapest: Történeti Hivatal, 2002), p. 143; p. 158.

151 See Szakács and Zinner, *A háború "megváltozott természete,"* p. 415; Klára Katona, "A MAORT-per előtörténete," p. 141.

152 Timár's personal recollection, cited in Szakács–Zinner, ibid., p. 417.

153 Gombosi was a member of the Board of Directors in five oil refineries and was the president of the Hungarian–Soviet Oil Company. In 1947 he was forced to resign because his currupt deals came to light. Katona, "A MAORT-per előtörténete," p. 143.

154 Szurovy, *A kőolaj regénye.* In 1946 oil production increased, but 60 percent of the natural gas was lost.

155 The Acting Secretary of State to the Representative in Hungary (Schoenfeld), 15 May 1945, *FRUS*, 1945, vol. IV, pp. 814–816.

156 A Külügyminisztérium feljegyzése [Memorandum by the Ministry of Foreign Affairs] July 1947, MOL, Küm, USA admin, 9. doboz, 4/a, ikt. sz. n; Nyersolajtermelés és MAORT felülvizsgálat [Grude oil production and MAORT investigation] 9 July 1947, MOL, 276 F., 68 cs., 73. őe.

157 General Key's memorandum on his special meeting with Marshal Voroshilov concerning the case of MAORT oil company, 24 January 1946, Cseh ed. *Documents of the Meetings of the Allied Control Committee in Hungary*, pp. 119–120.

158 Memorandum by the U.S. Legation in Budapest to Ministry of Foreign Affairs, MOL, Küm, USA admin, XIX-J-1-k, 4/a, 9. doboz, ikt. sz. n.

159 This meant that the Soviets felt entitled to MAORT under the Potsdam Declaration.

160 MOL, Küm, USA admin, XIX-J-1-k, 25/b, 55. doboz, 41132/4-6.

161 Szurovy, *A kőolaj regénye.*

162 Memorandum by the U.S. Legation in Budapest to the Ministry of Foreign Affairs, 6 April 1946, MOL, Küm, USA admin, XIX-J-1-k, 55. doboz, 3955 40739/4-1946.

163 Ibid.

164 Feljegyzés a Külügyminisztériumnak [Memorandum to the Ministry of Foreign Affairs], 1946, MOL, Küm, USA admin, XIX-J-1-k, 25/c, 55. doboz, 40.736/4-1946.

165 The Ministry of Foreign Affairs to the American Legation, 27 June 1946, MOL, KÜM, XIX-J-1-k, 25/c, 55. doboz, 41.133/4-1946.

166 Pető and Szakács, *A hazai gazdaság négy évtizedének története*, p. 74.

167 The Secretary of State (Marshall) to the Legation in Budapest, 29 May 1947, USNA, RG 59, 864.5034/5-2947.

168 Negotiations between the Hungarian and the U.S. governments, 16 July 1948, USNA, RG 59, 711. 64/7-1648.

169 Negotiations between the Hungarian and the U.S. governments, USNA, RG 59, 711.64/8-1248.

170 Article 30 provided that those Hungarian goods which had been forcefully taken away by the German army or authorities after 20 January 1945 had to be restored

to Hungary. Article 26 obliged Hungary to restore property belonging to the United Nations on its territory "as it now exists."

171 Discussion between Zoltán Vas and Harrison Lewis of the U.S. Legation, 21 May 1948, USNA, RG 59, 864.50/5-2148.

172 The U.S. minister in Hungary (Selden Chapin) to the State Department, 14 May 1948 USNA, RG 59, 711. 64/5-1448.

173 MOL, Küm, USA admin, XIX-J-1-k, 43 af, 9. doboz, ikt. sz. n.

174 The Deputy Director of the European Department (Hickerson) to the Deputy Secretary of State (Lovett), 22 November 1948, *FRUS*, 1948, vol. IV, p. 391.

175 MOL, Küm, USA admin, XIX-J-1-k, 23/d, 51. doboz, 6151.

176 MOL, Küm, USA admin, XIX-J-1-k, 23/d, 51. doboz, 9727.

177 MOL, Küm, XIX-J-1-j, USA admin, 23/d, 51. doboz, 12619.

178 MOL, Küm, USA admin, XIX-J-1-k, 3. doboz, 4/a ikt. sz. n.

179 Ibid.

180 Papp Simon ügye [The Simon Papp affair], 18 August 1948, MOL, 276. F., 67. cs., 155. őe.

181 Bannantine vallomása [Bannantine's confession], 19 September 1948, Ibid; Paul Ruedemann vallomása [Paul Ruedemann's confession] 20 September 1948, Ibid.

182 A gazdasági tanács feljegyzése [Memorandum of the economic committee], 9 July 1947, MOL, 276. F., 68. cs., 73 őe.

183 Jegyzőkönyv az MDP PB üléséről [Record of meeting of the MDP PB], 23 September 1948, MOL, 276. F., 53. cs., 10. őe.

184 Feljegyzés Kertay György kihallgatásáról [Memorandum of György Kertay's interrogation], 29 August 1948, MOL, 276. F., 67. cs, 155. őe.

185 Timár ezredes jelentése [Colonel Timár's report], 26 August 1948, MOL, 276. F., 67. cs., 155. őe.

186 Ibid.

187 Jegyzőkönyv az MDP PB üléséről, 23 September 1948, MOL, 276 F., 53. Cs, 10. őe.

188 MOL, Küm, USA admin, XIX-J-1-k, 11. doboz, 4/bd.

189 Lichtheim, *Imperialism*, p. 26.

CHAPTER V

EMPIRE BY COERCION

Towards the end of 1949 the bipolar structure of the world had already taken shape. Both the United States and the USSR had decided that there was no longer any ground for their cooperation, and moreover that to do so would threaten their own world position. Hence the most pressing issues that faced the victor powers remained unresolved. No collective peace treaty was signed with Japan, and Germany ended up as two separate states. German division was not premeditated, but with hindsight, it was probably inevitable.[1] As early as the Potsdam Conference, the U.S. had given up the idea of running Germany on a quadripartite basis because Secretary of State Byrnes had come to believe that cooperation with the USSR on the basis of common goals was not possible. After the Potsdam conference American policy in Germany was totally transformed, and this transformation—the idea that Germany and the rest of Europe would not be divided on a friendly basis—set the major powers at odds with each other.[2] It is also likely that Stalin and Molotov, in fear of a strong, remilitarized West Germany, kept on hoping for a united Germany with Soviet military presence until Stalin's note of 1952 was turned down by the Western powers. Stalin's successors would have been willing even to accept a unified and demilitarized Germany in order to avoid the FRG's membership in NATO and the EDC.[3] World politics seemed now to function as a zero sum game: a loss for one superpower was a gain for the other.

A case in point was China, where Mao Zedong's victory meant the "loss" of the country to the United States. Stalin exploited the victory of Mao's Communist movement by signing a pact of friendship that guaranteed military, political and economic gains for the Soviet Union. It is true that Moscow recognized Chinese sovereignty and the treaty reflected Mao's desire to preserve as much freedom of action and flexibility as possible in foreign policy matters and gave China license to operate on its own in matters concerning Asia.[4] In Korea the great powers got embroiled in unintended confrontation. Soon after the Sino-Soviet pact was concluded, the Kremlin, acting in the belief that a revolutionary situation existed in Korea, lent support to the North Korean dictator's attack on South Korea. Stalin, who thought that a friendly regime in the whole Korean peninsula was

needed in order to prevent a seemingly inevitable Japanese revanchist invasion of the Soviet Union, agreed to support Kim Il-sung. Moscow acted on
the basis of an assumption that the U.S. would not intervene.[5] This assumption was proven false when Washington launched a counter-attack under
UN auspices. The lessons of European diplomacy in the late 1930s and the
memory of the Japanese takeover of Manchuria shaped the American interpretation of the Korean War. In the late 1930s Western powers made the
mistake of taking each of Hitler's aggressive actions—the Anschluss, the
partition of Czechoslovakia—as his final move. As it later turned out, these
were only stepping stones toward more ambitious goals. Hence the U.S.
regarded the North Korean aggression as a mere prelude to further Communist expansion elsewhere orchestrated by Moscow.[6] Ignoring the actions of
Kim Il-sung would have entailed the risk of his aggression paying off, and
could have led to the collapse of self-confidence in the West. Truman was
sensitive to the loss of China and was personally committed to collective
security.[7] The Korean invasion hence gave a strong impetus for the United
States to drastically increase its military preparedness.[8]

Eastern Europe by this time had no hope for such American involvement and remained firmly under Soviet control. Political relations between
East and West were so hostile that virtually no contact was left between
them. Communication degenerated into mutually slanderous political cam-
paigns; the Soviet "lager" lined up behind the Soviet Union in all international questions. In fact the people's democracies by and large identified
their interests with those of the Soviet Union, and they were ready to shelve
mutual grievances—such as the fate of national minorities and territorial
disputes—to increase bloc solidarity.[9] Still, in 1948 a rift had appeared
within the Soviet bloc itself—Josip Broz Tito's otherwise Stalinist Yugoslavia was ostracized from the community of fraternal nations. Moscow's
allies slavishly followed the abrupt anti-Yugoslav course, even though for
instance Rákosi had praised Tito's policies. Minor armed clashes occurred
on the Hungarian–Yugoslav border in spite of the fact that the two countries
had signed a treaty of friendship in 1948. The Soviet bloc embarked on a
campaign of military build-up in 1948. Economic militarization was accelerated bloc-wide in January 1951 as a result of Stalin's decision,[10] which
aimed at forcing the newly created people's democracies to share the burden of preparing for the seemingly inevitable military conflict with the
"imperialists."

There was a fundamental difference in the attitude of Stalin and his
successors towards East Germany on the one hand and Eastern Europe on
the other. Except for a brief period between the spring of 1952 and Stalin's
death in March 1953 the "construction of socialism" in East Germany was
not Moscow's preferred option in the GDR. A united Germany remained

a preferable alternative to the two-state solution. This changed only after Beria's demise.[11] The introduction of the Soviet system in Eastern Europe was sanctioned in 1946 and accomplished by 1949. As Soviet policy towards Hungary will show, there is no indication that Moscow intended to make even the slightest concession on its grip on Eastern Europe.

The continental division involved economic relations. On the one hand the U.S. introduced an economic embargo against the Soviet bloc in 1948. America's European allies joined it reluctantly. Simultaneously, the Soviet Union, which had failed to secure East–West trade on its own terms, imposed a policy of economic autarchy on its allies and made preparations for close economic cooperation and even coordination among the members of the Soviet orbit.[12] Although the U.S. imposed embargo was never watertight, and the two halves of the continent remained economically interdependent, the Soviet bloc did remain largely outside the world economy. The flow of ideas and people came to a standstill: Western ideas reached people behind the iron curtain only illegally, through Western radio broadcasts and leaflets disseminated by balloons, and except for limited travel for business purposes East Europeans were not allowed to visit the non-Communist world. In these respects the Soviet border was extended to the satellite states.

There have been few studies of Soviet–Hungarian relations. This may seem surprising since the fate of Hungary was so closely intertwined with the Soviet Union that Hungarian history in the early 1950s is virtually unintelligible without a discussion of this relationship.[13] This chapter will analyze Soviet–Hungarian relations in the light of new research. The following questions will be asked. First, how was Hungary governed? What tools did the Soviets use to ensure that Hungary complied with the expectations of the dominant power? What kind of political climate was it in which Hungarian political leaders, those who were willing and able to meet those expectations, acted? Through an analysis of Soviet–Hungarian relations, this chapter will attempt to shed light on Hungary's role within the Soviet Empire. Moreover, what exactly was it that the Soviet Union expected of Hungary? Why did the Soviet Union want to exercise total control over a seemingly minor power like Hungary, even at the cost of squandering the political capital the USSR had as the liberator, not oppressor of colonized peoples?[14] Answering these questions should enable us to answer the third and final question; that is, what were the motives behind the Soviet Union's occupation of Hungary in the first place?

This chapter is divided into three segments. The first deals with the way Hungary was governed. It examines the institutional aspects of Soviet–Hungarian relations. Hungary's political and economic structure will show the relationship between ideological and practical affairs, i.e. the construction of a utopian social system and the satisfaction of a foreign power's imperial goals. The second part deals with the services Hungary provided for the dominant power. Finally, the third will discuss how the Soviet Union dealt with critical situations such as the revolution of 1956.

Politics

Octogon is a bustling square in Budapest, lined with eclectic and neo-renaissance buildings. It was built between 1872 and 1874 and was named after its geometrical shape. Later it was rechristianed after Stalin, then 7 November to remind Hungarians that the Bolshevik revolution was their historical reference. These names reflected Hungary's position in international politics. Now, following the Soviet withdrawal the square is called Octogon again. Today it shows a different reality. There are American fast food restaurants, demonstrating perhaps the different concepts of empire building of the two great powers. One power was widely rejected; the other is by and large accepted, perhaps even popular. But the point is not only that Moscow's rule was rejected by the Hungarian people. The Soviets wanted control, popularity did not matter. If the American Empire in Western Europe was in Geir Lundestad's phrase an "empire by invitation," the Soviet one in Hungary was undoubtedly an empire by coercion.

The Soviet imposition of Stalinism on the countries of Eastern Europe introduced a large degree of economic and political uniformity to nations with such divergent backgrounds as Czechoslovakia or Bulgaria by creating political systems that could exist only through complete economic and political dependence on the Soviet Union. The imposition of Stalinism sought to shape societies to the Soviet Union's image by attempting to destroy social autonomy.[15] Explained in terms of *Realpolitik*, the export of Stalinism allowed the Kremlin to dominate Eastern Europe. As a result, the Communist rulers of Eastern Europe had no alternative but to offer their unconditional loyalty to Stalin and his successors if they wished to remain in power.[16]

In the case of Hungary's Communist leadership, the key to Soviet control was an almost unquestioning ideological obedience and deference to the Soviets, although it occasionally gave priority to Hungary's national interests. The role of ideological commitment cannot be overestimated, and it was exactly this commitment which made the real difference in the control the Soviets had before and after the Communist seizure of power. Non-Communists, no matter how friendly to the Soviets, would not have thought of Soviet control as a desirable condition. Even a reform-minded Communist like Imre Nagy shelved dissent for the sake of pro-Soviet loyalty.

This in turn made continuous and direct Soviet interference in Hungarian internal affairs unnecessary. All the more so, since the Hungarian party first secretary Mátyás Rákosi and possibly other leaders as well sought policy guidance from the Soviet Union, sometimes even directly from Stalin, on a regular basis. As Rákosi explained in his memoirs, in Communist usage "advice" in actual fact meant "instruction."[17] In this sense there was no difference between reformers such as Nagy and dogmatic Stalinists like Rákosi. Both were ready to request Soviet mediation to decide domestic disputes, in fact Nagy is known to have initiated a Soviet arbitration to settle scores with his rival, Rákosi in January 1954.[18] Soviet ambassadors communicated the Kremlin's wishes in the form of recommendations and advice.[19] Moreover Communist functionaries used the Soviet ambassador in their domestic struggle for power. Of course this was complemented by the "hard" components of Soviet presence in Hungary: apart from Soviet troops, there were the significant number of advisors who worked in all the ministries, the army and the political police and economic establishments.

The significance of voluntary obedience is demonstrated by the fact that Hungarian leaders actually requested Soviet advisors, rather than having them imposed by Moscow.[20] Occasionally the Soviets did not send their advisors on time and the Hungarians had to urge them to do so.[21] This reveals what was meant by loyalty and unreserved commitment to the Soviet Union. However, this did in no way alter the fact that the Soviet Union directly determined the domestic politics of its satellites, Hungary included. An internal phenomenon in the USSR altered Soviet external policy, which in turn "had profound effects in internal developments in the countries of East-Central Europe,"[22] which is not to say, that Soviet policy alone was responsible for changes within the satellites. In addition Soviet economic predominance in itself provided political leverage.

In spite of all the efforts of the Kremlin and its Hungarian allies, the exercise of Soviet power over Hungary was by no means perfect, and it suffered from a considerable degree of misunderstanding between the two powers. Hungarians were sometimes unable to read the Kremlin's intentions and therefore made "mistakes" that they had to rectify upon Soviet request. A case in point was the establishment of a Hungarian Institute of Foreign Cultural Affairs based on the model of the Soviet Vsesoiuznaia Obschestvo Kulturnikh Sviazei (VOKS). Moscow protested because it regarded the Institute as the rival of the Soviet–Hungarian Friendship Association. It wanted the Friendship Association to monopolize bilateral cultural relations, and asserted that the Institute of Foreign Cultural Affairs would undermine Soviet–Hungarian friendship.[23] Moreover, Hungary tended to be over-anxious in implementing practice the tenets of Stalinism, which sometimes had an adverse effect on the Soviet–Hungarian relationship. For example, the fact that what appeared to be an excessive number of people having been imprisoned as enemies of the state was interpreted by the Soviet Union as a threat to the political stability of Hungary. The relationship also became tense on occasion due to sheer incompetence on the part of Hungary, since it often found itself unable to deliver the goods Moscow wished to purchase despite repeated Soviet protests.

During the 1950s, Hungary was arguably not a sovereign state. Hedley Bull described the relationship between the USSR and its satellites as hegemonic in the descending hierarchy of dominance, hegemony and primacy. But considering that the Kremlin changed the Hungarian leadership in 1953 without having to resort to violence and used Hungary for political, military and economic services, this relationship may have been what Bull classified as the stronger form of mastery, most flagrant "exploitation of preponderance, dominance."[24] Stephen Krasner articulated the Westphalian definition of sovereignty as an "institutional arrangement for organizing political life that is based on two principles: territoriality and the exclusion of external factors from domestic structures," which is violated either by voluntary or coercive action, that is intervention and invitation.[25] Based on these criteria Hungary's sovereignty was violated because it was subjected to external sources of authority. Similarly, according to Kenneth Waltz "to say that a state is sovereign means that it decides for itself how it will cope with its external and internal problems including whether or not to seek assistance from others and in doing so to limit its freedom by making commitments to them." That is to say sovereignty is violated by coercion. While Waltz appreciates that there could normally be constraints on nations' freedom of action, he does not regard a nation as sovereign unless it has surrendered its freedom of action voluntarily.[26] Hungary did not do so "voluntarily" in its literal meaning, since its leaders, who sought Soviet guidance for their actions, needed to be loyal to the Kremlin if they wished to remain in power. The Rákosi regime owed its existence and its highly centralized political structure to Moscow, and therefore Soviet control violated Hungarian sovereignty even by Waltz's standards.

The relationship between the two nations was never formalized.[27] The absence of any legal "arrangement" allowed the Soviet Union to use its leverage to meddle in Hungarian internal affairs with ease, without having to worry about breaching any formal agreement. Occasionally the Hungarian leadership invited Moscow's political intervention to settle its own domestic feuds. Furthermore, since the nation's "rights" and "obligations" remained undefined, the Hungarians had no method of expressing their grievances even if they were sometimes reluctant to comply with Soviet desiderata. Even under these conditions Soviet control required legitimacy. The aim was to create a common historical bondage and mission for the future so as to conceal the exploitative nature of the Soviet–Hungarian relationship.

Many Hungarians referred to the Soviet occupation of 1945 as a negative turning point. People in Budapest spoke of it as "before" and "after the siege." A government decree transformed it into something altogether positive by designating 4 April Hungary's liberation from German occupation. This date was from then on "the most decisive change in Hungary's thousand-year-long history," when the Soviet army "liberated the country from foreign, imperialist oppression." Hungarian independence was restored, which "opened the way [...] toward the construction of socialism." "Liberation day" was "the celebration of the Hungarian people's never ending gratitude, hot love, loyalty as a friend and ally toward its liberator, role model, protector of its independence, the leading defender of peace and its chief supporter, the Soviet Union, the Soviet Army and towards the teacher and true friend of our people and progressive humanity, the great Stalin."[28] Soviet occupation became a "stunde null"; the beginning of history, guaranteeing that historical development would come to fruition in the form of Communism. Since most people did not come to share the belief in this myth, the foundations of the regime remained shaky in spite of the hard power that stood behind it.

Hungary adopted a Stalinist political structure in both a formal and bureaucratic sense. At the same time, the political system in Hungary in the early 1950s amounted to not much more than the rule of Rákosi and perhaps two more of his political associates. The Rákosi regime made important political and military appointments only after consultation with the Soviets. For example, in 1950, the Chief of Staff of the Hungarian army was appointed "in agreement with the Soviet advisor comrades."[29] In a time of crisis, in June 1953, Moscow intervened directly to implement significant change in the make-up of the Hungarian leadership, and to steer the country onto a new political course.

The putatively highest decision-making organ of the party and the state, the Political Committee was seldom, if ever consulted on important policy issues. In June 1953, when Moscow demoted Rákosi, the members of the Politburo expressed their frustration that they had not been consulted on political matters prior to that time. According to one PB member, Károly Kiss, Rákosi and his associates had decided on issues of national importance in an informal fashion, often in private conversations. They did not rely on the Political or the Central Committee.[30] Soviet Ambassador Evgenii Kiselev remembered that "Rákosi was extremely stubborn and headstrong. He listened to nobody. Neither to his associates nor to him (Kiselev) or to Soviet state and party leaders except Stalin [...] (Kiselev) was never i nformed of the contents of Rákosi's private conversations with Stalin and was thus in a delicate situation since he had no way of knowing whether or not Rákosi's actions were based on a private arrangement with Stalin."[31]

In 1950, on Stalin's advice, a Committee of Defense was created, which included three members: Rákosi, Farkas and Gerő.[32] This committee was in charge of all issues related to political and economic affairs as well as national defense but was not responsible to any other authority. After 1953 the situation changed in the sense that several momentous political issues were decided *in* the Political Committee, including the political fates of Imre Nagy, Rákosi and Farkas. This was because Rákosi, as a result of the criticism he received in Moscow, was forced to return to "party democracy." Soon, however, Kiselev reported that Rákosi was returning to his old ways. On some occasions as in the critical deliberations on the fate of Rákosi in July 1956, a Soviet representative, Anastas Mikoyan participated in the discussion of the Political Committee, and influenced, but did not determine, the outcome.

Communication with the Kremlin was conducted through several channels. Contact with Stalin was Rákosi's own domain, and he preferred to travel to Moscow alone. Otherwise an obvious choice of communication was the Soviet embassy. This channel was most actively used during the summer of 1956, when the then Soviet ambassador in Budapest, Iurii Andropov, frequently consulted with Hungarian party leaders. Andropov's reports had a strong impact on Soviet thinking on the Hungarian crisis. Party leaders often used this channel to convey their views to Moscow. A more direct point of contact with the Kremlin was offered by a safe high frequency line, which connected the Party's first secretary to the Stalin secretariat. In Hungary such a line was installed in 1949, but other high frequency lines had already existed in Sofia for Dimitrov, and two were operational in Warsaw for Hilary Minc and the Polish Party's Central Committee. In Hungary this line of communication had already been at the disposal of the Soviet ambassador and the military attaché.[33] The first Hungarian record for its use dates from 1953 but it had almost certainly been used beforehand.[34] Rákosi is also known to have sent messages to the Kremlin in ciphered telegrams in Russian, the texts of which survive in Rákosi's red, hardbound diaries. These were addressed to "comrade Filipov." The Hungarian party chief asked for Moscow's policy guidance in twenty-two such messages, and since the addressee seldom bothered to answer, Moscow's silence was probably taken as consent.[35] Rákosi also sent letters, which were delivered by political emissaries. As with the ciphered telegrams these contained proposals and requests. Finally Stalin saw the party chief personally in Moscow or elsewhere in the Soviet Union on eight or nine occasions.

Unfortunately no written records of these meetings have yet been found. Lower level communication, for example between Hungarian ministries and their Soviet counterparts, was conducted through Soviet advisors.

Rákosi was surrounded by a cult of adulation, but he was only a "disciple" of Stalin's, even if, as he himself put it, the best one. Indeed, the international hierarchy was scrupulously observed by the state-controlled media. For example in 1951 the First Congress of the Hungarian Writers resolved that "contemporary Hungarian literature owes its success to the existence of the Soviet Union, the great Stalin and the triumphant Soviet Army."[36] Earlier on, as a reminder of the relations of power, Moscow's representatives in Budapest had unjustly criticized Gerő, Farkas and Rákosi for disregarding the interests of the Soviet Union in economic, cultural and propaganda affairs and for allegedly distancing themselves from the USSR and for deviating from "the correct line" toward a "nationalist" tendency.[37] The first secretary of the Hungarian Workers Party did his best to follow what he thought Stalin, whom he thought was the most suitable person to lead the CPSU, would expect him to do.[38] Rákosi's recently published memoirs attest to the fact, that like Molotov,[39] he remained a loyal Stalinist to the end. He devoted his life to the great cause and nothing would stand in his way. He regretted nothing he had done.

Although Rákosi knew his own and his country's limits, this did not mean that the Hungarian Communists and Rákosi personally did not have their own agendas. As for economic and financial issues, the Hungarian Communists were determined to assert their interests *vis-à-vis* those of the Soviet Union and tried to reduce the size of payments the Soviets demanded under various pretexts, but with almost no success. On at least two occasions they sought to protect the interests of the Hungarian minority in Slovakia after the Treaty of Friendship had been signed with Czechoslovakia, possibly to appease the Hungarian populists whom Révai sought to win over for the Communist cause. Rákosi objected to the Slovakian policy towards the Hungarian national minority, which "contradicted the Stalinist nationality policy, as well as the treatment of Hungarians in Romania and the Soviet Union." He criticized an article published in *Novoe Vremia*, describing its call for the limitation of the political rights of the Hungarian minority in Slovakia as "harmful." He demanded that the journal publicly renounce this "incorrect attitude." The party's chief ideologist, József Révai, asked his Soviet counterpart, Mikhail Suslov whether the Hungarians could raise the issue in the Informburo and asked for the help of the "fraternal parties" to resolve it. Suslov, however, recommended a bilateral approach.[40] It was all right to ask for political favors, but these were not necessarily granted. When a dispute with Romania arose over the same issue, Rákosi was loyal enough to the international Communist movement to support Bucharest's anti-Hungarian policy even though he disagreed with it.[41]

Some of Rákosi's initiatives suggest that he might have been after regional leadership. Rákosi sought to play an active role against Tito's Yugoslavia. He made recommendations as to the publication of an émigré Yugoslav paper to be edited in Moscow, or in one of the people's democracies—no doubt he was thinking of Hungary. He sought to organize a "unified Yugoslav center" and an illegal Communist party on Yugoslav territory and even suggested the establishment of military partisan activity against his southern neighbor.[42] On another occasion he proposed an armed struggle against Tito.[43] Interesting as these initiatives seem, it is important to note that the Hungarian regime never took any action without Moscow's approval.

Rákosi's anti-Yugoslav fervor stemmed in part from the need to rectify his previous pro-Yugoslav stance that had suddenly become unpalatable. His handling of László Rajk, his most potent domestic rival, was a case in point. It was in Rajk's show trial that Rákosi attempted to stretch Moscow's not exactly elastic leash the farthest and where his personal ambitions—as well as those of Farkas—became most apparent. Similar trials were taking place all over Eastern Europe, in Bulgaria, Albania, Poland and the Soviet Union itself. Although the Rajk trial was directly or indirectly initiated by the Soviet MGB, the Hungarian side and Rákosi in particular orchestrated the political campaign that accompanied the trial, did the selection of the defendants, made up some of the trial's motives as well as the sentences.[44]

Not all show trials in Eastern Europe ended with the execution of the defendants. While Rajk was tortured to obtain the necessary confession based on which the case was prepared, in Poland Gomułka was arrested only in 1951, was not tortured and did not confess to anything either. The Polish authorities could not come up with a case against him and Gomułka avoided Rajk's fate.[45] The idea that Rajk had been a police agent under Horthy came from the political police, while the other accusation, namely that the former minister of the interior was a Titoist agent, was developed by the MGB and Rákosi. Rákosi had no way of knowing that his role in the show trial would contribute to his political downfall. At the time it seemed to provide him a chance to refute some Soviet accusations. These were directed at Rákosi's position in the struggle against Hungarian Trockists, which was "incorrect" and allegedly was "impeding" the struggle of the Soviet and Hungarian security organs against them. The two security services hoped to "reveal" the international connotations of the Rajk case, thereby "helping" to "unmask" the enemy that had wormed its way into the ranks of the fraternal parties.[46]

To counter these allegations, Rákosi claimed that "a unified spy ring" existed in the people's democracies, "especially in Czechoslovakia."[47] He passed details and lists of alleged spies to Prague, Bucharest and Warsaw. His main target was Czechoslovakia and Czechoslovak party leader, Klement Gottwald in particular, whom he accused of doing nothing about unmasking spies and enemies in his party. There may even have been a personal motive involved, given Rákosi's anger at Gottwald's unrelenting campaign against the Hungarians in Slovakia, and the fact that for a long time Gottwald had refused to negotiate with the Hungarian Communists. In a letter to Gottwald, Rákosi named sixty-five alleged Anglo-American spies. Rákosi sent his brother, Zoltán Bíró, as his personal envoy to Prague, where Bíró charged that the Czechoslovak Minister of the Interior Nosek as well as the Minister of Defense Svoboda were spies.[48] Rákosi warned the Soviets that the Hungarians had "unmasked as spies such people as Nosek and Clementis," but "the Soviet organs and authorities give little assistance, what is more, they sometimes do not pay enough attention to the numerous spy groups that were arrested by the Hungarians."[49] He never received an answer.

The function of terror

The function of terror in a Stalinist society, according to George Schopflin, was to enforce compliance, destroy preexisting values, to break down preconceptions, to make it easier for the new revolutionary values to take root and to facilitate the politicization of society. Stalinism was an ideology of perfection; hence there could be, by definition, no problems that could not be solved. If a solution should fail, failure could be attributed not to the ideology, but to antagonists. Consequently, there was no place for error, there were no accidents or honest mistakes.[50]

It is hard to discover any kind of pattern among the victims of terror, which included former aristocrats, impoverished peasants, unskilled workers or university professors. The political police (ÁVH) answered only to Rákosi and were beyond control. The ÁVH terrorized the local population to such an extent that even Gerő complained about its actions. "Under the leadership of (ÁVH leader) Gábor Péter" Gerő once told the Soviet ambassador, "it did not matter to the ÁVH whether one was guilty or not."[51] Péter was the son of a poor Jewish family burdened with mental disability, was of low intellect and undereducated. After receiving training to be a tailor he joined the Communist Party. Traveling to Moscow he was recruited by the GPU, whose founder, Felix Dzherzhinskii, was Péter's role model. Subsequently Péter took control of the Hungarian party's counter intelligence and emerged as a leading figure of the domestic fraction of the Communist Party during World War II. Unscrupulous to the utmost, as the leader of the political police he arrested even the person who saved his life in the war. Péter played a crucial role in the show trials of 1949 and remained the all but omnipotent leader of the ÁVH till his arrest on New Year's Eve in 1953.[52]

The persecution of "class alien elements" was motivated only in part by ideological crusade. There were also other considerations. In 1950 approximately 10 thousand families that belonged to the "former ruling classes" were evicted from their homes in Budapest and deported to the countryside to perform agricultural labor. Propaganda depicted this event as a chapter in class struggle. This may have been so but the immediate cause was the lack of adequate housing for the growing number of police and army officers. Since the people that were thrown out were usually wealthy, their homes were suitable for the emerging new elite. Ultimately terror, no matter how irrational it appeared, was designed to uphold the political system.

Rákosi's campaign against enemies inside and outside the party was in tune with the Stalinist dogma of the sharpening of the class struggle and was meant to consolidate the regime. "Political consolidation and the increase of the class struggle were not contradictory conditions," argued the chief ideologist, József Révai. According to his explanation "as the enemy weakens its resistance grows" simultaneously. As another leading functionary put it, "on the higher stage of development class struggle intensifies" and this was something "inescapable."[53] Hungary was not alone in its quest to get rid of the "class enemy." Class struggle was said to be on the constant rise in Poland as well, where this dogma was introduced in 1948 as a method to combat "right wing nationalist deviations" and to fight enemies within and outside the party.[54] The Soviets noticed that Budapest's unrestrained persecution of political enemies had the opposite effect. Instead of consolidation it led to increased resentment of the regime. Occasionally, as the historian János M. Rainer observed, the Kremlin might even have exercised some restraint on the head of the HWP. Notably, Stalin vetoed the dismissal of Péter and Mihály Farkas. "Why do you want to shoot Farkas? What is wrong with Gábor Péter?" he asked. When the proconsul started to list their mistakes, Stalin waved him down and told him to "leave them alone." Rákosi could make nothing of his patron's unexpected resistance and convinced himself that his two prospective victims had got wind of what was in the making and alerted their patrons, Bulganin and Beria respectively, to save them.[55] Others were not so lucky.

On 2 June 1950 Rákosi mentioned to the Soviet ambassador the need to arrest 500 Social Democrats in the "near future" and to "organize concentration camps for them." It did not make a difference whether they were right or left wing, they were, according to Rákosi "all the same, informers all of them."[56] He later informed Stalin of his desire to arrest two former leaders the Social Democratic Party, György Marosán and István Ries and to organize open trials for them. Stalin agreed to their arrest, but insisted on a closed trial.[57] Terror soon caught up with those that helped build the police state. These included former president Árpád Szakasits, the ex-minister of the interior János Kádár and his successor, Sándor Zöld, foreign minister, Gyula Kállai and even the deputy head of the political police, Ernő Szűcs. Zöld was aware of what was in store for him when he was dismissed by the party boss at a meeting of the Political Committee on 20 April 1951. He went home, killed his family and committed suicide.[58]

Heavy purges were carried out in the army and the air force. In early 1951 many airforce officers were arrested and accused of "systematically disabling aircraft."[59] Persecution began with the cleansing of "bourgeois saboteurs" in 1948 followed by the trial of Archbishop Mindszenty and László Rajk in 1949 and the proceedings against "left wing Social Democrats." The trials of army generals then followed. In the course of the proceedings against László Sólyom, 44 people were convicted, of whom ten were executed.[60] The continuing struggle against "clerical reaction" was marked by the trial of Archbishop József Grősz. It is not hard to see that the proceedings followed the pattern of similar trials as they developed in the Soviet Union during the 1930s. In the implementation of terror against real and imagined "hostile elements," Hungary followed the Soviet model not only because Moscow required it, but also because the country's rulers believed in the dictatorship of the proletariat. Rákosi agreed with Lenin's definition: 'Rule founded on violence unconstrained by law'.[61] Even at the end of his life Rákosi still believed that Stalin's definition of the kulaks was valid. Terror in the Soviet Union had an immediate impact on Hungary.

On 13 January 1953 *Pravda* informed its readers that the Soviet security organs had unmasked a group of Zionist murderers. The "Zionist doctors" were allegedly in the service of an "international Jewish bourgeois–nationalist organization, Joint, which had been established by American intelligence services." Hungary's Communist daily, *Szabad Nép* carried *Pravda*'s account of the Zionist plot. On 11 February 1953, a few days after a bomb exploded at the Soviet embassy in Israel, sparking off massive arrests of Jewish intellectuals in the Soviet Union, Rákosi delivered a speech at a session of the Hungarian Workers Party Politburo on the Zionist threat. Rákosi, who was Jewish himself, and must have been feeling the heat as a result of the Soviet anti-Semitic campaign, had already expressed anti-Semitic sentiments in the Communist struggle for power, accused the United States of "mobilizing Zionism and Israel" and of stepping up the activity of spies and saboteurs in the people's democracies.[62] One would think, Rákosi claimed, that the Catholic Church was the largest center of intelligence; but in reality, "because Jews are everywhere," Zionism was the real center of espionage. Rákosi also claimed that in the Rajk trial most of the ones who were sentenced to death there were "petit-bourgeois Jews," in fact the original Hungarian concept had been to launch a campaign against "Jewish cosmopolitans." Rákosi alluded to the recent arrest of the Jewish chief of the political police, Gábor Péter, whom he accused of having worked with police informers who were either Nazis or Zionists. Finally, Rákosi pledged to "investigate" whether Zionists had infiltrated the party's midst, of which he was "convinced." He called for increased vigilance in view of the fact that for example the president of the Israelite church in Budapest had "turned out" to be a former "spy of the Gestapo."

Preparations for a large anti-Semitic campaign were launched in late 1952. Hungarian authorities prepared various scenarios based on the Slansky trial.[63] According to Slansky's confession, American and Israeli leaders agreed that the Zionist organizations in Eastern Europe would be the center of anti-Communist espionage and subversion. In return the U.S. would support Israel. As a result Zionist agents, who had previously served the Gestapo, had "wormed their way" into the higher echelons of Hungarian politics, economy, and state security organs as well. They supposedly received their instructions from the Jewish World Congress and Joint and provided the U.S. secret service with intelligence. Zionist engineers were sabotaging production and Zionist doctors were standing ready to murder party and state leaders.[64] This established a direct link with Stalin's doctor's plot.

The first phase in the preparation for the "trial of trials" was the arrest of the ÁVH leadership. The arrested leaders had been investigating the Zionist conspiracy themselves. The ÁVH was instructed to pursue the matter with a particular focus on Yugoslavia, the "Horthy police" the "Zionist line" and U.S. spying. An ÁVH doctor was accused of several murders and of deliberately maltreating senior comrades. Some 80 or 90 people were arrested, including Lajos Stöckler, the president of Magyar Izraeliták Országos Képviselete (National Representation of Hungarian Israelites), who was charged with being a former Gestapo spy. After Stalin's death the charges of Zionist conspiracy were dropped and new charges were cooked up with Soviet help. Many of the suspects were released.[65] Gábor Péter and "his gang" stood trial for economic crimes, such as selling passports to wealthy individuals. Their arrest provided a great opportunity for the Communist leaders to accuse Péter of "misleading" them about Rajk and the other Communist victims of the purges. It turned out that it was not Rákosi who was responsible, but Péter and his associates.[66] Ironically, in the summer of

1956 Péter took vengeance on Rákosi. He helped destroy him by revealing Rákosi's real role in the show trails of 1949.

The number of people employed by various organs of security was staggering. As of 1955, almost seventy thousand people worked for the Interior Ministry, most of which belonged to the border guards or wore uniform in one of the several police organizations.[67] This was equal to the size of the Hungarian army set down under the Peace Treaty of 1947. Their enemies were numerous as well. According to contemporary Soviet figures 362,000 people were taken to court in 1951, and in addition police investigations involved another 500,000 in the same year.[68] Despite this heavy security effort, Rákosi's brother, Zoltán Bíró, the deputy head of the Central Committee's Agitation and Propaganda division estimated in 1953 that there were still around 500,000 hostile elements[69] in the country of less than 10 million. Beria mentioned a figure of 1.5 million people who had been subjected to legal proceedings prior to 1953.[70] By the end of the first quarter of 1953 alone courts had tried 650,000 people and sentenced 387,000, while the police meted out punishment in 850,000 cases.[71] As a comparison, in Poland there were six million names on the list of "criminal and suspicious elements" in 1954, that is, one-third of the adult population. In 1950, 35,000 political prisoners were held in Polish jails.[72]

The massive hunt for "enemies" did not cease after 1953. József Révai's thoughts shed light on those whom the Hungarian leadership regarded as "enemies": "Zionists" and "Hungarian bourgeois nationalists," the "remnants of capitalists, kulaks and cosmopolitans." Révai wrote to Rákosi in February 1953 that: "It is impossible not to talk about the bourgeois remnants of ideology beside the remnants of capitalist classes, which nourishes the hostile forces. In Hungary this is much fatter and more dangerous than in the Soviet Union, because in Hungary there was hardly any struggle against it and the majority of our intelligentsia is a bourgeois one."[73]

Kulaks were singled out as the regime's chief targets. Rákosi borrowed Stalin's interpretation of the kulaks to conclude that they were "the most implacable enemies of Socialist construction." He aimed to liquidate them as a social class since they were part of the former "ruling strata."[74] In fact the enemy seemed to be everywhere: within the top and lower echelons of the party, in ministries, factories, mines and even places like the Soviet–Hungarian joint companies, where alleged saboteurs were "discovered" in the joint oil and bauxite companies. A report to the Political Committee claimed that both places had become "the reservoirs of hostile elements." These "shady" figures, former "Horthyite" officers or their offspring, as well as former landowners, occupied high positions, particularly positions around the Soviet comrades and were creating an anti-Soviet atmosphere. It was alleged that interpreters of bourgeois origin deliberately mistranslated in order to stir conflict.[75] Hungary in the 1950s was a place where few people were safe from persecution.[76]

As elsewhere in Eastern Europe, the judicial branch of government was reorganized on the basis of the Soviet model. Courts of law were supposed to protect the existing political establishment and the Hungarian legal system adopted the Stalinist concept of presumption of guilt. In practical terms, this meant that one did not have to commit a crime to be deemed dangerous to society. It was enough that the authorities *expected* someone to break the law for that person to end up in court. In one instance, a military tribunal tried a certain István Szabó because his adopted son was charged with treason. The judge admitted that Szabó knew nothing about his son's alleged spying activities. Nevertheless, he considered Szabó "dangerous to society since his close relative became a servant of the treasonous Titoist gangs, and as a result Szabó himself can be used for subversive activity against our people's democracy."[77]

Loyalty to the Party was expected to supercede other considerations such as family ties and influenced some people even in the name they chose for themselves. A woman whose husband was convicted in 1951 for "unknown reasons" petitioned the interior minister for a permission to retrieve her maiden name. The reason: her husband "failed to fulfill the confidence placed in him by our people's democracy." A man, who changed his German family name in 1945 to the name of a popular Communist politician, decided to undo the change in 1951. With his former hero disgraced, the man no longer wished to bear the name of "the basest foe of our people's democracy," which "is a great burden to me." In yet another case a person requested the Hungarianization of his name at the "instruction of the Budapest Party Committee."[78] After a leading functionary of the political police was arrested his wife chose to drop his name. Authorities expected people to report suspected crimes even if those involved close family members. In August 1953 a woman was sentenced to two years in jail in part because she failed to report her husband's "activities."[79]

In order to make the system of persecution more efficient, some 40 thousand informers were hired to report to the authorities.[80] Even this was not enough, and the obligation to report crimes was carried to the point of absurdity. Consequently, people were obliged to inform the authorities about crimes they suspected were about to happen. This is illustrated by judge Ferenc Andó's case against four defendants, who failed to report an alleged spy with whom they had conducted "illegal business activities" (purchasing nylon stockings) but of whose alleged spying they knew nothing. According to Andó, "actually none of them (the defendants) were told that Fazekas was an imperialist spy, his spying activities were unknown to any of them. But purely the things they knew about him [the alleged spy], in the present international situation with the obligatory political vigilance binding all Hungarian citizens, they could have been expected to conclude that Fazekas was spying. Today, when the sharpening of the class struggle and the ever increasing aggresso [sic] activities of the imperialists are proven by various forms of subversive activities camouflaged cunningly, [the law] which regulates reporting obligations of imperialist activities can be interpreted according to the demands of increased vigilance only."[81]

The authorities were not satisfied with sentencing political enemies. They made sure that they disappeared without a trace. This was the established pattern in the Soviet Union. On one occasion a junior airforce officer was arrested for "being a member of an imperialist spy ring composed of airforce officers." Almost two years later his father asked the first secretary of the party for information on the whereabouts of his son, who had given no sign of himself for two years. His family had no idea where he was or what crime he had committed. The letter, as instructed by the addressee, was left unanswered.[82]

The Hungarian Communists in their revolutionary zeal outdid Soviet expectations and persecuted more people than the Soviets thought desirable. In fact, the large number of mostly unjustified sentences seemed to threaten the stability of the system and this was one of the reasons why Rákosi was reprimanded in June 1953. On one occasion the Budapest party secretary went as far as accusing the Soviet companies in Hungary for employing too many old cadres. He told the Soviet ambassador that the Hungarians wanted these companies to be rid of "unreliable" and "hostile elements" and recommended that more attention be devoted to the selection of employees to the Soviet companies.[83] Kiselev refuted the allegations, and he in fact sought to restrain the Hungarians from overt abuses. In one instance he protested against the police beating of kulaks,[84] and condemned the Hungarian party's attitude towards the technical intelligentsia. He felt that the regime's "disdain" towards them was alienating many intellectuals who would otherwise cooperate with it.[85] The Soviet ambassador argued that far too many cases on subversion and other crimes that reached the judicial organs were based on unfounded accusations, and recommended an overhaul of the judicial system in order to restore "socialist legality." He claimed that Soviet experts had revealed numerous structural mistakes in the Ministry of Justice.[86]

Kiselev deplored many elements of Rákosi's policies, including political persecution and industrialization. Rákosi would not even listen to Stalin.[87] Beria called the reign of terror in Hungary inadmissible and intolerable. This would suggest that he regarded terror as a means rather than an end in itself. In 1953 Imre Nagy relaxed persecution by overhauling the justice system, by eliminating forced labor camps and releasing Communist and Social Democratic political prisoners, but the machinery of terror was left intact.

The Stalinist economy

The Hungarian Stalinist system's weakest point was its economy and there is little doubt that economic deficiencies ultimately helped to bring the Communist system to its knees in 1989. In 1949 the Soviet Union established COMECON, which was meant to coordinate planning and production among the socialist nations in order to achieve economic independence from the Western world. It aimed to create a common raw material base and the division of labor in industry among its members.[88] In reality, the organization failed to get off the ground and economic relations within the Soviet bloc operated essentially on a bilateral basis. As Lavrentii Beria put it in 1953, the organization was "working poorly" and "plays no positive role in the coordination of the countries of the people's democracies whatsoever."[89] In fact, the newly created people's democracies did their best to earn Western currency, and sold whatever marketable goods they had on the "capitalist" market. Hungary lacked most raw materials, yet it was often unable to obtain them from its fellow East European countries, which possessed them. Poor intra-Comecon relations led to serious difficulties in production. Imre Nagy once complained that "we get less and less coke than the factories need every day. There are no stocks. Neither the Czechs, nor the Poles carry out their obligations. The factories cannot fulfill production plans, this diminishes wages, leading to the workers' dissatisfaction, who know that it is the government's job to take care of supplies."[90]

It goes without saying that for a nation which lacked the necessary economic base, traditions and raw materials, such ambitious plans as super-industrialization based on Communist doctrine and the imperative of military build-up had appalling consequences. These included a serious decline in the standard of living and the neglect of traditional branches, including the agricultural and food processing sectors, as well as the light industry. Industrial development instead concentrated on steel and iron production and means of production in general. The economy's phenomenal growth was due to the fact that in the course of the first five-year plan (after 1948) 25 percent of the national income was allocated to investment, out of which almost 50 percent went to industry (including construction) and only 14 percent to agriculture.[91] The percentage allocated to investment was higher than Bulgaria's (19.6 percent), Czechoslovakia's (22.3 percent), and Poland's (21.6 percent) first five-year plan, or the Soviet Union's (21 percent) between 1946 and 1950. The share of industry in investment was also higher than in these countries, just like the share of heavy industry and construction within industrial investments, which amounted to over 90 percent in Hungary.[92]

As in the Soviet Union from the early 1930s, resources were diverted from agriculture to industry. In such a way the government killed two birds with one stone: carried out its economic program, and at the same time made progress in the liquidation of the peasantry as a social class. The government's economic policy inevitably had a serious effect on the standard of living.

In the period between 1949–1953 the level of consumption for all important foodstuffs was lower than in 1938 save for wheat and sugar. The deterioration in the quality of consumer goods added another 10 percent to the consumer price index, which in 1955 was 35 percent higher than at the beginning of the decade.[93] The Poles experienced similar hardships, in 1953 the meat and sugar consumption fell below the 1949 level.[94] The price increases imposed by the Czechoslovak government in 1953 resulted in a roughly 40 percent drop in living standards for the citizens of Czechoslovakia.[95]

Hungary, which had been traditionally a major exporter of wheat, now had to import it from the Soviet Union and elsewhere, because its own was used to service the country's ever growing foreign debt. In January 1956, the Hungarian leadership turned to the Soviet Union for the shipment of 100,000 tons of wheat, while in September 1956 another 350,000 tons were requested for 1957. Such requests could only increase Hungary's subordinated position *vis-à-vis* the hegemonic power. Because of the acute wheat shortage extraordinary methods were used to curb consumption, which whether intentionally or not, helped the regime's war on the peasantry. For the "hoarding" of a few kilos of bread or flour people were sent to jail for years. In January 1953 Ferenc Reisz received a sentence of two years in jail and a fine of 1000 forints for buying seven kilos of bread and 65 croissants. In the same year Károly Bod received three years in prison for "hoarding" 139 kilos of flour and twenty kilos of sugar. József Fábián bought ten kilos of flour even though he possessed flour. The price: three and a half years in jail. Another man, Károly Csorba had 150 kilos of flour, but was greedy enough to buy bread from the local cooperative. He even hid 20 kilos of lard in his garden, which earned him a spell in jail.[96] This is how economic decline was used in the battle to transform society.

If the quality of goods a nation is able to produce is indicative of how developed that nation is, what happened in Hungary in terms of production was a sure and dismal sign of decline. Hungary had been renowned around the world for the high quality of its food processing and light industry, as well as the machine building industry. By the 1950s, it was clear that Hungary's reputation was being undermined because Hungarian salami or canned food shipments were being returned from abroad due to their poor quality.

The decline can be linked directly to the introduction of the central command system. The result was immediate. As early as in 1950, only a year after the Stalinist system had been introduced, the director of the Soviet–Hungarian bauxite company complained of typical symptoms: negligence and low standard of production which were leading to the continuous growth of waste. The only thing that mattered was to fulfill the plan, which meant that production was cyclical: very little was done at the beginning of the month, while at the end of it work was carried out in great haste.[97]

The country's economic dictator, Ernő Gerő complained: "What is happening in the area of quality is absolutely intolerable and untenable. It has to be said that in [earlier years] when we were economically much weaker, there were not so many and so well-founded complaints against the commodities we produce, what is more, there are more now, in 1952 than there were in 1951." In the shoe industry, which according to Gerő had once been famous for its quality, the customers returned only one percent as waste in 1950, but by 1951 this had reached 25 percent. On one occasion the USSR sent back 4900 pairs from a shipment of 5000.[98] In 1952 and 1953 Austria, Sweden, Italy and Belgium returned a variety of machine tools because of their poor quality.[99] The Vörös Csillag (Red Star) tractor factory sent 140 tractors to Romania in the fall of 1952 and by February 1953 *all* of them had broken down. Only six of these could be mended in 1954 partly because the factory did not make spare parts for them. The machine tools sent to Argentine had no paint on them, because it came off while being shipped. Their electronic guidance compartment could not be opened because the screws on it had rusted away. Argentina also purchased Hungarian locomotives before the war but no longer wanted them by the 1950s. Machine tools and motorcycles could no longer be sold in Sweden.[100] Hungarian sugar was rejected in the Far East because it was filthy,[101] poultry, pasta asciutta, Hungarian salami, cattle, canned food could not be sold because of "low quality."[102] The list goes on. These failures had no impact on production because soft budgetary constraints ruled out bankruptcy. Another peculiar trait of the central command economy, which plagued it while it lasted, was the poor quality of packaging, which occurred as soon as this economic system was introduced. Elevators sent to Poland got soaked because of the "primitive manner" in which they had been packaged, their screws fell apart or rusted. Similarly, x-ray machines exported to the USSR fell to pieces.[103]

Central bureaucracy determined which company would manufacture which product. "Profiling," as this was called, resulted in a shortage of spare parts. In 1951 no spare parts were available for important export items such as buses. Belated delivery was one another chronic symptom. Out of twenty lathes ordered from the Szerszámgépgyár (Machine Tool Factory) in 1950 ten were still undelivered two years later.[104]

An alarming consequence of heavy industrialization was that instead of becoming independent from the Western world in terms of foreign trade, the Hungarian economy became increasingly reliant on it in terms of importing machine tools and raw materials in particular. This was especially true in the period after 1953, when the Soviet Union began to reduce the amount and variety of ores and other materials it exported to Hungary. This, and the inability to export enough goods of sufficient quality to pay for the imports led to the rapid increase of the Hungarian debt and an alarming decrease of its gold reserve, which was being used to finance imports. Without imports, however, the heavy industry could not function. "Forced imports which were connected to investments and the demand for raw materials had to be balanced by forced exports," argue historians Pető and Szakács. "Foreign trade was becoming increasingly self-serving: Hungary was importing so as to have enough to export for the next import."[105]

In late May 1953, only weeks before Rákosi was summoned to Moscow for consultations, the Soviet ambassador warned that the Hungarians were struggling with a debt of 534 million forints to the capitalist countries including West Germany and also to the East. They owed 221 million forints to the Soviet Union and 244 million to China.[106] Industry was to be blamed for the indebtedness, since Hungary's imports exceeded its exports, the worst year being 1952, when it accumulated a trade deficit of 1,686 million forints.[107] The situation in 1953 was worse than the Soviets had anticipated. In reality Hungary's short-term debt was 865 million forints, an increase of over 200 million forints since 1950. One reason for the growing indebtedness was that, although both the Eastern and the Western trading partners wanted Hungary to sell them agricultural products, Hungary only offered industrial goods.[108] In this respect, the situation did not improve during the years of Imre Nagy's "new course" either. Agricultural imports increased while the export of such products declined. Between 1953 and the end of 1954 the debt to the Western world increased 2.5 times, and in 1955 it increased by another 800 million forints. In some months the nation's debt service was actually higher than its total annual earnings from Western exports,[109] even though the country managed to increase its exports to the West by 60 percent.

The national debt reached a total of 2.6 billion forints by the end of 1955, despite a trade surplus with the COMECON. But trade with the Soviet bloc was decreasing in 1954 and 1955: from 72 percent of the turnover in 1953 to 53 percent in 1955. More raw materials came from the West than previously.[110] As a result of its inability to finance its imports from the sale of goods abroad, Hungary used its gold reserve to pay for them. While in 1949 the freely disposable national gold reserve (the part not tied down to finance imports) was 36.1 tons, it plummeted to only five tons in late 1955.[111] The new Soviet ambassador, Iurii Andropov, informed the Kremlin of the deteriorating economic situation, which in turn decided to call Rákosi's attention (he was staying in Moscow) to "the deficiencies in the development of the Hungarian national economy and the work of the Political Committee of the HWP."[112] Nothing could have pleased the disgraced dictator more than such reports, as he had been trying to engineer his rival's removal almost since Nagy had been installed in June 1953. Poor performance of the economy was a major cause of Soviet anxiety concerning Hungarian affairs and was also the major theme of domestic rivalry between reformers and orthodox Stalinists. In 1955 it was used to kill reform.

Hungary as a client state—Economic services

Hungarian leaders often voluntarily consulted with the Soviet Union before deciding on matters of significance, and constructed a political system modeled on the Soviet Union in almost every detail. Hungarian–Soviet bilateral relations in the early part of the 1950s are best described by Edward Luttwak's paradigm of a "Leninist client state," which satisfied the "growing hierarchy of Soviet imperial needs,"[113] namely, provided services in foreign and military policy and economic affairs. In matters of foreign policy for instance, Hungary served Moscow by aligning itself completely with the Soviet line even if it was detrimental to the national interest. It consulted with the Kremlin even on minor issues such as closing the U.S. library in Budapest and offered Hungarian services in foreign intelligence. In order to strengthen the cohesion of the Soviet bloc Hungarian leaders dropped the problem of the treatment of Hungarian minorities outside Hungary from their political agenda.

On one count Edward Luttwak's assessment of Soviet expectations from the client states is definitely flawed. He claims that Moscow was not interested in economic gains, there were no merchants in the Kremlin. In fact, economic services formed a crucial part in Soviet–Hungarian relations, and Moscow derived great benefit from them. The satisfaction of the USSR's military requirements was a large burden for the Hungarian economy. The Soviet model of modernization and military needs launched Eastern Europe on a frantic pace of industrialization. Hungary's five-year plan of 1949 envisioned a rapid increase of industrial production, with a growth of 86 percent. In 1951, however, when Stalin decided that the people's democracies should reach peak military preparedness by 1953, the planned growth rate was raised to 310 percent. This figure was far higher than Poland's, where the revised plan of 1950 envisioned an industrial growth of 158 percent.[114] As a result, the Hungarian GNP grew by 50 percent, and the gross industrial production was 88 percent higher in 1954 than in 1949. However, Hungary lacked the necessary resources for massive industrialization, and as a result the Hungarian economy rapidly declined. Paradoxically some of the resources required by the Soviet-dictated industrial program were procured from Western sources. Thus for example a 1951 Franco-Hungarian "hors d'accord" agreement provided that in return for 750 million francs worth of Hungarian wheat and sugar France would deliver iron and steel products, steel alloys and the export of a plant for the production of sulphuric acid by the French firm Krebs. In addition the agreement provided that France would raise the delivery of certain "rare items" such as special metals envisioned in the bilateral trade accord France and Hungary signed the same year.[115]

The early 1950s saw the need to increase foreign trade to improve the economy. Hungary's most important trading partner, of course, was the Soviet Union. Its share in Hungary's foreign trade turnover reached 34 percent in 1953 and then declined somewhat to 22 percent by 1955. The rest of the COMECON countries accounted for 34.6 percent in 1950 and 32 percent in 1955.[116] The Hungarian economy was so heavily reliant on the Soviet Union's shipments for the development of its economy and for the Soviet market to be able to pay for the imports that this in itself provided a strong measure of political control. Albert Hirschmann argues that foreign trade has two principal effects upon the power position of an imperialist country. First, economic profits from trade increase the economic power of the dominant country. Second, foreign trade becomes a direct source of power if other countries become economically dependent on the dominant state and thus provide it with an instrument of coercion. The power to interrupt and redefine commercial relations with any country is the root cause of the power position that the dominant country acquires over other nations. This ability is achieved through the creation of exclusive complementarity.[117] Trade instruments are useful also in creating economic satellites that provide guaranteed markets and sources of supply, of which Soviet–Hungarian commercial relations were a good example.[118]

The second effect became apparent when in 1955 the Soviet Ministry of Foreign Trade refused to accept the list of goods Hungary desired to sell to, and purchase from, the Soviet Union. Hungary presented its list in the usual manner in July 1954 but had to wait until January 1955 for a reply . It turned out to be disastrous, because the Soviets rejected many of the commodities Budapest offered, and simultaneously refused to deliver much of what the Hungarians requested.[119] Moscow simply refused to offer anthracite, lead, furnace raw iron, steel raw iron, which Hungary asked for. In other goods like crude oil or raw phosphates Moscow promised less than half the amount the Hungarian government requested.[120] No explanation was given and the refusal threatened the fundamentals of the country's economy. In this critical situation the Central Committee dispatched Deputy Minister of Foreign Affairs Andor Berei, a person of high standing in the Party hierarchy and Minister of Foreign Trade László Háy to consult with Soviet Minister of Foreign Trade Ivan G. Kabanov and the director of the Soviet Planning Office, Gosplan. However, the meeting proved that the Soviets were less than helpful. They insisted that Hungary, as other East European countries, should resolve the problems by itself.

Consequently, Rákosi traveled to Moscow and took up the matter with the Soviet leadership himself, and as a result Moscow agreed to raise exports by 130 million rubles, and its imports by 94 million rubles. A number of Soviet products were "offered" which were not on the original list and quite a few Hungarian goods were purchased which the Soviets originally did not wish to take. This compromise was still insufficient, especially in cotton, iron and crude oil,[121] but the Soviet government refused to raise the value of its shipments to the 1954 level. This forced Hungary to purchase the missing items from Western Europe, which in turn aggravated the country's debt situation. Lacking the relevant Soviet sources one can only speculate on the Soviet motives. One of these may have been political, namely to weaken Imre Nagy's position. This assumption is supported by the fact that Moscow agreed to be more cooperative in this matter after Nagy had been ousted. Economic relations thus provided Moscow with one more lever with which to assert political dominance.

The rapid decline of the economy soured Hungary's relationship with the Soviets, who were increasingly irritated by the fact that Hungary was unable to satisfy its export obligations to the USSR. This was a case when all the efforts designed to satisfy the hegemonic power floundered on the country's general decline, the incompetence of its leaders, as well as the fact that the Stalinist economic system proved to be unworkable. In November 1952 the Soviet ambassador in Budapest instructed the consul in the city of Győr (who acted as a kind of Soviet political representative in the western part of the country) to discuss a solution of Soviet economic grievances with the county party secretary. The Győri Vagon- és Gépgyár (Győr Vagon and Machine Plant) there had not fulfilled its obligations to deliver goods to the Soviet Union. The consul demanded that the party secretary intervene, but nothing came of it.[122] On 23 May 1953 the Soviet ambassador arranged to meet Rákosi to "discuss how Hungary's delay in fulfilling its delivery obligations to the USSR could be resolved."[123]

The ambassador was so troubled by the state of affairs that two days later he sent Molotov two memoranda on the issue. Both dealt with economic problems. He wrote that, although the socialist countries in general were "usually unable to tackle the problem of the mutual shipment of goods," the chief culprit was Hungary, the tardiness of which in this respect was often more significant than the others. Several factors seemed to be responsible for this: on the one hand "the careless work of the planning organs, the low standard of organization on the part of the leading Hungarian firms." On the other hand the country's leaders were to blame: the top party cadres, the economic ministries, and "other responsible persons" were underestimating the importance of foreign trade in the nations' economy. Significantly, Kiselev deplored the fact that the "remnants of bourgeois–nationalist methods in the Hungarian Ministry of Foreign Trade were not thoroughly eradicated" and accused the Hungarians of "systematically delaying the delivery of important industrial equipment to the Soviet Union."[124] Anastas Mikoyan instructed the Soviet economic advisor in Hungary to draw Gerő's attention to the matter. While Gerő promised to resolve it by the end of the year and personally took charge of exports to the Soviet Union, neither he, nor the rest of the Hungarian leaders, in fact, felt able to do anything about it.[125] In July the Soviet economic advisor repeatedly warned Gerő that Hungary was still falling behind in exports to the Soviet Union and would not be able to fulfill the plans in ships, locomobiles, locomotives and many other articles.

Some of Kiselev's criticisms concerning the Hungarian political leadership were unjust. Gerő was well aware of the importance of foreign trade and attempted to improve it. The foreign trade sector had been thoroughly purged of "bourgeois experts," in fact, politically reliable cadres, who had little or no training in business or foreign trade were promoted to important positions. What concerned the Soviet leadership even more was Hungary's accelerated descent into the quagmire of indebtedness, especially towards the Western world.

In order to keep the economy running the Hungarian regime had to ask the Soviet Union for favors such as loans to reduce debts or to be used for building industrial sites. Thus, in 1952, the USSR agreed to extend a gold loan of 48 million rubles for the construction of a metallurgical plant.[126] This was in addition to a large commodity credit that had already been granted "in order to combat the economic hardships caused by the drought and the poor crop."[127] In May 1953 Rákosi asked for a commodity credit in gold in an effort to reduce Hungary's balance of payment deficit.[128] This proved to be insufficient for the ailing Hungarian economy to survive the year, therefore the government turned to the Kremlin for more money. This time for a loan of 200 million rubles in commodities such as wheat and agricultural products in general, as well as coal and other raw materials needed for steel production was requested, but Moscow agreed to only half that amount.[129]

Rákosi later lamented that when the Hungarian delegation arrived in Moscow to put forward this latter request, the reception was rather cool. The Soviets explained that Hungary had no need for the loan and the mistake must be in the leadership if in such a year, when the crop was good, they could not balance their trade. Lazar Kaganovich remarked that the Hungarian request was "hoarding" (rvachestvo).[130] When in 1956 the Rákosi regime recommended that the USSR should purchase the Hungarian short term Western debt and convert it into a long-term one, the response was a decisive *niet*.[131] Moreover, what the Soviets gave with one hand, they took away with the other. For instance the Soviets received reparation payments, the claims of German companies which the Soviets took over under the Potsdam agreement, the Hungarian debt on the clearing account with Nazi Germany, compensation for war damages in former German assets, the profits and the consultation fees of the joint companies, and the cost of the Soviet-owned companies that were sold by the USSR in 1952.

Up until the end of 1954 the Soviet Union had significant control over the Hungarian economy through its enterprises in Hungary. These gave the Soviets control over, *inter alia*, the bauxite, aluminum, oil and oil refining industries, as well as Danube shipping and much of coal mining.[132] Hungary's only manganese mine, located in Urkut, was Soviet-owned. In 1952 the Soviet Union centralized and expanded the activities of the Soviet–Hungarian companies, but at the same time decided to sell the assets of those companies where the Soviet share was less than 50 percent, back to Hungary. According to the agreement signed with the Soviet Union on 30 September 1952, Hungary was to pay 990 million forints payable until 1956 for these companies.[133] This was slightly better than the original proposal, according to which the payment would have had to be made during the course of three years only. Payments included the delivery of 500,000 tons of bauxite in 1955 alone, which was over a third of the nation's entire annual production of 1.4 million tons.[134] Two years later the Soviet Union offered the sale of its share of the joint companies except the Hungarian–Soviet Oil Company, which was the most profitable of them all, plus the Soviet Bank and eleven houses, but Soviet prices were too high for Hungary. This occasioned the most significant Hungarian–Soviet disputes of the period. Moscow valued the assets at 1.2 billion forints. Ernő Gerő supported the proposal with the reservation that Hungary would not be able to pay any installments in 1955 or 1956, since its payments to the USSR under the 1952 agreement and earlier obligations amounted to 253 million forints in 1955 and 265 million the following year.[135]

Because of the country's grave financial situation, the Political Committee decided to accept the Soviet offer with the proviso that Hungary would not pay more in the forthcoming years than it would otherwise have done as consultation fees and profit transfer. Hungary announced that it wished to extend the period of payment in the Soviet offer from five years to ten, and that they wanted to purchase the joint Oil Company as well.[136] Budapest also wanted the Soviet Union to omit a clause from the proposed agreement according to which Hungary would have to take responsibility for all further claims against the joint companies.[137] That provision caused problems in the Austro-Hungarian treaty that was under negotiation at that point, since Vienna insisted that Hungary should compensate Austria for its former assets in Hungary that the Soviets had taken after 1945. The Russians made only a few concessions: they agreed to sell the joint oil company, but insisted that they receive a payment of 2–2.5 billion forints in five years starting in 1955, albeit in increasing installments. Furthermore, Moscow rejected all responsibility for any future claims against these companies.[138] Although the reacquisition of the joint companies returned economic sovereignty to Hungary, the exploitation of its resources continued with the Soviet use of Hungarian uranium. This was done under terms reminiscent of colonial arrangements: the USSR was in charge of the exploration and extraction of the ore, while the Hungarians were obliged to provide the infrastructure. Moscow was the sole buyer and set the price it would pay unilaterally. It also dictated the pace at which the ore would be exploited and of the construction of the necessary installations.

The exploration of Hungarian uranium resources began in 1953 by Soviet experts at a time the Soviets were accelerating their nuclear weapon program, which relied on uranium from the GDR, Czechoslovakia and Bulgaria. Large deposits were found in the Mecsek mountains in southern Hungary. According to the preliminary estimates there was a reserve of 15 million tons of ore, which made it one of the largest deposits in the world. The uranium content was average.[139] Well after the initial works for the exploitation of the uranium had actually begun, the two countries signed a protocol on 8 June 1955. This dealt with how the uranium of the Mecsek would be explored, mined and sold. It provided for the exploration of radioactive elements and for production to begin while exploration was going on. The Hungarian government was obligated to place the sites at the geological expedition's disposal free of charge and to exempt the equipment imported by the Soviet members, as well as the ore taken to the Soviet Union, from all taxes and charges. Housing, installations and electricity would be provided by the Hungarians. In return the USSR provided scientific and technical assistance, experts and technical equipment for the exploration of radioactive ore. The contacting parties agreed to spend 60 million forints on exploration in 1955, to be financed in equal parts.

The protocol was surrounded by great secrecy and the parties were not allowed to include it into their economic plans or statistical data. The ore would be sold to the USSR, except for the quantity required by Hungary—which was, and would continue to be for a long time to come, zero. Prices would be calculated on the basis of the cost of production plus a 10 percent profit[140]—the same price formula they applied for the Czechoslovak uranium in 1947.[141] In order to pursue the contract, the Hungarian government established a company under the code name "Bauxite" in 1956. It would receive the production site free of charge and would be exempted from all taxes and duties except for the taxes on wages; for shipping it would use the internal tariff. Besides the technical assistance and experts, the Soviets also agreed to finance 75 percent of the investment and exploration costs in the form of long-term loans. The agreement was to last for 20 years and the USSR would be allowed to purchase all the company's products the Hungarian government did not need.[142] The infrastructure, roads and installations had to be built, and 960 flats had to be ready by the end of 1957. Because of secrecy, no documentation whatsoever was prepared for the project, which was to cost 380 million forints in the first year alone.[143] By the end of 1957 the investments exceeded 650 million forints, and the Soviet side owed the Hungarians 300 million.[144] The parties disagreed on how the production costs should be calculated. This was a fundamental problem, since the "production costs" formed the basis of the price the Russians agreed to pay for the uranium.

In order to make production profitable, the Hungarians thought that t he Soviets should pay for everything produced by the company, down to a metal content of 0.03 per cent. On the other hand, the Soviets were unwilling to finance the production of the low quality ore, even though without it the 0.2 percent quality they desired could not be produced. It was calculated that on the basis of the Soviet position Hungary would receive approximately 60 percent of the production cost until the time it would become capable of processing the lower quality ore.[145] Hence, it was the Soviet Union, the sole user of the uranium, who dictated the price unilaterally. In fact the revision of the uranium agreement became one of the demands that the revolutionaries leveled against the country's leadership in 1956. Nonetheless, the Soviets continued to want to pay less for the uranium than the producer wanted, which would have been acceptable had the Hungarians had the chance to sell it to anyone else, but that was not the case. Moreover, Soviet experts demanded that the quality and quantity of production be raised at a pace that would have been tantamount to "robbing" the mine.[146] The difference between this and the situation with the joint companies was that the Hungarian government actually owned the uranium mines. However, this did not alter the fact that they served only the Soviet Union's needs. The Soviet government determined the terms of its operations, although the Hungarians made attempts to assert their national interest.

Economic Stalinism was fraught with a paradox. Firm political control over the economy ensured that Hungary would provide for Soviet needs. But the economic decline engendered by Soviet control and the Stalinist system accentuated the need to rebuild economic ties with the West. This in turn led to indebtedness and economic dependence on the Western world— precisely what the Communists wanted to avoid in the first place. Economic penetration ensured Soviet control in the short run, but the flaws inherent in the central command system helped undermine the Communist system in the long run.

Hungary as a client state in defense

Security concerns may have been one of the USSR's chief motives in the lasting occupation of Eastern Europe. Charles Bohlen held that "the essential Soviet objective in Eastern Europe was [...] to ensure Soviet control [...] for strategic purposes. The post war Soviet takeover in Eastern Europe was inspired primarily by strategic considerations and only secondarily by the spread of Communism for ideological reasons."[147] Vojtech Mastny explained the contradiction between the lack of an external threat to the Soviet Union and Stalin's frantic "quest for security" with the element of irrationality.[148] Stalin's psychotic personality and Communist ideology blew the potential Western threat to the Soviet Union out of proportion. Soviet presence in Eastern Europe alleviated Stalin's security concern by extending the Soviet Union's defensive perimeter. Hungary's importance for Soviet security was illuminated by the assumptions of Hungarian defense planning in the early 50s. In case of a successful attack Hungary could be used as a staging ground for an invasion of the Soviet Union; the Soviet Union's lines of communication to Austria could be cut off and the enemy would be in the back of the Soviet occupation troops in Austria; a wedge would be driven into the alliance cutting off the communication lines between Czechoslovakia and Romania and opening the way for an attack on Czechoslovakia from the South (much the same the Anschluss did after March 1938).[149]

The Hungarian Communist Party had exercised almost total control over the small Hungarian armed forces since 1945. In the course of the political transition the Soviet Union had asserted its control over the Hungarian army through its advisors. In addition to this, the Hungarian leadership did its best to follow the Soviet guidelines in military strategy and to provide for the Soviet units stationed in Hungary. In 1950 the Hungarian army was transformed along the Soviet model. Some 1100 officers were removed and by 1951 81 percent of the officer corps consisted of "new cadres."[150] Although the Paris Peace Treaty maximized the size of the Hungarian army to 70,000, in 1952 it numbered 210,000. The Soviets were well aware that this provision was being violated and therefore rejected a Hungarian proposal to have the UN investigate alleged American violations of the treaty of peace so as to avoid discussion of their own.[151] The Hungarian army's growth rate was the same as Poland's. There the army increased from 140 thousand in 1949 to 410 thousand in 1953, but Soviet penetration in the Polish army was deeper. The Polish armed forces were virtually commanded by Red Army generals and officers and Soviet 200 advisors,[152] but there were no Soviet commanders in the Hungarian military.

Hungarian services to the Soviet army were established by a series of bilateral agreements signed on 6 December 1946, according to which the Soviet Army in Hungary secured the communication lines to the Soviet zone in Austria.[153] New agreements were signed in February 1948. These contained no time limit or any other restriction concerning the presence of the Soviet army in Hungary. In fact the "guest" units, as they were euphemistically called, were entitled to use the maneuvering grounds of the Hungarian army and even privately or collectively owned agricultural areas. They were entitled to all sorts of benefits, such as exemption from duties on equipment brought into the country, and enjoyed a 50 percent discount on utilities and railway fares. The Hungarian budget covered most of the costs of installations constructed for the Soviet units. In order to expand military collaboration, further agreements were signed for the transfer of military technology and licenses, for sending Soviet military advisors to Hungary and for training Hungarian officers in the Soviet Union. The Hungarians hoped to obtain facts and figures on the organizational principles and size of the Soviet army, but did not get them.[154]

The Soviet advisors were to assist in preparing the Hungarian army for the possibility of a world conflict and to create a mass army based on the lessons of the Great Patriotic War.[155] Thus an army of a little over 30 thousand in 1948 grew to the nation's largest peacetime armada of 210 thousand in 1952. In order to achieve the ambitious military targets a massive program of industrialization was needed, which in turn required a sharp, 30–35 percent reduction of the standard of living. As the "international situation" was growing "tenser and tenser," Moscow demanded increasing East European contribution to its military efforts. Therefore Stalin invited the party and military leaders of the satellites to Moscow in January 1951. There general Shtemenko briefed them on the international political and military situation concluding that NATO would be able to launch an attack on the socialist world in 1953. This required the people's democracies to accelerate their military preparations.

The announcement and the target figures caused consternation. Bulgarian leader Vlko Chervenkov was the most outspoken and protested that his country lacked the necessary industrial capacity, therefore the Soviets should supply the necessary hardware for the armament program. At first Stalin pretended to be sympathetic to the concerns but according to the usual choreography Shtemenko "demonstrated" that the Bulgarian view was unacceptable leaving Stalin no choice but to agree.[156] Although the Hungarians seconded the Soviet views concerning the aggressive designs of the imperialists, in reality the Korean developments caused great anxiety.[157] Hungary was shocked by the Soviet demands, which made it necessary to revise the annual production plan and to increase industrialization at an accelerated pace. This in turn meant that further resources had to be diverted from consumption and other sectors of the economy, chiefly agriculture. Nonetheless they followed suit.

Moscow did not hesitate to intervene whenever the development of the Hungarian army was threatened. One of the reasons why Moscow backed Rákosi against Imre Nagy in 1955 may have been Khrushchev's fear that Nagy was neglecting military investments and that the rift within the HWP was threatening military modernization.[158] In 1955 the USSR institutionalized its military domination of Eastern Europe by establishing the Warsaw Pact. The pretext for this undoubtedly was West Germany's rearmament and integration into NATO, which seemed to threaten the European military balance. The treaty allowed Soviet forces to remain in Hungary and Romania even after the Austrian treaty was signed.

In November 1954 the Soviet leadership instructed Czechoslovakia and Hungary to broach the idea of a conference on collective security in Europe with the participation of the Western states. As expected, the West turned down the invitation. Therefore at Khrushchev's initiative the Soviet bloc convened a meeting in December and agreed to place their armies under joint command in case the Paris agreement was ratified. Molotov opined that West Germany's rearmament was a dangerous development, perhaps even an indication of war. If the Western powers continue to rearm, "the peace-loving nations would be compelled to take joint defensive measures."[159] When the Paris agreements were ratified, Khrushchev circulated the Soviet draft of the Warsaw Pact among the people's democracies in February 1955 with an invitation for a secret conference.[160] Hungary accepted the invitation without reserve on 10 March 1955. Even though Imre Nagy thought of the Austrian treaty as an opportunity to achieve Hungarian neutrality, the country's Stalinist leadership was worried that the Austrian

Treaty would end the presence of Soviet troops in Hungary. In order to forestall this alarming prospect they petitioned Moscow to retain at least one
Soviet division in Hungary in case the idea of withdrawing the Soviet units
should crop up, under the pretext that the Hungarian army was "not fully
prepared." Apparently they had no illusions about their popular support.
The Warsaw Pact was expected to prop up their unpopular regime.

    Soviet needs took precedence over Hungarian domestic concerns. In
1954 the Soviet government requested the construction of a military airport
capable of receiving heavy bombers. Although the investment, the cost of
which was estimated at 330 million forints was at odds with Prime Minister
Imre Nagy's program of reducing military expenditures, the Defense Council (not to be confused with the Defense Committee) accepted the proposal.
The Soviets did not take any chances, their chief advisor at the Ministry of
Defense Mikhail Fiodorovich Tikhonov put pressure on both Nagy and
Rákosi[161] to ensure a positive reply. Furthermore, the Hungarian government agreed to receive some of the Soviet forces that had to be removed
from Austria pursuant the state treaty. Hungary agreed to reconstruct a military airport at Szolnok and to build 350 apartments for the new arrivals.[162]

    Loyalty to the USSR was guaranteed by the fact that the Hungarian
political and military leadership accepted the tenets of Soviet military strategy and estimates of the world situation. Thus in October 1953 Minister
of Defense István Bata argued that only the increase of military power
could keep the imperialist warmongers from launching a world war. Nothing reflected more the Hungarian Communists' loyalty to the Kremlin than
their attitude to the use of nuclear weapons in combat. In September 1954
a military exercise took place in the South Urals military district with a
nuclear explosion. The Defense Ministers and chiefs of staff of the people's
democracies were invited as observers.[163] As a result of the "experience"
the minister of defense saw to it that the necessary measures were taken in
order to train an army capable of fighting in a nuclear war.[164] Even he must
have understood that such a war would end with the annihilation of his
army.

    In terms of the services and the favors demanded by the Soviet Union
and provided by Hungary the balance tilted clearly towards the former. The
Soviet decisions about Hungary can be interpreted within the framework of
providing services to satisfy the USSR's imperial needs although the power
relations within the Kremlin also shaped Soviet decisions. Hungary's political instability, growing indebtedness to the Western world and its general
economic malaise were beginning to change the country from a "bastion"
to a gaping crack through which imperialist influence could infiltrate. Ultimately only military force would keep it from collapsing altogether. In 1953
less persuasive methods were sufficient.

Crisis behind the Iron Curtain—Peaceful solutions

Following Stalin's death on 5 March 1953 Beria, Malenkov and Khrushchev were the main contenders for power. They thought of collective leadership as a compromise arrangement, which sooner or later would give way to a dominant figure. The intensity of their power struggle was due more to personal ambitions than to fundamental policy differences.[165] Shortly after Stalin's passing Malenkov announced a peace initiative and the Soviet leaders showed readiness to conclude the Korean War and even to deal with such thorny issues as Austria, even though in the latter case there was no breakthrough till 1955. They were soon to deal with problems inside their own empire as well, where cracks on the edifice of Soviet control began to appear. While Moscow was ready to bargain over the fate of the GDR at least initially, there was no prospect for any change in the status of Eastern Europe.

The Czechoslovak leadership was making "dangerous mistakes" and Soviet intelligence sources warned of "extremely detrimental conditions and disruption in Romania."[166] In East Germany the Communist regime was on the brink of collapse, the resentment of SED leader Walter Ulbricht was more widespread than many in the West had come to believe.[167] Alarming signs had already reached the Kremlin as early as March, when there were signs of a worsening class struggle in East Germany. At first it was not clear in Moscow how quickly the situation was deteriorating. In May Beria circulated a report according to which the dramatic rise in the number of refugees could be explained by the discontent caused by the crash program of building socialism introduced the previous summer.[168] The Soviet Council of Ministers found that "as a result of incorrect policies, many mistakes were made in the GDR. Among the German population there was huge dissatisfaction." Mass emigration of Germans showed that East Germany was "facing an internal catastrophe" and "without the presence of Soviet troops the existing regime there is not stable."[169] Importantly, Beria recognized that the critical situation was due not only to hostile propaganda, but also to legitimate fears and grievances of the population.[170] A report by the Soviet Control Commission in Berlin criticized the accelerated construction of socialism and recommended measures to reduce economic malcontent and steps to alleviate terror. In a similar vein the Soviet government called for an end to the "artificial establishment of agricultural production cooperatives," for an increase in production for mass consumption at the expense of heavy industry and the elimination of the rationing system. Ulbricht was summoned to Moscow, where the Soviet leaders, expressing concern for the situation in the GDR, demanded a new course.[171] The CPSU Presidium denounced Walter Ulbricht's speech of 5 May on the construction of socialism as "politically misguided" that could damage the cause of German reunification "on a peace loving and democratic basis." He had to refrain from mentioning his harmful statement again.[172]

There is evidence to suggest that the Soviet leadership may have been ready to accept German unification on the basis of the Western political model and the withdrawal of occupation forces in order to avert catastrophe in the GDR and to forestall West German membership in the NATO. But the denunciation and arrest of Beria altered the thrust of Moscow's German policy in spite of the previous consensus within the leadership since the rival leaders dared not risk being accused of a sell out and surrender of the GDR.[173] On the other hand Christian Ostermann noted that Beria's alleged plan may have been simply a fabrication of his political enemies.[174] Nevertheless, Ulbricht, whose prestige both within the East German party leadership and the Kremlin had declined seriously, was saved. In June the Soviets almost had him ousted, but he managed to cling on until the situation in Moscow changed in July and Soviet leaders were no longer willing to support his opponents.[175]

Political repression and economic hardship led to strikes and "chaotic demonstrations" with the participation of several hundred workers in Bulgaria on 3 May 1953.[176] In Czechoslovakia an ill-conceived currency reform against the backdrop of political terror sparked strikes around the country in April and May. On 1 June the workers of the Skoda plant rebelled in Plzen. They articulated political demands for the overthrow of the government, free elections and the end of Communist rule. The outbreak, which was put down with armed force, was serious enough for the authorities to acknowledge that "large segments of the working class [in Eastern Europe] do not support the Communist Party."[177]

Disquieting news came from Hungary as well. Critical accounts of the Rákosi regime's rampant terror and the faltering economy had been reaching the Soviet capital for a while. Already in October 1952 a report from Budapest described the rightful dissatisfaction of the population whose needs were overlooked by the local Soviets, which in turn were "separated from the masses."[178] The Soviet leadership seemed to have been losing its confidence in Rákosi's leadership ever since the Kremlin had to reach into its pocket to salvage it in 1952. The dictator was summoned to Moscow in the midst of the Czechoslovak and the East German crises. It was clear that Soviet patience was running out, with Hungary's virtual bankruptcy and Rákosi's reign of terror threatening with the political stability there. The meeting in Moscow did not take the form of a regular diplomatic consultation. It was held between two highly unequal states. The Soviets put forth their claims in terms of a *diktat* over which no bargaining was possible.

The criticisms were often of a highly personal character—the Soviets held Rákosi, Gerő, Farkas and Révai personally accountable for the "mistakes"—and encompassed almost everything the confused Hungarian Stalinists had accomplished. They were chastised for the irrational pace of industrialization, the drive for forced collectivization, the oversized army, as well as the regime's punitive policies. The verbal assaults against the Hungarians contained an element of anti-Semitism. According to one account of the meeting Beria called Rákosi, with whom he had had a personal feud, the "Jewish king of Hungary." Although the official records do not contain this slur, it is true that the Russians—especially Khrushchev, Malenkov, Beria, Molotov—criticized the ethnic composition of the party leadership, which uniquely in Eastern Europe, was composed almost entirely of Hungarians of Jewish descent. This criticism was particularly unjust given that they, particularly Gerő and Rákosi, had disclaimed their Jewish roots and their policies occasionally assumed an anti-Semitic character.

The new Soviet leadership needed scapegoats and the Rákosi group was more than perfect for this role. They insisted that a "real" Hungarian, namely Imre Nagy, should replace Rákosi as the Prime Minister and that other cadres of Hungarian stock be given leading positions in the party hierarchy. They condemned the low morale of the Hungarian army, which was attributed to "cleansing" and deplored the low standard of ideological work. In response the Hungarian delegation drafted a document, which contained the measures designed to remedy the "mistakes." Economic policy would change, the pace of industrialization would slow down, and investments would be reviewed. Agricultural investments would rise while collectivization would be "decisively" slower. More support would be given to individual peasants, the kulak list would be abolished. More houses would be built or renovated. As a result the standard of living would rise. "Legality" would be introduced by putting the political police under government control and a Supreme Attorney's Office would be established. The Politburo and the government would be reshuffled along Moscow's guidelines. The Soviet leaders thought that the draft was "basically not bad," although the economic measures were not concrete enough, and the leading triumvirate's responsibility had to be clearly stated. It is revealing of the Soviet stance towards Hungary that the last and therefore emphatic point on the agenda was a virulent verbal assault on Rákosi's alleged rapprochement with the United States. Given his anti-American attitude and loyalty to Moscow Rákosi could hardly have embarked on such a course and the Russians were probably aware of this. Their agitated response to the alleged initiative indicated that there were well-defined geographical limits of their tolerance of Western influence. Rákosi, disgraced and intimidated, vowed to do his best to correct the mistakes[179] and upon his return to Hungary he confessed all the crimes cited by the Soviet Presidium. His self-criticism was insincere. It was in part motivated by the dramatic developments in the GDR, of which he learned upon his return from Moscow. Nagy rapidly enacted reform. Heavy industry received less attention, more money went to the consumer and agricultural sectors of the economy. The pressure on the peasantry was relaxed, forced collectivization was halted, in fact peasants were allowed under certain conditions to leave agricultural collectives. Internment camps were closed and left-wing political prisoners were released. Despite the limited nature of the reforms there was a collective sigh of relief and a measure of optimism concerning the future.

However, it soon turned out that Rákosi would seize every opportunity to bring back Stalinism. Rákosi called the new course a set of "incomprehensible and incorrect" measures, which "emboldened the enemies of socialism."[180] He attacked Nagy relentlessly and used every chance to smear his policies, never losing faith that fortunes would turn and the Soviets would reinstall him. He did not have to wait long for the first break. Only a few weeks after the June meeting he, Nagy and Gerő were invited to the Soviet capital. Romania's Gheorghiu-Dej and Chervenkov of Bulgaria were also present. Khrushchev informed them that Beria had been arrested as the "enemy of the state." Rákosi correctly sensed that the criticism he had received a few weeks earlier, in which the arrested former NKVD chief had taken the lead, might have lost some of its bite. Khrushchev declared that Beria had been "impudent" towards the Hungarian party leader and that Beria's view that the first secretary of the party had no right to interfere in the affairs of state security had been incorrect. "The question immediately arose," wrote Rákosi in his memoirs, "what remained of the agreement of three weeks ago?" Other concrete issues like the kolkhoz-movement were not mentioned, but this was the first step in the Soviet retreat from radical reform.[181] In fact the Soviet leaders did not intend to overhaul the Stalinist system. Their instructions in the GDR or Hungary were designed to implement the necessary corrections in order to forestall the collapse of the Soviet sponsored regimes. Imre Nagy's mistake was to think that the Soviet strategy had changed.

Unlike in the other people's democracies, however, where reforms were terminated even before they could begin, Imre Nagy managed to implement many of the ideas that he believed would transform the system to socialism with a human face. For Nagy, reform was not merely an order to be carried out. Jovial and corpulent, Nagy was not the typically inhuman and ascetic Communist revolutionary. Révai once complained that Nagy saw important political issues through the lens of his family. Born at the turn of the century in the small town of Kaposvár as the son of a poor peasant family, he had childhood experience of what it was like to be socially and economically underprivileged. Nagy saw military action on the Russian front in World War I. He was indoctrinated as a prisoner of war and entered the Bolshevik party. Nagy came to be involved in the illegal Communist movement in Hungary after the fall of Kun's Bolshevik dictatorship, but went to Moscow in 1929. He regarded Soviet Russia as the "Promised Land." He worked on the topic of his choice, agricultural politics in the International Agrarian Institute. A Russian colleague remembered his corpulent figure, jovial character and pleasant complexion, and that, "like all Hungarians, he liked women." An apparent contradiction of character appeared: although he liked comfort, together with his family Nagy was able to live for 15 years in the Spartan conditions offered in Moscow. At Béla Kun's initiative Nagy was expelled from the party in 1936. Kun's own demise may explain why this event did not end in disaster for Nagy. In fact during the war he worked himself up into the leadership of the Hungarian party.

After returning to Hungary he held a variety of cabinet posts, including the agricultural one, and he came to be remembered as the man that distributed land. Nagy accepted Soviet control and believed in spite of his personal experiences in a livable version of Soviet-style socialism. Still, the Smallholder Prime Minister, Ferenc Nagy thought that among the Communists Imre Nagy was the most Hungarian and had a "friendly attitude. Not a great politician, but does what his party tells him obediently." The peasant politician Imre Kovács remembered that Nagy "loved the people" and never disavowed his peasant origins. Yet, his long exile distanced him from his motherland. "Like all Muscovites, he was initially suspicious, a complete stranger, who did not know Hungary," remembered a middle-class official. Unlike his fellow Muscovites he looked sincere with a far-flung personality, lacking ambition, and passed as a Hungarian. Nonetheless after his political defeat in 1949 he was loyal enough to assist a policy that destroyed agriculture even though he did not agree with it. The new course presented a chance for them to go back to his old notion of peaceful and organic road to socialism.[182] With hindsight, Nagy's reforms appear rather limited. But at the time they offered a ray of hope for a livable future in the bleak and desperate days of Rákosi's unlimited reign of misery, where for many the richness of life was reduced to mere survival. Collectivization was arrested, the pace of industrialization was slowed down, persecution was relaxed and a small measure of political pluralism in the form of the Popular Front was reintroduced. For a while Nagy was able to outmaneuver his arch rival, Rákosi by making temporary alignments with Farkas and Gerő against the common enemy.

Nagy's political, social and economic reforms were more ambitious than Malenkov's, because Nagy realized that the party itself was in crisis.[183] Nagy's most drastic measures were directed at reorienting economic priori-

ties, without, however, touching the institutional system of the central command economy, or restoring any significant degree of market economy,
although "economic regulators" were restored in agriculture. In order to
raise consumption, the 1954 plan reduced the amount allocated for investment while at the same time increased the share of agriculture in it. Industrial investments were reduced from 46.3 percent to 35.2 percent and proportion of heavy industry was reduced from 41 to 30 percent.[184] Nagy's
reforms enabled peasants to leave agricultural cooperatives, agricultural
taxes were reduced and tax breaks were granted not only to cooperatives
but to individual peasants as well. The government reduced the amount of
compulsory delivery. Unfortunately, however, economic performance did
not improve, and in a number of respects it even declined. Although the
production of some crops, like maize, increased, that of others, like wheat,
decreased significantly and the share of agriculture in the GNP did not
change.[185] The gross national product stagnated. Furthermore, in the year
1954 Hungary's indebtedness to the West increased significantly, partly
because the country was unable to sell the planned amount of goods in exchange for the growing import of agricultural products and raw materials
for the industry.

The economic disarray helped Rákosi's conspiracy against Nagy in
Moscow and his attack of his rival's reforms at home. Rákosi did not hide
his aversion to reform and advocated heavy industrialization soon after it
had been disavowed in the Kremlin. The conflict within the Hungarian
leadership was becoming so tense that Nagy proposed an arbitration by
Moscow to iron it out. The screenplay was the same as before. The meeting
took place on 5 May 1954 with the participation of Malenkov, Khrushchev,
Voroshilov, Kaganovich, Bulganin, Mikoyan, and Suslov from the Soviet
leadership, and Rákosi, Nagy, Gerő and Farkas from the Hungarian one.[186]
Khrushchev and Voroshilov were interested in the most pertinent question
of unity in the Hungarian Politburo, Kaganovich inquired about the class
struggle in the provinces and the urban areas. Mikoyan was worried about
the growing foreign trade deficit and claimed that the production of soap,
textiles and shoes was below the 1952 level. Hungary's plans for the development of heavy industry were still too ambitious, which meant that the
reform would not be halted altogether.[187] Malenkov agreed and condemned
the renewed attempts to accelerate industrialization.[188] Khrushchev then
proceeded to pronounce an evenly divided criticism of Nagy and Rákosi.
The latter was guilty of sticking to his old policies and did not recognize his
mistakes, which was harmful for party unity. He strengthened Nagy's hand
by making it clear that to some extent Moscow was still committed to
reform: it was incorrect to explain Soviet criticism with "Beria's provoca-
tion." "He thinks," said Khrushchev of his Hungarian counterpart, "that

after we shot Beria, we also shot criticism. This is not so." Khrushchev also declared that Rákosi was responsible for the sentencing of many innocent people.[189] He then scolded Nagy for dwelling too much on the mistakes of the past and not talking about the "results."[190] This, and the statement that "the mistakes will have to be corrected in such a way as not to destroy comrade Rákosi's authority" was a clear signal that Khrushchev was no longer firmly behind the 1953 line, although he was not ready to return to the conservative course either. The way Khrushchev treated the collectivization theme was particularly important and to a certain degree cast a shadow on the future course of reform. He stated that he did not want the collectivization movement to be speeded up in Hungary, but did not wish to see it held back either. Khrushchev candidly referred to his own experience in the Ukraine as a positive example, where collectivization was pursued among "very tense class struggle, but was still concluded three years earlier than in the neighboring Byelorussia."[191]

Moscow's criticism crystallized around the themes of party unity and economic policy and it was evident that Khrushchev and the Kremlin's old guard did not see eye-to-eye in the question of economic policy. Party unity and economy were closely interrelated, since the question of industrial development and the future course of agriculture were the most controversial issues within the Hungarian leadership. Of course economy was important in itself, thus the Soviets reinstalled Gerő as the nation's economic dictator.

The struggle for power in Budapest was in full swing. The competing parties used the Soviet ambassador as a vehicle to convey their views to Moscow and to win the Kremlin's support. Gerő and Rákosi tried to convince Andropov that the new government was responsible for the economic ailments because of its (non-repressive) peasant policies and because it allowed the standard of living to surpass the level the economy was able to support. Gerő's recommendation to alleviate the problems by reducing the standard of living startled even the ambassador.[192] Nagy was able to counter the proposals of the party conservatives and threatened to get rid of those who failed to support the new course. In his effort to put Gerő out of the way Nagy enjoyed the support of Mihály Farkas who tried to convince Andropov that Gerő was responsible for the economic malaise.[193] Although Nagy won over the Central Committee, he violated party norms by publishing an article in *Szabad Nép*, which publicized the dispute within the party leadership. This, according to the Soviet ambassador, created an "intolerable and abnormal situation" where "the authority of the party leaders was destroyed in the eyes of a whole range of party organizations."[194] Andropov was sending other signals of alarm as well. Based on information received from Nagy's opposition, in late 1954 he reiterated the view that the Hungarian economy was in a poor shape. He was particularly concerned with agricultural production, claiming that the yield of crops like potato, maize, sugar beet and sunflower was too low, and that allegedly there were losses in livestock, including the loss of 250,000 pigs because they were poorly kept. Deputy Foreign Minister Zorin introduced the report to the Central Committee,[195] which was then sent to the Gosplan in order to help preparations for the economic consultations requested by the Hungarians. Rákosi's attention was called to the "deficiencies in the development of the Hungarian national economy and the work of the Central Committee."[196] All this made Rákosi's task much easier.

In the meantime changes were occurring in Moscow and these were strengthening the conservative opposition in Hungary. After Beria was ousted Georgii Malenkov was appointed prime minister. Malenkov had been Stalin's most important aide after Beria. During the war he emerged as the dominant figure behind the industrial empire, and together with Beria headed the Soviet nuclear arms program. Malenkov openly questioned the dogma of the inevitability of war and declared "that there is no objective grounds for a collision between the United States and the USSR."[197] Moreover he asserted that the reduction of tensions was the only alternative to "the policy of preparing for a new world war." Such a war, he declared, would destroy "world civilization."[198] Khrushchev, whose ideas still revolved around the destruction of the capitalist bourgeoisie, rejected these ideas. He forced Malenkov to publicly repudiate his heretic thoughts. On 31 January 1955 Malenkov resigned.[199]

Malenkov's downfall coincided with Nagy's decline and the strengthening of the Stalinist line within the Hungarian party. The collusion between the two events may not have been a coincidence.[200] Nagy, who received his mandate for change in Moscow, gradually lost the Kremlin's support as Beria was executed and Malenkov steadily lost his influence. This should not obscure the fact that the dynamics of Hungarian domestic politics was the opposite of those of the Soviet Union. Stalin's heirs engineered Beria's downfall so as to mask their own role in Stalinist repression. On the other hand, Nagy did his best to find and uncover those responsible for Hungary's own political repression. He refused to apply the Soviet model of finding one scapegoat for all crimes. Nagy also refused to accept the former chief of the political police as the scapegoat even though Rákosi tried to hide behind Péter's back. Of course, it was easier for Nagy than for his Soviet colleagues. The latter were involved in the Stalinist crimes while Nagy was not.

Seeing black clouds gathering on the Hungarian horizon, Moscow "offered" yet another consultation. Sensing his imminent demise, Nagy tried to convince his party's Political Committee to turn down the proposal, but this time the party organ failed him and sided with Rákosi.[201] Stalin's "best disciple" now turned the table on his foe, the inquisition in Moscow showered its admonitions on Nagy, and to a lesser extent on Farkas. Even Malenkov turned against Nagy, which reflected his dwindling influence in the Politburo. Nagy's incriminated article in *Szabad Nép* was in the focal point of the attacks, especially because it demonstrated that its author violated the sacred principle of party unity. Malenkov "read it with great anxiety" and if Nagy had not signed the article, Malenkov would have thought it was written by someone alien to Marxism. "Rotten" trends were hiding behind Nagy. Khrushchev claimed that Nagy's article was "the best gift for the bourgeoisie, Churchill is rubbing his hands" in the hope that Hungary would become a second Yugoslavia.[202] Molotov added that without the Soviet Union's assistance the Hungarian People's Democracy could not survive.[203]

These statements revealed that Moscow was not worried so much about the domestic conditions within Hungary but about the prospect that Nagy would challenge Soviet supremacy in Hungary. The recommendations of 1953 were conveniently blamed on Beria. There was, however, one significant difference from the situation of 1953. Then the Soviets actually appointed Nagy and dismissed Rákosi on the spot. Now they made no concrete "proposal," but offered the prime minister a chance to exercise self-criticism. Nagy himself offered his resignation, but this was rejected, as it would have revealed the rift within the party. Both the Kremlin and the Hungarian Politburo expected self-criticism in public, in the absence of which the Hungarian Politburo rejected Nagy's resignation.

On the other hand Nagy had to accept all elements of Soviet criticism and implement the required changes without reserve.[204] Although Nagy was not completely inimical to some measure of self-criticism, which he expressed in a letter to Rákosi, he was not willing to do so publicly as required by his adversaries. Therefore Mikhail Suslov, who was knowledgeable in Hungarian affairs, was sent to Budapest to solve the impasse. Suslov had been Moscow's plenipotentiary in Lithuania in 1944 from where he went on to the Information Bureau of the Central Committee, then to its secretary of ideological and foreign affairs, where he received regular information on Hungarian domestic developments. In what became the pattern for solving important Hungarian domestic issues, the Soviet emissary met Nagy on two occasions and participated in the March 12–14 session of the Central Committee. Nagy was forced to resign and was expelled first from the Politburo, then from the party itself. The fact that this move came too late, and the genie of change was already out of the bottle, was another matter entirely.

From Moscow's perspective Nagy's reforms were alarming. Hungary, as we have seen rendered important military services to the Soviet Union.

Khrushchev criticized Nagy's military policy by stressing that it was "not enough to have adequate supplies of bacon, aircraft are needed."[205] If Nagy had his way, Hungary may not have been able to contribute to imperial defense. Moreover, the Prime Minister was unable to reduce indebtedness to the West, and this situation actually worsened while he was in power. It did not matter that there was nothing much he or anybody else could do about this. The trend had to be arrested, because it was destabilizing the economy and was increasing Hungary's reliance on countries like the Federal Republic of Germany. But if the Stalinists thought that the time had come to go back to the old ways, they were mistaken. The seemingly unpredictable Soviet leadership produced yet another volte-face. Soviet domestic developments had influenced the Hungarian domestic sphere directly in the past, but seldom as dramatically as the impact of Khrushchev's "Secret Speech" at the CPSU's 20th Congress. The impact was tremendous and led to an open split within the party between reformers and conservatives as well as to the mass expression of discontent and in the final analysis to the first revolution behind the iron curtain.

Crisis behind the Iron Curtain—Military solution

Looking back at the events one is struck by the inappropriate responses the Soviet and the Hungarian party leadership gave to the political crisis in Hungary, namely the rapid decline of Rákosi's personal prestige within the party, the widening rift within the Hungarian Communist leadership, the increasing manifestations of public discontent coupled with open criticism of party politics and even of Soviet domination in Hungary. Instead of calming the stormy sea of Hungarian politics the Politburo was inadvertently pouring oil on the fire. A case in point was the appointment of Rákosi's successor in the person of a hide-bound Stalinist, Ernő Gerő, who was obviously just as inappropriate to implement the measures required to stabilize the situation as the man he replaced. When Gerő was nominated as Rákosi's successor in July 1956, the veteran Muscovite, Zoltán Vas warned Anastas Mikoyan that in half a year's time "we will be facing a Gerő problem and consequently [the party] will hardly be able to strengthen control."[206]

There was no lack of information on the Hungarian scene. It is apparent that the Soviet leadership received enough intelligence to help deal with the political crisis. The problem was the selection of the sources and the interpretation of the intelligence. Ideological preconceptions determined the interpretation of developments and distorted the Soviet response to them. In fact, ideology consistently shaped the Soviet leadership's image of the world. The Soviets saw the root cause of the Hungarian political crisis in the subversive activity of the class enemy. Gerő was expected to combat these forces and save the party. But Gerő was utterly incapable of addressing the real problems that caused widespread popular dissatisfaction. In 1955 he warned Andropov that capitalism was being restored in Hungary. Had the Russians identified and understood the social and economic causes they might have avoided this disastrous choice and perhaps the escalation of the conflict into an armed revolution. By the time Imre Nagy was reappointed, it may have been too late. Ambassador Andropov played an important role in the escalation of the crisis. In the summer of 1956 he still supported Rákosi. His reports caused anxiety in the Soviet leadership. Andropov supported the anti-reformist forces because he believed that they guaranteed Soviet interests in Hungary. Andropov, who was driven by personal ambitions, reported of the increasing activities of "hostile forces," claiming that the Hungarian party was indecisive in its struggle against them. Therefore the Hungarians needed Soviet assistance to stay in power. On the basis of Andropov's reports the Soviet foreign ministry advocated tough policies. Andropov also played a key role in the Soviet military intervention of 24 October.[207] It is ironic that as his party's General Secretary in later years, Andropov would be seen as an advocate of reform. The Hungarian crisis strengthened Khruschev's conservative opposition, which attributed the Soviet Union's domestic and international problems to the 20th Congress and Khruschev's policies.

The Soviets failed to fully appreciate that resentment of the unequal political and economic relationship with the Soviet Union, the widespread belief that the Soviets were robbing Hungary's natural resources, hatred of the political police, declining standard of living, the desperate housing situation, the dull, regimented and poor quality of everyday existence or the yearning for political and cultural pluralism was behind the growing Hungarian dissatisfaction.[208] Only a few days before the revolution Zoltán Vas attempted to convince Andropov that in order to stabilize the situation popular support would be needed, but Gerő and some other members of the Politburo "do not command such support." Vas thought that only drastic economic reform could have stopped Nagy's now inevitable return to power. He neglected to mention that Nagy was the only figure of national standing who was able and willing to introduce the required measures. Characteristically, Andropov attributed Vas's observations to his alleged "extreme rightist" political bias and sympathy toward the "Yugoslav model of constructing socialism."[209]

The Soviet observers failed to grasp that the Hungarian working class was turning against them; instead they assumed that anti-Soviet and anti-Communist sentiment sprang from the nefarious influence of hostile forces. Less than a fortnight before the revolution broke out Gerő explained to the

Soviet ambassador that anti-Soviet feeling in Hungary had increased, but Andropov thought that the statement concerning the growth of dissatisfaction and the "dangerous spread of anti-Soviet tendencies in the midst of the working class" were "imprecise." "It would be more precise to say," he claimed, "that the agitation from the part of the reactionary circles of the intelligentsia is disorienting the workers to a significant extent."[210] Although the "objective political and economic situation in the country was satisfactory" there was political tension because of the opposition within the HWP, and because the hostile elements, which enjoyed the support of Western propaganda were attempting to "weaken the dictatorship of the proletariat and reduce the leading role of the HWP."[211]

This appraisal of the situation coincided with that of the Hungarian Stalinists on two counts: the "danger" posed by Nagy and subversion by hostile forces. Andropov claimed that "mistakes and blunders were committed in the country's economic leadership," which led to the "uneven development of the national economy, a great decline of foreign trade, and beside the negative economic consequences caused political harm to the party."[212] Hence, all one had to do was to find the culprit, in this case Rákosi, and his removal would put things right. Unfortunately, hostile elements and "reactionaries"—of which apparently quite a few remained in spite of the extensive purges—were attempting to exploit the situation in order to "discredit the party leadership in the eyes of the Communists."[213] The Soviets and their Hungarian allies seemed to agree also in the fact that Yugoslavia was exerting a malicious influence on the Hungarian intelligentsia, many of whom found the Yugoslav model more appealing than the Hungarian one.[214] Furthermore, the Yugoslav embassy was allegedly supporting Imre Nagy and his group.[215] The Soviets and Hungarian conservatives agreed that Nagy's activities were detrimental to the party's interests. As Mikoyan put it, "he made new mistakes, launched a struggle against the party and incited the anti-party elements to launch an attack on the party."[216] Prime Minister András Hegedűs claimed that "the activities of the right wing opposition are directed at Imre Nagy, who embarked on the road of open struggle against the party."[217] Besides hostile influence, the party's weakness was held responsible for the loss of power. The Russians deplored the fact that the party was not taking "tough measures against the enemy and demagogues and is not utilizing the support of the workers, peasants and the better part of the intelligentsia."[218]

In the summer of 1956 Rákosi's position was becoming increasingly precarious. The reason was his role in the illegal trials of 1949, a role he could no longer hide. Since it was clear that the situation could easily spin out of control, Andropov urged the CPSU Presidium to provide greater support and assistance to Rákosi so as to prevent Rákosi's opponents from extracting more concessions for "the right wing and demagogic elements."[219] In June the Presidium sent Suslov to Budapest in order to appraise the situation. Suslov reported that although dissatisfaction had not yet spread to the peasant and working classes, urban intellectuals and the party apparatus was dissatisfied with the Central Committee's leadership, and moreover the relations between the Central Committee and the Politburo were "cold." Disgruntled party cadres were preparing an attack on Rákosi on the pretext of the Farkas affair. In spite of all this the situation was not yet critical.[220]

Yet, as time went by, the Soviets perceived a turn for the worse. The opposition, it seemed to them, was becoming increasingly audacious and was beginning to feel confident that their activities would be unpunished. The Politburo was wavering about taking the necessary measures to curb "opportunistic and hostile elements" and even the political police was indecisive against the "counterrevolutionaries." Prompted by his distrust of Nagy and his incapability to make sense of what was going on, Andropov called Rákosi one of the "most valuable cadres," who the enemy wanted to oust from the party.[221] The situation caused anxiety for Khrushchev, who confided to Tito that he would go to any lengths to keep Hungary,[222] where the opposition was acting more and more audaciously against the party line in the major issues concerning the construction of socialism.[223] It gradually became evident that Rákosi would have to be sacrificed and that Soviet assistance would be needed to take the necessary steps, since the Hungarian party was too divided to do it on its own. Many Hungarian functionaries shared this view. As János Kádár put it, "in Hungary they often say that the Soviets intervene in Hungarian affairs too often and it always misfires. Why don't they intervene now, maybe it will succeed this time."[224] The situation in Hungary was ripe for Soviet intervention once more. The Presidium dispatched Mikoyan to take care of the Rákosi issue. He stayed in Budapest from 13 to 21 July.

In the meantime another crisis erupted in an even more sensitive area, Poland. On 28 June 1956 a strike broke out in Poznań. The demonstrators proceeded toward the local centers of administration, shouted political slogans, attacked the prisons and penetrated public buildings. They attacked the Office of Security and the demonstration turned into an armed rebellion, which the insurgents experienced as a national uprising. The Polish government forces suppressed the revolt in 24 hours.[225] Gerő's remark concerning the Polish crisis reveals the true nature of relations between the "fraternal parties": he complained that he was not notified of the events by the Polish "comrades," and learned of the events from the "Western bourgeois press."[226] The Soviet leadership feared that unrest would flare up again elsewhere unless strict ideological controls were reimposed. Khrushchev claimed that the violence had been provoked by "the subversive activities of the imperialists" and was aimed at "fomenting disunity" with the Soviet bloc and "destroying [the socialist countries] one by one."[227] This lent a special urgency to Mikoyan's mission who perceived similar symptoms in Hungary. On 9 July Andropov reported that "class alien" circles were striving to restore capitalism.[228] Mikoyan received no instructions on how to go about removing Rákosi, nor was he instructed of the Soviet choice for the dictator's replacement. Mikoyan was appalled at what he found in the Hungarian capital, where "hostile elements were active without being punished" and were using workers to remove the party leadership. He deplored the schism within the Central Committee and the fact that the Hungarian "comrades" were losing the reigns of power, as well as their control of the media. Therefore he recommended that Rákosi resign of his own accord, so as to demonstrate party unity and urged the co-optation of "Hungarian" cadres into the leadership. He demanded an assault on the "ideological front," the restoration of party discipline and unity. He lashed out against the Petőfi Circle, a forum for intellectuals to criticize the regime, calling it "an ideological Poznań without shooting." He asserted that "coexistence and détente [...] exclude ideological concessions and opportunism to hostile ideas."[229] The slogans that applied to interstate relations were inapplicable for the domestic affairs of the satellites.

Mikoyan's role in removing Rákosi is revealing of how the domestic scene of the satellites were an intrinsic part of Soviet foreign policy. He participated at the session of the highest decision-making organ of a foreign country. He made recommendations as to what measures should be taken and put forth proposals for the posts of party first secretary and Prime Minister. But he allowed the Hungarians to reject his proposal and he did not participate in the Politburo meeting of 14 July, which decided on the matter. Thereby Mikoyan managed to avoid having to assume responsibility if the wrong decision was made, while at the same time ensuring that Rákosi's replacement was satisfactory to him. After Gerő was selected, the Hungarians asked Mikoyan whether he had any objections. He had none and neither did "his party."[230] Although Gerő promised to take the steps which the Soviets demanded to curb "hostile" activity and to "restore party unity," i.e. to silence the opposition, it should have been obvious that the man was not suitable for the job. In 1953 Mikoyan had condemned the policies Gerő stood for. Now the Soviet leadership gave him mandate without any strings attached as far as reforms were concerned. This in itself underscores the notion that rivalries in the Kremlin had as much to do with personal changes in Hungary as political issues themselves.

On 6 October a state funeral was held for László Rajk and other political victims in Budapest, which turned into a mass demonstration. The date was symbolic as it marked the anniversary of the execution by the Habsburgs of the military leaders that led the Hungarian Revolution of 1848. From then on events unfolded at an accelerated pace. Soviet observers found the new party leader in a "nervous and uncertain state." Gerő warned that if Nagy came to power the political system would take on an even less socialist character than Yugoslavia. Therefore he urged Khrushchev, who was scheduled for an official visit on 20 November to come to Hungary as soon as possible.[231] At that particular moment the Polish crisis erupted and the Soviet leader had more important things to take care of. Gomułka was ready for power and the Soviets feared that he would remove the most pro-Soviet members of the Polish leadership and steer Poland to a more independent course in foreign policy.[232] Gomułka demanded the dismissal of the Polish army's Soviet commanding officers including the Defense Minister Rokossovskii. In response Soviet units approached Warsaw and a delegation headed by Khrushchev paid a surprise visit, but the Polish leader reiterated his demands. In the midst of the exchanges the Poles learned of a large scale mobilization of Soviet troops—probably intended as a form of coercive diplomacy—and responded by placing Polish troops around Warsaw. Although Khrushchev withdrew the troops, Gomułka was elected and the Soviets removed Rokossovskii. Tension mounted on 20 and 21 October, but the CPSU Presidium decided to "refrain from military intervention" and to "display patience."[233] The prospect of having to fight the Poles pushed Khrushchev toward finding a *modus vivendi* by granting greater leeway for the Polish road to socialism. In addition, the moderating role of the Chinese leadership that opposed military intervention in Poland, may also have played a key role in the peaceful resolution of the Polish crisis. Gomułka reciprocated by assuring him that Poland would remain in the Warsaw Pact and called for stronger military ties with the Soviet Union. This concession and the deteriorating situation in Hungary helped Khrushchev swallow Rokossovskii's ouster, and the threat of military intervention passed.

Meanwhile the situation in Budapest was explosive. On 22 October students of the Technical University drafted their demands in 12 points and requested permission to organize a demonstration for the following day. Gerő, who returned from Belgrade one day later, had to decide whether to allow the demonstration. At first the Political Committee decided to ban the demonstration, in fact two members, Révai and the former Social Democratic baker, György Marosán advocated all measures necessary to defend the "dictatorship of the proletariat," including firing at the crowd. For most Politburo members this was unacceptable and the moral of the armed forces seemed questionable anyway. In the absence of viable alternatives, the demonstration was permitted after all.[234] This kind of indecisiveness and helplessness characterized the party leadership throughout much of the revolution. Like the Soviets, they were captives of ideology.

By six o'clock on 23 October tens of thousands of Hungarians were demonstrating in front of the parliament building awaiting Imre Nagy's speech. Nagy was not a good speaker, his thoughts were straitjacketed by ideological conditioning. He was virtually paralyzed by the sight of the crowd. His speech turned out to be a great disappointment, which in turn launched the revolutionary spiral. Gerő's radio address, which branded the demonstrators "fascists," caused public outrage. By that time as Hungary's "greatest contribution to political semiotics,"[235] Stalin's gigantic sculpture had been pulled down, the radio and the party newspaper buildings were surrounded by hostile crowds. Members of the political police fired at the people around the Radio, provoking the militarization of the demonstration. The Soviet Special Corps were standing ready based on a contingency plan designed to put down large-scale disturbances in Hungary. Similar plans had been worked out in the rest of the people's democracies after the East German crisis in 1953, which had caught the Russians off guard.[236]

According to the official historiography of the Kádár era, the Soviet intervention of 23 October came at the Hungarian government's request. Such a request had in fact been made, but *post festam* and was ante-dated to 23 October. The precise course of events that led to the first military intervention is still obscure. We know that Gerő requested it. It was definitely precipitated by Andropov's report, which depicted the situation in Hungary as desperate, and one that could only be resolved by Soviet intervention. The Hungarian Political Committee did not take part in the decision-making process and Khrushchev had probably made up his mind before the Soviet Presidium met at nine p.m. that night.

After Gerő phoned the Soviet embassy to ask for military intervention, Andropov called Commander of the Special Corps Laschenko at five o'clock in the afternoon, who informed him that in order to carry out the operation, authorization from Defense Minister Georgii Zhukov was needed. Khrushchev then consulted with Andropov and Gerő on the high frequency line. Gerő, in contrast to his statement to Andropov, indicated that he would be able to deal with the situation. Khrushchev, who initially was reluctant to intervene, consulted with Zhukov and Andropov and concluded that intervention was necessary. With or without Gerő's knowledge the Soviet troops were placed at a state of military readiness at eight p.m. The Presidium met an hour later and only Mikoyan voted against military action. At 9 p.m. Marshall Vasilii D. Sokolovskii instructed Laschenko to move in on Budapest and assist local forces in "restoring order." The Presidium also decided to send Suslov, Mikoyan and KGB Chairman Ivan

Serov to Budapest to appraise the situation.[237] Only a decade after the German invasion another foreign power, this time the Soviet Union, used military force to maintain a political status quo that most Hungarians wanted to change.[238]

Simultaneously the Soviet leadership searched for a political solution. Khrushchev stated that Imre Nagy should be brought back into politics, although not as prime minister. By that time the Hungarian Politburo had reached the same conclusion in its deliberations through the night of 23 October. In contrast with Khrushchev's wish, the Central Committee decided to appoint Nagy as prime minister. This was a great leap towards the restoration of national sovereignty, because they made the decision without consulting the Soviets. They also elected Nagy as a member of the new Politburo, but Gerő briefly managed to hang on as first secretary, since the other candidate, János Kádár refused to take the job.

On the 24th the Soviet emissaries arrived in Budapest. By then the Hungarian authorities had labeled the events of the previous night as counter-revolution, had proclaimed a state of emergency and had declared that they were ready to take the harshest measures necessary to restore order. Mikoyan and Suslov, failing to appreciate the gravity of the crisis found that the Hungarian Communists were underestimating their own, and overestimating the enemy's strength. They saw no cause for alarm, since they believed that all the centers of resistance had been liquidated except the Radio, which was also in the process of being eliminated. The Soviet military intervention, according to the myopic Soviets, was allegedly conducted "without friction," and to "public satisfaction."[239] The situation, Mikoyan and Suslov reported, was not as dreadful as the Soviet ambassador and the Hungarians depicted it. They expected that things would be back to normal by the following morning. The newly appointed Prime Minister was described as acting "decisively and courageously," the population was seemingly not hostile to the USSR.[240] In reality the prospect for a peaceful settlement of the crisis was becoming more and more remote.

A mass demonstration was held in front of the parliament on 25 October. From a rooftop the political police opened fire on the crowd. The ensuing bloodbath was aggravated by rallies fired by Soviet troops. Gerő's position became untenable. Mikoyan and Suslov participated at the session of the Politburo, which replaced him with Kádár, but their precise role in this important decision is not known. Nevertheless, Kádár accepted the appointment because he secured Russian support. At the same session a newly elected member of the Politburo raised the issue of Soviet troop withdrawal from Hungary much to the consternation of the Soviet guests, who held that the recommendation was an invitation for American troops to occupy the country. Although the Politburo rejected the recommendation, Nagy

announced that the Hungarian government would start negotiations with its
Soviet counterpart for a complete withdrawal of Soviet troops.[241] This was
a move the Soviets would soon come to consider.

Far from subsiding, the revolution was gaining momentum and the
Communist leadership seemed unable to keep it under control. Troubling
news reached Moscow on 26 October: the masses were "out of [the HWP's]
control, the party's standing plummeted [...] strong anti-Semitic and anti-
Soviet feelings prevail among the workers and the population." On the positive side for Moscow the Spanish veteran Ferenc Münnich was appointed as
minister of defense[242] and Khrushchev was satisfied that the military situation seemed to be under control.[243] But from the Soviet perspective the situation was deteriorating. On the 28th Nagy finally reversed the official party
position and announced that the uprising could not be called a counterrevolution. The prime minister, who after days of hesitation cast his lot with the
revolutionaries, pledged that insurgents would not be harmed and promised
comprehensive talks with the Soviets on bilateral relations. The Soviets
learned that Kádár, the new first secretary was contemplating negotiation
with the centers of resistance and that the workers were supporting the revolution. Serov reported that two Americans had talked to a Soviet informer
and implied that Hungary could become a 'second Korea' with UN intervention. Early in the afternoon the government announced a general and
immediate cease-fire. The party Central Committee, which had been unable
to keep abreast of the situation, dissolved itself and a new organ, a party
Presidium was formed under the former peasant party politician, István
Dobi. The former Smallholder president of the republic, Zoltán Tildy, who
had been held under house arrest for years, had been appointed into the
government as state minister a day earlier. Khrushchev, who presided the
Presidium's session as *primus inter pares*, gave the most important assessment of the Presidium's debate, which highlighted the differences among
the Soviet leadership.

Khrushchev gave a pessimistic appraisal of the situation, which was
supported by Voroshilov. The former chairman of the Hungarian ACC criticized Mikoyan and Suslov's performance in Budapest and declared that the
troops would not be withdrawn. Kaganovich found that the counterrevolution was coming alive, but was less sanguine about putting it down than
Voroshilov. Khrushchev's alternative was the following: either there would
be a pro-Soviet government in Hungary, or one that would be against the
Soviet Union, which would demand troop withdrawal. In the first instance
the revolution could be "over quickly" with Soviet assistance, but if Nagy
turned against the USSR, and demanded a cease-fire and Soviet troop withdrawal, capitulation would ensue. There were two further options: either

a committee could be set up to assume power, or the present government could be supported. Khrushchev opted for the latter. At this point the tide of the debate turned and the previously hawkish Bulganin stated his backing of the Hungarian government. To do otherwise, he said, would entail occupation and "lead to adventurism." Malenkov talked about supporting the government and amnesty to the rebels. The minister of defense recommended the withdrawal of Soviet units from the streets of Budapest and their grouping into specified areas. Khrushchev agreed and proposed a cease-fire, which in turn would lead to the withdrawal of troops from Budapest. This was too much for Bulganin, who warned that "people's democracy collapsed" in Hungary and the party leadership ceased to exist.

Khrushchev on the other hand wanted to save face without getting into a "mess" like the British and the French in Egypt. Suslov, who had returned from the Hungarian capital, warned that public sentiment had turned against the Soviet military. He advocated the inclusion of "several democrats" into the government.[244] It therefore appeared that the Soviets were willing to give Nagy a chance and also to withdraw from Budapest in order to avoid getting embroiled in a military campaign with unforeseeable consequences. The British ambassador in Moscow understood the gist of the Soviet position: "build on [Nagy] as a Gomułka, leave it to him to return order in Budapest if he can, rely on him to secure retention of Soviet troops in Hungary under the Warsaw Pact."[245] In the meantime the Hungarian public wanted the full withdrawal of Soviet troops, the dissolution of the political police, national independence and political democracy in one package. Nagy thought that the party had given enough concessions and thought of waging a political, perhaps even armed struggle against the extremists. Talks on a general cease-fire collapsed.[246]

In the meantime yet another crisis was developing in another part of the world. Frustrated by American unwillingness to put strong pressure on Egyptian leader Gamel Abdul Nasser to undo the Suez Canal's nationalization, Great Britain and France decided to solve the problem with their own methods. On 16 October British Prime Minister Anthony Eden and his French counterpart, Guy Mollet decided on a military solution. They prompted Israel to attack Egypt, which would provide an opportunity for their military intervention. On 29 October Israel invaded its Arab neighbor, taking the American leadership by surprise. American intelligence sources had been serving notice on the trilateral military preparations since the middle of October, and the CIA reported on a large concentration of heavy bombers and transport planes in Cyprus. Nevertheless, President Eisenhower and Secretary of State John Foster Dulles dismissed the evidence because it conflicted with other sources.[247] Egypt had been the target of Soviet encroach-

ments since 1954 and Moscow made significant inroads as a result of its
support of Nasser's move to nationalize the Suez Canal. Soviet interests
were threatened on two fronts.

The CPSU Presidium did not discuss the Hungarian crisis on the 29th
but turned to it the following day with the participation of the representatives of the Chinese Communist Party. On 30 October Nagy announced the
government's reorganization on a multi-party basis, which included the former Smallholder General Secretary Béla Kovács and ex-President Zoltán
Tildy. The composition of the new government still reflected Nagy's prefer-
ence for people's democracy. János Kádár entered the cabinet, which meant
that power shifted from the party to the government.[248] Nagy was now in
a precarious position: his government had to suit the mood of the masses,
which was getting ever more radical, whilst also staying within the tolerance level of the Soviets, which was quite unpredictable. Moreover, a "revolutionary defense council" of the armed forces was set up, which called for
the withdrawal of Soviet troops from the country within the shortest time
possible. Nagy promised to approach the Soviet government about this
without delay. While all this was happening in Budapest, Khrushchev proposed what could have been the most important development in Eastern
Europe since the descent of the iron curtain. He suggested a declaration
"on the withdrawal of troops from the countries of people's democracies
[...] taking into account the views of the countries in which our troops are
based."[249] Molotov supported an appeal to the Hungarians so that they
"promptly enter into negotiations about the withdrawal of troops." Shepilov, who saw a crisis in the relations between the USSR and the satellites,
supported the principle of non-interference and expressed the Soviet
Union's readiness to withdraw troops. Zhukov declared that troops should
be pulled out of Budapest and if necessary from Hungary as a whole.

This was a momentous turnaround since just four days before, Suslov
and Mikoyan had told the Hungarians that Soviet troop withdrawal was
out of the question. Khrushchev, who thought that party first secretary
Kádár was "behaving well," proposed measures to support the Hungarian
government. In this spirit a declaration was drafted on the relationship
between socialist countries expressing respect for their sovereignty, territorial integrity and independence, as well as pledging non-interference in
home affairs. As far as Hungary was concerned, it was recognized that the
continued presence of Soviet troops may make things worse, and envisioned
troop withdrawal from Budapest and negotiations with the Hungarian government on their stationing in Hungary.[250]

Although the declaration was potentially of great significance, it did
not mean that Moscow was ready to give up Hungary. Khrushchev saw the
declaration as a means for a peaceful solution. Even if they were withdrawn,
Soviet units could be easily reintroduced through the Carpatho-Ukraine,

which Stalin had taken over in 1945. Moreover, the document was carefully worded to avoid a statement on party relations, which, as Molotov pointed out, were distinct from state-to-state contacts. The Chinese, who had previously expressed that Soviet–Hungarian relations should be based on the principles of Pancha Shila, indicated that according to the CPC's position Soviet troops should remain in Hungary and in Budapest.[251] According to the Beijing Revue Mao became convinced that Russia was making a mistake in adopting a policy of capitulation and abandoning Hungary to counter-revolution. Mao himself recalled the Chinese embassy in Budapest's report according to which the counter-revolution was spreading at an alarming speed and which warned that if the Soviet Union failed to act, capitalism would be restored. Therefore he urged military action.[252]

At a reception on the 30th Zhukov told the U.S. ambassador that the Soviet units had received an order to withdraw from Budapest.[253] But the next day the Soviet leadership decided to reverse this decision and to send troops to suppress the revolution. With the exception of Saburov, everyone agreed with Khrushchev that the Soviet Union "should take the initiative to restore order in Hungary." Marshall Konev would issue the order for military intervention, the plans for which would be worked out by Zhukov. Khrushchev and Malenkov would consult with Tito, while Brezhnev, Pospelov and Furtseva would take care of the propaganda part.[254] The satellites were informed. Molotov and Malenkov consulted with the Poles in Brest on the first of November. Soviet units crossed the Hungarian border. Gomułka attempted to dissuade the Russians from marching in, but to no avail. In response Nagy declared neutrality, renounced the Warsaw Pact and called on the UN to guarantee it. Nagy had no illusions about the Soviet stance to Hungarian neutrality, but he thought that the request, which he believed was the only way to cause complication for the Soviets, could be used as a bargaining chip to forestall Soviet intervention. If the Russians agreed to halt their military preparations Hungary would withdraw its plea to the UN for the four-power guarantee.[255] Mikoyan argued for talks but to no avail. Suslov warned that the "danger of bourgeois restoration has reached its peak," and only occupation could avert disaster. Zhukov saw no reason to accept Mikoyan's argument either. Kádár was flown to Moscow to be appointed to the post of Party first secretary. As a ploy, the Soviets continued to discuss troop withdrawal with a Hungarian delegation, but Serov, who had been involved in deportation of Balts and Soviet national minorities during the war, surprised even the Russian negotiators by halting these discussions on 3 November and arresting the Hungarian negotiators.

Based on the available evidence there is no clear explanation for the abrupt shift. Of course, military intervention was a strong option throughout the crisis. Yet, the Soviet leadership's volte-face requires explanation. Mark Kramer points to the importance of the alarming reports Mikoyan and

Suslov were sending from Budapest.[256] Immediately before the session of
the Presidium on the 30th the two envoys reported that the situation was
getting worse, hooligans were occupying local party headquarters and killing
Communists. They feared that the Hungarian units might go over to the side
of the insurgents in which case it may become necessary for the Soviet military to resume operations. They added that they had no final opinion on the
matter and would report of the developments.[257] Soon after sending the
message Mikoyan and Suslov learned about the grisly siege of the Budapest
party headquarters, including the lynching of members of the political
police. The fact that some Hungarian tanks took side with the attackers confirmed their fears.[258] Kramer also emphasizes the importance of remaining
in the Soviet bloc. Had Gomułka not been willing to keep Poland in the
Soviet bloc, a military confrontation might have ensued. It seems likely,
Kramer concludes, that Nagy's expressed desire to renounce Hungarian
membership in the Warsaw Pact was one of the factors that induced the
Soviets to reverse their decision on 30 October.[259] In the afternoon of 31
October Imre Nagy announced that Hungary would start negotiations on
Soviet troop withdrawal and on "renouncing our obligations under the Warsaw Pact."[260] Unfortunately we do not know whether Nagy's announcement
came before or after the Presidium's session. Therefore it is hard to establish a direct link between the announcement and the decision to intervene.
Moreover Nagy's announcement came after he learned that Soviet troops
were entering Hungarian territory. Suslov and Mikoyan reported to Moscow
that Nagy was worried about these troop-movements. Domestic developments may not have been the only factor that influenced Soviet decision-
making.

On 30 October Britain and France issued a joint ultimatum to Israel
and Egypt that threatened with invasion unless the two parties complied
with their demands. On 31 October they joined Israel in the aggression
against Egypt by bombing its military airfields. This may have been highly
important in the abrupt shift of Soviet policy. Khrushchev made a reference
to it when he announced his decision to intervene: "if we depart from Hungary, it will give a great boost to the Americans, English and the French—
the imperialists [...] To Egypt they will then add Hungary."[261] Prime Minister Bulganin gave a briefing on the decision on the first of November. He
explicitly referred to international developments. Since the decision of 30
October, Bulganin explained, "the international situation changed."[262] In
fact, Khrushchev claimed in June 1957 that steps made by Soviet "foreign
policy" during the "Anglo–French–Israeli aggression and the counterrevolutionary putsch in Hungary averted the outbreak of a new, world war."[263]
From the remarks of the Soviet leaders it is fairly clear that they worried
about the loss of Hungary and the deteriorating situation in the Middle East.
The Americans were making reassuring remarks about non-intervention in

Hungary, but these may have sounded suspicious to Soviet ears.[264] Conflu-
ence of the Anglo-French military aggression against Egypt and the critical
situation in Hungary may have caused the Kremlin to take immediate preventive measures. It is safe to say, therefore, that without the Anglo-French
intervention on 31 October the Soviet leadership would not have been so
hard pressed to crack down in Hungary. The role of Suez in the Hungarian
crisis was that it precipitated the Soviet invasion, while making it difficult
for the U.S. to condemn it.

Of course military intervention was on the Soviet agenda all throughout the crisis. But there were serious political risks involved both in and
out of Hungary, therefore for a while Khrushchev and Mikoyan were able
to convince the Presidium to search for a political solution. But all along
there were opponents within the Presidium of the peaceful approach, notably
Molotov, Bulganin, Kaganovich, while Zhukov wavered. Deliberations
about Hungary reflected the struggle for power within the Kremlin. In these
circumstances Khrushchev's position may have become untenable if he had
insisted on further patience and talks with the Hungarians. Hence the dynamics of Kremlin politics, the perceived deterioration of the Hungarian scene
and international developments determined that there would be no experimentation with democracy in Eastern Europe.

In 1956 the Soviet Union was not ready to surrender Eastern Europe.
Khrushchev's vision of Europe did not resemble Gorbachev's. Eastern
Europe was still an asset and not a liability, as it had become by the late
1980s. In the final days of the revolution Hungary went too far, its role as a
client state was in serious jeopardy. Still, a negotiated settlement of the crisis as envisioned on 30 October would have allowed a measure of political
pluralism to survive under a more equal relationship with the Soviet Union.
On the other hand full independence required liberation by a foreign power.
The last chapter will explore whether liberation was a real alternative.

NOTES

1 See on this Adomeit, *Imperial Overstretch.*
2 Mark Trachtenberg, *Constructed Peace,* pp. 27–28, p. 33.
3 For an argument that Stalin would have accepted a unified Germany in 1952
  under certain conditions see Mark Kramer, "The Early Post-Stalin Succession
  Struggle and Upheavals in East-Central Europe: Internal–External Linkages in
  Soviet Policy Making" (Part 3), *Journal of Cold War Studies,* vol. I, no. 3, (Fall
  1999), pp. 9–14. Stein Bjørnstad, *The Soviet Union and German Unification
  During Stalin's Last Years* (Oslo: Defense Studies, 1998/1). Wilfried Loth argues
  that "Stalin really wanted what be said: the speady conclusion of a peace treaty
  and a natural Germany." See Wilfried Loth, "The Origins of Stalin's Note of 10
  March 1952," *Cold War History,* vol. IV, no. 2 (January 2004), p, 84. On the other

hand Adomeit believes that "the diplomatic note and its sequels were a tactical device designed to [...] gain a greater degree of influence on West German public opinion [...] to delay or prevent West Germany's defense integration in the framework of the EDC [...] " and other ends. Adomeit, *Imperial Overstretch*, p. 88.

4 See Goncharev, Litai and Lewis, *Uncertain Partners*, pp. 115–116.

5 On the Soviet Union and the Korean War see Kathryn Weathersby, "Soviet Aims in Korea and the Origins of the Korean War, 1945–1950: New Evidence from Russian Archives," Cold War International History Project, Working Paper No. 8. (Washington D.C.: Woodrow Wilson Center, 1993).

6 On the U.S. perception of Soviet involvement in the Korean attack see Robert Jervis, *Perception and Misperception in International Politics* (Princeton: Princeton University Press, 1973), p. 34.

7 Gaddis, *We Now Know*, p. 75.

8 See Robert Bowie and Richard H. Immerman, *Waging Peace: How Eisenhower Shaped an Enduring Cold War Strategy* (Oxford: Oxford University Press, 1998), pp. 17–24.

9 A case in point is the Hungarian–Czechoslovak treaty of friendship that was concluded in 1948 in spite of the very serious differences between the two countries regarding the fate of the Hungarian minority in Slovakia.

10 Rákosi, *Visszaemlékezések*, vol. II, pp. 860–862.

11 Kramer, "The Early Post-Stalin Succession Struggle and the Upheavals in East-Central Europe," part 3, p. 12.

12 Reshenie Politbiuro TsK VKP (b) ob ekonomicheskikh otnosheniakh mezhdu SSR i starane narodnoi demokratii [Resolution of the Central Committee of the CPSU on the economic relations between the USSR and the people's democracies] 23 December 1948, *VEDRA*, vol. I, document 308, pp. 847–853.

13 On the establishment of Communist regimes after 1948 see T.V. Volokitina, et al., *Moskva i vostochnaia Evropa–Stanovlenie politicheskikh rezhimov sovietskogo tipa, 1949–1953* (Moscow: Rosspen, 2002).

14 On Soviet efforts to capitalize on its image as the liberator of colonized peoples, its success with experimentation with neutralism in the Third World as a tool for expanding political influence at the expense of the West see David J. Dallin, *Soviet Foreign Policy after Stalin* (Philadelphia, Chicago, New York: J. B. Lippincott Company, 1961), pp. 286–321.

15 George Schopflin, *Politics in Eastern Europe, 1945–1992*.

16 Ibid.

17 Rákosi, *Visszaemlékezések,* vol. II. p. 165.

18 See János M. Rainer, *Nagy Imre, 1953–1958—Politikai Életrajz, II* [Imre Nagy, 1953–1958—A political biography, II] (Budapest: 1956-os Intézet, 1999), p. 45. On one occasion the Hungarian government wanted to turn to the UN with a protest against "U.S. intervention in Hungary's internal affairs," but asked for Soviet advice (i.e. instruction) whether they should do so. The way this was handled says something about the decision-making process in Moscow: the request for advice went to Vishinskii. Yet, the minister of foreign affairs did not commit

himself in a matter of this magnitude and turned to Stalin himself. Pismo A. Ia. Vishinskogo I. V. Stalinu po povodu namerenia pravitelstvo Vengrii obratitsia v OON s zhaloboi na SshA [Letter by A. Ia. Vishinskii in connection with the intention of the Hungarian government to turn the UN with complaint against the U.S.] 8 September 8 1951, in *Vostochnaia Evropa v Dokumentakh Rossiiskikh Arkhivov*, vol. II, 1949–1953, (hereafter cited as *VEDRA*, vol. II), (Moscow: Sibirskii Khronograf, 1998), pp. 609–610, Document 220. On another occasion Deputy Foreign Minister Andor Berei turned to the Soviet ambassador for "advice" whether the Hungarians should close the U.S. Legation's library in Budapest. Iz dnevnika Kiseleva. Zapis besedi so stats-sekretarem MID Vengrii A. Berei ob ogranichenii peredvizheniia diplomaticheskikh rabotnikov, zapreshchenii izdaniia biuletenei angliiskoi i amerikanskoi missii, namerenii zakrit biblioteku amerikanskoi missii [From Kiselev's diary. Record of conversation with state secretary of foreign affairs A. Berei on the restriction of movement of diplomatic personnel, banning the publication of the bulletin of the British and American missions and the intention to close the library of the American mission] 17 November 1950, pp. 441–442, document 150.

19 A revealing example of how the soviets interfered with government appoitments was when at a reception Ambassador Ievgenii Kiselev informed Ernő Gerő that although "he had no wish to interfere in the issue, but was surprised by the fact that we want to appoint Kossa as minister of heavy industry and not Zsofinyecz. Their economic men in here think that Zsofinyecz is more solid than Kossa." Gerő's letter to Nagy and Rákosi is cited in Magdolna Baráth ed., *Szovjet nagyköveti iratok Magyarországról 1953–1956—Kiszeljov és Andropov titkos jelentései* [Soviet ambassadorial documents on Hungary 1953–1956—the secret reports of Kiselev and Andropov] (Budapest: Napvilág Kiadó, 2002), p. 12.

20 Hence for example the Soviet Union's Council of Ministers resolved to send to Hungary forty-five expert advisors to ministries including Machine Construction, Heavy Industry, Agriculture, etc. at the Hungarian government's request. Postanovlenie Sovieta Ministrov SSSR [Resolution of the Council of Ministers] 30 April 30 1956, *VEDRA*, vol. II, pp. 296–297, document 96. In the same year Rákosi requested the sending of six Soviet experts to work in the oil industry. "Pismo Rákosi Stalinu s informatsiei o merakh po ukrepleniiu armii i oboronosposobnosti Vengrii i s prosboi prislat spetsialistov po dobiche nefti [Rákosi's letter to Stalin with information on measures to strengthen the army and Hungarian defense capability and request to send specialists in the production of oil] 31 October 1951, *VEDRA*, vol. II, pp. 437–439, document 147.

21 Pismo Rákosi sekretariiu Ts. K. VKP (b) M. Suslovu s informatsiei o podgotovke k viboram, vengero-chekhoslovatskikh otnosheniakh i sotrudnichestve s SSSR po oboronnim voprosam [Rákosi's letter to the secretary of the Central Committee of the CPSU Suslov with information on the preparation for the elections, Hungarian-Czechoslovak relations and cooperation with the USSR in defense matters] 13 April 1949, *VEDRA*, vol. II, pp. 70–74, document 22.

22 Kramer, "The Early Post-Stalin Succession Struggle and Upheavals in East-Central Europe," Part 1, p. 5.

23 Informatsionnaiia Spravka Sovietnika Posoltsvo SSSR v Vengrii Smirnova [Information by the counselor of the Soviet Embassy in Hungary Smirnov] 20 October 1950. *VEDRA*, vol. II, pp. 425-429, document 144.

24 Hedley Bull, *The Anarchical Society—A Study of Order in World Politics* (New York: Columbia University Press, 1977), pp. 213–217.

25 Stephen Krasner, *Sovereignty—Organized Hypocrisy*, p. 20.

26 Kenneth Waltz, *Theory of International Politics*, p. 96. Martin Wight argued that a nation can be sovereign without full national independence. Martin Wight, *Power Politics*. Hedley Bull described the relationship between the Soviet Union and the countries of Eastern Europe as "hegemony." He defined this relationship as "the great power is ready to violate the rights of sovereignty, equality and independence enjoyed by the lesser states, but it does not disregard them; it recognizes that these rights exist." Hedley Bull, *The Anarchical Society*, pp. 215–216. This statement contradicts Morgenthau's view to wit that only one nation can exercise sovereignty over a given territory, sovereignty is indivisible. Hans Morgenthau, *Politics among Nations*, pp. 328–346.

27 Austrian–Hungarian relations in the 18th century and in the 19th century up to 1867 for example were governed by the Pragmatic Sanction of 1723 and Article 10 of 1790. These laid down the legal framework of the relationship, as well as the *services* Hungary was obligated to render the Habsburg-Lotharingian sovereign (in some interpretations to the *crown*) in return for an explicit recognition of Hungary's "freedom and independence." Hungary was endowed with the constitutional right to dispute with the court in Vienna. Similar imperial arrangements were not unknown in different dimensions of time and space.

28 1950. évi 10. számú törvényerejű rendelet április 4.-ének, Magyarország felszabadulása napjának nemzeti ünneppé nyilvanításáról [Decree 10 of 1950 on the designation of 4 April, the day of the liberation of Hungary as a day of national commemoration] undated, Sándor Balogh ed., *Nehéz esztendők krónikája, 1949–1953* [The Chronicle of Hard Years, 1949–1953], (Budapest: Gondolat, 1986), p. 236.

29 Pismo Rákosi Stalinu [Rákosi's letter to Stalin] 31 October 1951, op. cit., *VEDRA*, vol. II, pp. 437–439, document 147.

30 Feljegyzés az MDP PB üléséről [Record of meeting of the Political Committee of the HWP] 20 June 1953, MOL, MDP, 276. F., 53. cs., 122 őe., vol. I.

31 Kiszeljov beszélgetése Zágor György kairói magyar követtel [Kiselev's conversation with Hungarian minister György Zágor in Cairo] 4 December 1956, cited in Baráth, *Szovjet nagyköveti iratok*, p. 21.

32 Pismo Rákosi Stalinu [Rákosi's letter to Stalin] 31 October 1950, op. cit, *VEDRA*, vol. II, pp. 437–439, document 147.

33 Friss István feljegyzése Rákosinak [Memorandum by István Friss to Rákosi] 12 March 1949, MOL, 276. F., 65. cs., 114. őe.

34 See János M. Rainer, "Sztálin és Rákosi, Sztálin és Magyarország, 1949–1953" [Stalin, Rákosi, Stalin and Hungary] in András Hegedűs B., et al. eds., *Évköny 1956* (Budapest: 1956-os Intézet, 1998), p. 92.

35 Ibid., p. 93.

36 A magyar írók első kongresszusának határozata [Resolution of the First Congress of Hungarian Writers] 30 April 1952, in *Nehéz Esztendők Krónikája*, pp. 330–335.

37 Spravka OVP TsK VKP (b) 'o natsionalisticheskikh oshibkakh rukovodstva kommunisticheskoi partii i burzhoaznom vliianii v vengerskoi kommunisticheskoi pechati [Information of the foreign affairs division of the CPSU Central Committee on the nationalistic mistakes of the leadership of the Communist Party and the bourgeois influence in Hungarian Communist press] *VEDRA*, vol. I, pp. 802–806, document 269.

38 Rákosi, *Visszaemlékezések*, vol. II, p. 753. Rákosi considered Stalin an all-round talent, who was better than his former rivals like Bukharin or Trotsky if all requirements for a politician are taken together even if in one or another field they may have been more able than Stalin.

39 See Albert Resis, ed., *Molotov Remembers: Inside Kremlin Politics. Conversations with Felix Chuev* (Chicago, 1993).

40 Pismo Rákosi Suslovu [Rákosi's letter to Suslov] 13 April 1949, *VEDRA*, vol. II, op. cit., pp. 70–74; Iz zapisi besedi M.A. Suslova s chlenom Politburo J. Révai [From record of conversation between A. Suslov and Politburo member J. Révai] *VEDRA* vol. I, pp. 872–875, document 283.

41 Feljegyzés a Rákosi Mátyással folytatott beszélgetésről [Record of conversation with Mátyás Rákosi] 15 April 1955 in Baráth, *Szovjet nagyköveti iratok Magyarországról*, pp. 234–238.

42 Dokladnaia zapiska S. G. Zabolzhskogo N. N. Pukhlobu o predlozheniakh M. Rákosi po organizatsii edinogo pechatnogo organa i radiostantsii yugoslavskikh emigrantov v Moskve ili v odnoi iz stran narodnoi demokratii [Report by S. G. Zabolzhskii, N. N. Pukhlob on the proposal by Rákosi to organize an émigré Yugoslav press organ and radio station in Moscow or one of the people's democracies] 29 September 1949, *VEDRA*, vol. II, pp. 237–238, document 74; Zapis besedi S.G. Zabolzhskogo s M. Rákosi o neobhodimosti aktivizatsii borbi protiv politicheskogo rezhima v Yugoslavii i o sviazakh riada kommunistov s inostrannimi razvedkami [Record of conversation between S. G. Zabolzhskii and M. Rákosi on the indispensability of stepping up the struggle against the political regime in Yugoslavia and the links of Communists across the border with foreign intelligence services] 31 January 1950, *VEDRA*, vol. II, pp. 297–298, document 97.

43 Dokladnaia zapiska Zabolzhskogo Barananovu o besede s M. Rákosi o "dele" L. Rajk, predstoiaschikh arestakh v vengerskoi armii, razvertivanii vooruzhennoi borbi v Yugoslavii i dr. [Zabolzhskii's report to Baranov on conversation with M. Rákosi on L. Rajk's "matters," on the imminent arrests in the Hungarian army, on the development of armed struggle in Yugoslavia, etc.] 11 July 1949, *VEDRA*, vol. II, pp. 181–183, document 55.

44 On the Rajk trial see Tibor Hajdu, "A Rajk-per háttere és fázisai" [The background and phases of the Rajk trial] *Társadalmi Szemle*, 1992, no. 11, pp. 17–36; János M. Rainer, "Sztálin és Rákosi, Sztálin és Magyarország."

45 Paczkowski, *Lengyelország története,* p. 177.

46 On these accusations see János M. Rainer, "Távirat Filippov elvtársnak" [Telegram to Comrade Filipov] in András Hegedűs B. et al. eds., *Évkönyv 1998* (Budapest: 1956-os Intézet, 1998), p. 106.

47 Dokladnaya zapiska Zabolzhskogo Baranovu o besede s Rakosi, op. cit., 11 July 1949, *VEDRA*, vol. II, pp. 181–183, document 55.

48 Annotatsia dokladnoi zapiski chlena TsK VPT Z. Bíró o besedakh s Gottwaldom i Slanskim [Summary of report by HWP Central Committee member Bíró's conversation with Gottwald and Slansky] 26 September 1949, *VEDRA*, vol. II, pp. 219–224, document 69.

49 Dokladnaya zapiska Zabolzhskogo Grigorianu s poluchennoi ot M. Rákosi informatsiei o vengerskikh i zarubezhnikh kommunistakh [Zabolzhskii's report to Grigorianu with information from M. Rákosi on Hungarian and foreign Communists] 9 March 1950, *VEDRA*, vol. II, pp. 316–319, document 105.

50 George Schöpflin, *Politics in Eastern Europe*.

51 Feljegyzés Gerő Ernővel folytatott megbeszélésről [Record of conversation with Ernő Gerő] 18 February 1954 in Baráth, *Szovjet nagyköveti iratok Magyarországról*, p. 139.

52 Little is known about Péter's (born Benjámin Eisenberger) biography. For an attempt to assess Péter's personality and to piece together the basic facts of his early career see György Gyarmati, "Péter Gábor fiatalsága 1906–1945," [Gábor Péter's youth] in György Gyarmati ed., *A Történeti Hivatal Évkönyve* (Budapest: 2002), pp. 25–78.

53 Elméleti feladataink és a pártoktatás. Vázlat az Országos Oktatási Értekezleten tartandó referátumhoz [Our theoretical tasks and party education. Outline for presentation to be given at the National Education conference] 1948, undated, Contribution by József Révai and Erzsébet Andics. MOL, 276. F., 53. cs., 10. őe.

54 Paczkowski, *Lengyelország története*, p. 173.

55 Rákosi, *Visszaemlékezések*, vol. II, p. 899.

56 Iz dnevnika posla SSSR v Vengrii. Zapis besedi s M. Rákosi o hode peregovorov s episkopnim sovietom i dr. [From the diary of the ambassador in Hungary. Record of converstion with Rákosi on the status of talks with the council of bishops, etc.] 2 June 1950, *VEDRA*, vol. II, pp. 371–372, document 126.

57 Pismo Stalina Rákosi [Stalin's letter to Rákosi] 23 June 1950, in Rainer, Távirat Filippov elvtársnak [Telegram to Comrade Filipov] in Hegedűs, ed., *Évkönyv 1956*, p. 113.

58 In his memoirs Rákosi expressed his lack of comprehension of Zöld's awful act. Rákosi, *Visszaemlékezések*, vol. II, p. 895. He neglected to mention that he had already been planning to arrest him together with Kádár and Kállai. Zöld committed suicide on 20 April, Kádár and Kállai were arrested soon after. Pismo Rákosi Stalinu [Rákosi's letter to Stalin] 27 March 1951, op. cit, *VEDRA*, vol. II, pp. 497–498, document 171. Rákosi reported to Stalin on Zöld's suicide on 21 April noting that Kádár and Kállai would be arrested when they find out about it. Rákosi Filippovu [Rákosi to Filippov] 21 April 195, in Rainer, "Távirat Filippov elvtársnak," op. cit. pp. 116–117.

59 Pismo Rákosi Stalinu, 27 March 1951, *VEDRA*, op. cit., vol. II, pp. 497–498, document 171.

60 See Izsák, *Rendszerváltástól rendszerváltásig*, pp. 110–111.
61 Rákosi, *Visszaemlékezések*, vol. II, p. 756.
62 Rákosi hozzászólása az MDP PB ülésén [Rákosi's speech at the meeting of the HWP Political Committee] 11 February 1953, MOL, 276. F., 65. cs., 30. őe.
63 In writing this passage I used Mária Schmidt, "'Ez lesz a perek pere'—Adalékok egy torzóban maradt tisztogatási akcióhoz," ['This will be the trial of trials' - Addenda to an unfinished campaign of purges] in Mária Schmidt, *Diktatúrák ördögszekéren* [Dictatorships on Eringium] (Budapest: Magvető, 1998).
64 Ibid.
65 Ibid.
66 Ibid.
67 The figure is from Javaslat az MDP PB-nek [Proposal to the Political Committee of the HWP] 6 December 1955, MOL, 276. F., 53. cs., 260. őe.
68 Soprovoditelnoe pismo E. D. Kiseleva A. Ia. Vishinskomu k spravke o podpolnoi deyatelnosti vrazhdebnikh elementov v Vengrii i o borbe s nimi [E. D. Kiselev's cover letter to A. Ia. Vishinskii to the report on the underground activity of enemy elements and the struggle against them] 25 December 1952, *VEDRA*, vol. II, pp. 853–854, document 309.
69 Iz dnevnika sovietnika posolstva SSSR v Vengrii Filippova. Zapis besedi s Z. Bíró [From the diary of the counsellor of the USSR's Embassy in Hungary Filippov. Record of conversation with Z. Bíró] 3 February 1956, *VEDRA*, vol. II, pp. 866–871, document 312.
70 See György T. Varga, ed., "Jegyzőkönyv a szovjet és magyar párt- és állami vezetők tárgyalásairól—1953. június 13–16" [Minutes of the negotiations of Hungarian and Soviet party leaders, 13–16 June 1956], *Múltunk*, 1992, no. 3., p. 242. The document is published in English in Csaba Békés, Malcolm Byrne and János M. Rainer eds., *The 1956 Hungarian Revolution.*
71 Izsák, *Rendszerváltástól rendszerváltásig*, p. 112.
72 Paczkowski, *Lengyelország története*, p. 175.
73 Révai feljegyzése Rákosinak [Révai's memorandum to Rákosi] MOL, 276. F., 65. cs., 16. őe.
74 Rákosi planned the "liquidation of kulaks" in the "second five-year plan." Feljegyzés a Minisztertanács elnökével, Rákosival, helyettesével, Gerővel, az MDP KV titkárával, Révaival és a honvédelmi miniszterrel, Farkassal folytatott beszélgetésről [Memorandum on conversation with Prime Minister Rákosi, his deputy Gerő, HWP Central Committee secretary Révai and Defense Minister Farkas] 10 May 1953 in Baráth, *Szovjet nagyköveti iratok Magyarországról*, p. 53.
75 Feljegyzés az MDP PB számára [Memorandum for the HWP Politburo] 29 October 1953, MOL, 276. F., 53. cs., 146. őe.
76 Budapest Party First Secretary, Imre Kovács reported his own brother, a veteran of the British army crippled in war, to the AVH for spying. No evidence was found to implicate him, but Kovács tried and tried until his brother was eventually arrested and incarcerated innocently.
77 Szabó István és társai [István Szabó and associates] 1951, Történeti Hivatal (hereafter cited as TH), 10-51048-952, V-93057.

78 All the cases are cited in István Kozma, "Névváltoztatás és történelem (1894–1956)," [Name change and history 1894-1956] *Századok,* vol. 37, no. 2, 1997, pp. 383–453.

79 Szabó István és társai, TH, 10-51048-952 V-93057.

80 Izsák, *Rendszerváltástól rendszerváltásig,* p. 113.

81 Szabó István és társai, 1951, TH, 10-51048-952, V-93057, op. cit.

82 Levél Rákosinak, MOL, 276. F., 65. cs., 82. őe.

83 Iz dnevnika Kiseleva. Zapis besedi s sekretarem Ts. K. VPT Kovacsem [From Kiselev's diary. Record of conversation with HWP Central Committee secretary Kovács] 16 June 1951, *VEDRA,* vol. II, pp. 567–570, document 204.

84 Iz dnevnika Kiseleva. Zapis besedi s ministrom vnutrennikh del Vengrii [From Kiselev's diary. Record of conversation with Hungary's Minister of the Interior] 28 August 1951, *VEDRA,* vol. II, pp. 600–601, Document 215.

85 Iz dnevnika Kiseleva. Beseda s ministrom inostrannikh del [From Kiselev's diary. Conversation with the minister of foreign affairs] 5 September 1951, *VEDRA,* vol. II, pp. 604–605, document 217.

86 Soprovoditelnoe pismo Kiseleva Vishinskomu [Kiselev's cover letter to Vishinskii] 25 December 1952, VEDRA, document 309.

87 Kiszeljov nagykövet emlékiratainak kérdése [The question of Ambassador Kiselev's memoirs] 4 December 1954, MOL, Küm, XIX-J-1-j, Szu tük, IV-100-1, 5. doboz, 056-16/1956.

88 See Pető and Szakács, *A hazai gazdaság négy évtizedének története,* p. 162.

89 Soprovoditelnoe pismo L. Berii G. Malenkovu i soobshchenia sovietnika MVD SSSR v Chekhoslovakii A. D. Beschastnova o massovikh besporiadkakh v Prage i Plzeni v sviazi s denezhnim reformom [Cover letter by L. Beria to G. Malenkov and report by Soviet Interior Ministry advisor in Czechoslovakia A. D. Beschast-nov on massive unrest in Prague and Plzen in connection with the monetary reform] 1–2 June 1953, *VEDRA,* vol. II, p. 918, document 329.

90 Feljegyzés Nagy Imrével, a Magyar Népköztársaság Miniszterelnökével folyta-tott beszélgetésről [Memorandum of conversation with the Prime Minister of the People's Republic of Hungary Imre Nagy] 16 July 1953 in Baráth, *Szovjet nagy-követi iratok Magyarországról,* pp. 54–62.

91 See Pető and Szakács, *A hazai gazdaság négy évtizedének története,* pp. 152–167; Izsák, *Rendszerváltástól rendszerváltásig,* pp. 114–115.

92 Source Pető and Szakács, *A hazai gazdaság történetének négy évtizede,* p. 168.

93 Ibid., pp. 212–233.

94 Paczkowski, *Lengyelország története,* p. 160.

95 Mark Kramer, "The Early Post-Stalin Succession Struggle and Upheavals in East-Central Europe," Part 1, p. 17.

96 Feljegyzés a Belügyminisztérium helyi tanács osztálya beszolgáltatási csoport számára [Memorandum for the delivery group of the local council department of the Ministry of the Interior] 22 January 1953, MOL, XIX-A-1-2-ee, F tük, 198. doboz, 39. dosszié.

97 A magyar-szovjet bauxit társaság vezérigazgató-helyettesének feljegyzése [Memorandum by the deputy managing director of the Hungarian-Soviet bauxite com-pany] 13 December 1950, MOL, XIXX F 35, 2 doboz. ikt. sz. n.

98 Külkereskedelmi vezetők értekezlete Gerő Ernőnél [Meeting of foreign trade leaders at Ernő Gerő] 3 June 1952, MOL MDP, 276 F., 66 cs., 69 őe.

99 Feljegyzés minőségi kifogások miatt visszaküldött árukról [Memorandum on goods returned because of qualitative deficiency] 27 August 1953, MOL, 276. F., 67. cs., 178. őe.

100 Jelentés a külkereskedelemről [Report on foreign trade] 15 August 1954, MOL, 276. F., 66. cs., 69. őe.

101 Külkereskedelmi vezetők értekezlete Gerő Ernőnél, 3 June 1952, op. cit.

102 1952-es export elmaradások [Export arrears in 1952] 1952, undated, MOL, XIX-A-2-ee, A/tük, 6. doboz, 8. dosszié.

103 Külkereskedelmi vezetők értekezlete Gerő Ernőnél, 3 June 1952, op. cit.

104 Ibid.

105 Pető and Szakács, *A hazai gazdaság négy évtizedének története*, p. 166.

106 Kiselev Molotovu [Kiselev to Molotov] 30 May 1953, AVPRF, Fond 077, opis 33, papka 166, delo 240.

107 Source Pető and Szakács, *A hazai gazdaság történetének négy évtizede*, p. 164. The debt was calculated in "deviza forints," which was equal to two forints. The exchange rate for the forint was 12 to a dollar.

108 Háy László külkereskedelmi miniszter feljegyzése a külkereskedelmi helyzetről [Memorandum by minister of foreign trade László Háy on the foreign trade situation] 13 October 1953, MOL, 276. f., 67. cs., 178. őe.

109 Feljegyzés az adóssághelyzetről [Memorandum on the debt situation] 1955, undated, MOL, 276. F., 65. cs., 283. őe.

110 Feljegyzés az MDP PB üléséről [Record of meeting of the HWP Politburo] 2 January 1956, MOL, 276. F., 53. cs., 264. őe.

111 Feljegyzés az MDP PB részére [Memorandum for the HWP Politburo] 11 October 1954, MOL, 276. F., 53. cs., 199. őe.

112 Zimyanin Molotovu [Zimyanin to Molotov] 12 November 1954, AVPRF, Fond 077, opis 34, papka 178, delo 260.

113 Luttwak, *The Grand Strategy of the Soviet Union*, p. 177.

114 Paczkowski, *Lengyelország története*, p. 157.

115 Étude sur la Hongrie [Study on Hungary] prepared by the French Legation in Budapest, June 1952. Archives de Quai d'Orsay, Europe 1944–1960, Hongrie, vol. 40, pp. 215–230.

116 Kálmán Pécsi, *A magyar–szovjet gazdasági kapcsolatok 30 éve* [Thirty years of Hungarian–Soviet economic relations] (Budapest: Közgazdasági Kiadó, 1979) pp. 190–192.

117 See Paul Marer, "The 'Soviet Bloc' as an Integration Model," pp. 64–65.

118 Holsti, *International Politics*, pp. 282–283.

119 Károly Urbán, *Sztálin halálától a forradalom kitöréséig – a magyar-szovjet kapcsolatok története*, (Budapest: unpublished manuscript), p. 37.

120 Ibid., pp. 34-37.

121 Háy László feljegyzése [Memorandum by László Háy] 24 February 1956, MOL, 276. F., 65. cs., 283. őe.

122 Zaveduiuschii otdelom Balkanskih stran (V. Valkov) konsulu soiuza SSR v
Győr (Iniushkinu) [Head of the Balkan states department, V. Valkov to the
Soviet consul in Győr, Inyushkin) 26 January 1953, AVPRF, Fond 077, opis 33,
papka 164, delo 200.

123 In order to see Rákosi on this matter Kiselev needed the permission of deputy
foreign minister Zorin. Zamestitel ministr inostrannikh del (V. Zorin) zamestitelyu ministra vnutrennei i vneshnei torgovli SSSR (P. I. Kumikinu) [The Deputy
Minister of Foreign Affairs, V. Zorin to the Deputy Minister of Foreign and
Internal Trade, P. I. Kumikin] 23 May 1953, AVPRF, Fond 077, opis 33, papka
164, delo 210.

124 Kiselev ministru inostrannikh del SSR Molotovu [Kiselev to Minister of Foreign Affairs Molotov] 25 May 1953, AVPRF, Fond 077, opis 33, papka 164,
delo 210 and 211.

125 Kiselev to Molotovu [Kiselev to Molotov] 25 May 1953, ibid. delo 210;
Kumikin zamestitelyu ministra inostrannikh del SSSR Zorinu [Kumikin to
Deputy Minister of Foreign Affairs Zorin] 4 June 1953, AVPRF, Fond 077, opis
33, papka 164, delo 210.

126 Protokol [Protocol] November 1952. AVPRF, Fond 077, opis 33, papka, 164
delo 211.

127 See Urbán, *Sztálin halálától a forradalom kitöréséig.*

128 Kiselev ministru inostrannikh del SSR Molotovu [Kiselev to Foreign Minister
Molotov] 30 May 1953, Fond 077, opis 33, papka 166, delo 240.

129 Urbán, *Sztálin halálától a forradalom kitöréséig,* p. 27.

130 Rákosi, *Visszaemlékezések,* vol. II, p. 948.

131 Az MDP PB ülése [Meeting of the HWP Politburo] 2 January 1956, MOL, 276.
F., 53. cs., 264. őe; Nachalniku Glavnogo upravleniya po delam ekonomiches-
kih sviazei so storoni narodnoi demokratii [Head of the chief directorate for
economic relations with the people's democracies] 3 March 1955, AVPRF,
Fond 077, opis 36, papka 183, delo 240.

132 The coalmines of the Pécs region, which was among the country's most important coal regions, had been attached the Soviet–Hungarian Navigation company.

133 A Szovjetuniótól megvásárolt vállalatokkal kapcsolatos kötelezettségek [Oblig-
ations in connection with companies purchased from the Soviet Union] 1952,
undated, MOL, 276. F., 66. cs., 71. őe.

134 Feljegyzés az MDP PB-nek a Szovjetuniónak történő bauxit szállításokról
[Memorandum for the HWP Politburo on bauxite shipments to the USSR]
1955, undated, MOL, 276. F., 53. cs., 223. őe.

135 Urbán, *Sztálin halálától a forradalom kitöréséig,* p. 31.

136 Jegyzőkönyv az MDP PB üléséről [Record of meeting of the HWP Politburo]
18 August 1954, MOL, 276. F., 53. cs., 190. őe.

137 Feljegyzés az MDP PB-nek a magyar–szovjet vegyesvállalatok megvételéről
[Memorandum on the purchase of Hungarian–Soviet joint companies] 10 October 1954, MOL, 276. F., 53., cs., 198 őe.

138 Soglashenie o prodazhe Vengerskoi NR sovietskoi doli v sovietsko-vengerskikh
smeshannikh obshchestvakh [Agreement on the sale of the Soviet shares in

Soviet–Hungarian joint companies] 6 November 1954, AVPRF Fond 077 opis 34 papka 178 delo 256.

139 Feljegyzés az MSZMP PB-nek [Memorandum for the Political Committee of the Hungarian Socialist Workers Party] 19 November 1957, MOL, XIX-F-17-ah, 1. doboz, ikt. sz. n.

140 Jegyzőkönyv radioaktív elemek geológiai feltárásáról Magyarországon [Protocol on the geological excavation of radioactive elements in Hungary] 8 June 1955, MOL, MDP, 276 F., 53 cs., 234 őe.

141 Marer, "The 'Soviet bloc' as an Integration Model," p. 36.

142 Egyezmény a MNK kormánya és a Szovjet SzSzK kormánya között vállalat létrehozásáról uránlelőhelyek felkutatására és kiaknázására Magyarországon [Agreement between the government of the HPR and the government of the USSR on the establishment of joint company for the discovery and exploitation of uranium in Hungary] 1956, undated, MOL, XIX-F-17-ah, 1. doboz, ikt. sz. n.

143 A Magyar Népköztársaság Minisztertanácsának 3351/V.21./1956 Határozata a Bauxitbánya Vállalat fejlesztése és működtetéséről [Resolution No. 3351/V.21/ 1956 of the Council of Ministers of the People's Republic of Hungary on the development and operation of Bauxitbánya Vállalat, 17 May 1956, MOL, XIX-F-17-ah, 1. doboz, ikt. sz. n; Feljegyzés Hegedűs Andrásnak [Memorandum for András Hegedűs] 21 August 1956, MOL, XIX-F-ah, 1. doboz, ikt. sz. n.

144 Előterjesztés a gazdasági bizottsághoz [Memorandum for the economic committee] 18 december 1957, MOL, XIX-F-ah, 1. doboz, ikt. sz. n.

145 Ibid.

146 Ibid.

147 Telegram from Charles Bohlen (Moscow) to the Secretary of State, 10 December 1956, USNA, RG 59, PPS Lot 66 D 487, 1956, Box 76, (Soviet Union)

148 Mastny, *Soviet Insecurity and the Cold War*.

149 Hadtörténeti Levéltár (Archive of Military History), Magyar Néphadsereg vezérkara (Staff of the Hungarian People's Republic Army), Hadműveleti Csoportfőnökség (Strategic Planning Group), 1951, 24. doboz, 1. csoport, p. 40. cited by Imre Okváth, "A Magyar Néphadsereg háborús haditervei, 1948–1962," [The war plans of the Hungarian People's Army] *Paper prepared for the conference NATO, the Warsaw Pact, and the European non-Aligned 1949–1979: Threat Assessments, Doctrines and War Plans,* Longyearbyen, Norway, June 2003.

150 Iz dnevnika sovietnika Posoltsva SSSR v Vengrii, S. T. Kuzmina. Zapis besedi s ministrom oboroni M. Farkas o sostoyanii vengerskoi armii [From the diary of the counselor of the Soviet embassy in Hungary S. T. Kuzmin. Record of conversation with Defense Minister Farkas on the composition of the Hungarian Army] 4 January 1951, *VEDRA*, vol. II, pp. 453–457, document 156.

151 Pismo A. Ya. Vishinskogo I. V. Stalinu [Vishinskii's letter to Stalin] 8 September 1951, op. cit., VEDRA, vol. II, pp. 609–610, document 220.

152 Paczkowski, *Lengyelország története*, p.178.

153 The agreements are published István Pataki, ed., "Magyar–szovjet katonai egyezmények," *Múltunk*, 1995, vol. 40, no. 3, pp. 123–158.

154 The forthcoming passage relies on Imre Okváth, *Bástya a béke frontján—Magyar haderő és katonapolitika, 1945–1956* [Bastion on the peace front—Hungarian military policy, 1945–1956] (Budapest: Aquila, 1998), pp. 149–165.

155 Ibid., pp. 194–217.

156 Rákosi, *Visszaemlékezések*, vol. II, pp. 860–863.

157 The Soviet ambassador in Budapest noticed that the Korean events caused great anxiety and a certain amount of confusion in the Hungarian leadership. Iz dnevnika Kiseleva. Zapis besedi s ministrom oboroni M. Farkas o politicheskih repressiah, hode peregovorov s episkopami, reaktsii rukovodstva VPT na voinu v Koree i dr. [From Kiselev's diary. Record of converastion with Defense Minister Farkas on political repressions, on the status of talks with the bishops, the reaction of Hungarian party leaders to the Korean war, etc.] 18 July 1950, *VEDRA*, vol. II, pp. 386–388, Document 130.

158 See Okváth, *Bástya a béke frontján*, pp. 339–346.

159 Ibid., p. 334.

160 Hruscsov levele Rákosinak [Khrushchev's letter to Rákosi] 9 March 1955, MOL, 276. F., 53. cs., 229. őe.

161 A honvédelmi miniszter feljegyzése Rákosinak [Memorandum by the minister of defense to Rákosi] 15 March 1954; A Honvédelmi Tanács 45/24/1954 sz. határozata [The Resolution No. 45/24/1954 of the Defense Council] 29 March 1954, MOL, 276. F., 65. cs., 195. őe; Okváth, *Bástya a béke frontján*, p. 387.

162 A honvédelmi miniszter feljegyzése a Honvédelmi Tanácsnak [Memorandum by the minister of defense to the Council of Defense] 31 May 31 1955, MOL, 276. F., 53. cs., 234. őe; Okváth, *Bástya a béke frontján*, p. 341

163 For a description of the exercise see Holloway, *Stalin and the Bomb*, pp. 326–328.

164 Okváth, *Bástya a béke frontján*, pp. 310-311.

165 Mark Kramer, "The Early Post-Stalin succession Struggle and Upheavals in East-Central Europe," part 1, pp. 8–9.

166 Ibid., pp. 6–7.

167 "This is not a Politburo but a Madhouse—The Post-Stalin Succession Struggle, Soviet *Deutschlandpolitik* and the SED: New Evidence from Russian, German and Hungarian Archives." Introduced and annotated by Christian Ostermann, CWIHP Bulletin Issue 10, March 1998, p. 61. On the East German refugee crisis see also Mark Kramer, "The Early Post-Stalin Succession Struggle and Upheavals in East-Central Europe," Part 1, pp. 12–13.

168 Ibid., p. 63

169 Quoted in Hannes Adomeit, *Imperial Overstretch*, p. 93.

170 See Ostermann ed., *Uprising in East Germany, 1953* (Budapest–New York: Central European University Press, 2001) pp. 8–14.

171 Ostermann, "New Evidence from Russian, German and Hungarian Archives," pp. 65–66.

172 Kramer, "The Early Post-Stalin Succession Struggle and Upheavals in East-Central Europe," part 1, pp. 24–25.

173 Kramer, "The Early Post-Stalin Succession Struggle and Upheavals in East-Central Europe," part 3. According to Adomeit the policy reversal was caused

by the fear that a unified Germany could not be neutral, the GDR's importance as an anti-imperialist obstacle and psychological reasons. Adomeit, *Imperial Overstrech*, p. 98.

174 Osterman, *Uprising in East Germany*, p. 15.

175 Mark Kramer, "The Early Post-Stalin Succession Struggle and Upheavals in East Central Europe," p. 27, p. 33.

176 Ibid., pp. 15–17.

177 Ibid., p. 21.

178 Iz dnevnika vtoroga sekretarya Posoltsva SSSR v Vengrii N. N. Sikacheva. Zapis besedi s zamestitelem ministra vnutrennikh del A. Varga o podbore kadrov v mestnie organi vlasti [From the diary of the second secretary of the Soviet Embassy in Hungary N.N. Sikachev. Record of conversation with deputy minister of the interior A. Varga on the selection of cadres for the local organs of power] 14 October 1956, *VEDRA*, vol. II, pp. 821–824, document 297.

179 For the documentation of the 13–16 June meeting see T. Varga, ed., *Jegyzőkönyv a szovjet és a magyar párt- és állami vezetők tárgyalásairól*, pp. 234–269. A part of the minutes were published in English translation in Ostermann, "This is not a Politburo but a Madhouse," pp. 81–86.

180 Rákosi, *Visszaemlékezések,* vol. II, pp. 936–937.

181 Ibid., pp. 937–939.

182 For the brief biography of Imre Nagy I used János M. Rainer, *Nagy Imre* (Budapest: Vince Kiadó, 2002).

183 Urbán, "Nagy Imre és G. M. Malenkov – Két miniszterelnök Sztálin után" [Imre Nagy and G. M. Malenkov - Two prime ministers after Stalin] *Múltunk*, 1996, vol. 41, no. 1. pp. 150–152.

184 Pető and Szakács, *A hazai gazdaság négy évtizedének története*, pp. 248–249.

185 Ibid., p. 272.

186 The transcripts of the meeting are not verbatim records and were compiled from the notes of several Hungarian participants. These do not include the reflections of the Hungarian side. See János M. Rainer and Urbán Károly, eds., "'Konzultációk'. Dokumentumok a magyar és szovjet pártvezetők két moszkvai találkozójáról 1954–1955-ben," ["Consultations." Documents on the two Moscow meetings of the Hungarian and the Soviet Party Leaders in 1954–1955] *Múltunk*, 1992, vol. 37, no. 4, pp. 124–148.

187 Ibid., p. 135.

188 Ibid., p.140. In reality the Political Committee discarded István Friss's proposal to halt the economic reforms and supported Nagy in the reduction of investments by 11 billion forints.

189 Ibid., pp. 135–136.

190 Ibid., p.136.

191 Ibid., p.137.

192 Magdolna Baráth, ed., "A szovjet nagykövet 1954. őszi beszélgetései," [Conversations of the Soviet ambassador in fall 1954] in *1956-os Évkönyv*, op. cit., pp. 121–122.

193 Ibid., p. 126.

194 Ibid.

195 Spravka Andropova Zorinu [Andropov's report to Zorin] 12 October 1954, AVPRF, Fond 077, opis 34, papka 178, delo 260. The document contains an appendix with Zorin's writing to Zimianin: "Nuzhno informirovat TsK, daite predlozhenie." [Must inform the Central Committee, give advise]

196 Spravka Zimyanina Molotovu [Zimyanin's report to Molotov] 12 November 1954, AVPRF, Fond 077, opis 34, papka 178, delo 203.

197 Zubok–Pleshakov, *Inside the Kremlin's Cold War*, p. 164.

198 Ibid., p. 164; p. 166.

199 Ibid., p. 168.

200 The parallel features of Malenkov's and Imre Nagy's course between 1953–1955 are discussed in Urbán, *Nagy Imre és G. M. Malenkov*, pp. 129–180.

201 Rainer and Urbán, eds., *Konzultációk*, p. 126.

202 Ibid., p. 145.

203 Ibid., p. 143.

204 Urbán, *Nagy Imre és G. M. Malenkov*, p. 170.

205 Rainer and Urbán, *Konzultációk*, p. 147.

206 Telegramma A. I. Mikoyana iz Budapesta v Ts. K. KPSS o podgotovke i pervom dne raboti iyulskogo plenuma TsK VPT [Mikoyan's telegram from Budapest to the CPSU Central Commitee on the preparations and first days of the July plenum of the HWP Central Committee] 18 July 1956, V. K. Volkov et al., *Sovietskii Soiuz i Vengerskii Krizis 1956 g. Dokumenti* (hereafter cited as *SSVK*). (Moscow: Rosspen, 1998), pp. 176–181, document 38; Viacheslav Sereda, Aleksandr Stikalin, eds., *Hiányzó lapok 1956 történetéből* [hereafter cited as HL] (Budapest: Móra Ferenc Kiadó, 1993), pp. 59–65.

207 On Andropov's role see Baráth, *Szovjet nagyköveti iratok Magyarországról*, pp. 38–42; See also Aleksandr Stikalin, "A szovjet nagykövetség és az MDP-n belüli harc 1956 tavaszán-kora őszén," [The Soviet Embassy and the struggle within the HWP in the spring-early fall of 1956] *Múltunk*, 1998, vol 43, no. 2, p. 36.

208 According to party first secretary Gerő anti-Soviet "propaganda" focused around the following: protest against the stationing of Soviet troops; protest against Hungarian payments to the USSR for German property; protest that Hungary was selling uranium to the Soviets at a low price; Hungary's trade with the USSR was disadvantageous. Andropov jelentése [Andropov's report] 12 October 1956, HL, pp. 83–90.

209 Telegramma Andropova v MID SSSR o besede s Vas [Andropov's telegram to the Soviet Foreign Ministry on conversation with Vas] 14 October 1956, *SSVK*, pp. 306–309, document 71; *HL*, pp. 92–96.

210 Andropov jelentése [Andropov's report] 12 October 1956, op. cit., *HL*, pp. 83–90.

211 Zapis besedi Iu. Andropova s E. Gerő o berlinskoi sessii SEV, usilenie v Vengrii politicheskoi napryazhennosti i oppozitsii Rákosi [Record of conversation between Iu. Andropov with E Gerő on the Berlin session of SEV, the rising political tension in Hungary and Rákosi's opposition] 6 June 1954, *SSVK*, pp. 78-81, document 12.

212 Zapis besedi Iu. V. Andropova s A. Hegedűs o nedostatkakh v rabote Politbiuro i Sekretariata TsR VPT i raznoglasiyah v sviazi s delom M. Farkas [Record of conversation between Iu. Andropov and A. Hegedűs on the shortcomings in the work of the party secretariat and the contradictions of the Farkas case] 4 May 1956, *SSVK*, pp. 67–69, document 8.

213 Zapis besedi Iu. V. Andropova s I. Kovács o vistupleniyakh uchastnikov partiinih aktivistov v Budapeste protiv M. Rákosi [Record of conversation between Iu. V. Andropov and E. Gerő on the speeches of the participants of the party aktiv in Budapest against M. Rákosi] 30 March 1956, *SSVK*, pp. 51–53, document 2.

214 Zapis besedi Iu. V. Andropova s E. Gerő o yugoslavskom vlianii na deyatel-nosti oppozitsii v Vengrii i o polozhenii v TsR VPT posle iulskogo plenuma [Record of conversation between Iu. V. Andropov and E. Gerő on the Yugoslav influence on the activity of the opposition in Hungary and the situation in the party leadership after the July plenum] 2 August 1956, *SSVK*, pp. 210–214, document 45.

215 Zapis besedi Iu. V. Andropova s E. Gerő o rezultatakh vstrechi chlenov TsR VPT s I. Nagy [Record of converastion between Iu. Andropov and E. Gerő on the results of the meeting of party leaders with I. Nagy] 15 August 1956, *SSVK*, pp. 231–233, document 51; *HL*, pp. 72–74.

216 Telegramma A. I. Mikoyana iz Budapesta v TsK KPSS o podgotovke i pervom dne raboti iyulskogo plenuma TsK VPT [A. I. Mikoyan's telegram from Buda-pest to the CPSU Central Committee on the preparation and first days of the July plenum of the HWP Central Committee] *SSVK*, pp. 176–181, document 38; *HL*, pp. 59–65.

217 Zapis besed Iu. V. Andropova s A. Hegedűs i E. Gerő ob usilenii 'podrivnikh deistvii' pravoi oppozitsii [Record of conversation between Iu. V. Andropov, A. Hegedűs and E. Gerő on the growing 'subversive activity' of the rightist opposition] 19 June 1956, *SSVK*, pp. 89–91, document 16.

218 Telegramma Iu. V. Andropova v MID SSR o besede s E. Gerő o narastanii obshchestvenno-politicheskogo krizisa v Vengrii [Telegram by Iu. V. Andropov on the conservation with Gerő on the growth of social-political crisis in Hun-gary] 9 July 1956, *SSVK*, pp. 137–142, document 27.

219 As quoted by Mark Kramer, "New Evidence on Soviet Decision-Making and the 1956 Polish and Hungarian Crises," in *Cold War International History Pro-ject Bulletin*, Issues 8–9. Winter, 1996/1997, p. 363.

220 Telefonogramma Suslova iz Budapesta v TsK KPSS o nastroeniyakh v venger-skom obschestve i besedakh s rukovodstvom VPT [Suslov's telephone message from Budapest to the CPSU Central Committee on the mood of the Hungarian society and the conversations with the HWP leadership] 13 June 1956, *SSVK*, pp. 85–87, document 14; *HL*, pp. 21–23.

221 Zapis besedi Andropova s Gerő [Record of Andropov's conversation with Gerő] 4 June 1956, op. cit., *SSVK*, pp. 78–81.

222 See János M. Rainer, "Döntés a Kremlben," [Decision in the Kremlin] in Gál Éva, et al. eds., *A "Jelcin Dosszié—Szovjet Dokumentumok 1956-ról* [The "Yeltsin File"—Soviet Documents on 1956] (hereafter cited as JD) (Budapest: Századvég, 1956-os Intézet, 1993), p. 115.

223 Zapis besed Andropova s Hegedűs i Gerő [Record of Andropov's conversation with Hegedűs and Gerő] 19 June 1956, *SSVK*, op. cit., pp. 89–91.

224 Telegramma A. I. Mikoyana iz Budapesta v TsK KPSS o vidvizhenii kandidatur na posti pervogo sekretarya TsK VPT i ego zamestitelei na zasedanii Politbiuro TsK VPT [A. I. Mikoyan's telegram from Budapest to the CPSU Central Committee on candidacy for the post of first secretary of the HWP and its deputies at the meeting of the HWP Central Committee] 14 July 1956, *SSVK*, pp. 172–173, document 36; *HL*, pp. 57–58.

225 Paczkowski, *Lengyelország története*, pp. 201–202.

226 Zapis besedi Iu. V. Andropova s E. Gerő o meropriatiyakh, namechennikh Politbiuro TsK VPT v svazi s obostreniem vnutripoliticheskoi obstanovki v strane i sobitiami v Poznani [Iu. A. Andropov's conversation with E. Gerő on the measures forseen by the HWP Politbro in connection with the worsening internal political situation in the country and the events in Poznan] *SSVK*, pp. 127–128, document 23.

227 See Kramer, "New Evidence on Soviet Decision-Making and the 1956 Polish and Hungarian Crises," p. 360.

228 Telegramma Andropova v MID SSR, 9 July 1956, op. cit., *SSVK*, pp. 137–142.

229 Telegrama A. I. Mikoyana iz Budapesta v TsK KPSS o soveshchanii v Politbiuro TsK VPT i plane meropriyatii po normalizatsii obstanovki v partii vkluchaya otstavku M. Rákosi [A.I. Mikoyan's telegram from Budapest to the CPSU Central Committee on the meeting of the HWP Central Committee and the planned measures for the normalization of the situation including M. Rákosi's resignation] 14 July 1956, *SSVK*, pp. 152–157, document 33; *HL*, pp. 40–46.

230 Telegramma A. I. Mikoyana iz Budapesta v TsK KPSS o predvoritelnom obsuzhdenii kandidatur na posti pervogo sekretarya TsK VPT i ego zamestitelei i resheniakh Politbiuro po etomu voprosu [A. I. Mikoyan's telegram from Budapest to the CPSU Central Committee on the preliminary discussions on candidacy for the post of first party secretary and its deputies and the resolution of the Politburo in this question] 14 July 1956, *SSVK*, pp. 168–171, document 35. The telegram was only partly published in *HL*, pp. 47–48.

231 Telegramma Iu. V. Andropova v MID SSSR o besede s E. Gerő o rezkom uhudshenii obshchestvenno-politicheskoi obstanovki v Vengrii [Iu. V. Andropov's telegram to the Foreign Ministry of the USSR on the discussion with E. Gerő on the drastic worsening of the social-political situation in Hungary] 12 October 1956, *SSVK*, pp. 300–305, document 70; *HL*, pp. 83–90.

232 Discussion of the Polish crisis is based on Kramer, "New Evidence on Soviet Decision-Making and the 1956 Polish and Hungarian Crisis," p. 360.

233 Ibid., p. 361.

234 For a detailed account see Zoltán Ripp, "A pártvezetés végnapjai, október 24–október 28," [The final days of the Party leadership] in *Ötvenhat októbere és a hatalom* [October Fifty-six and power] (Budapest: Napvilág kiadó, 1997), pp. 170–179.

235 This term was used by Sanford Levinson, *Written in Stone—Public Monuments in Changing Societies* (Durham, London: Duke University Press, 1998) p. 12.

236 See Kramer, "New Evidence on Soviet Decision-Making and the 1956 Polish and Hungarian Crises," pp. 364–365.

237 See Ripp, *A pártvezetés végnapjai*, pp. 183–185; Kramer, "New Evidence on Soviet Decision-Making and the 1956 Polish and Hungarian Crises," pp. 366; *Döntés a Kremlben*, 1956, p. 26; "The 'Malin notes' on the Crises in Hungary and Poland, 1956," Translated and annotated by Mark Kramer, *CWHIP Bulletin* Issue 8-9. Winter, 1996/97, document 3, p. 388. The Malin notes are published in English also in Békés, Byrne and Rainer, eds., *The 1956 Hungarian Revolution*.

238 On 19 March 1944 Germany occupied Hungary to keep it in the war and to shore up the Reich's defense against the expected Anglo-American and Russian invasion.

239 Telegramma Mikoyana i Suslova iz Budapesta v TsK KPSS ob obstanovke v stolitse Vengrii [Mikoyan and Suslov's telegram from Budapest to the Central Committee of the CPSU on the situation in the Hungarian capital] 24 October 1956, *SSVK*, pp. 371–374, document 87; *JD*, pp. 47–49; *HL*, pp. 101–105.

240 Ibid.

241 Telegramma Mikoyana i Suslova iz Budapesta v TsK KPSS o novih vooruzhennikh stolknovenniakh v gorode, izmeneniakh v vishem rukovodstve VPT i vistuplenii I. Nagy po radio [Telegram by Mikoyan and Suslov from Budapest to the CPSU Central Committee on the new armed clashes in the city, changes in the top leadership of the HWP and Nagy's radio speech] 25 October 1956, *SSVK*, 385-386, document 93; *JD*, pp. 50-51.

242 Telefonogramma Mikoyana i Suslova v TsK KPSS o o planakh vengerskogo rukovodstva po stabilizatsii politicheskoi obstanovki [Telegram by Mikoian and Suslov to the CPSU Cental Committee the plans of the Hungarian leadership for the stabilization of the political situation] 26 October 1956, *SSVK*, pp. 403–407, document 96; *HL*, pp. 109–113.

243 Report to the Foreign Office by Ambassador Hayter on discussion with Khruschev, 27 October 1956, in Eva Haraszti-Taylor ed., *The Hungarian Revolution of 1956. A Collection of Documents from the British Foreign Office* (Nottingham: Astra Press, 1995), p. 109.

244 Working notes from the Session of the CPSU CC Presidium on 28 October 1956, *The Malin Notes*, pp. 389–391.

245 Hayter to the Foreign Office, 29 October 1956, *The Hungarian Revolution of 1956*, p. 129.

246 Rainer, *Nagy Imre*, pp. 105–106.

247 See Peter L. Hahn, *The United States, Great Britain and Egypt, 1945-1956: Strategy and Diplomacy in the Early Cold War* (Chapel Hill and London: The University of North Carolina Press, 1991), pp. 223–229.

248 See Ripp, *Ötvenhat októbere és a hatalom*, pp. 299–300.

249 Working Notes from the Session of the CPSU CC Presidium, 30 October 1956, *The Malin notes*, pp. 392–393; *JD*, pp. 51–57.

250 Szovjet kormány-nyilatkozat a szocialista országok közötti kapcsolatokról [The declaration of the Soviet government on the relationships of socialist states] *JD*, pp. 64–65.

251 *The Malin notes*, Ibid., p. 393.

252 Janos Radvanyi, *Hungary and the Superpowers, The 1956 Revolution and Realpolitik* (Stanford: Stanford University Press, 1972), pp. 12; 27.

253 The American Embassy in Moscow to the State Department, 30 October, 1956 10 p.m., *FRUS*, 1955–1957, vol. XXV, pp. 346–347.

254 Working Notes from the Session of the CPSU CC Presidium, 31 October 1956, *The Malin notes*, pp. 393–394; *JD*, pp. 62–65.

255 See Csaba Békés, "Az Egyesült Államok és a magyar semlegesség 1956-ban," [The United States and Hungarian neutrality in 1956] in János Bak et al. eds., *1956 Évkönyv 1994* (Budapest: 1956-os Intézet, 1994), pp. 171–174.

256 Mark Kramer, "The Soviet Union and the 1956 Crises in Hungary and Poland: Reassessments and New Findings," *Journal of Contemporary History* vol. 33, no. 2, 1998, pp. 163–214.

257 Telefonogramma A. I. Mikoyana i M. A. Suslova iz Budapesta v TsK KPSS ob uhudshenii politicheskoi obstanovki v Vengrii [Telegam by Mikoyan and Suslov from Budapest to the CPSU Central Committee on the deterioration of the political situation in Hungary] 30 October 1956, *SSVK* document 117, pp. 467-468; Vistuplenie I. Nagy po radio o likvidatsii odnopartiinoi sistemi [I. Nagy's radio speech on the liquidation of the monoparty system] 30 October 1956, 2 p.m., Ibid., document 120, pp. 470-471.

258 As Kramer notes, the lynching was an isolated case. The revolution lacked the kinds of atrocities that historically accompany such events. Characteristically, when Budapest police chief, Sándor Kopácsy told Serov that the Hungarians did not shoot their prisoners, Serov retorted: "Why didn't you shoot them? Men sprout like weeds."

259 Kramer, "The Soviet Union and the 1956 crises in Hungary and Poland," p. 175, p. 189.

260 See Ripp, *Ötvenhat októbere és a hatalom*, p. 309.

261 Working Notes from the Session of the CPSU CC Presidium, 31 October 1956, *The Malin Notes*, p. 393; *JD*, p. 62.

262 Working Notes from the Session of the CPSU CC Presidium, 1 November 1956, *The Malin Notes*, p. 394; *JD*, p. 69.

263 Meeting of the CPSU Central Committee,s 28 June 1957, Vladislav Zubok ed., "CPSU Plenums, Leadership Struggles and Cold War Politics" in *CWIHP Bulletin*, Issue 10. March, 1998.

264 Henry Kissinger observed that "far from proving reassuring, that staple of American diplomatic rhetoric—the claim to an absence of ulterior motive—has usually been interpreted as signs of either unpredictability or arbitrariness, even among non-Marxist leaders." Henry Kissinger, *Diplomacy* (New York: Simon and Schuster, 1994), p. 558.

CHAPTER VI

CONTAINMENT, ROLLBACK, LIBERATION
OR INACTION?

On 4 November 1956, Marshal Ivan Konev, the commander in chief of the Warsaw Pact's joint armed forces, oversaw the large-scale deployment of Soviet tanks into Hungary to crush an armed uprising against Soviet rule in Eastern Europe. President Dwight Eisenhower promptly sent an appeal to Soviet premier Nikolai Bulganin calling on Soviet forces to pull out. This mild response was in stark contrast to the expectations of many participants in the revolution, who hoped for some form of Western military assistance and were disappointed by Eisenhower's "do nothing attitude."[1] The American response to the 1956 Hungarian Revolution encapsulated Washington's Janus-faced attitude toward the liberation of Eastern Europe. Although U.S. officials worried that the Soviet presence in Eastern Europe extended Soviet power to the heart of Europe, the "rollback" of Communism ultimately was subordinated to efforts to improve Soviet–American relations and avoid a general war.

American inaction seemed all the more puzzling in view of the significance that the United States placed on the elimination of Soviet power in Eastern Europe. By themselves, the East European states were of "secondary importance" only. The primary threat caused by Soviet occupation, the State Department Policy Planning Staff argued in 1949, was their potential use as staging ground for the Soviet occupation of Western Europe. By reducing the Soviet control in those countries, the U.S. would lessen the threat to its Western European allies.[2] In July 1956, the U.S. National Security Council (NSC) declared that a permanent Soviet presence in Eastern Europe "would represent a serious threat to the security of Western Europe and the United States."[3] The NSC reaffirmed America's "traditional policy to recognize the right of all people to independence and to governments of their own choosing. The elimination of Soviet domination of the satellites is, therefore, in the fundamental interest of the United States."[4] These statements implied that Soviet control had to be withdrawn from Hungary as well as from the rest of Eastern Europe. The gap between these stated imperatives and actual policies in 1956 seemed to lend credence to the conviction of many Hungarians that Washington had "struck a deal" with Moscow at Yalta in February 1945 and was keeping its part of the agreement by ignor-

269

ing the Soviet domination of Hungary. Statements by senior U.S. officials in 1956, especially John Foster Dulles's speech on 27 October, the essence of which was that the U.S. was not counting on the countries of Eastern Europe as potential allies, were widely interpreted as having given a de facto green light to Soviet intervention in the Hungarian crisis. On the other hand, a more aggressive stance might have entailed a full-scale military confrontation with the Soviet Union, including the use of nuclear weapons by both sides. The United States ultimately refused to use force to dislodge the Soviet Union from Eastern Europe.

This chapter discusses the Eisenhower administration's policy toward Hungary in the years leading up to the 1956 revolution, setting it in the broader context of U.S. Cold War strategy. It begins by briefly describing the genesis and evolution of U.S. "rollback" plans for Eastern Europe under the Truman and Eisenhower administrations. It then looks at the policy of "economic warfare," which encompassed a range of efforts by both administrations to deny essential goods to the Soviet bloc, including all items of a military nature. This will be followed by an examination of the more aggressive policies that some U.S. officials advocated implementing rollback, including covert operations and military supplies. I shall also discuss the Eisenhower administration's attempt to strike a negotiated settlement with the Soviet Union that would provide a status for Eastern Europe akin to that of Finland. This effort ultimately failed, but the very fact that talks were pursued was a tacit U.S. acknowledgement of Soviet security interests in the region.

The penultimate two sections of the chapter focus more specifically on U.S. policy toward Hungary. They firstly describe the tentative improvement of U.S.–Hungarian relations in the summer of 1956 and then turn to the events of October–November 1956, when the Eisenhower administration had to decide how to respond to the uprising. These two sections, combined with the earlier discussion, lead to the questions addressed in the final section of the chapter: Did U.S. policy either deliberately or inadvertently encourage the violent rebellion in Hungary? If so, were U.S. officials aware of the grim consequences that would befall Hungary? The answers to these questions reflect more broadly on the nature of U.S. foreign policy towards Eastern Europe in the 1950s.

The Context of U.S. policy

In 1948 the first official document on U.S. policy on Eastern Europe, NSC 58/2 concluded that "efforts to bring about the direct replacement of existing satellite regimes with non-Communist governments do not seem feasible." Therefore, as "a practical immediate expedient" the U.S. was supposed to "foster Communist heresy among the satellite states" and encourage "the emergence of non-Stalinist regimes as temporary administrations even though they may be Communist in nature." The paper was inspired by an appraisal of the Yugoslav–Soviet schism according to which Tito had broken with the Soviet Union in favor of an independent road to Communism. This was a mistaken analysis as it was Stalin that broke with Tito. By 1951, it turned out that the encouragement of Communist heresy "had proven to be an unrewarding and unrealistic policy,"[5] therefore the policy recommendations of NSC 58/2 were abandoned. Simultaneously, a more aggressive policy option, the rollback of Soviet influence in Eastern Europe, was explored. However, U.S. passivity in the 1956 Hungarian crisis was part of a gradual retreat from the declared aim of "rolling back" Soviet influence in Eastern Europe. The notion of "rollback" had surfaced in the late 1940s, but it gained wider currency when the Truman administration approved a document known as NSC 68 just after the outbreak of the Korean War in 1950.[6] NSC 68 had set rollback as an objective, but it failed to specify how to achieve that goal. The document explicitly ruled out most of the measures (e.g., preemptive war) that would have been needed to pursue rollback in a realistic way. Nevertheless, the Truman administration's attitude toward the Soviet bloc was less complacent than previously imagined. In June 1948, the president and the NSC committed the U.S. government to an unprecedented counterforce against Communism to authorize "preventive direct action, including sabotage, countersabotage and subversion against hostile states." The latter included assistance to underground resistance movements, guerillas and refugee liberation groups to be carried out in such a way that the U.S. could "plausibly disclaim responsibility." General funding and direction of these operations would come from the government.[7]

At George Kennan's recommendation, the Office of Policy Coordination was set up under the leadership of an OSS veteran, Frank Wisner. OPC was an ultra secret organization in charge of psychological warfare operations, and by 1952 had almost three thousand persons on its payroll. The Pentagon contributed to the strategy of rollback by training guerillas among East European refugees.[8] In November 1948, NSC 20/4 committed the U.S. to use all methods short of war to reduce the power and influence of the USSR in Eastern Europe to a point where it no longer constituted a "threat to peace." Thus, American policy shifted from solely a defensive posture to the elimination of the Communist bloc altogether. National security planners, in their belief that the Soviets were susceptible to psychological warfare, which had a potential to cause the collapse of the Soviet system, wanted the policy to be carried out with the acceptance of the risk of war. American monopoly of nuclear arms made this policy safe to conduct.

Although NSC 10/5 of 1951 called for an intensification of covert operations, the Truman administration was not prepared to provoke revolt, con-
tending that such policy would be morally indefensible because it could
lead to brutal repression.[9]

In the final years of the Truman administration, the basic objectives of
NSC 68 were nominally reaffirmed, but many of its more specific policy
recommendations were modified or discarded. According to NSC 135/3, a
new assessment of Soviet intentions put forth at the very end of the Truman
administration in January 1953, the Soviet Union's top priority was the security of the Communist regime. This formulation suggested that the Kremlin
did not want to start a full-scale war, in spite of the growth of Soviet and
East-bloc military capabilities. NSC 135/3 proposed the abandonment of
aggressive versions of rollback, and recommended that the United States
pursue indirect policies that would merely erode Soviet influence in Eastern
Europe. The aim would be to exploit divisions between the Soviet Union and
the Eastern bloc and to harness popular discontent within Eastern Europe.
U.S. officials hoped that these policies, if applied consistently over time,
would cause the Soviet system to disintegrate without the use of force.[10]
Two developments dashed any hope that the status quo in Eastern Europe
could be changed forcefully. First, news that the Soviets had developed an
atomic bomb shattered the foundations of NSC/4. According to a reevalua-
tion of national security strategy, the Soviet Union would soon possess the
nuclear capability to cause irreversible damage to the U.S. and its allies.
Global war in a time of such American vulnerability would have been so
disastrous that they needed to reconsider any policy that risked conflict.

Second, the assessment of the Soviet threat also changed. The Soviets
would not deliberately start a war at a given date. Soviet power, it was now
believed, was directed at preserving the regime, and the Kremlin would
not take any action that it believed could lead to a collapse of its power at
home, such as nuclear war. Nevertheless, the Soviets would respond with
preemptive nuclear strike if the U.S. threatened the Soviet hold on Eastern
Europe or the stability of the Soviet regime itself. Not even military superiority could shield the U.S. from a Soviet attack when attempting to destabilize the Soviet zone.[11] If American efforts to overthrow Communism were
the only factors that would bring about a Soviet attack, it followed that
aggressive designs to roll back Communism were far too dangerous and
counterproductive, such plans therefore had to be surrendered. Thus American nuclear policy operated two ways: it kept the Russians out of Western
Europe but at the same time consolidated the Soviet position in the eastern
part of the continent.

Although the rhetoric of the incoming Eisenhower administration was
more strident than that of its predecessor, the new President similarly rejected

the contention that the United States faced a "year of maximum danger" from Communist aggression.[12] He believed that the Soviet Union could easily be deterred from launching a nuclear attack or risking a general war. The new administration expected that the build-up of the U.S. nuclear arsenal would "create a stalemate, with both sides reluctant to initiate general warfare."[13]

U.S. policy toward the Soviet Union was a contentious issue throughout the first few years of Eisenhower's presidency.[14] Although the president himself was cautious, his Defense Department and Joint Chiefs of Staff (JCS), having been alarmed by the growth of Soviet nuclear capabilities, began looking anew at the possibilities for rollback. The JCS urged the Eisenhower administration not to rule out forceful action, since that would be "self-defeating and directly contrary to the positive, dynamic policy required to reduce the Soviet threat before it reaches critical proportions."[15] In their view, a program of positive action could be adopted without undue risk of general war.

By contrast, the State Department strongly opposed the policy of rollback and sought to avoid the use of force against the Soviet Union and the Eastern bloc. Eisenhower's Secretary of State, John Foster Dulles, spoke against the JCS plan to use force against the Soviet Union. He did not believe that splitting the Soviet bloc would solve the basic problem of the Soviet Union's growing nuclear capacity. Attempts to detach Soviet satellites would, in his view, increase the risk of general war, but would do little to alter the central balance of power. Furthermore, aggressive action might imperil the Western coalition and would destroy any chances of reaching agreement with the Soviet Union.[16]

In the end, Eisenhower resolved the debate within the government by deciding against measures that risked provoking nuclear war. After the Soviet Union exploded its own hydrogen bomb in 1953 both Eisenhower and Dulles recognized that a general nuclear war was no longer any better than suicide.[17] In 1954, Eisenhower stated that no moment would be right for starting war, and that the United States would be prepared only to retaliate against a Soviet nuclear attack. Over time, Secretary of Defense Charles Wilson came to agree with Dulles's view, and he too began to advocate a policy of containment.[18] Nonetheless, the administration sought, in NSC-162/2, to alleviate some of the concerns of the JCS and Defense Department. Although an earlier draft stated that the United States should not "initiate aggressive actions involving force against Soviet bloc territory,"[19] this explicit prohibition was omitted from the final document, signaling the Eisenhower administration's ambivalence about aggressive rollback. Still, those who expected the President to employ psychological warfare to its fullest potential were disappointed. Eisenhower failed to launch an aggressive campaign of liberation and within a year concluded that the threat of thermonuclear war dictated accommodation with the Kremlin. As under Truman, Eastern Europe remained the captive of Soviet atomic deterrence.

By 1956, a fundamental tension had appeared in U.S. policy toward the Eastern bloc. On the one hand, the United States hoped to encourage East European countries to break away from the bloc through their own efforts. On the other hand, U.S. officials wished to avoid a U.S.–Soviet military confrontation, fearing escalation into nuclear war. For these reasons, U.S. policymakers had to consider other means of diminishing Soviet influence in Eastern Europe. This led to the development of policies such as economic and psychological warfare (psyops), covert operations, and, at a later stage, negotiation with the Soviet Union regarding the status of the East-bloc states.

Economic warfare

The United States initiated "economic warfare" (the denial of all goods that might be adapted for weapons) against the Soviet bloc in 1948.[20] The aim of the policy was to diminish the Soviet Union's military potential. The policy was also designed to put strain on relations between the USSR and the East European states by forcing the Soviet Union to supply scarce materials to its allies.[21] In addition, the United States hoped to impede economic growth in the Communist countries, and perhaps bring about their economic collapse.

W. Averell Harriman, the Secretary of Commerce under President Harry Truman, first devised economic warfare in 1947 and 1948. Ironically, Harriman had been one of the strongest advocates of expanded economic relations with the Soviet Union during World War II. In a letter sent to the NSC on 17 December 1947, Harriman declared that the Soviet Union and its satellites were not taking part in the European Reconstruction Program (ERP) and were therefore hindering European reconstruction, menacing world peace, and threatening the security of the United States. Harriman recommended the "termination, for an indefinite period, of shipments from the United States to the USSR and its satellites of all commodities which are critically short in the United States and which would contribute to the Soviet military potential." This was to be done without severely punishing Eastern Europe. A multilateral Coordinating Committee (CoCom) was set up with West European countries to create a list of goods to be embargoed.[22]

On the domestic front, the U.S. Congress fully backed Harriman's policy, insisting that the embargo be strictly enforced to prevent the United States from contributing to the military capacity of its enemy. Congress passed the Battle Act and the Kem Amendment in 1951, both of which imposed strict export controls and stipulated that the United States must deny or suspend military and economic assistance to countries exporting items of strategic significance. The JCS similarly desired to reduce Soviet military might. All these officials sought a continuous expansion of the embargo list, and a requirement that West Europeans adhere to the terms of the embargo.[23]

The State Department argued for a less stringent approach. Department officials recognized that if the West Europeans followed American guidelines, the consequent decline in East–West trade would seriously impede the reconstruction of Western Europe. Moreover, if the West European economies were weakened, Soviet subversive efforts would be harder to resist. In the final analysis, according to the State Department, an economic embargo would be counterproductive. The State Department persuaded Truman's cabinet to support the position that only essential commodities could be embargoed, commodities that would be determined in a selective licensing procedure. The procedure would be carefully designed to avoid a total economic war against Eastern Europe. The flow of goods from East to West would be ensured, and the Soviet Union would continue to sell manganese, chrome, iridium, and platinum to the United States. In the end, the Cabinet adopted three mutually incompatible goals in its economic warfare policy: to prevent or delay the build-up of Soviet military potential; to ensure that the West European countries received needed imports from Eastern Europe, including timber, coal, and potash; and finally, to ensure the flow of essential commodities from Eastern Europe to the United States. Licensed goods were grouped into four classes, ranging from commodities of direct military value to articles of little military value. [24]

Throughout the 1950s, interdepartmental wrangling continued over the number of embargoed commodities and the definition of strategic goods. The JCS came out strongly in favor of tightening restrictions on Eastern Europe. The Joint Chiefs were convinced that an effective "economic Iron Curtain" would paralyze the Soviet economy within five to ten years.[25] Charles Sawyer, the U.S. secretary of commerce from 1948 to 1953, also sought to pressure Western Europe to conform to the embargo. The U.S. business community supported Sawyer, having been discouraged that their West European competitors were exploiting the embargo to get favorable trade deals. Congress passed a series of measures to penalize countries that shipped embargoed goods to the Soviet Union and the Eastern bloc.[26]

Soon after North Korea's attack on South Korea in June 1950, the NSC surveyed departmental views of the relationship between national security and export controls. The departments of commerce and defense and the National Security Resources Board all recommended expanding the embargo, arguing that national security considerations should govern export control.[27] Some reports indicated that the embargo had already significantly retarded military development in the Soviet bloc. Furthermore, the ERP countries had made significant headway in their economic recovery, which meant that the significance of East–West trade was diminishing. Hence, the cost-benefit analysis tilted in favor of more radical controls.[28]

Nevertheless, State Department officials believed that East–West trade was still crucial to the health of the West European economies. As that department gradually took precedence in determining export control policy, it increasingly advocated a balance between free trade and control. In 1951, the Truman administration officially embraced this moderate position, arguing in NSC 104 that the Soviet bloc's reliance on outside resources was limited and therefore the effect of the embargo was limited as well.[29]

When Eisenhower became president in January 1953 he favored the approach of the State Department, and decided to further change the direction of American export control policy by relaxing trade controls.[30] At this point, U.S. pressure on Western Europe to comply with the embargo was seriously straining alliance relations. Furthermore, Eisenhower remained unconvinced that economic warfare was having the desired effect on either the Soviet Union or the satellites. He argued that an expansion of trade would be more successful in weaning the Eastern bloc away from the Soviet orbit. In July 1953 he decided on a "gradual and moderate relaxation" of trade controls. The U.S. and CoCom lists were shortened. This new policy was opposed by the JCS, who believed that the difficulty of distinguishing between strategic and non-strategic commodities was too great. The Joint Chiefs insisted that the embargo was already causing bottlenecks in Soviet industry.[31]

Eisenhower's policy of moderation was supported by evidence from a National Intelligence Estimate (NIE) prepared by the Central Intelligence Agency (CIA) in 1954. After analyzing the results of the first years of economic warfare, the CIA concluded that a relaxation of controls would enhance the Soviet bloc's strategic position, but would not significantly affect its production of goods and services. The CIA did suggest that the Eastern bloc's military potential would slightly increase after a relaxation of trade controls. However, it added that such a relaxation of controls would improve inter-allied relations, and that CoCom countries would be supportive of the remaining aspects of the embargo.[32]

Eisenhower's new policy was codified by NSC 5609 in June 1956, and from then on, economic incentives began to play a larger role in U.S. policy toward the Soviet bloc. NSC 5609 recommended that Congress selectively relax trade restrictions on East-bloc countries, treating each state as a separate case. If circumstances warranted, some countries could be granted "most favored nation" status.[33] If economic controls were aimed at strangling the satellite economies, the relaxation of the embargo was poorly timed. After

1954, the Soviet Union began to reduce its shipment of raw materials and countries like Hungary, which relied on external sources as their raw material base, became increasingly reliant on Western sources.[34]

Economic policy shifts behind the Iron Curtain favored the relaxation of trade controls. In 1954, the Council for Mutual Economic Assistance (CMEA) officially rescinded the policy of economic autarky it had adopted in 1949. The CMEA resolution affirmed that "the development of trade with capitalist countries that strive to do the same is in line with the foreign policy of democratic nations."[35] Hungary's chief economic planner, Ernő Gerő, had already called for an expansion of trade with the capitalist world in the summer of 1952, even before Georgii Malenkov, the Soviet prime minister, raised the issue at the Nineteenth Congress of the Soviet Communist Party (CPSU) in October 1952. On 20 January 1954, the Hungarian Foreign Ministry instructed the Hungarian delegation in Washington to explore opportunities "to expand trade relations with the United States, and to determine what circles to approach."[36]

Nonetheless, Eisenhower's idea of using trade as a diplomatic tool was implemented only gradually. The United States did not negotiate with an East-bloc country until February 1957, when it approached the Polish government. The obstacles to trade relations were partly of an economic nature. East Europeans were short of hard currency and had difficulty paying for imports. In Hungary, for example, the chronic shortage of Western currency was coupled with an equally chronic balance of trade deficit, which reached 2.7 billion forints (over 200 million contemporary dollars) by 1956. To alleviate the deficit, the Hungarian finance minister prescribed a drastic curtailment of Western imports.[37] However, the ban on imports proved impossible to sustain because the Soviet Union had sharply cut its shipment of raw materials to Hungary in 1955. Hungary had become dependent on Western goods.[38]

To get around the currency problem, the State Department advocated barter arrangements for raw materials.[39] Such an arrangement was unworkable for Hungary, which was poor in raw materials except for bauxite and uranium, both of which were purchased by the Soviet Union. Hungarian industrial goods were virtually worthless because they were outdated and qualitatively deficient.[40] The poor quality of industrial products was in part caused by the embargo, which had rendered Hungary unable to modernize its capital equipment. In 1955, the Hungarians began to make overtures to the U.S. Legation in Budapest, asking to purchase American wheat and cotton. The talks collapsed because the United States would not grant Hungary the necessary credit, since tensions between the two countries were still high and Budapest was still unwilling to make the necessary political concessions. The United States engineered the rejection of a similar Hungarian overture to West Germany.[41] It would take another decade until Eisen-hower's plan to use trade to detach countries from Soviet control came into effect in Hungary, eventually with excellent results.

Ultimately, it is difficult to assess the full effects of U.S. economic war-fare against the Communist states. An estimate by the Operations Coordi-nating Board (OCB) in February 1956 claimed that the embargo had dimin-ished the Soviet bloc's economic and military potential. According to the OCB, the restrictions on technology transfer compelled the Soviet bloc to use largely outdated equipment and production methods. At the same time, the OCB conceded that the embargo was unlikely to erode Soviet power in Eastern Europe.[42] It was also clear that the embargo was not airtight. Accord-ing to intelligence from Hungary, the Hungarian economy, "although seri-ously hindered by shortages of technical equipment, has been able to func-tion […] partly as a result of a successful evasion of Western trade con-trols."[43] One way to obtain embargoed goods was to establish trading com-panies that would purchase retransfer items.[44] Mátyás Rákosi, leader of the Hungarian Workers' Party (MDP) until July 1956 and prime minister until July 1953, remembered that "America's Western partners assisted the eva-sion of the American embargo and export controls in the hope of receiving the appropriate profits."[45] Israel sold ball bearings in return for the relax-ation of controls on Jewish emigration, and Sweden also was a source for this important commodity. The American Legation in Vienna named Aus-tria, Finland, and Egypt as the most important sources of goods "procured in contravention of Western controls."[46] France sold ball bearings and spe-cial steel alloys in the framework of a Franco-Hungarian commercial agree-ment.[47] Many raw materials needed for Hungarian industry were supplied from the West. All of Hungary's rubber and leather, 92 percent of its copper, 72 percent of its coke, 66 percent of its tin, and 41 percent of its cotton came from capitalist states in 1955.[48]

Despite the high incidence of evasion, Rákosi was merely blustering when he maintained that the embargo was proving beneficial for the Social-ist bloc because it had forced CMEA countries to rely on each other and to make better efforts to find and exploit their own natural resources.[49] In real-ity, cooperation among the CMEA members was virtually non-existent, and the embargo significantly impaired the Hungarian economy, which was plagued by serious shortages of all types of precision and measuring instru-ments, industrial diamonds, and grinding and abrasive equipment. Ball-bear-ing measuring equipment and certain spiral drills for the weapons industry were in especially short supply, and Hungary was suffering from a lack of instruments to measure the hardness of steel—a major necessity for Hun-gary's crash project of heavy industrialization.[50] Hungarian industrial goods became obsolete and so inferior to their Western counterparts that they could not be sold in Western markets. To obtain hard currency, Hungary was forced to sell agricultural products such as wheat, which was in short supply because of the persecution of the peasantry and forced collectivization. Food shortages and low-quality consumer goods were, in turn, the major sources of popular discontent.[51]

Psychological warfare

Winning over the minds of the public was as important to the United States as its efforts to bankrupt the Communist regimes. Eastern Europe was effectively sealed from contact with the non-Communist world. Travel across the Iron Curtain was virtually impossible. Barbed wire, minefields, and armed guards on the Hungarian–Austrian border dissuaded potential Hungarian defectors. A nation of almost ten million exchanged a mere fifty thousand letters with the Western world annually.[52] Communist media conveyed official propaganda. One of the unique aspects of modern political relationships is the deliberate attempt by governments to influence the attitudes and behavior of foreign populations or of specific groups of those populations.[53] These may be class, ethnic, religious, economic or linguistic groups. U.S. propaganda cut through these lines and targeted a political group, one that was diverse in all respects except in the presumed opposition to foreign rule and Communism.

In February 1953 the U.S. Legation in Budapest summed up its goals for psychological warfare in Hungary: "We can maintain the spirit of opposition and preserve resistance to the present regime which will prevent Moscow from putting any real trust in Hungary or have any confidence in the stability of the government or the loyalty of the armed forces in case of war." On the other hand, the Legation was sober in its conclusion that "we cannot hope to build up a resistance movement or other type of active opposition, which might overthrow the present regime in the foreseeable future." Similarly, there was little chance that Hungary would defect from Soviet control, "à la Tito."[54] Three years later N. Spencer Barnes, the American minister in Budapest, asked himself whether "any possibilities exist for the Hungarian people to offer effective resistance to a thoroughly unpopular regime without military aid from the outside?" Barnes stressed that "any suggestion for mass action can be worked out abroad and presented to a target audience of literally millions within a very short time." This meant that there was a "possibility of coordinating mass action, without the need of direct contact between individuals and with a minimum risk to anyone." Some "trivial" action could be selected that could be taken by any individual who wished to express protest against Hungary's present status or the regime. Suggested acts included dropping pieces of paper with torn-off edges on sidewalks. The idea was that if thousands of such pieces appeared in Hungarian cities every day ("each one a testimony of an individual citizen's hatred of the regime"), they would mitigate the regime's prestige "and perhaps even stability." Similarly conceived attacks could be made on economic viability and the government bureaucracy.[55] Although the minister recommended great caution in implementing these sorts of schemes, his proposals represented a more ambitious and hence a more reckless side of psychological warfare.

The creation of the CIA in 1947 provided a bureaucratic system that could facilitate the coordination of psychological warfare operations.[56] On 20 April 1950, President Truman announced that the propaganda offensive would be a "struggle for the minds of men," which would be waged by "getting the real story across to people in other countries."[57] NSC 68 called for large-scale covert operations, through which strategists intended to foment revolutionary activities within the satellite states. More intensive efforts in economic, political and psychological warfare were meant to foment and support unrest in selected satellite countries. In April 1951 the Truman administration created an umbrella organization, the Psychological Strategy Board (PSB), for the spread of information and propaganda. The Board acted as the "nerve center" for psychological operations, which now became one of Washington's chief instruments in undercutting Soviet power in Eastern Europe. In 1953 Eisenhower continued the psychological warfare programs. Because the PSB was criticized for failing to pursue its purpose vigorously and effectively enough, Eisenhower replaced it with the OCB, which was meant to coordinate planning between information programs and covert operations. The United States Information Agency (USIA) was created to implement OCB planning. It assumed responsibility for overt efforts to disseminate information abroad.[58]

These attempts to sow the seeds of discontent and promote the disintegration of Communist regimes fell on fertile ground in Eastern Europe because of the widespread dissatisfaction with Communism and the popularity of the United States. For example, the U.S. minister in Budapest, Christian Ravndal, reported that his wife's Buick Century was habitually flocked by Hungarians. Evidently, the crowd was occasionally so large that traffic police officers were needed. Part of the reason that the Buick was so popular is that it was a rare sight, only around five thousand motorcars were in Hungary at the time, most of which were obsolete, pre-war models. Ravndal highlighted the propaganda value of American cars at a top-secret meeting on psychological warfare, held in Washington in March 1953.[59] The popularity of American goods was also made clear in the small town of Cegléd in 1955. The local agricultural cooperative sought to sell children's clothes found in a warehouse belonging to the National Office of Israelites. Rumors spread that the American government had sent the clothes to the victims of the 1954 flood. The clothing allegedly still had American labels. The local party secretary reported that "interest in the goods was so great that the windows of the cooperative were smashed" by the crowd that tried to get hold of them. Therefore, the local party boss suspended the sale, claiming that it provided opportunities for "hostile propaganda and agitation."[60]

Radio broadcasts were by far the most effective means of influencing ordinary East Europeans.[61] Because of jamming the sound kept drifting on and off. Although the messages were sent from European transmitters, this unintended sound effect made it seem as though the broadcast was coming from the United States itself, increasing its authenticity. Voice of America (VOA) was launched in 1947. The following year, the East-bloc states were already jamming it. This was offset by a costly but effective counter-jamming drive, and in 1951, the VOA increased its daily programming and managed to broadcast in 45 languages. Radio Free Europe (RFE), set up by the Free Europe Committee, began broadcasting in 1950. When RFE began operations, its vice president, Frederick Dolbeare, declared that it would express Hungary's ancient aspiration for freedom.[62] Before 1956, however, RFE did not directly address resistance groups and instead targeted youth groups, workers, and peasants.

The U.S.-sponsored radio campaign was meant to keep alive the spirit of anti-Communism by appealing to nationalist and religious sentiments and by spotlighting grievances. It was also designed to sustain popular hopes that Communism would eventually be overthrown. Even so, it could not openly advocate revolt against Communist rule, nor could it suggest that the United States would intervene on behalf of such a revolt. The dilemmas of this policy were reflected in the guidance given to RFE in 1951. On the one hand, broadcasters were to disseminate anti-Soviet propaganda and avoid words such as "peace" and "disarmament" that might signal international acceptance of Soviet control of East Europe. On the other hand, no broadcaster was allowed to promise armed liberation. Any such statements would have fundamentally misled the East European audience. The reporters were supposed to advocate reversing the "tide of Soviet imperialism" and to suggest that the Western world would stand up to Soviet aggression anywhere, but they had to make clear that this did not amount to a pledge of military intervention.[63] The events of 1956 in Hungary demonstrated that the line between keeping hope alive and arousing unjustified expectations was often blurred. The guidance for broadcasters was ambiguous enough to be stretched quite far, causing some in the audience to believe that armed liberation was imminent.

In 1953, Columbia University conducted a survey of Hungarian citizens' reactions to the RFE, VOA, and British Broadcasting Corporation

(BBC). Hungarian defectors—some of the most anti-Communist elements of society—claimed that the programming of the VOA and BBC was sufficiently anti-Communist. However, when their hopes for the armed liberation of their homeland failed to materialize, they blamed the radio stations as well as the British and U.S. governments for stirring these hopes. Therefore, the Columbia survey recommended that the radio broadcasts strive, on the one hand, to keep the hopes of the audience alive, but, on the other hand, to avoid giving any impression that Western countries could perform miracles.[64]

Until well into the 1950s, however, some Hungarians were convinced that the United States would liberate them even if it required war. A 19-year-old defector told his interrogator that although "the Hungarians realize that direct Western intervention would mean war" and were aware of the horrors of war, "they would still prefer it to continued slavery [...] They fear that the United States may have become reconciled to Hungary's status as a Soviet satellite. Hungarian young people strongly believe that only the U.S. can force Russia to make concessions."[65] Another defector claimed that people were widely quoting alleged statements by the RFE and the BBC to the effect that Hungary would soon be free. He declared that the VOA was the best radio station because of its well-presented, pertinent information and its "forthright, encouraging, anti-Soviet stand."[66] Yet, another informant claimed that "people listened avidly to news from the West and particularly from the United States [...] People continue to hope for the outbreak of the war, which they believe the United States would win."[67]

There is not enough evidence to determine exactly how widespread these expectations of armed assistance were. An RFE survey in 1957 indicated that one-half of the 620 U.S.-bound refugees who were questioned had expected American intervention in support of the revolution. Some of the men arrested by the Hungarian regime for conspiracy told their interrogators that they were inspired by Western broadcasts. Béla Halász, arrested for spying, claimed during his interrogation that he and his fellow conspirators "believed the news and the propaganda of the imperialist radio and expected a (political) transition."[68] In 1951, Győző Flossmann organized a group to overthrow the Communist system. He confessed to the police that he had regularly listened to the broadcasts of Western stations, "especially the American Hungarian broadcasts and the Voice of Free Europe [sic]." Based on these broadcasts, he claimed, he "expected war, or an American occupation of the country."[69] His comrade, Zsiga Tiborc, confessed that he sought "to shake the country with explosions and terror attacks and to sabotage industrial production," when the expected war with the Soviet Union broke out.[70] Another conspiracy led by a clergyman, Ottmár Faddi, hoped to establish a Catholic government "with American military assistance."[71]

　　Hungarian conspirators often planned to coordinate their attacks on the regime with American assistance. Kálmán Horváth organized a conspiracy on behalf of a Hungarian émigré organization working in conjunction with the U.S. Counter Intelligence Corps and the Gehlen organization.[72] His group acted in the firm belief that armies arriving from West Germany would occupy Hungary. He believed his group would receive arms, clothing, and other military items thrown from American warplanes. After their arrest, the conspirators claimed to have been influenced by U.S. propaganda. As one leader confessed: "We believed the news and propaganda of the imperialist radio stations and expected an imminent transformation of our political system."[73] Gedeon Ráth organized one of the most significant anti-Communist plots in the early 1950s. The conspirators disseminated leaflets in the manner encouraged by the RFE. They worked to acquire arms in order to assist an expected influx of Western troops. In May 1950, Ráth thought that "the Americans or the Tito group" would supply weapons to the conspirators. They aimed to "overthrow the system" and to "support the invaders."[74]

　　The Hungarian regime was understandably concerned about the effect of the VOA and RFE on Hungarian conspirators. In his indictment speech in the case of Győző Flossmann, the judge Vilmos Olti blamed RFE and VOA for stirring trouble. Olti claimed that "in order to arouse panic and incite counterrevolution [RFE and VOA] disseminate information that gives the impression that war will soon break out and that American forces will occupy Hungary and restore the old imperialist system."[75]

　　To some extent, Hungarian secret police exaggerated the effect of radio propaganda to justify censorship and repression. In the summer of 1956, the Hungarian government itself acknowledged that it had been unduly harsh in dealing with supposed conspirators. This is not to say that the allegations were completely unfounded.[76] Plots did exist, even if they were blown out of proportion. Hungarians expected Western assistance, and this encouraged them to take up arms against the regime.[77] In this respect, American propaganda was somewhat callous to the fate of East Europeans. Knowing the nature of Communist regimes, U.S. officials and radio broadcasters might have warned against resorting to measures that the Americans had no intention of supporting.

　　On the more positive side, the foreign broadcasts did make it much harder for Soviet officials to retain their monopoly on information. Radio propaganda also sustained the morale of the people. Some defectors testified that Hungarians would otherwise have been left with "a distorted view of the world."[78] Ernst Halperin of the *Neue Zuricher Zeitung*, who had visited Hungary in 1954 claimed that "public thinking on foreign affairs was formed not by the Hungarian newspapers, which nobody reads, but in the editorial rooms of the Western broadcasting services."[79] Western radio worked against

Communist indoctrination,[80] and many believed that, without the radio broad-casts, Hungarians would have lost "all hope for the future."[81]

A USIA program that distributed two thousand bulletins and some three thousand newspapers, periodicals and pamphlets each month supplemented radio propaganda.[82] Balloons carrying propaganda leaflets were sent into Communist airspace, allowing them to cover wide areas. Balloon operations commenced in 1951, and by the time these operations were terminated in 1956, over 300 million leaflets had been dropped onto Communist territory. The leaflets carried messages such as, "The regime is weaker than you think, the hope lies with the people."[83]

In Hungary, these messages from the sky encountered a mixed recep-tion. Some defectors complained that the "leaflets did more harm than good" because they "gave the police a chance to step up their persecution of the 'class alien elements', providing additional reasons to justify the search of their homes." People were persecuted even if no leaflets were found on them. The residents of the village of Nyögér considered the operations a failure for the same reason. Police searched their homes when they saw a balloon approaching.[84] Even if no such problems had arisen, the leaflets did not seem to contain any information "that has not been broadcast over and over again."[85] Because most of the balloons were shot down near border regions, their audience was far smaller than that of the radio programs.[86] Nonethe-less, some defectors thought the balloons were effective against the regime because they "boosted the morale of the population," and were "encourag-ing popular resistance to the regime and shaking Communist power."[87] According to the 1957 RFE survey of Hungarian defectors, fifteen percent of the population relied on leaflets for their news.[88]

The Communist authorities reacted harshly to the balloons. In 1956 the Hungarian Workers Party Central Committee claimed that the regime had collected 2.6 million leaflets in 1955. The Central Committee also declared that "interest in leaflets sent from the West is diminishing, but they still have a mobilizing effect on hostile elements."[89] The Czechoslovak and Hungarian regimes protested to American diplomats and used fighter planes to shoot down the balloons. On 8 February 1956 Hungarian Deputy Foreign Minister Endre Sík summoned the U.S. chargé and protested against the balloon operation. Sík claimed that balloons were sent to gather intelligence and to disseminate "filthy documents slandering the government and the political system." These actions, according to the foreign minister, consti-tuted interference in Hungarian internal affairs and violated Hungarian sov-ereignty. Sík also alleged that the balloons had caused the downing of air-craft and the death of two pilots. The Hungarian government demanded the termination of such flights and "reserved the right" to seek reparations for the casualties and damage they caused.[90] The American side dismissed the accusations by incorrectly stating that the balloons in question were launched by private organizations or served meteorological purposes.[91] The Hungarian authorities lodged another protest on 28 July, arguing that 293 balloons had been sighted since February, one of which had caused an airplane to crash, killing its pilot. The government threatened to force international aircraft land whenever balloons were sighted so that they would "avoid disaster." The Hungarians also claimed that the operations were hindering the improvement of bilateral relations, which was Hungary's "profound desire."[92]

In the end, the Hungarian regime was largely unable to block Western propaganda. Jamming was difficult, and even the Soviet Union could not provide effective help in blocking radio transmissions because the VOA constantly altered its frequency.[93] The protests against the balloons were a sign that U.S. tactics were successful. By 1955, the regime was losing the battle to win "hearts and minds." That year, the Hungarian authorities confiscated twelve thousand "hostile" letters, propaganda brochures, and private presses.[94] Rákosi was forced to admit that party cadres were increasingly unable to sell the party line. In his words, "In the course of our ever livelier debates we have seen that some comrades cannot come up with convincing arguments and are incapable of defending the party's position in the face of the enemy [...] Many an honest comrade has begun to waver, indeed, has fallen under enemy influence. In the debates of the past few weeks [these comrades] have heard incorrect or hostile views, which were well-prepared and expressed more convincingly."[95] Western propaganda thus appears to have fallen on fertile ground. Less than a decade later, a member of the party Politburo was forced to admit that Communist ideology had lost all appeal for young people in Hungary. Even the party youth magazine was disseminating Western popular culture.[96] Although twenty-five more years would elapse until the political system followed suit, communism as an ideology was already losing its influence in Hungary. By facilitating Western cultural penetration and countering Communist indoctrination, Western propaganda in this period helped pave the way for the downfall of Hungarian Communism.

Covert warfare

In the early 1950s, the United States began to explore various possibilities for covert activities behind the Iron Curtain. In 1951, legislation known as the Kersten amendment appropriated $100 million for the recruitment of refugees from the Soviet bloc for military service.[97] The head of the PSB, Gordon Gray, praised this action as the first positive step against Soviet aggression since the war.[98] General Ladislav Anders, an Polish émigré leader, had originally promised over six million men for the anti-Soviet cause, but the U.S. military had shown no interest until 18 December 1951, when the secretary of defense instructed the JCS to take steps to implement the Kersten Amendment. Twenty-five light regiments of former refugees were to be integrated into the military structures of the North Atlantic Treaty Organization (NATO). By 1955, some 60,000 men were supposed to receive military training, and the best were to be trained for psychological, intelligence, and unconventional warfare. All branches of the military prepared their own plans. The U.S. Air Force, for example, hoped to encourage defections of East European and Soviet air force personnel.[99]

Soon, however, the secretary of defense began to question the feasibility of implementing the Kersten Amendment.[100] Because European governments were opposed to the refugee regiments, the relationship between these units and NATO or the European Defense Community (EDC) became problematic.[101] In light of these concerns, the JCS concluded in 1953 that the Kersten Amendment was unfeasible. U.S. military commanders in Europe also concluded that refugee units were neither practicable nor desirable, and they recommended against them.[102]

The Eisenhower administration broached the idea of creating a refugee paramilitary force, called the "Volunteer Freedom Corps" (VFC).[103] In May 1953, the president approved the establishment of a VFC under NSC 143/2.[104] This idea, however, suffered the same fate as the Kersten Amendment. West European opposition to the project was too strong to ignore. In early 1956, the administration decided to defer any further consideration of the Corps.[105]

Other covert schemes were explored in the early 1950s. For example, in 1951 and 1952 an effort was made to reconstitute the Home Army in Poland.[106] In Czechoslovakia the United States staged border incidents, violated Czechoslovak airspace, and dropped radio transmitters for undercover agents. From January 1951 to December 1953, some 1,200 "Western agents" were reported arrested or killed by the Czechoslovak authorities. From 1951 through 1956, 79 murders were attributed to foreign agents.[107] Varieties of penetration missions were designed to collect intelligence in the Eastern bloc and to assemble paramilitary units that could resist a possible Soviet invasion. Hundreds of agents were dispatched behind the Iron Curtain to contact and encourage anti-Communist resistance forces.[108]

In 1955, the NSC stated that covert operations were designed to "develop underground resistance, and facilitate covert and guerrilla operations and ensure the availability of those forces in the event of war, including wherever practicable provision of a base upon which the military may expand these forces in time of war within active theaters of operations..." If operations were discovered, the U.S. government had to be prepared to plausibly deny responsibility.[109]

In July 1956, Mátyás Rákosi, the first secretary of the MDP, claimed that each month, Hungary's state security forces (ÁVH) "uncovered an average of two counterrevolutionary underground conspiracies, whose strings led to the imperialists. Thirty-seven spies sent into Hungary from the West were unmasked."[110] Between 1949 and 1953 the regime investigated 120 cases of foreign intelligence, 41 of which were U.S.-sponsored. In the same period the ÁVH arrested the members of 14 alleged spy rings organized before 1949, all with alleged American connections. In 1955, some 61 percent of the spies discovered in Hungary were American.[111] In fact, based on interrogations of captured CIC agents, the Hungarian Ministry of Internal Affairs concluded that the United States was organizing a nucleus of armed anti-Communist resistance and was instigating acts of sabotage in Hungary. Now there is evidence to suggest that this accusation may not be groundless.

In 1949, an agent by the name of Gordon Mason was dispatched to Romania to contact resistance groups active in Transylvania in the hope of igniting widespread insurrection. Mason's networks positioned resistance fighters to harass Soviet troops in case of a world war. Two years later two agents were dropped into the Romanian–Hungarian inhabited region of Fogaras in Romania. They were arrested with radio transmitting and receiving sets, weapons and money in gold and local currency. Their mission was to set up clusters of resistance among the locals and send intelligence.[112] Similar arrests were made in Hungary. They too claimed that the Americans were setting up resistance groups to commit acts of terrorism and to combat the Soviets in case a war broke out.[113]

Aggressive rollback

When the Eisenhower administration took office in early 1953, a more aggressive American policy toward the Eastern bloc seemed to be in the offing. John Foster Dulles had promised to support an "explosive and dynamic" policy of "liberation."[114] Stalin's death in March 1953 provided Dulles with an opportunity to launch a strident propaganda campaign. He instructed U.S. embassies "to sow doubt, confusion, [and] uncertainty about the new regime not only among both Soviet and satellite masses, but among local Communist parties outside the Soviet Union."[115] Eisenhower himself was skeptical about aggressive rollback, but some of his aides, particularly his chief national security adviser, C. D. Jackson, wanted to convert the policy into action as soon as possible.[116] Eisenhower and even Dulles were more cautious, but the fate of rollback was still an open question when events on the ground in mid-1953 largely settled the matter.

The East German uprising in June 1953 and its suppression by Soviet troops shattered the notion of aggressive rollback.[117] Dulles, who initially perceived the crisis as an opportunity for Western victory against the Soviet Union, was unable to find a way to capitalize on it. Although Eisenhower would have been willing to intervene had the uprising spread to China, and if there was a real prospect of success, he believed that helping the East German movement was premature. As he put it "the time to roll them out for keeps" had not "quite" arrived. Even C. D. Jackson, who had initially advocated sending arms to the protestors, had to admit that the U.S. did not have the power to eject the Soviets from East Germany through coercion.[118] In the end, the administration merely decided to distribute food packages to East German residents, beginning in late August 1953. Although this response did prove to be highly effective politically, it was far more commensurate with the earlier strategy of containment than with aggressive rollback.[119] Because the administration was unwilling to run the risks that stronger action would have entailed, Eisenhower's notion of relying on peaceful means to achieve liberation now seemed the most feasible—or at least most palatable—option to pursue.[120] The inability of the West to do more once violence had erupted in June 1953 led many U.S. officials to conclude that if "another uprising" broke out in East-Central Europe, the United States once again would be forced to watch helplessly as the Soviets put them down. The Eisenhower administration's strategic reassessment, called Operation Solarium, disavowed the "rollback" concept and affirmed that "we do not want to [...] incur blame for [the] consequences" of "a mass open rebellion" in the Soviet bloc.[121]

The retreat from aggressive rollback was reaffirmed in December 1953, when the administration adopted NSC 174, which fell well short of the "explosive and dynamic" policy that Dulles had promised earlier in the year. NSC 174 described the restoration of East European independence as only a long-term U.S. aim. Care had to be taken not to incite "premature" rebellion. No promises could be made about the timing and nature of American liberation efforts, nor were there plans for direct military action. In the short run, the United States would merely strive to "undermine" the local regimes, create favorable conditions for liberation, and preserve all forces that could contribute to independence and the assertion of American interests. No mention was made of sponsoring "Titoism" as an intermediate stage between Kremlin domination and democratic freedom as advocated by the first U.S. policy paper on Eastern Europe, NSC 58/2.

This is not to say that NSC 174 was simply a writ for passivity. The document called for, among other things, the stepped-up use of psychological warfare to prepare the ground for possible armed resistance against the Soviet Union. In particular, the United States would support the growth of nationalist sentiments, which were seen as antithetical to "Soviet imperialism." The United States would also exploit rifts within the Communist regimes, foster dissatisfaction in the armed forces, take advantage of "Titoist" sentiments, and encourage "key elements" to defect.[122] These policies were by no means insignificant, but they were far less ambitious overall than Dulles's initial promises had envisaged.

Part of the reason that the move away from rollback was so pronounced is that Dulles's perspective had changed by late 1953. He began to view rollback as a costly and risk-laden strategy that could reduce the Soviet threat, but that could also destroy the free world.[123] Dulles's views continued to moderate over time. By 1955, he acknowledged the relaxation of the Cold War, describing the Soviet Union as "less menacing." He told the Senate Foreign Relations committee that "the U.S. is getting closer to a relationship [where] we can deal [with the Soviet Union] on a basis comparable to that where we deal with differences between friendly nations."[124] In 1956, when the challenger for the presidency, Adlai Stevenson, mentioned the "pledge" of liberation, Dulles responded that "there is no such pledge." Containment was again the line pursued by the State Department.[125] According to the Policy Planning Staff, liberation meant keeping the spirit of hope and liberty alive, not the use of military force.[126]

The cautiousness of the administration's new policy was evident in 1955 when Ferenc Nagy, Hungary's former prime minister who was removed when the Communists took over in 1947, asked a high-ranking State Department official to speak at the 10-year commemoration of Hungary's 1945 election. The State Department declined, claiming it did not wish to identify "publicly and officially" with ideas expressed by the Hungarian émigrés.[127] Whenever department officials received an inquiry about U.S. policy toward Eastern Europe, they were careful not to give the impression that forceful liberation was an option.[128] Ultimately the possibility of nuclear war in Europe ruled out forceful liberation. Eisenhower was convinced that a war against the USSR would inevitably be a nuclear one. The argument about deterrence, the idea that both sides would hold back from nuclear use, was in his view mistaken.[129]

Even so, Dulles and other high-ranking officials continued to make statements about liberation, conveying an ambiguous picture of U.S. policy that could easily mislead the populations of East-bloc countries.[130] These mixed signals were not necessarily arbitrary; rather, they resulted from the continued belief on the part of many administration officials that resistance to totalitarian rule in Eastern Europe was "less hopeless than has been imagined." The administration still desired "to nourish resistance to Communist oppression throughout satellite Europe, short of mass rebellion in areas under Soviet control, and without compromising its spontaneous nature."[131] These strands of U.S. policy, no matter how they were viewed in Washington, led many in Hungary to expect more support once the revolution had begun.

Negotiation

The aftermath of Joseph Stalin's death is often described as a missed opportunity for the United States to relax East–West tension. The U.S. administration seemed unprepared for the eventuality; Eisenhower failed to respond to Malenkov's overtures, to Churchill's suggestion for a summit meeting or to such phenomena as the alleviation of Soviet occupation policy in Austria.[132] Yet, the Eisenhower administration was not as passive as it suggested, in fact an offer was made to Hungarian party leader to meet with the U.S. President soon after the Russian dictator passed on. A window of opportunity for the Austrian treaty was opened, based on some form of neutrality, but this did not seem to be an option for Eastern Europe. Popular unrest in East Germany was nipped in the bud. The Soviet leadership severely reprimanded the Hungarians for their alleged overture to the West in the summer of 1953 and in the same year, Soviet experts began the exploration of Hungarian uranium. Nevertheless, after Stalin's death the United States also began to pursue a new means of solving the East European problem: negotiation. This is not surprising in view of the appraisal that open revolts would simply cause bloodshed without hope of success and the fact that the U.S. was unwilling to engage in war for the sake of liberation. Dulles advised Eisenhower to propose that the United States and the Soviet Union mutually withdraw their forces from Europe. Dulles also suggested that the two countries could agree to some formula for international control of nuclear weapons and missiles.[133] Although he soon changed his mind, the State Department Policy Planning Staff (PPS) began developing ideas for a negotiated settlement in 1953. The PPS suggested capitalizing on the power struggle in Moscow. A senior official of the PPS, Louis Halle, argued that in light of the turmoil in the Soviet Union, negotiations could spur Soviet concessions in return for smaller concessions from the United States. Halle surmised that the Iron Curtain might even be raised if the European Defense Community were not extended to the boundary of the Soviet Empire.[134] The PPS also began to explore the controversial idea that the Soviet Union was occupying its vassal countries to maintain a buffer zone against the West.[135] Some papers prepared by the PPS argued that the Soviet Union's withdrawal from Eastern Europe could be achieved by assuring Moscow that the West would not threaten Soviet security. According to a memorandum prepared in July 1953, the countries adjacent to the Baltic, Black, Aegean, and Adriatic seas could be considered territories crucial to Soviet security. Western demands of free elections would have to consider these "legitimate" Soviet security concerns. Measures would be taken to ensure that states bordering the Soviet Union would not become "overtly or actively hostile to her or free to engage in operations adversely affecting her security."[136]

As a compromise, the Soviet Union would withdraw its troops behind its boundaries and return to Eastern Europe only "on invitation of freely elected governments." Existing regimes would be disbanded and elections would be held and "assured by some international supervisory body." Newly elected governments would be free to make their own foreign and domestic policies, but would be obliged to subordinate their security policies to Moscow's interests. In short, the Eastern bloc countries would be granted a status "closely analogous to that of Finland today."[137] For the sake of an agreement, the West could grant further concessions to satisfy Soviet defense needs, including assurances that Germany would not be united.[138] The authors acknowledged that serious risks would be involved, but they argued that "as a price of removing Soviet control from the whole satellite area, [it would be desirable] to make certain agreements on the level of armaments and the location of forces in Europe."[139] These negotiating points, which Mikhail Gorbachev would accept in 1989, were not acceptable to the Soviet Union in 1953–1954. Therefore, the proposal was stillborn.

In late 1954, the NSC began to debate the policy of negotiation. Although the JCS were still willing to take greater risks, John Foster Dulles, speaking for the majority in the NSC, advocated a middle course: "we should recognize that there is tenable ground in between military commitment to save these nations from Communism and the total abandonment of the areas to Communism."[140] The result of the deliberations, NSC 5501, recommended that the United States encourage the East European regimes to break away from Soviet dominance. Under the new policy, the East-bloc states would be urged to pursue their own interests. The logic was that once they did so, the Soviet bloc would disintegrate of its own accord.[141]

The Austrian State treaty, signed by Great Britain, France, the United States, and the Soviet Union on 15 May 1955, seemed to present a new opportunity to come to an agreement on Eastern Europe and perhaps even to end the Cold War. The treaty guaranteed Austria's armed neutrality, and provided for the end of the four-power occupation of Austria. Soviet leader Nikita Khrushchev agreed to the treaty for a variety of reasons: to prevent Austria's military integration into Western Europe, to strengthen "neutralism" in Europe, and to give a boost to East–West relations, including talks about the status of Germany. Austria was to be the showcase for Khrushchev's policy of "peaceful coexistence." His flexibility on the matter aroused hopes in the West that comparable deals might be feasible for other countries in which Soviet troops were stationed.[142] The possibility for a negotiated settlement that would take account of Soviet security interests was discussed again within the State Department.[143]

The Geneva Summit on 18 July 1955 afforded a perfect opportunity to test the new negotiation strategy. The State Department proposed that the United States push for increased self-determination for the Eastern bloc. A PPS memorandum suggested that the United States draw up a proposal for German unification, which would be followed by Soviet withdrawal from the GDR and Poland and subsequently, when the Austrian Treaty came into force, from Romania and Hungary.[144] This proposal was in line with NSC 5524/1, which had been approved shortly before the summit. The NSC document declared that the elimination of Soviet control over Eastern Europe was to be pursued by means short of war and possibly by negotiation with the Soviet Union, using the Austrian state treaty as an avenue for further agreements.[145]

New ideas on the future of Germany were behind the planned overture on Eastern Europe. The Americans were beginning to be attracted to the idea of a disengagement agreement and the reunification of Germany outside NATO. In 1955 Dulles was ready to accept a reunified neutral Germany under some sort of international control in which the USSR would have a voice. He was even willing to consider an undertaking whereby the U.S. would engage itself on the Soviet side if the USSR were attacked. What lay behind the new policy was the desire of Eisenhower and Dulles to disengage from NATO. A reunified, neutral Germany was their device to "get out of Europe" and make the Europeans carry the burden of their own defense.[146] Getting the Soviets out of Eastern Europe would improve the chance that their plan succeeded.

In pre-summit briefings, Dulles suggested to Eisenhower that they discuss the question of Eastern Europe during private conversations in Geneva with Soviet leaders. At the summit, the president and the secretary of state each brought up the question of Eastern Europe in a separate discussion with Soviet Premier Nikolai Bulganin. Both men informed Bulganin that the United States attached great significance to the status of the East European countries, partly because of the domestic influence of East European émigré groups. At the same time, they assured Bulganin that the United States "had no desire that the Soviet Union should be ringed by a group of hostile states." Dulles advocated a solution—allowing the Eastern bloc to develop according to the Finnish model, without, however offering the Soviets anything in return. Bulganin, as expected, refused to discuss the issue.[147] But the American offer was not timely anyway. The changes that occurred in Soviet policy after Stalin's death did not express a new political thinking or strategy on the part of the Soviet Union. As the historian Vladislav Zubok put it, domestic power struggle was the single most crucial factor in the formulation of Soviet foreign policy aims at the time. Khrushchev believed that the Soviet expansion into Central Europe fulfilled Communist dreams and "saved" the occupied people from the "capitalist yoke." Khrushchev feared that NATO would expand eastward and consolidation of the empire in Eastern Europe was still a top priority of Soviet foreign policy.[148]

In July 1956, the NSC again revised U.S. policy toward Eastern Europe with the approval of NSC 5608. These latest documents reemphasized old objectives, including attempts to divide the Eastern bloc and spur the East European populations to revolt. The United States would adapt its tactics to suit the situation in each country, but the general approach was one of under-cutting Soviet influence. It seemed as if the policy of negotiation, aimed at the "Finlandization" of Eastern Europe, had been abandoned.[149]

U.S.–Hungarian relations on the eve of the 1956 revolution

In the summer of 1956, relations between Hungary and the United States slowly began to improve. At that time, the United States responded very favorably to Hungary's overtures about a possible expansion of bilateral trade relations.[150] Shortly after Mátyás Rákosi was removed from his post as head of the Hungarian Communist Party in July 1956, the State Department invited his successor, Ernő Gerő, "to study the two party electoral process whereby the chief executive and the members of the Congress of the United States are chosen." The U.S. government was prepared to cover the costs of the trip, and an itinerary was put together to permit the "most advantageous observation of the two party campaign." The invitation "assumed that on the next appropriate occasion Americans would be invited to view elections in Hungary." Although the Hungarian Foreign Ministry did compile a list of recommended participants, the offer was eventually turned down.[151] Nonetheless, in the wake of the Twentieth Party Congress of the Soviet Communist Party (CPSU) in February 1956, which had featured Khrushchev's "Secret Speech" denouncing Stalin, the Hungarians continued to show interest in the improvement of bilateral relations. In the spirit of the CPSU Congress, the Hungarian Foreign Ministry worked out a set of "guiding principles" to restore the independence of Hungarian foreign policy.[152]

Hungary's desire for better relations was partly attributable to the country's catastrophic economic situation. In the 1950s, the Hungarian economy lost most of its gold reserve, as a result of an increased trade deficit. Christian Ravndal, the U.S. minister in Hungary, reported that Hungarian deputy foreign minister Károly Szarka was "almost pleading for the resumption of preparations for [trade] discussions."[153] The Hungarians desired U.S. imports and credit, and they particularly needed wheat and cotton on favorable credit terms. Endre Sík, Hungary's deputy foreign minister, indicated that Hungary could lift travel restrictions in 1955 if that would facilitate trade agreements with the United States.[154] Before any results could be achieved, however, the Hungarian Ministry of Internal Affairs, which feared that better relations with the West might weaken Communist rule in Hungary, slowed the pace of negotiations. Early in 1956 two U.S. citizens and two employees of the American Legation in Budapest were arrested. In response the U.S. banned its citizens from traveling to Hungary and suspended talks on economic issues.

In May 1956, Christian Ravndal discussed a possible normalization of ties with Hungarian officials. He told them that bilateral relations could improve only if the Hungarian "secret police were brought under control," because the police had become "a state within the state."[155] Party secretary Lajos Ács assured Ravndal that he would rein in the police. Furthermore, a deputy defense minister told Ravndal that "we now have an opportunity to listen to each other's grievances and fundamentally change the existing situation." His tone was a remarkable shift after years of harsh rhetoric against the United States. Ravndal responded that it was "the most constructive statement" he had heard during his time in Hungary. The most significant issue to be resolved was that of the secret police's treatment of Americans in Hungary.[156] Robert M. McKisson of the State Department's Office of Eastern European Affairs told the Hungarian minister in Washington, Péter Kós (who incidentally was also a Soviet citizen), that the first step would be to settle the question of the arrested employees of the U.S. Legation in Budapest.[157] In June 1956 the College of the Hungarian Foreign Ministry prepared a position paper on U.S.–Hungarian relations and proposed Hungarian initiatives, including the "revision" of the cases of the arrested U.S. citizens. The College also proposed that the Ministry of the Interior consult with the Foreign Ministry in cases involving diplomatic missions and the relaxation of the controls applying to the U.S. Legation. It was expected that talks could be started on the settlement of outstanding financial claims, the expansion of trade and cultural relations.[158] In the bitter debate that followed all agreed that the activities of the Interior Ministry, although justifiable, were sometimes contrary to Hungary's international interests. But some high level officials, including the dogmatic Foreign Minister, János Boldoczky, argued that the initiative to improve relations should come from the U.S. because if Hungary took the initiative, it would mean the success of American "power politics." Boldoczki reprimanded the author of the position paper, László Helmeczi for defending Ravndal's position in the debate, whom he called "one of the best trained, most cunning diplomats of my diplomatic career, who is a hidebound enemy of the socialist system." Helmeczi, and others, including Hungary's future chargé in Washington, Tibor Zádor defended the thesis arguing that other socialist states, including the Soviet Union had much better relations with the U.S. than Hungary. Moreover, they argued that Hungary was not a great power, therefore cannot deal with the U.S. on the same terms as Moscow.[159] It would be a simplification to say that the debate mirrored the antagonism between reformers and conservatives in the Hungarian party leadership. Rákosi in his discussion with Senator Kefauver advocated the expansion of bilateral trade, and said that he would be pleased to visit the U.S. should the occasion arise.[160] Nevertheless, Ravndal got the wrong impression that the Hungarians were pleading to better relations with the U.S. for trade benefits, because many officials opposed the relatively radical steps as envisioned in the College's position paper. Still, change was taking place.

In late August 1956, Hungary abolished the regulation compelling U.S. diplomatic personnel to have their travel plans approved in advance. The United States reciprocated this move. Hungarian minister Péter Kós informed the State Department that the number of regions closed to foreigners would be reduced as well. Kós assured Herbert Hoover, Jr., who was then the U.S. Under Secretary of State, that the improvement of relations was his mission's "primary objective." Hoover told Kós that Washington expected further concessions, which would be reciprocated by the United States.[161] The Hungarian initiative to eliminate areas restricted for foreign diplomats received Soviet blessing.[162] In return, the Hungarians were allowed to step up their information activities in Washington.

Although the State Department informed Hungary of its satisfaction with the improvement of relations between the two countries, it also made clear that the detained U.S. Legation employees had to be set free before the United States would lift its travel ban. The department promised that once the ban had been lifted, commercial and cultural delegations and tourists would be allowed to visit Hungary, and vice versa. Eager to meet these conditions, the new Hungarian Foreign Minister Imre Horváth asked the minister of the internal affairs, László Piros, for further information on the arrested Americans. Piros failed to respond. On 23 October 1956, the very day that the revolution began, Horváth made a second request for information so that he could report it to the forthcoming session of the United Nations (UN) General Assembly.[163] He did not realize that larger events were about to overshadow his difficulties with the Ministry of Internal Affairs, and that more serious matters concerning Hungary would be discussed at the UN session.

The U.S. response to the revolution of 1956

The American response to the 1956 Hungarian revolution encapsulated Washington's Janus-faced attitude toward the liberation of Eastern Europe.[164] The Eisenhower administration wanted to respond in some manner, but military intervention of any sort was quickly ruled out. The administration was left with a variety of policy options ranging from negotiations with the Soviet Union to the encouragement of popular unrest against the Communist regime. Given that Soviet presence in Eastern Europe was regarded as a potential staging ground for a Soviet attack on Western Europe,[165] by rolling back Soviet influence the United States could have reduced the political and military tension in Europe. The revolution in Hungary provided an excellent opportunity to do so. Eisenhower firmly believed that the tension in Europe could not be relaxed until the Soviet Union released Eastern Europe from its hold.[166]

Although Washington's official policy was at odds with the bolder side of psychological warfare and with the administration's more belligerent remarks, the cautious U.S. approach did have a sound inner logic. American strategy was predicated on the slight hope that if Washington showed restraint, Moscow might be willing to accept the Finlandization of Hungary.

In 1956, senior administration officials in Washington had been hoping that unrest would grow within the Eastern bloc, but they were completely unprepared for open, armed revolt against Soviet power that occurred in Hungary. Earlier on, they had believed that any such revolt would fail.[167] When the uprising broke out, John Foster Dulles stated that U.S. policy would remain aimed at promoting peaceful transformation in Hungary. On 25 October, two days after the revolution began, he cabled to the U.S. Embassy in Belgrade: "As in Poland we welcome all steps by any people toward national independence and freedom from Soviet domination [...] Nevertheless [it is] difficult to see how unarmed people no matter how heroic can overcome Soviet tanks. In circumstances therefore we desire to minimize bloodshed, keep the Nagy–Kádár regime from taking reprisals and [...] encourage it to proceed with rapid democratization."[168] When events in Hungary continued to spiral out of U.S. (and Soviet) control, the Eisenhower administration found itself scrambling for an appropriate policy.

Eisenhower's initial response was to deplore the Soviet intervention of 23 October and to express sympathy for the Hungarian people. Dulles believed that the United States had been successful in preserving the "yearning for freedom" in the Eastern bloc, and he hoped that the "great monolith of Communism is crumbling."[169] In the absence of reliable information about developments in Hungary and Moscow, U.S. officials sought to forestall a decisive Soviet crackdown. Both Dulles and Eisenhower tried not to give the impression that "they were selling [the Hungarians] out or dealing with their hated masters behind their backs."[170]

The NSC was convened on 26 October to formulate a strategy. Presidential adviser Harold Stassen suggested that they immediately assure Moscow that the independence of Hungary and the rest of the Eastern bloc would in no way threaten Soviet security.[171] The NSC rejected this proposal, but supporters of Stassen's idea convinced Eisenhower to propose the Austrian model as a solution to the Hungarian question, a model that would give Hungary its independence while safeguarding Soviet security.[172] The assumption underlying this strategy was the same as the assumption made by the State Department's Policy Planning Staff in 1953, namely that the Soviet Union needed the Eastern bloc as a buffer zone for its security. If Soviet security was adequately guaranteed, the argument went, East European independence might become possible. The PPS reiterated this position on 29 October 1956, arguing that if the United States "recognized the Soviet Union's legitimate interests in those territories," Soviet military intervention would be forestalled and Hungarian independence would be achieved.[173] Stassen claimed that if the United States assured Moscow that Hungary would not be admitted to NATO, there was a chance that the Soviet Union would feel confident in granting independence to Hungary.[174]

Stassen was hopeful that this kind of solution would be appealing to Soviet Defense Minister Marshal Georgii Zhukov, who, in Stassen's view, "must be reluctant to deploy the Red Army throughout the Balkans in increased numbers to hold down indigenous populations." Stassen warned that Zhukov "may be unable to prevent this deployment [of Soviet troops] if his internal opposition can raise the specter of U.S. bases in Hungary, etc. and the affiliation of these Balkan [sic] countries with NATO."[175] Stassen was worried that Dulles had been too ambiguous in his statements about Soviet security.[176] Stassen's concern about Dulles's statements had been confirmed by a recent incident involving preparations for a speech by Eisenhower in Dallas. The President had requested that Dulles formulate a statement about U.S. willingness to guarantee Soviet security, but Dulles watered down the passage to suggest only that the United States did not see the countries of Eastern Europe as potential allies. Eisenhower's willingness to accept non-alignment in Eastern Europe was not fully shared by Dulles. To make sure that Dulles's weaker message was heard in Moscow, Ambassador Charles Bohlen was instructed to repeat the crucial passage (that the East European states were not seen as potential allies) to Soviet leaders, which he did at a reception on 29 October. Eisenhower himself did the same in a speech on 31 October offering economic assistance to Eastern Europe.[177]

The initial Soviet intervention in Hungary was discussed in the UN Security Council on 27 October in the light of Article 34 of the UN Charter. Péter Kós, who was now the chief Hungarian representative at the UN, protested, thus making the position of the Western powers more difficult. The Soviet representative, Arkadii Sobolev, justified the Soviet intervention by claiming that Hungary had failed to fulfill its obligation to "suppress fascist movements," as stipulated by Article 4 of the Paris Peace Treaty signed in 1947. The British and American representative condemned what they regarded as Moscow's violation of UN principles, but they failed to specify which articles of the Charter had been violated. The chief British representative, Sir Pearson Dixon, referred to the section of the Paris Peace Treaty that guaranteed Hungarians the free exercise of their democratic rights, but Pearson's lack of specificity weakened the Western case. Sobolev dominated the proceedings, and at one point he even accused the Americans of siding with "Hitler's former collaborators," a statement that caused the chief U.S. representative, Henry Cabot Lodge, to lose his composure. Lodge declared it "inadmissible that murderers of women and children were pointing their finger at those who were sending Christmas packages." The meeting ended inconclusively, but on an optimistic note, as news came that Soviet troops were leaving Budapest.[178]

On 30 October the CPSU Presidium did in fact decide to remove Soviet forces from Budapest and expressed the Soviet government's readiness to negotiate with the Hungarian government about a complete withdrawal of Soviet troops from the country. The same day, at a reception before the CPSU Presidium meeting, Marshal Zhukov spoke to Western ambassadors about Hungary. Referring to the Polish crisis, he stated that the Soviet Union had shown restraint but "could have crushed them [the Poles] like flies."[179] During the CPSU Presidium meeting itself, Zhukov spoke in favor of withdrawing Soviet troops from Budapest. At a later reception in the Kremlin the same day, Zhukov told Bohlen about the decision to withdraw troops.[180] To some observers at least the Soviet Presidium's October 30 decision to pull out of Budapest and to renegotiate Soviet presence in Eastern Europe marked the beginning of a new era. The Indian Government was "firm in its belief that when the Soviets announced withdrawal of their troops they in fact intended to withdraw completely."[181] According to the French embassy in Moscow, in the light of the October 30 declaration the Soviet Union seemed prepared to renounce its economic empire, and "under certain conditions" even its military empire in Eastern Europe.[182]

At this point, U.S. officials believed that their negotiation strategy was succeeding. On 30 October, Eisenhower optimistically told Edward Wailes, the newly appointed minister to Budapest, that if Eastern Europe became neutral and independent, a more constructive period in world politics would ensue.[183] A top-secret State Department memorandum that day, citing the U.S. Legation in Budapest, reported that Soviet troops were leaving the capital. According to the memorandum, the outcome, achieved without inordinate Western pressure, was evidence "of the tremendous strength of the popular movement, which is undoubtedly having a profound effect on Soviet policy [...] [T]he Soviets must be considering departing from Hungary within a short time."[184] The JCS were similarly optimistic in predicting that the Soviet troops would leave without American military intervention.[185] As late as 2 November, two days after the Soviet Union reversed its decision of 30 October and decided to undertake a much larger invasion, Bohlen claimed that Soviet leaders were not preparing for military action and were simply trying to buy time. Based on what Zhukov and Soviet foreign minister Dmitrii Shepilov had told him, Bohlen surmised that the "Soviet decision was to support the Nagy government to the end [...] thereby hoping to avoid total military occupation of Hungary."[186]

Because U.S. officials assumed there was no immediate danger of Soviet military intervention in Hungary, the NSC turned to the more pressing Suez crisis on 1 November. Great Britain and France, in their effort to regain control of the Suez Canal, issued a joint ultimatum to Israel and Egypt on 30 October, threatening to invade unless the two countries withdrew from the lines of battle. Dulles was outraged: "Just when the Soviet orbit was crumbling and we could point to a contrast between the Western world and the Soviets, it appeared that the West was producing a similar situation."[187]

On 31 October, U.S. officials still assumed that "national Communist governments" could emerge in the Eastern bloc. At an NSC meeting, they considered three options they might pursue to promote national Communism in Hungary: (1) exerting pressure on the Soviet Union through the UN and public declarations; (2) providing clandestine or open military aid to the rebels as long as they remained capable of controlling territory and forming a government; or (3) attempting to secure a Soviet troop withdrawal and Hungary's neutrality on the Austrian model.[188]

The Communist regime in Hungary later accused the United States of providing clandestine military assistance to the rebels, but this claim is largely groundless. To be sure, the United States had earlier set up a military base in Munich under the codename Operation Red Sox/Red Cap, where

East European refugees were trained and equipped to perform paramilitary operations in support of uprisings against Soviet control. It is unclear whether Operation Red Sox/Red Cap was implemented in Hungary, but the evidence suggests that it was not.[189] There is no doubt, for example, that Washington refused to support Spanish plans for covert assistance to the rebels, a position that would be very odd if the United States itself was already providing such aid. Otto Habsburg got in touch with Spanish dictator Francesco Franco through an intermediary and requested him to send aid to Hungarian freedom fighters. A decision was made to dispatch a volunteer unit to be led by the former commander of the Spanish Blue Division on 4 November.[190] Two days later, on 6 November, Spanish Foreign Minister Alberto Martin Artajo had told Cabot Lodge that his government "stood ready to send an armed force to Hungary." Artajo suggested that the United States send "two airplanes to Spain to be loaded with arms to be dropped in Hungary. Franco and his cabinet had instructed him to take up this matter." Washington's response, sent out by the State Department, was unequivocal: "The U.S. government can lend *no* support, overt or covert, to any military intervention in Hungary in present circumstances." The Department also expressed its hope that Spain would take no precipitate action without consulting the United States "in the light of our common objectives and obligations for the maintenance of international peace." In return for Spanish restraint, the State Department promised that appropriate measures would be taken at the UN.[191]

In a further attempt to avert a Soviet crackdown, the Eisenhower administration continued its policy of assuring Moscow that the United States did not regard Hungary as a potential ally. On 31 October, the NSC endorsed the Policy Planning Staff's idea of proposing mutual troop withdrawals from Europe in exchange for neutral status for the East-bloc countries.[192]

On 1 November 1956, in response to news that the Soviet Union was sending troops back into Hungary, the Nagy government declared Hungary a neutral country and annulled its membership in the Warsaw Pact. The British and French sought to divert attention from their own plight by enthusiastically recognizing Hungarian neutrality at the UN. Because of the "difficulties" in Suez, the British representative at the United Nations was told to "arrange for his American colleague to take the initiative" and to give him "close and firm support."[193] On 3 November, the French representative at the United Nations was ordered both to "press for neutrality" and to emphasize "the need to allow the Hungarian people to express their opinion on their future in free elections."[194] Lodge was instructed otherwise. On 2 November, Dulles cabled Lodge to tell him to "make every possible effort to distance the French from tabling substantive resolution at tonight's meeting." Dulles wanted Lodge to defer the vote, even if it was tabled on the grounds that the UN lacked full and current information on Hungary. Dulles referred to "obvious reasons" for his attitude, but in retrospect, it is not clear what those "obvious reasons" were.[195] He may have feared putting the Soviet Union on the defensive. U.S. relations with London and Paris were strained at the time, and Washington had joined Moscow in condemning the Suez invasion. Alternatively, it may be that Dulles was simply worried that a demand for Hungarian neutrality would reopen the question of German neutrality, a question that the United States wished to forestall.[196] The episode seems to underscore the views of those historians who argued that Eisenhower and Dulles could not stomach neutralism[197] although they seemed ready to negotiate about it directly with Moscow. Whatever Dulles's motives may have been, the chance to condemn the Soviet Union was lost. On 4 November Soviet tanks deposed Imre Nagy's revolutionary government and installed a new regime under János Kádár. Although armed resistance continued for several days, the revolution was defeated.

Passivity of rollback

The ineffective U.S. response to the Hungarian crisis of 1956 is difficult to explain. Poor intelligence was part of the problem. The Eisenhower administration was caught off guard not only by the Hungarian uprising, but also by the Polish and the Suez crises. At a meeting of senior State Department officials on 2 November, Robert Murphy complained that in all three crises, U.S. intelligence agencies had failed to anticipate events.[198] In a particularly glaring example of what this shortcoming meant, the NSC's report of 27 June 1956—just four months before the revolution began—had ruled out the possibility of open popular revolt in Hungary.[199]

Deficient intelligence gathering was not the only problem, however. The Suez crisis played an extremely important role in hampering the U.S. response to the Hungarian crisis. The problem was not that Suez distracted U.S. attention from Hungary,[200] but that it made the condemnation of Soviet actions very difficult. As Richard Nixon later explained: "We couldn't on one hand, complain about the Soviets intervening in Hungary and, on the other hand, approve of the British and the French picking that particular time to intervene against [Gamel Abdel] Nasser."[201]

Another factor that influenced U.S. policy toward Hungary was the Eisenhower administration's distrust of Imre Nagy's government. Unlike the Polish leader Władysław Gomułka, Nagy was regarded with open hostility in Washington. This view did not change until after the second Soviet intervention. The administration's aversion to Nagy dated back to mid-1953 when Nagy had first come to power. U.S. officials believed that Nagy's New

Course, introduced in 1953, was no more than a tactical measure that failed to improve the economy or appease the people. (Interestingly, Moscow shared this negative view of Nagy's first government.)[202] Moreover, unlike Gomułka, Nagy was seen as insufficiently anti-Soviet.[203] During his earlier stint as prime minister in 1953–1955, Nagy had made no effort to alter Hungarian foreign policy and had not sought to improve Hungary's relations with the United States. U.S. officials had expressed few regrets when Nagy was removed in April 1955. When he returned to power after the revolution began in October 1956, the Eisenhower administration maintained its distance. On 29 October, Dulles still believed that Nagy's government was "not one we want much to do with."[204] Edward Wailes, who became the new U.S. minister in Budapest on 2 November, was instructed not to present his credentials to the Nagy government.[205]

The administration's divergent views of Gomułka and Nagy reflected a broader pattern in U.S. foreign policy that impeded U.S. actions during the Hungarian revolution. In almost every respect, Poland had priority over Hungary in U.S. calculations. This was underscored shortly after the 1956 crises, when the administration endorsed NSC 5616/2, which called for a feasibility study of military intervention in Poland, but not in Hungary. In a striking contrast to the cautious U.S. position on Hungary the NSC called for studies "immediately to be made to determine whether, if the USSR uses military force to repress the Gomułka regime or to reverse a future trend toward national independence, and if the Polish regime resists and makes timely request to the UN, the United States should be prepared to support any UN action, *including the use of force*, necessary to prevent the USSR from successfully reimposing its control by force"(emphasis mine).[206] On 23 November 1956 the Assistant Secretary of Defense instructed the JCS to prepare an estimate of the feasibility of UN military intervention in Poland and the risk of global conflict.[207] The JCS responded with three points:

(a) UN military intervention in Poland was feasible;
(b) The UN (led by the United States) should initially rely on air strikes carried out by forces in Western Europe, and should be prepared to cripple Soviet air defenses by attacking Soviet communication lines and sources of Soviet air potential; and
(c) If the United States resorted to these measures, it would incur the risk of general war.

Under NSC 5616/2, an attempt by the Soviet Army to restore control in Poland would require the administration to inform Moscow that the UN would immediately take steps to reverse the situation.[208] The JCS in its assessment had counted on the participation of Polish forces. The Chief of

Staff of the U.S. Air Force estimated that the combined forces of the Polish army, NATO, the U.S. Air Force, and the UN would be able to defeat the forces of the Soviet bloc if the objective were limited.[209] To bolster this contingency planning, the JCS drafted a statement warning Moscow that the United States was willing to use force against the Soviet Union if needed to restore Polish independence.[210]

No comparable preparations were ever made for Hungary. During the revolution, military intervention was ruled out from the very start, although one CIA official, Robert Cutler, did come up with the idea of a nuclear strike on Soviet logistical lines near the Hungarian border. An intelligence estimate from 1955 stated that Moscow would go to any lengths to keep Hungary in the Eastern bloc, and that any U.S. intervention would therefore escalate into a wider war.[211] On 30 October 1956, the PPS concluded that "effective action would probably involve hostilities with the Soviets."[212] Similarly, the State Department's response to the Spanish request for armed intervention explained that intervention was infeasible because it would risk war with the Soviet Union.[213] In terms of simple logistics, military supplies could not be sent to the Hungarians without crossing the territories or airspace of Austria, Yugoslavia, or Czechoslovakia.[214] Robert Murphy later recalled that Dulles "like everybody else in the State Department was terribly distressed, but no one had whatever imagination it took to discover any other solution."[215]

The central question is whether the fear of nuclear escalation was real, or it was only a pretext for inaction. In view of the estimate that the Soviet Union would attack in the defense of its vital interests, and the intelligence that the Soviets would do anything to keep Hungary in their orbit, there could have been little doubt that intervention would lead to war. Moreover, the President believed that with so much at stake both sides would use whatever forces they had, including nuclear arms. In such a war, national survival would have been at stake.[216]

Lacking any other viable strategy, the administration hoped that by reassuring the Soviet Union about Western intentions, the United States could persuade Moscow to grant Hungary its independence. The U.S. strategy was clear to the British: "It is evident that the U.S. administration is anxious to dispel any Soviet fears that the U.S. intends to exploit the present situation in the Satellite area to the point of creating a strategic threat to the USSR. Foster Dulles made this quite clear in his speech in Dallas."[217] Whether the strategy was at all practical was a different matter.

Eisenhower is usually praised for his moderation in handling the crisis, even though Hungarians felt that they were let down. H. W. Brands wrote that in certain times and places such as Hungary Eisenhower's inclination not to interfere in events served the cause of world peace well. Although these were not victories for American diplomacy, the president grasped the risks of an activist foreign policy and accepted a minor failure rather than risk a great catastrophe.[218] Back in the 19th century John Stuart Mill, who in general subscribed to the principle of non-intervention and self-help, had thought that these principles could be suspended and intervention could be justified in case a foreign power was already intervening in the domestic affairs and the self-determination of a community. This was clearly the case in 1956. However, in the nuclear age, as Michael Walzer has argued, the case was not so simple. Political prudence required the intervening power to weigh the danger to itself. That power must "for moral reasons weigh the dangers its action will impose on the people it is designed to benefit and on all other people who may be affected. An intervention is not just if it subjects third parties to terrible risks: the subjection cancels the justice [...] And clearly, an American threat of atomic war in 1956 would have been morally and politically irresponsible."[219] When Robert Cutler recommended dropping A bombs on Soviet supply lines in the Carpathians, Eisenhower brushed him aside: the U.S. could not destroy the people it want to save.

John Lewis Gaddis pointed to an important contradiction. "American nuclear superiority had been useless in the crisis. Eisenhower's caution [...] illustrated very clearly the limits of nuclear superiority [...] Indeed, fear of the Soviet Union's wholly inferior nuclear capability had convinced Eisenhower of the need to reassure the Russians, rather than to deter them."[220] Eastern Europe, then, was a captive of nuclear policy. Paradoxically the revolution strengthened, rather than weakened Moscow's hold on Eastern Europe. It became apparent that no power on Earth could wrest it from them.

The final question then remains, did the United States unfairly encourage Hungarians to revolt? As far as covert operations were concerned, CIA director Allen Dulles declined to recommend any steps for approval by the NSC. On the other hand, Cord Meyer, the chief of the CIA's psychological warfare division, ordered RFE to support the Hungarian rebels, although he later denied having tried to incite revolution.[221] Meyer's action was questionable if judged by the guidelines of the NSC's July 1956 report, which stipulated that the United States must avoid inciting actions that could lead to reprisals and other consequences detrimental to U.S. foreign policy goals. Although spontaneous manifestations of anti-Communism and dissatisfaction could not be prevented by public statements alone (even if individual lives were endangered), the RFE broadcasts had the opposite effect.[222] After the crisis ended, the CIA acknowledged that "the RFE occasionally went beyond the authorized factual broadcasting [...] to provide tactical advice to patriots as to the course the rebellion should take and the individuals best qualified to lead it." Although the CIA went on to claim that the RFE broadcasts before the Revolution "could not be construed as inciting armed revolt," that conclusion is at best highly problematic.[223]

The newly available transcripts of RFE Hungarian language broadcasts from 1956 reveal how incautious, even reckless, some of the programming was. In one instance, a broadcaster assured listeners that "the Soviet forces deployed against Hungary are not invincible. The troops available [to the Soviets] have been used up [...] The Hungarian forces are superior to these [...] Every weapon that is not being used now will turn against its holder. Every weapon that procrastinates will be victim to the Nagy government's deceptive tactics." In an even more reckless broadcast transmitted on 28 November a speaker ander Julián Borsányi's pseudonym advocated a full-blown war against the Soviets to be fought by regular formations of the Hungarian People's Army. The broadcast claimed that "if the Hungarian national forces are clever and their leadership is quick-witted, then the Soviet reinforcement [...] will not even reach the Danube line within two or three weeks." Borsányi invoked the tactics used by Serbian partisan forces against the Germans in 1943.[224] Such broadcasts were allegedly conceived by William Griffith, a senior official at RFE/RL. They were relayed under the pen name of Colonel Bell, used by the famous RFE commentator, Julián Borsányi. Borsányi himself refused to relay the messages, but they still went out under his pseudonym.[225] Defectors later remembered these and other such programs very well and considered them to be effective in encouraging revolt.[226] In 1953 at least some of the East Germans expected that "Western tanks will come to their aid"[227] and so did many Hungarians. One rebel claimed later that "the demands of the Hungarian insurgents grew because RFE broadcasts encouraged the belief that decisive aid would come from the West," although he admitted "RFE made no specific promises to this effect." The former rebel insisted that "the mere reiteration of the need to continue the fight convinced the Hungarian populace that they would not be fighting for long [...] RFE would have better served Hungary's cause by frankly informing the Hungarian people that the only aid which the West was able to supply was food and medicine."[228]

RFE broadcasts were thus at odds with the administration's desire to avoid active intervention and to seek Hungary's independence through nego-tiation. One rebel later stated that the West should have broadcast its inten-tion not to send military aid.[229] No effort was made to convey Dulles's view that the Hungarian revolutionaries did not stand a chance. Exactly the oppo-site was broadcast, even after Soviet troops moved in a second time on 4 November. The American attitude was remarkably different in June 1953. Then the deputy director of the CIA, Frank Wisner, argued that the United States "should do nothing at this time to incite the East Germans to further actions which will jeopardize their lives," and this view was shared by CIA

Director Allen Dulles. On the evening of 17 June 1953 the American radio
station RIAS urged the rebels to obey the orders of Soviet officials and to
avoid clashes with Soviet troops.[230] No such effort was made to stop the
Hungarians, in fact the opposite happened. In 1953, the American leadership concluded that the Soviets would not allow the satellites to secede,
the United States cannot liberate them without resorting to war, which was
impossible.[231] Self-liberation was the only possibility despite its dangers.
It is therefore difficult to escape the conclusion that RFE broadcasts were
tolerated because they were part of an alternative foreign policy, one that
actively encouraged armed revolt, and one that could plausibly be denied
later.

In the end, torn between the desire to act and the fear of the consequences
of direct intervention, the United States pursued a policy that sent mixed
signals, both to the Soviet Union and to the Hungarian people. On the one
hand, Eisenhower and Dulles pursued negotiations with Moscow, seeking
to alleviate Soviet fears that the United States was encouraging or supporting anti-Soviet protests. On the other hand, the administration pursued an
aggressive propaganda campaign designed to give hope to the Hungarian
rebels. At least inadvertently, this campaign encouraged them to fight the
Soviet invasion with everything they had. These contradictory policies sabotaged the overall approach. The harder the insurgents fought, the less chance
there was for a negotiated settlement. However, the unwillingness of the
United States to counter Soviet military action meant that the Hungarian
quest for liberation was suicidal.

These contradictions underscore what can only be described as a measure of cynicism in U.S. policy toward Hungary. Although chances for the
success of the Hungarian revolt were low, the Eisenhower administration
may well have perceived the rebellion as a low-cost effort to destabilize the
Soviet Union. If the effort failed, the administration could always disclaim
involvement in the rebellion, leaving the rebels to fend for themselves.

Hungarian and American historians have argued that the United States
sacrificed Hungary because peaceful relations with the Soviet Union were
more important, and the status quo was "preferable to a complete breakdown
in the existing power balance."[232] In this view, "Western passivity" was
caused by a de facto acceptance of the division of Eastern Europe into "spheres
of influence."[233] In reality, the United States was limited only by its fear
that intervention in Hungary would mean escalation into war.[234] U.S. perceptions of the Soviet Union's determination to hold onto Eastern Europe
suggested that even measures short of active intervention would have very
little chance of success. The historian Bennett Kovrig has asserted that "the
prompt recognition of Hungary's independence and neutrality by the United
States [...] and a dispatch of an international observation commission could

have at least delayed the Soviet decision to intervene and any delay would have increased the chances of consolidating the gains of the revolution."[235] This conclusion is dubious. What is now known about the Soviet decision on 31 October to suppress the revolution undermines the premise of Kovrig's argument. Nor is it at all plausible that mere "observers" would have impeded the Soviet invasion, quite the contrary.

The heroic fight the Hungarians put up against their oppressors were not in vain. They fought for noble causes. Their struggle became the beacon in the fight against ruthless tyranny. It showed that in Europe the clock of history, which went past the age of despotism cannot be turned back. Hungary exposed the true nature of Soviet rule at a time when for a great many people this was not at all obvious. Few would continue to think that Communism was the way of the future.

Still, the 1956 Hungarian crisis demonstrated that the fate of Eastern Europe depended far more on the Soviet Union than on the East Europeans themselves or the United States. Washington's policies before and after 1956 did contribute to the long process of disintegration in Hungary, which reached its climax in 1989, but lasting change in the region ultimately required a fundamental change in Soviet foreign policy. Khrushchev may have briefly contemplated such a move on 30 October 1956, but even if he did, he quickly backed away from it. For the next 33 years, Eastern Europe, and Hungary in it was firmly within the Soviet Union's sphere.

NOTES

1 "Hungarian Refugee Opinion," Radio Free Europe Munich Audience Analysis Section, Special Report no. 6, January 1957, National Security Archive, Washington D.C. (NS Archive), Soviet Flashpoints Collection (SFC), Record no. 64450. Eight hundred escapees were asked to evaluate the performance of Western broadcasts to Hungary and to recall whether the broadcasts had led them to expect Western military intervention. Ninety percent of those interviewed expected some form of intervention after the 4 November 1956 invasion of Hungary. Twenty per cent expected the United States to intervene, 48 percent expected the United Nations to intervene, and the rest expected help from the "free world." According to another survey conducted among Hungarian refugees in Austria, 96 percent of those questioned had expected some form of American assistance in Hungary, and 77 percent believed it would come in the form of military support. Statistics cited in James Marchio, *Rhetoric and Reality: The Eisenhower Administration and Unrest in Eastern Europe, 1953–1956* (Ph.D. dissertation 1990), p. 417. Cited from "Miscellaneous Comments by Hungarian National," 3 January 1957, AmCongen Frankfurt to the State Department, USNA, RG 59, 764.00/1-357.

2 Cited in Gregory Mitrovich, *Undermining the Kremlin,* pp. 39–40.

3 National Security Council Staff Study, Annex to NSC 5608, U.S. Policy Toward the Satellites in Eastern Europe, 6 July 1956, in U.S. Department of State, *FRUS,* 1955–1957, vol. XXV, p. 199.

4 Ibid., p. 199.

5 Memorandum by Bohlen to Barbour, 15 May 1952. NSC 58/2 U.S. Policy Toward the Soviet Satellite States in Eastern Europe. USNA, RG 59, PPS 64 D 563, box 717.

6 United States Objectives and Programs for National Security, NSC 68, 14 April 1950, *FRUS,* 1950, vol. I, pp. 237–290.

7 Peter Grose, *Operation Rollback: America's Secret War Behind the Iron Curtain* (Boston, New York, Houghton Mifflin Co., 2000), pp. 7–8.

8 Ibid., pp. 104–111.

9 See Gregory Mitrovich, *Undermining the Kremlin*, pp. 10–72.

10 Robert Bowie and Richard H. Immerman, *Waging Peace: How Eisenhower Shaped an Enduring Cold War Strategy* (Oxford: Oxford University Press, 1998), p. 31.

11 Mitrovich, *Undermining the Kremlin,* pp. 99–100.

12 The phrase comes from NSC 68, 14 April 1950, *FRUS,* 1950, vol. I, p. 264.

13 Bowie and Immerman, *Waging Peace*, p. 154.

14 A historiographical overview of Eisenhower's national security policy is provided in the introduction written by Günter Bischof and Stephen E. Ambrose, eds., *Eisenhower—A Centenary Assessment* (Baton Rouge and London: Louisiana State University Press, 1995). Revisionists praised Eisenhower for his calibrated New Look national security strategy and his restraint on the arms race. Other historians contended that on the contrary, Eisenhower was unable to control the Pentagon, promoted the growth of the military–industrial complex and fueled the Cold War by his overblown rhetoric.

15 Ibid., p. 161.

16 Ibid., pp. 176–177.

17 For the Eisenhower administration and the hydrogen bomb see: McGeorge Bundy, *Danger and Survival—Choices about the Bomb in the First Fifty Years* (New York: Vintage Books, 1990), pp. 236–260.

18 Ibid., pp. 176–177.

19 Saki Dockrill, *Eisenhower's New Look National Security Policy, 1953–1961* (London: Macmillan, 1996), p. 46.

20 According to Tor Egil Førland, economic warfare "can be defined by its end, which is to weaken the economic foundation of the adversary's power." It can be conducted by means of a strategic embargo, the institution of export control on strategic goods, by either the common sense, or the economists' definition. Tor Egil Førland, *Cold Economic Warfare: The Creation and Prime of Cocom, 1948–1954* (Oslo: Norwegian University Press, 1991), p. 22.

21 John Lewis Gaddis, *The Long Peace: Inquiries into the History of the Cold War.* (Oxford: Oxford University Press, 1987), p. 159.

22 Paper submitted by Averell Harriman to the National Security Council, *FRUS,* 1948, vol. IV, pp. 506–507.

23 Tor Egil Førland, "'Selling Firearms to the Indians': Eisenhower's Export Control Policy, 1953–1954," *Diplomatic History*, vol. 15, no. 2 (Spring 1991), pp. 231–232.

24 See Forland, *Cold Economic Warfare*, p. 45.

25 Report by the Joint Chiefs of Staff to the Secretary of Defense, 26 June 1950, *FRUS*, 1950, vol. 4, pp. 152–253.

26 Forland, *Cold Economic Warfare*, p. 45.

27 Report by the Secretary of the NSC, 21 August 1950, *FRUS*, 1950, vol. 4, p. 163.

28 See Førland, *Cold Economic Warfare*, p. 124.

29 U.S. Policies and Programs in the Economic Field Which may Effect the War Potential of the Soviet Bloc, April 1951, *FRUS*, 1951, vol. I, pp. 1059–1064, 1069.

30 For a discussion of the New Look embargo policies, see Robert Spaulding Jr., A Graduate and Moderate Relaxation: Eisenhower and the Revision of American Export Control Policy, 1953–1955, *Diplomatic History*, vol. 17, no. 2. (Spring 1993), pp. 223–250.

31 Memorandum by the Joint Logistical Committee to the JCS on the revision of the relaxation of the export of strategic commodities to the Soviet bloc; July 1953, USNA, RG 218, Records of the Joint Chiefs of Staff (RJCS) 1951–53, CCS 091 (12-9-49); Memorandum to the Secretary of Defense on the export controls of the United States; 1954, USNA, RG 218, RJCS 1954–56, CCS 091.31 (9-28-45), Section 26.

32 Consequences of a Relaxation of Non-Communist Controls on Trade with the Soviet Bloc, CIA National Intelligence Estimate, 23 March 1954, *FRUS*, 1952–1954, vol. I, pp. 1121–1132.

33 Trends in National Security Programs and the Fiscal and Budgetary Outlook Through Fiscal Year 1959, NSC 5609/2, 27 June 1956, USNA, RG 273.

34 See the previous chapter.

35 Rákosi beszámolója a KGST határozatáról az MDP PB-nek [Rákosi's report to the HWP Politburo on the resolution of the Comecon] 27 May 1954, MOL, 276. F., 65. cs., 283., őe.

36 A külügyminiszter a washingtoni követnek [The foreign minister to the minister in Washington] 20 January 1954, MOL, Küm, USA tük, XIX-J-1-k, 25/c, 55. doboz, 01134 titk. I. 1954.

37 Olt Károly pénzügyminiszter jelentése a keményvaluta helyzetről [Finance Minister Károly Olt's report on the hard currency situation] 15 April 1956, MOL, 276. F., 66. cs., 71. őe.

38 See Urbán, *Sztálin halálától a forradalom kitöréséig*, pp. 25–39.

39 Memorandum by the Deputy Assistant Secretary of State for Economic Affairs (Kalijarvi) to the Secretary of State, 18 July 1956, USNA, RG 59, lot file 76 D 232.

40 In the course of one year, 1.7 billion forints worth of capital equipment were returned to Hungary from Western Europe because of qualitative deficiencies. Even the Soviet Union returned some commodities for the same reason. See Háy László külkereskedelmi miniszter feljegyzése a külkereskedelem helyzetéről [Report by Minister of Foreign Trade László Háy on the position of foreign trade] 13 October 1953, MOL, 267. F., 67. Cs., 178. őe.

41 Hungarian Interest in U.S. Wheat and Cotton, Amleg Budapest to the State Department, 2 April 1955, USNA, RG 59, 411.6441/4-2255; see also Hungarian interest in United States Trade, Amleg Budapest to the State Department, 24 June and 9 August 1955, USNA, RG 59, 411.6441/6-2455 and 411.6441/8-955 respectively.

42 Progress Report on NSC 174, United States Policy toward the Satellites of Eastern Europe, Progress Report Submitted by the Operations Coordinating Board to the National Security Council, 29 February 1956, *FRUS, 1955–1957*, vol. XXV, pp. 121–128. It is interesting to note that an Office of Intelligence and Research report in 1950 concluded that neither the embargo nor the offer of Western economic assistance would be sufficient to cause the satellites to break away from the Soviet bloc.

43 The American Embassy in Vienna to the State Department, 20 October 1953, USNA, RG 59, 864.00/20-2056. The information was gathered from a Hungarian immigrant who supplied the Hungarian government with technical equipment.

44 I have not actually found records of any such companies, but in a memorandum prepared for the HWP general secretary, Mátyás Rákosi expressed the need to set up companies in countries such as Belgium, the Netherlands, and Sweden. Feljegyzés operatív külkereskedelmi vállalat létesítéséről [Memorandum on the establishment of operative foreign trading company] 21 April 1949, MOL, 276 F., 65. cs., 28. őe.

45 Rákosi, *Visszaemlékezések, 1945–1956*, vol. 2, p. 847.

46 The American Legation in Budapest to the State Department, 25 July 1952, USNA, RG 59, 864.00/10-2552.

47 This contained a provision for Hungary to purchase spare parts for French automobiles, but Hungarians used it to acquire spare parts for British and American automobiles, which were embargoed, in France. Étude sur la Hongrie, op. cit.

48 Feljegyzés az MDP PB üléséről [Record of meeting of the HWP Political Committee] 2 January 1956, MOL, 276. F., 53. cs., 264. őe.

49 Feljegyzés az MDP PB üléséről [Record of meeting of the HWP Political Committee] 19 June 1956, MOL, 276. F., 53. cs., 101. őe.

50 The American Embassy in Vienna to the State Department, 20 October 1953, USNA, RG 59, 864.00/20-2056. The 1948 list of commodities Hungary wished to buy from the U.S. shows the type of goods Hungary needed, but could not legally get, included milling machines, turners lathes, grinders, trucks, ball bearings, concrete mixers, cadmium, etc. Hungary received only about eight percent of these products. See also Rákosi, *Visszaemlékezések*, vol. 2, p. 846, p. 863.

51 The price index of consumer goods was 166 percent higher than that of capital equipment in 1952. The price of clothing had risen to 17 times since 1938, and the price of food had risen 12 times. Services were somewhat cheaper. The purchasing power of the forint declined 40 percent between 1946 and 1949 and a further 27 percent by 1955. In 1951 rationing was introduced for meat, lard, sugar, flour, and soap. This was lifted seven months later, when prices rose by 40 percent, while wages rose only by 20 percent. Between 1949 and 1953 food consumption was below the 1948 level (except in wheat and sugar). In 1953 even the consumption of wheat fell below the 1938 level. The deterioration of quality

added another 10 percent to the increase of the official price level, which in 1955 surpassed the 1951 figure by 30 percent. See Pető and Szakács, *A hazai gazdaság négy évtizedének története*, pp. 212–233.

52 Feljegyzés az MSZMP PB üléséről [Record of meeting of the Political Committee of the Hungarian Socialist Workers Party] 23 November 1965, MOL, 288. F., 5., cs., 380 őe.

53 Holsti, *International Politics*, p. 248

54 The American Legation to the State Department, 2 February 1953, USNA, RG 59, 764.00/2-1953.

55 The American Legation to the State Department, Pattern of Democratic Action under a Totalitarian Regime, 6 February 1956, USNA, RG 59, 764.00/2-656.

56 For further discussion of psychological warfare, see Walter L. Hixson, *Parting the Curtain: Propaganda, Culture and the Cold War 1945–1961* (London: Macmillan, 1997), pp. 12–13. See also Peter Grose, *Gentleman Spy: The Life of Allen Dulles* (Boston: Houghton-Mifflin Co., 1994). According to Grose "Some of what was proposed [regarding psychological warfare] to be sure, might be a little close to the illegal, the unethical, or the downright immoral." Ibid., p. 36.

57 Hixson, *Parting the Iron Curtain*, pp. 12–13.

58 Ibid. pp. 26–27.

59 The U.S. Legation in Budapest to the State Department, 6 October 1954, USNA, RG 59, 764.00/10-654.

60 Kiss Károly feljegyzése Rákosinak [Károly Kiss's memorandum to Rákosi] 5 April 1955, MOL, 276. F., 65. cs., 283. őe.

61 See James Critchlow, "Western Cold War Broadcasting: A Review Essay," *Journal of Cold War Studies*, vol. l, no. 3 (Fall 1999), pp. 168–175. According to the 1957 survey, 93 percent of Hungarians relied on foreign radio and 15 percent relied on balloons for news. Only two per cent relied on domestic media for information. "Hungarian Refugee Opinion," Radio Free Europe Munich Audience Analysis Section, Special Report no. 6, January 1957, NS Archive, SFC, Record no. 64450.

62 *Az állam biztonsága ellen kifejtett tevékenység és az ellene folytatott harc, 1949–1956* [Activity against the Security of the State and the Struggle against it, 1949–1956], vol. 2, unpublished manuscript, undated. The manuscript is found in the Ministry of the Interior Historical Office, Történeti Hivatal (TH), A-1364/2, p. 150.

63 RFE Handbook, 30 November 1951, NS Archive, SFC, Record no. 66 367.

64 Columbia University Bureau of Applied Research on listening to VOA and other foreign stations in Hungary, November 1953, NS Archive, Record no. 64 444.

65 Amcongen Frankfurt to the State Department, 14 November 1956, USNA, RG 59, 764.00/11-1456.

66 Amcongen Frankfurt to the State Department, 16 July 1956, USNA, RG 59, 764.00/7-1656. According to the RFE survey of January 1957, the VOA was Hungary's most popular foreign station.

67 AmEmbassy, Tel Aviv to the State Department, Interview with Recent Arrival from Hungary, 12 May 1955, USNA, RG 59, 764.00/5-1255.

68 Flossmann Győző és társai (Magyar Függetlenségi Front) [Győző Flossmann and associates—Hungarian Independence Front] 1952, TH, 10-50986-52, V-73203.

69 Flossmann Győző és társai, 1952, ibid. Győző Flossmann was an unskilled laborer who regularly listened to foreign radio stations. It is interesting to note that during World War II many Hungarians, including members of the political elite, expected the British and Americans to parachute into Hungary and occupy it.

70 Ibid.

71 Faddi Ottmár és társai, az ÁVH feljegyzése a Belügyminisztériumnak [Ottmár Faddi and associates. Memorandum of the ÁVH to the Ministry of Interior] 19 June 1954, TH, 10-5114-54, V-127 372.

72 The Counter Intelligence Corps, originally founded as the Counter Intelligence Police in 1917, had the purpose of hunting down Nazis after World War II. After 1947, its mission changed to include the gathering of intelligence in the Soviet bloc. The Gehlen organization similarly had the purpose of recruiting former Nazis for the task of gathering intelligence on the Soviet bloc. See Douglas Botting, *America's Secret Army: The Untold Story of the Counter Intelligence Corps* (New York: F. Watts, 1989), pp. 319–321, p. 341.

73 Horváth Kálmán és társai, kihallgatási jegyzőkönyv [Kálmán Horváth and associates, record of interrogation] 1954, TH, 10-5114-54, V-111 790. The alleged plot was revealed in the town of Kecskemét, which had one of the most significant military airfields in the country. Similarly, a certain István Dudás was allegedly asked by his brother in 1951 "to organize a group of partisans in case war breaks out, so as to lend armed support to the Americans in Hungary." He was told that "Americans will supply the arms when the time comes." They would be "parachuted near the hamlet." Since Dudás did not get the instruction to launch the conspiracy, he took no action. He and his brother were executed nonetheless. Dudás Imre és társai [Imre Dudás and associates] 1951, TH, 10-5575-51, V-81 337-2.

74 Ráth Gedeon és társai, kihallgatási jegyzőkönyv [Gedeon Ráth and associates, record of interrogation] 1950, TH, 37-5079/1952, V-112 524/1.

75 Flossmann Győző és társai, 1952, TH 10-50986-52, V-73203, op. cit.

76 On one occasion a Hungarian man, Ferenc Alföldi, wrote the U.S. Legation in Budapest a handwritten letter, in which he requested explosives in the name of the "Hungarian People's Party." His request indicated to Legation officials that he was "not only somewhat of a specialist in this field but has a definite scheme for utilizing the particular type of material he asks for." Amlegation Budapest to the State Department, 2 February 1956, USNA, RG 59, 764.00/3-256.

77 This is known from reports to the interrogators by informers in the prison cells.

78 Interrogation of Hungarian Defector, Frankfurt, Germany, 31 May 1956, USNA, RG 59, 764.00/5-356.

79 Cited in Briefing memorandum on the current situation in Hungary prepared in anticipation of the visit of Mr. William A. Crawford, Deputy Director, Office of Eastern European Affairs, the U.S. Legation to the Department of State, 7 January 1955. USNA, RG 59, 764.00/1-755.

80 See Amcongen Frankfurt to the State Department, 19 July 1956, USNA, RG 59, 764.00/7-1656; Amcongen Frankfurt to the State Department, 16 November 1956, USNA, RG 59, 764.00/11-1456.

81 Interview with recently escaped man, Amcongen Munich to Francis M. Stevens, Director of East European Affairs, State Department, 23 August 1956, USNA, RG 59, 764.00/8-2356.

82 Amlegation Budapest to the State Department, 11 February 1955, USNA, RG 59, 764.00/2-1156.

83 See Hixson, *Parting the Iron Curtain*, pp. 65–66; Marchio, *Rhetoric and Reality*, p. 216.

84 Amcongen Frankfurt to the State Department, 14 March 1956, USNA, RG 59, 764.00/3-1456; AmEmbassy Vienna to the State Department, 3 October 1956, USNA, RG 59, 764.00/10-356.

85 Amcongen Frankfurt to the State Department, 14 March 1956, USNA, RG 59, 764.00/3-1456.

86 Amcongen Frankfurt to the State Department, 16 July 1956, USNA, RG 59, 764.00/7-1656. An official Hungarian report on balloon sightings from July to September 1956 seems to confirm that they were seen mostly along the borders, although on four occasions out of 22 they were seen in the Budapest area as well.

87 Amcongen Frankfurt to the State Department, 16 July 1956, USNA, RG 59, 764.00/7-1656.

88 Hungarian Refugee Opinion, Radio Free Europe Munich Audience Analysis Section, Special Report no. 6, January 1957, National Security Archive, Washington D.C. (NS Archive), Soviet Flashpoints Collection (SFC), Record no. 64450.

89 Az MDP Politikai Bizottságának határozata a Belügyminisztérium belső reakció elleni munkájáról [Resolution on the work of the Ministry of Interior against domestic reaction] 11 May 1956, MOL, 276. F., 53. cs., 286. őe.

90 The Hungarian Ministry of Foreign Affairs to the U.S. Legation in Budapest, 8 February 1956, MOL, Küm, USA tük, XIX-J-1-j, 4-fh, 6. doboz, 002 118/56.

91 The U.S. Legation in Budapest to the Foreign Ministry, 9 February 1956, MOL, Küm, USA tük, XIX-J-1-j, 6. doboz, 002 118/2.

92 Note from the Hungarian Foreign Ministry to the U.S. Legation in Budapest, 28 July 1956, MOL, Küm, USA tük, XIX-J-1-j 1-b, 6. doboz, 112 118/1.

93 Feljegyzés Rákosinak [Memorandum to Rákosi] 23 February 1952, MOL, 276. F., 65. cs., 95. őe.

94 Az MDP Politikai Bizottságának határozata a Belügyminisztérium belső reakció elleni munkájáról, op. cit.

95 Feljegyzés az MDP PB üléséről [Record of meeting of the HWP Politburo] 25 June 1956, MOL, 276. F., 65., cs., 26 őe.

96 Feljegyzés az MSZMP PB üléséről, 23 November 1965, op. cit.

97 For more on the Kersten amendment see Bennett Kovrig, *Of Walls and Bridges: The United States and Eastern Europe* (New York: New York University Press, 1991), pp. 64–65.

98 Charles Kersten's letter to Dean Acheson, 1 October 1952, USNA, RG 218, RJCS 1951-1953, 385 (6-4-46), box 48.

99 Memorandum to the Secretary of Defense, January 1952, USNA, RG 330, Records of the Office of the Secretary of Defense (OSD), CD 091.3.

100 JCS memorandum to the Secretary of Defense, 17 March 1952, USNA, RG 330, OSD, CD 091.3.

101 Memorandum to the Secretary of Defense, 12 September 1952, USNA, RG 330, OSD, CD 091.3.

102 Implementation of Section 101 (A) of the Mutual Security Act of 1951 (Kersten Amendment), Enclosure: A Draft—Joint Strategic Plans Committee 808/116 JSPC—Implementation of Section (A) (1) of the Mutual Security Act 1951 (Kersten Amendment) Reference JSPC 808/115/D. Signed G.E. Stevens, B. R. Eggenman, Joint Secretariat, 13 February 1953, USNA, RG 218, RJCS 1951-53, 385 (6-4-46), Box 149.

103 James Jay Carafano, "Mobilizing Europe's Stateless: America's Plan for a Cold War Army," *Journal of Cold War Studies*, vol. 1, no. 2 (Summer 1999), pp. 61–85.

104 Hixson, *Parting the Iron Curtain*, p. 68.

105 Ibid., p. 70.

106 Gaddis, *The Long Peace*, p. 174.

107 Vojtech Mastny, *The Cold War and Soviet Insecurity*, p. 118.

108 Grose, *Gentleman Spy*, p. 322.

109 "National Security Directive," 28 December 1955, NS Archive, Record no. 62351.

110 Rákosi feljegyzése az MDP Politikai Bizottságának [Rákosi's memorandum to the HWP Politburo] 13 July 1956, MOL, 276. F., 65. cs., 26. őe.

111 Az MDP PB határozata a Belügyminisztérium belső reakció elleni munkájáról, op. cit.

112 Grose, *Operation Rollback,* pp. 167–173.

113 *Az állam biztonsága ellen kifejtett tevékenység és az ellene folytatott harc*, op cit.vol. 2. Among the files of interrogation records in the Ministry of the Interior I found a number of cases where alleged conspirators confessed to organizing armed groups in Hungary and in Transylvania. They claimed that they acted on the instructions of the CIC, preparing for possible war and the American invasion of Hungary. According to János Weissengruber, an alleged agent of the CIC, the CIC was planning to establish guerillas in Transylvania who would infiltrate Hungary to commit terrorist attacks. They would be supported by pre-established bases. During a war, these groups would help cut supply lines from the East. Weissengruber János és társai [János Weissengruber and associates] December 1952, TH, 10-50910/52, V-82 932; András Lada, another CIC agent, was allegedly sent to sabotage targets in the heavy industrial town of Sztálin-város. Lada András és társai [András Lada and associates] 1954, TH, 10-514 75-954, V-1116 808-2; Sándor Dudás was allegedly instructed by the CIC to set up illegal armed groups, who would provide resistance against the Communists in case of war. Imre és társai [Imre Dudás and associates] October 1951, TH, 10-50775-51, V-81 337. These stories have not been adequately checked for their reliability.

114 John Lewis Gaddis wrote that liberation "had long been quietly endorsed by Truman himself." Gaddis, *The Long Peace*, p. 174.

115 Ibid., p. 174.

116 Bowie and Immerman, *Waging Peace*, pp. 158–177; Richard H. Immerman, *John Foster Dulles: Piety, Pragmatism, and Power in U.S. Foreign Policy.* (Wilmington, DE: SR Books, 1999), pp. 39–55; 60–85; Gaddis, *The Long Peace*, pp. 149–189.

117 For a comprehensive analysis of the East German uprising and its effects on Soviet and Western policies in East-Central Europe, see the three-part article by Mark Kramer, "The Early Post-Stalin Succession Struggle and Upheavals in East-Central Europe," no. 1 (Winter 1999), pp. 3–55 (part 1); vol. 1, no. 2 (Summer 1999), pp. 3–42 (part 2); and vol. 1, no. 3, pp. 3–64 (part 3), esp. parts 1 and 3.

118 See Christian F. Ostermann ed., *Uprising in East Germany, 1953*, pp. 176–177; p. 327.

119 Kramer, "The Early Post-Stalin Succession Struggle and Upheavals in East-Central Europe," part 3, pp. 19–20. Marchio, *Rhetoric and Reality*, pp. 210–211. In July and August 200 thousand people a day collected food packages, all in all 5.5 million food packages were distributed. East German authorities were dismayed that the U.S. was able to win over large segments of the population. The food program combined humanitarian motives with political–psychological objectives. As the U.S. expected, the food program sharply raised tension within the GDR and prevented the SED regime from consolidating its hold over the population. The program helped hungry Germans to a substantial amount of food, highlighted the shortcomings of the shortages of the GDR. It gave the East Germans contact with the West, offering hope of eventual freedom, thereby undercutting Communist unity propaganda. Ostermann, *Uprising in East Germany*, pp. 322–325.

120 Immerman, *John Foster Dulles: Piety, Pragmatism, and Power*, p. 81.

121 See Kramer, "The Early Post-Stalin Succession Struggle and Upheavals in East-Central Europe," part 3, pp. 26–27.

122 Statement of Policy by the National Security Council on United States Policy toward Soviet Satellites in Eastern Europe, NSC 174, 11 December 1953, *FRUS*, 1952–1954, vol. VIII, pp. 111–127.

123 Ibid., p. 82.

124 See Ronald W. Preussen, "John Foster Dulles and the Predicaments of Power," in Richard H. Immerman, ed., *John Foster Dulles and the Diplomacy of the Cold War* (Princeton, NJ: Princeton University Press, 1990), p. 35.

125 In a discussion with Polish émigré leaders in March 1953, State Department officials declared that "the liberation of the enslaved nations cannot be achieved by their own efforts and requires for its realization a fundamental change of the international situation." In other words, rollback was not possible at that time. "Memorandum of Conversation, Subject: Liberation of Eastern Europe, Rowmund Pilsudski, Jerzy Lerski and Allan Vedeler," 20 March 1953, NS Archive, SFC, Record no. 66171. Provenance: Department of State Office of the Assistant Secretary of State for European Affairs.

126 Memorandum by Fuller to Stelle, 3 December 1956, USNA, RG 59, PPS 1956, lot File 66 D 487, L.W. Fuller, box 78.

127 Memorandum by William Crawford to Walwourth Balbour, 28 September 1955, USNA, RG 59, 764.00/9-2855.

128 Memorandum by McKisson, 1 July 1955, USNA, RG 59, 764.00-7-155. In its standard response, the State Department stated that it was "looking forward" to the day when the peoples of the region would regain their "freedom and independence."

129 Trachtenberg, *Constructed Peace*, p. 160.

130 See Immerman, *John Foster Dulles: Piety, Pragmatism, and Power*, p. 83; and Marchio, *Rhetoric and Reality*, p. 214.

131 Report by the National Security Council on Interim Objectives and Actions to Exploit Unrest in the Satellite States, 29 June 1953, NS Archive, SFC, Record no. 62113.

132 Günter Bischof, "Eisenhower and the Austrian Treaty," in *Eisenhower—A Centenary Assessment*, pp. 138–144.

133 Immerman, *John Foster Dulles: Piety, Pragmatism, and Power*, pp. 77–79.

134 Memorandum by Halle to Bowie and Beam, 27 July 1953, USNA, RG 59, PPS 1947–53, Members Chronological File, Louis Halle Jr., box 47.

135 This notion had such prominent adherents as Charles Bohlen, who held that "The essential Soviet objective in East Europe was and still remains to ensure Soviet control [...] for strategic purposes. The post-war Soviet takeover in East Europe was inspired primarily by strategic considerations and only secondarily by spread of communism for ideological reasons." Moscow to the Secretary of State, 10 December 1956, USNA, RG 59, PPS 1956, lot file 66 D 487, box 76, (Soviet Union).

136 Memorandum by L. W. Fuller, 21 July 1953, USNA, RG 69, PPS 1947–1953, lot 64 D 563, box 29, Europe.

137 Memorandum by L. W. Fuller, 21 July 1953, USNA, RG 69, PPS 1947–1953, lot 64 D 563, box 29, Europe.

138 A Dialectical Approach to the Possibilities of Accommodation by Negotiation between the Free World and the Soviet Bloc [no date, 1953], USNA, RG 59, PPS 1947–53, lot 64 D 563, box 47.

139 United States Policy Respecting Europe, 5 March 1954, USNA, RG 59, PPS, lot 65 D 101, box 88.

140 Marchio, *Rhetoric and Reality*, p. 232.

141 Ibid., pp. 232–233.

142 Bischof, *Austria in the First Cold War*, pp. 150–151.

143 According to a summary paper approved by the OCB on 5 January 1955, "there is little likelihood of detaching a major satellite at any time without the grave risk of war except by negotiation." *FRUS*, 1955–1957, vol. XXV, pp. 8–9.

144 Memorandum by John C. Campbell to the PPS, 31 May 1955, USNA, RG 59, PPS 1955, lot file 66 D, box 64. Campbell proposed the following compromise: If the Soviet Union allowed German unification, withdraw from Czechoslovakia and Poland, and give the Eastern bloc a chance to choose military align-

ment, and remove troops from Czechoslovakia and Poland, then the U.S. would withdraw from all NATO countries except Britain. Alternatively, a united Germany, Poland, and Czechoslovakia would all receive non-aligned status.

145 Basic U.S. Policy in Relation to the Four-Power Negotiations, 11 July 1956, NSC 5224-1, *FRUS*, vol. XXV, 1955–1957, p. 287.

146 Trachtenberg, *Constructed Peace*, pp. 136–145.

147 Marchio, *Rhetoric and Reality*, p. 247.

148 Vladislav Zubok, "Soviet Policy Aims at the Geneva Conference of 1955," in Günter Bischof and Saki Dockrill eds., *Cold War Respite—The Geneva Summit of 1955* (Baton Rouge: Louisiana State University Press, 2001), pp. 55–74.

149 Statement of Policy on U.S. Policy Toward the Soviet Satellites in Eastern Europe, NSC-5608/1, 18 July 1956, *FRUS*, vol. XXV, 1955–1957, pp. 217–221.

150 At an NSC meeting in February 1956, Eisenhower declared that U.S. trade with the Eastern bloc might prove to be a "centrifugal force." *FRUS*, 1955–1957, vol. XXV, p. 120.

151 A Külügyminisztérium V. Területi Osztályának feljegyzése a külügyminiszternek [Memorandum of the 5th division of the Ministry of Foreign Affairs to the minister of foreign affairs] 19 September 1956, MOL, Küm, XIX-J-1-j, USA tük, 4/a, 4. doboz, 007682/1956.

152 Irányelvek kiküldése [Dispatch of directives] 1956, undated, MOL, Küm, XIX-J-1-j, USA tük, 1/b, 1. doboz, 00664/1956. Hungary wanted to develop diplomatic, economic, cultural, scientific and technological relations with the "capitalist" states and wanted to initiate the "restoration" of the "atmosphere of confidence." The Foreign Ministry claimed that the improvement of relations were impeded by diplomatic representatives, who "are honest and loyal to the party" but whose deficient general knowledge and diplomatic training stops them from exploiting the new opportunities. See also: A külügyminisztérium feljegyzése a moszkvai követségnek [Memoramdum of the Ministry of Foreign Affairs to the Embassy in Moscow] 1956, undated, MOL, Küm, Moszkva tük, XIX-J-1-j, IV-100/1, sz. n.

153 AmLegation Budapest to the State Department, 7 July 1956, USNA, RG 59, 611.64/7-1356. The Hungarian side suggested that Ravndal had initiated the trade discussions. The Ministry of Foreign Trade believed that increased Hungarian exports to the United States were desirable because of the need for hard currency, but it cautioned that the U.S. offer had political strings attached. A külkereskedelmi minisztérium feljegyzése Rákosinak [Memorandum of the Ministry of Foreign Trade to Rákosi] 20 June 1955, MOL, 276. F., 53. cs., 283. őe.

154 Meeting with Sík, Amlegation Budapest to the Secretary of State, 22 July 1956, USNA, RG 59, 411. 6441/7-2255; Amlegation Budapest to the State Department, 29 August 1955, USNA, RG 59, 411.6441/8-955.

155 Memorandum on Minister Ravndal's visit, 8 May 1956, MOL, Küm, USA tük, XIX-J-1-j 4/a, 4. box, 004782/1.

156 Ravndal to the Secretary of State, 5 May 1956, *FRUS*, 1955–1957, vol. XXV, p. 162.

Hungary in the Cold War

157 Discussion with McKisson, 24 July 1956, MOL, Küm, USA tük, XIX-J-1-j, 5/e, box 15, 00594/1. In 1955 the Hungarian authorities had arrested two Hungarian employees of the Legation and sentenced them for "intelligence activity on behalf of a foreign power, seditious acts and other crimes." Seven other employees had been arrested earlier, their fate and whereabouts were undisclosed. In 1955 the Hungarians also arrested and sentenced two U.S. correspondents, Andrew Marton and his wife.

158 Kollégiumi előterjesztés a magyar–amerikai kapcsolatok megjavításának lehetőségeiről [Memorandum of the "Kollégium" on the possibilities of improving Hungarian–American relations] 4 June 1956, MOL, Küm, USA tük, XIX-J-1-j, 26/a, 1948-58, 6. doboz.

159 Jegyzőkönyv a Külügyminisztérium Kollégiuma üléséről [Minutes of meeting of the "Kollégium" of the Ministry of Foreign Affairs] 11 June 1956, MOL, Küm, USA tük, XIX-J-1-j, 26/a, 1948-58, 6. doboz.

160 Feljegyzés Kefauver amerikai demokrata párti szenátor látogatásáról Rákosi és Hegedűs elvtársnál [Memorandum on the visit of the American Democratic Party Senator Kefauver at Comrades Rákosi and Hegedűs] 20 September 1956. MOL, Küm, USA tük, XIX-J-1-j, 26/a, 1948–1958.

161 Az utazási korlátozások feloldásának bejelentése [Announcement of lifting travel restrictions] 24 August 1956, MOL, Küm, USA tük, XIX-J-1-j, 15. doboz, 007151/1956; Memo of Conversation between Hoover, Leverich, and Kós, 4 September 1956, USNA, RG 59, 611.6411/9-456.

162 A szovjet nagykövet (Andropov) a külügyminiszternél (Horváth) [Soviet ambassador (Andropov) at the minister of foreign affairs (Horváth)] 12 September 1956, MOL, Küm, Szu tük, XIX-J-1-j, IV-102, 1/d, 5. doboz, 1455/56.

163 A külügyminiszter (Horváth) feljegyzése a belügyminiszternek (Piros) [Memorandum of the minister of foreign affairs (Horváth) to the minister of internal affairs (Piros)] 4 October and 23 October 1956, MOL, Küm, Szu tük, XIX-J-1-j, 4/a, 4 doboz, 007425-1956.

164 For a thorough reassessment of the Soviet Union's response to the Hungarian and Polish crises, based on multi-archive research, see Mark Kramer, "New Evidence on Soviet Decision-Making and the 1956 Polish and Hungarian Crises," *Cold War International History Project Bulletin*, Issue 8–9 (Winter 1996/1997), pp. 358–384, which was published in expanded form as "The Soviet Union and the 1956 Crises in Hungary and Poland: Reassessments and New Findings," *Journal of Contemporary History*, vol. 33, no. 2 (April 1998), pp. 163–214. Kramer also has provided an annotated English translation of the Malin notes, "The 'Malin Notes' on the Crises in Hungary and Poland, 1956," *Cold War International History Project Bulletin*, Issue 8–9, pp. 385–410. Kramer argues that the sudden reversal of the Kremlin's 30 October decision not to intervene in Hungary was caused by the combination of seemingly alarming developments in Hungary and the British–French bombing of Egypt, which commenced on 31 October. On the Soviet role see also János M. Rainer, "Döntés a Kremlben—Kísérlet a feljegyzések értelmezésére" [Decision in the Kremlin—Attempt at understanding the memoranda] in Vyacheslav Sereda and. János

M. Rainer, eds., *Döntés a Kremlben—A szovjet pártelnökség vitái Magyar-országról* [Decision in the Kremlin—Discussions of the Soviet party Presidium about Hungary] (Budapest: 1956-os Intézet, 1996), pp. 111–155; László Borhi, "The Great Powers and the Hungarian Crisis of 1956," *Hungarian Studies*, vol. 12, no. 2 (Spring 1997), pp. 237–279.

165 For a typical assessment of the significance of Eastern Europe for U.S. policy see: Policy Planning Staff Paper, 25 August 1949, U.S. policy Toward the Soviet Satellite States in Eastern Europe, *FRUS*, 1949, vol. V, pp. 21–26. As the paper put it, "These states in themselves are of secondary importance [...] but in the current two-world struggle they have meaning primarily because they [...] extend (Soviet) power into the heart of Europe. It is assumed that there is general agreement that, so long as the USSR represents the only major threat to our security [...] our objective [...] must be the elimination of Soviet control from those countries."

166 Eisenhower to Tito, NS Archive, SFC, Record no. 66 140.

167 In 1953 State Department officials expressed their view that "any armed resist-ance in the Moscow controlled countries of East-Central Europe has no chance of success and its outcome could bring only biological annihilation of the nations concerned." Memorandum of Conversation with Polish émigrés, 20 March 1953, NS Archive, SFC, Record no. 66171. In a memorandum of 14 January 1956 to Francis B. Stevens of the Office of Eastern European Affairs, Robert F. Delaney of the Office of Policy and Programs, Soviet Orbit Division, United States Information Agency, stated that the U.S. policy toward a potential Hun-garian uprising should be the same as policy during the Berlin uprising in 1953. He declared that the United States must not "cause the premature uprising and consequent annihilation of dissident elements on the basis of exhortations or promises which we are not able to support." *FRUS*, 1955–1957, vol. XXV, pp. 10–11.

168 Dulles to the American Embassy in Belgrade, 25 October 1956, USNA, RG 59, 764.00/10-2556. In 1950 he similarly wrote, "The people have no arms, and violent revolt would be futile. Indeed it would be worse than futile, for it would precipitate massacre." Quoted in Ronald W. Preussen, "Walking a Tightrope in the Twilight: John Foster Dulles and Eastern Europe in 1953." Paper delivered in Paris at the Conference "Europe and the Cold War" (November 1998).

169 Quoted in Kovrig, *Of Walls and Bridges*, p. 89.

170 Ibid, p. 91

171 See Csaba Békés, *The 1956 Hungarian Revolution and World Politics*, Cold War International History Project Working Paper no. 16 (Washington, DC: Woodrow Wilson Center, 1996), p. 15.

172 Ibid., p. 15.

173 Policy Planning Staff Position Paper, 29 October 1956, USNA, RG 59, PPS, lot 66 D 487 1956, box 80.

174 Interview with Harold Stassen on J. F. Dulles; NS Archive, SFC, Record no. 65 102. Stassen did admit to having doubts that the Soviet Union would accept the expulsion of the Soviet Army from Hungary.

175 Memorandum by the Special Assistant to the President, 26 October 1956, NS Archive, SFC, Record no. 64 493.

176 There is no indication in the currently available Soviet records that U.S. policies had any direct impact on the Soviet decision-making process. Other records, not yet released, may eventually provide a different picture.

177 Kovrig, *Of Walls and Bridges*, p. 95.

178 Minutes of the Meeting of the Security Council, 28 October 1956, Archives de Quai d'Orsay, Serie Europe 1944–1960, Hongrie, vol. 62, folio 207-216.

179 Bohlen to the Secretary of State, 30 October 1956. NS Archive, SFC, Record no. 65 692. Zhukov's words were also picked up by the French chargé. Soutou to Pineau, 30 October 1956, in Ministère des Affaires Étrangères, Commission de Publication des Documents Français, *Documents Diplomatiques Français* (Paris), 1956, vol. III, pp. 82–83.

180 The Embassy in the Soviet Union to the State Department, 30 October 1956 10 p.m., *FRUS*, 1955–1957, vol. XXV, pp. 346–347.

181 The information came from the Indian ambassador in Moscow, Krishna Menon. The American Legation in Budapest to the Department of State, 8 January 1957, USNA, RG 59, 611.64/1-857.

182 L'URSS parait disposée, dans la déclaration du 30 Octobre á renonçer á l'empire économique et, sous certaines conditions, á l'empire militaire qu'elle exerçait sur les états satellites depuis la fin de la guerre. 2 November 1956. The French embassy in Moscow to the Foreign Ministry, Archives de Quai d'Orsay, Europe 1944–1960, vol. 116, fol. 39.

183 As cited by Békés, "Az Egyesült Államok és a magyar semlegesség 1956-ban" [The USA and Hungary's neutrality in 1956] in András Hegedűs, György Litván, and János M. Rainer, eds., *Évkönyv 1994* (Budapest: 1956-os Intézet, 1994), p. 176.

184 State Department Memorandum, 31 October 1956, NS Archive, SFC, Record no. 65 283.

185 Report by the Joint Strategic Survey Committee to the NSC, 31 October 1956, USNA, RG 218.

186 Bohlen to the Secretary of State, 2 November 1956, USNA, RG 59, 764.00/11-256. On 1 November the British minister in Budapest thought that the Soviets "reversed their position and will impose on the country with force of arms." Fry to the Foreign Office, *The Hungarian Revolution of 1956,* pp. 155–156.

187 On the Suez crisis and for the citation see Peter L. Hahn, *The United States, Great Britain and Egypt 1945–1956,* p. 231.

188 Draft Statement of Policy by the Planning Board of the NSC—U.S. Policy on developments in Poland and Hungary, NSC 5616/1, 31 October 1956, *FRUS,* 1955–1957, vol. XXV, pp. 354–359.

189 Kovrig, *Of Walls and Bridges*, pp. 79, 92;

190 See Gyula Borbándi, *Magyarok az Angol Kertben—A Szabad Európa Rádió története* [Hungarians in the English garden—The history of Radio Free Europe] (Budapest: Európa, 1996), p. 225.

191 Lodge's Talk with the Spanish Foreign Minister, 6 November 1956, USNA, RG 59, 764.00/11-656; Fischer Howe to the Acting Secretary of State (Hoover),

11 August 1956, USNA, RG 59, 764.00/11-856; Acting Secretary to the U.S. Embassy in Madrid, 8 November 1956, USNA, RG 59, 764.00/11-856.

192 Draft Statement of Policy by the Planning Board of the NSC—U.S. Policy on developments in Poland and Hungary, NSC 5616/1, 31 October 1956, *FRUS*, 1955–1957, vol. XXV, pp. 354–359. The JCS were opposed to this policy.

193 Draft to the UK Delegation in New York by the Foreign Office, 2 November 1956, *Hungarian Revolution of 1956*, p. 161.

194 Pineau to Cornut-Gentille, 3 November 1956, in Ministère des Affaires Ètrangères, *Documents Diplomatiques Français*, vol. III, p. 159. The French draft resolution "invited" the Moscow government to "withdraw its forces from Hungary" and to "recognize and respect the neutrality of Hungary." The U.S. Mission in New York to the Secretary of State, 25 November 1956, USNA, RG 59, 764.00/11-256.

195 Dulles to USUN New York, 2 November 1956, USNA, RG 59, 764.00/11-256. See also Caroline Pruden, *Conditional Partners—Eisenhower, the United Nations, and the Search for a Permanent Peace* (Baton Rouge: Louisiana State University Press, 1998), p. 243. According to Pruden, Eisenhower and Dulles may have feared that the British–French motion was a ploy to divert attention from Suez.

196 In a conversation with Manlio Brosio, the Italian ambassador in Washington, Burke C. Elbrick, Acting Assistant Secretary of State, explained that "neutralization was a delicate subject because it inevitably led to a consideration of East Germany and possible neutralization of Germany as a whole [...] However [...] the U.S. has no intention of creating a cordon sanitaire around the Soviet Union nor do we expect the satellites, if their status changed, to take sides against the Soviet Union." 27 December 1956, USNA, RG 59, 764.00/12-2756.

197 Bischof and Ambrose, *Eisenhower*, p. 11.

198 The Acting Secretary's Meeting, 2 November 1956, *FRUS*, 1955–1957, vol. XXV, p. 364.

199 NSC Staff Study: The United States Policy toward the Satellites in Eastern Europe, 27 June 1956, NS Archive, Record no. 62 596. The United States was not alone in its lack of foresight. The French Foreign Ministry's analysis stated that "For the moment we cannot say whether the Hungarian people would be resolved [...] to show proof of similar courage as the workers of Poznań." Archives Diplomatiques de Quai d'Orsay, Serie Europe 1944–1960, Hongrie, vol. 88.

200 It is often argued that the crisis in Suez, which erupted simultaneously with the end game in Hungary, eclipsed the Hungarian revolution in significance. The evidence for this is derived from the November 1 meeting of the NSC, where the council after hearing the report on Hungary turned immediately to the discussion of the Middle East. It is quite clear that this did not happen because Suez was more important. The situation in Hungary was reportedly improving, the Soviets seemed to be pulling out, negotiations between them and the Hungarians were launched. In this light Suez was simply more *urgent* to deal with.

201 Interview with Richard Nixon concerning J. F. Dulles, NS Archive, Record no. 65 106.

202 Report on the Satellites, 7 June 1956, USNA, RG 59, PPS, lot file 66 D 487, box 78; See also a report by W. Park Armstrong to Dulles: The new course "failed to resolve the problems of industry and agriculture [...] living conditions did not improve in 1954." Memorandum on NIE 12.5-55, Current Situation and Probable Developments in Hungary, 4 July 1956, USNA, RG 59, 764.00/4-755; The U.S. Legation in Budapest sent a damning critique of the Nagy regime, stating that "Hungarians retained the same degree of antipathy towards the regime as before June 1953 and they were at least as willing, and perhaps more so, to express this feeling openly and to engage in passive resistance towards the state." The American Legation in Budapest to the State Department, Briefing memorandum on the current situation in Hungary Prepared in Anticipation of Mr. William A. Crawford, Deputy Director, Office of Eastern European Affairs, 7 January 1955, USNA, RG 59, 764.00/1-755.

203 Memorandum to the chairman of the JCS, 25 October 1956, USNA, RG 218, RJCS 1953–1957, 091 (Poland), box 15. The memorandum stated "Gomułka may very well be anti-Russian unlike Nagy, he has not spent considerable time in the USSR."

204 Telephone Call to Mr. Shanley to J. F. Dulles, 29 October 1956. Cited in Bennett Kovrig, *Of Walls and Bridges*, p. 92.

205 Hoover to the Legation in Budapest, 31 October 1956, USNA, RG 59, 764.00/ 10-3156.

206 NSC 5616/2 Interim US Policy on Developments in Poland and Hungary, 19 November 1956. The full document with this previously classified paragraph is published in *The 1956 Hungarian Revolution,* p. 439.

207 Memorandum by Arthur Radford to the Secretary of Defense on the Polish Policy of the United States, 3 December 1956, NS Archive, SFC, Record no. 71 515.

208 Ibid.

209 Memorandum by the Chief of Staff of the U.S. Air Force to the JCS on the Polish Policy of the U.S., 30 November 1956, NS Archive, Record no. 71 527.

210 JCS Draft Statement, 6 May 1957, USNA, RG 218, RJCS 1957, 062 (5-26-45), box 3. "The USSR should be informed that the U.S. is determined to apply force against the USSR itself if necessary in fulfillment of U.S. objectives and that these objectives are limited to the restoration of Polish independence. However, even though the U.S. made this position clear to the Soviet leaders, it is highly unlikely they would back down."

211 Quoted in Hixson, *Parting the Curtain*, p. 80.

212 Policy Planning Staff Meeting, 30 October 1956, NS Archive, SFC, Record no. 66 148.

213 Hoover to the American Embassy in Madrid, 8 November 1956, USNA, RG 59, 764.00/11-856.

214 Memorandum of Conversation: Carlton, Senator Flander's assistant; Beam, EU. Reports of Proposed Spanish Intervention in Hungary. 12 April 1957, USNA, RG 59, 764.00/4-1257.

215 Interview with R. Murphy regarding J. F. Dulles, NS Archive, SFC, Record no. 65 105. In his memoirs, Henry Kissinger similarly criticizes U.S. officials for lacking imagination in their approach to the Hungarian crisis. He argues that

experts such as Charles Bohlen and George Kennan could have given the administration better advice. This criticism is somewhat off the mark. Bohlen was involved in policy making during the crisis, and Kennan's views on containment suggest that he would hardly have argued for active intervention. See Kissinger, *Diplomacy*, p. 562.

216 Trachtenberg, *Constructed Peace*, p. 161. Eisenhower was prepared to use tactical nuclear weapons in case of a Soviet aggression and may have been ready for a preemptive nuclear strike at the USSR in case the Soviets were perceived to be preparing for war. See Ibid., chapter 5.

217 The British Embassy in Washington to the Foreign Office, 1 November 1956, in *Hungarian Revolution*, pp. 152–153.

218 H. W. Brand, *The Devil We Knew—Americans and the Cold War* (New York, Oxford: Oxford University Press, 1993).

219 Michael Walzer, *Just and Unjust Wars—A Moral Argument with Historical Illustrations* (Basic Books, Third Edition, 2000), pp. 86–95.

220 Gaddis, *We Now Know,* p. 235.

221 Grose, *Gentleman Spy*, p. 437.

222 See Ronald W. Preussen, "John Foster Dulles és Kelet-Európa," [John Foster Dulles and Eastern Europe] and Raymond Garthoff, "A magyar forradalom és Washington," [The Hungarian revolution and Washington] in András Hegedűs, György Litván, and János M. Rainer, eds., *Évkönyv 1996–1997* (Budapest: 1956-os Intézet, 1997), pp. 228–237 and 314–327, respectively.

223 Quoted by Hixson, *Parting the Iron Curtain*, p. 85.

224 Transcript of RFE Programs, title Armed Forces Special no. B-1, 28 October 1956. Published in *The 1956 Hungarian Revolution*, pp. 286–288.

225 George R. Urban, *Radio Free Europe and the Pursuit of Democracy: My War within the Cold War* (New Haven: Yale University Press, 1997), pp. 218–219. In a similar message László Béry told his audience that the army that Hungary must face "is not invincible." Rebels "had to count not with the full force of the Soviet Union but only with those that were sent to restore order. According to all common sense and rational calculation there is a chance that the Hungarian army can stand the ground against the Soviet army deployed against the people and can be victorious." Cited in Borbándi, *Magyarok az Angol Kertben*, p. 239. On October the 30th, when Nagy abolished the one-party system the RFE warned the freedom fighters not to "hang [their] weapons on the wall." As cited by Kissinger, *Diplomacy*, p. 557.

226 Report on Hungarian Refugee Opinion, RFE Audience Analysis Section, Munich; Amcongen Frankfurt Germany to the State Department. Comments by Hungarian Defector, 4 February 1957, USNA, RG 59, 764.00/2-457.

227 Kramer, "The Early Post-Stalin Succession Struggle and Upheavals in East Central Europe," p. 24.

228 Amcongen Frankfurt to the State Department, Western Radio Listening in Hungary before and after the Uprising. Comments by a Hungarian National, 3 January 1957, USNA, RG 59, 764.00/1-357.

229 Amcongen Frankfurt to the State Department, Hungarian Uprising, Comment by Hungarian National, 4 February 1957, USNA, RG 59, 764.00/2-457.

230 Kramer, "The Early Post Stalin Succession Struggle and the Upheavals in East Central Europe," part 3, p. 25; p. 28.

231 Ibid., pp. 26–27.

232 Brian McCauley, "Hungary and the Suez, 1956: The Limits of Soviet and American Power." *Journal of Contemporary History*, vol. 16, no. 4 (October 1981), pp. 794–795.

233 Békés, *The 1956 Hungarian Revolution and World Politics*, pp. 20–21.

234 Békés wrote that "the United States did not have the political tools with which to force the Soviet Union to give up Hungary and any direct military intervention would probably have resulted in the [...] outbreak of World War III." Csaba Békés, "Hidegháború, enyhülés és az 1956-os forradalom" [Cold war, Détente and the 1956 Revolution] in *Évkönyv, 1996–97*, p. 207. Bennett Kovrig put it bluntly: "The United States was not going to risk war for Hungary. It was an unpleasant moment of truth for America and the West, not to speak of the Hungarians." Bennett Kovrig, "The Liberators: The Great Powers and Hungary in 1956," in Ignác Romsics, ed., *Twentieth Century Hungary and the Great Powers* (Boulder, CO: East European Monographs, 1996), p. 263.

235 Kovrig, *Of Walls and Bridges*, p. 102.

CONCLUSION

In 1945 the Soviet Union was an Empire on a roll. It had already annexed the Baltic States, and parts of Poland, Romania and Finland. The non-annexed Soviet sphere in Europe not including Yugoslavia extended to a territory of over 392 000 square miles with a population larger than 92 million. Aside from Europe the Kremlin demonstrated its interest in territory or influence in the non-European parts of Turkey, Iran, North Africa and the Far East. Nevertheless, many historians ascribe Soviet expansion to rational or irrational security concerns. There is much in favor of this argument. The USSR lost 20 million of its people in World War II. It was, despite having the largest land army in the world, in many ways militarily inferior to its capitalist rivals, Great Britain and the United States. The Soviets suffered tremendous economic losses during the war, and their industrial base was technologically under developed. The traditional Russian feeling of vulnerability to the West was reinforced by Stalin's own sense of paranoia. As Robert Jervis and others have pointed out, what from one perspective appears to be expansion, can be seen from another as measures designed to enhance security.[1] Defense and offense are the two sides of the same coin. Many historians tend to explain postwar Soviet expansion into Eastern Europe and the imposition of Stalinist regimes as a response to American interference in a sphere the Soviets rightfully regarded their own. That is to say, Soviet policy in Eastern Europe was reactive.

This study of Soviet penetration in Hungary suggests that the Soviet Union was an expansionist power. Most studies of Soviet conduct have concentrated on the ideological and military aspects of Soviet foreign policy. It is true that the Soviet Union used its adjacent lands in Eastern Europe as a buffer zone, signing agreements with the satellites that amounted to the extension of the Soviet military perimeter to Eastern Europe. Soviet ideological proselytism is illustrated by the fact that Moscow helped to power Communist parties that constructed ideological states, were devoted to the world-wide triumph of Soviet ideology over capitalism and accepted the leading role of the Soviet Union in the world Communist movement. But ideological states were not necessarily erected only because the Soviet Union wanted to live up to its historical mission of guiding humanity to an allegedly higher form of social, economic and political organization. There were more mundane reasons, such as securing the unhindered performance of imperial services to the USSR by the satellite states. In fact the ideological motive may have been only a secondary one. It is true that Stalinism was omnipresent, both in everyday life and in official culture. But ideological penetration was only superficial. There was no forced Russification. Although the instruction of the Russian language was compulsory, few Hungarians ever spoke it to a satisfactory degree. Cultural and scientific exchange was centrally controlled and the Soviets rarely bothered about it: many Soviet participants of the cultural exchange programs did not even arrive. Contact between the two peoples was almost non-existent and was limited to official exchanges. Although experts of Marxism–Leninism were trained on various levels, instruction of ideological disciplines failed to produce cadres of sufficient quality. Communist ideology did penetrate Hungarian culture. Although a Soviet diplomat complained that the Hungarian attendance of Soviet movies was low, he had to accept party leader Rákosi's explanation that those movies were not good enough.

In many respects the Soviet Union behaved as a traditional imperial power. First of all, it must be emphasized that the Soviet Union regarded Hungary as a prize of the Soviet victory in World War II. Vladimir Dekanozov put it bluntly in 1949: "The victorious country demands to assert its rights for the reason that the vanquished country [Hungary] started war against it." Hungary, as did all Eastern Europe, satisfied Moscow's unbridled economic needs and served as its military base. In fact, economic expansion may have been one of the chief motives of Soviet penetration into Eastern Europe. Although economic factors have always been the focal point of political thinkers and historians concerned with the history of imperialism, this aspect of postwar Soviet policy has received very little attention and has rarely been identified as a possible motive of postwar Soviet conduct.

The Hungarian experience suggests that economic motives played a crucial role in Soviet expansion. Economic penetration was used for two purposes: to further political penetration, and equally importantly, to satisfy the needs of Soviet reconstruction and military build-up. Through the Supreme Economic Council the Soviet Union indirectly controlled Hungarian economic policy. Reparation payments, requisitions and looting provided a flow of wealth into the Soviet Union, and the establishment of fully or partly Soviet-owned companies ensured Soviet control of important branches of the Hungarian economy and almost unlimited, cheap access to strategic raw materials. Dismantled industrial plants were taken to the USSR with all their machinery and inventory, providing among other things new technology for the Soviet industry. This net transfer of assets was not counterbalanced by the loans Moscow provided to keep the Hungarian economy afloat. Ironically the Soviet Union was unable to make full use of these assets, and many of the machines destined for the USSR rusted away on railway tracks before they ever reached their destinations. The reorientation of foreign trade provided additional political leverage. The Hungarian economy, which was restructured according to Soviet needs, required raw materials supplied by the Soviet Union to function. Had Moscow decided not to furnish them the Hungarian economy could have been brought to a standstill.

Historians differ in their analysis of the origins of Soviet rule in Eastern Europe. Some say it was premeditated by Stalin, others argue that at least Hungary and Czechoslovakia could have avoided it were it not for ill-conceived or imperialistic U.S. foreign policy. Most studies still claim that up to 1947 in Hungary (and up to 1948 in Czechoslovakia) the Soviet Union exercised great self-restraint, the Communist Party shared power in a coalition government and only in the second half of 1947 did the Communists decide to establish a proletarian dictatorship. Newly available records, however, reveal that the establishment of a proletarian dictatorship may have been the aim from the outset, and Communist policies aimed at the seizure of power were more relentless than hitherto believed. Even though Hungary elected a democratic parliament with a coalition government in 1945, that government and parliament had very little authority. Local governments, the army and the police were, by and large, Communist controlled. Under Communist control the political police persecuted democratic elements. The Soviet controlled Allied Control Commission treated Hungary as a closed sector. Travelling to and from the country was strictly restricted by the Soviet authorities. Hungarian airspace was under Soviet military control. By 1946 the most important segments of the Hungarian economy were under Soviet ownership, the Hungarian government had little control over much of the nation's natural assets such as bauxite. The Communist-led Supreme Economic Council formulated economic policy and transferred foreign and Hungarian assets to the Soviet Union. With Soviet assistance the Communists pursued a conscious policy of driving out Western economic interests and placed their assets under state or Soviet control. By 1947 the Soviet Union was Hungary's number one trading partner, even though prior to the war bilateral trade between the two countries had been below one percent. Although as in other eastern countries Communist rhetoric eschewed mention of the proletarian dictatorship, in closed circles it was revealed that moderation served tactical purposes. First domestic conditions had to be ripened by driving out the bourgeoisie and the former ruling classes. In addition Soviet interest in retaining cooperation with the Western powers had to be considered. Even so, in May 1946 party leader Rákosi announced the construction of a proletarian dictatorship in Hungary irrespective of foreign or domestic conditions. By the time the Marshall

Plan was announced the backbone of the democratic opposition was broken, the Smallholders' powerful General Secretary was under Soviet arrest, and Prime Minister Nagy had been forced to resign. Communist authorities rigged the 1947 election and the Communist controlled Interior Ministry destroyed what remained of the opposition piecemeal.

A critical question, therefore is, why Communist seizure of power was so smooth. Many factors played a role. First of all Moscow used the ACC to assert Soviet political will with little resistance from the ACC's Western members. Thus, for example, in 1945 Molotov used this body to alter the composition of the democratically elected government. Soviet representatives in Hungary, including Soviet minister Pushkin regularly interfered in domestic political disputes whenever the Communist Party was unable to prevail over its opponents. Unchallenged Soviet power was a further crucial factor, as well as unscrupulous Communist tactics. The Communists used clandestine party members in other parties to disrupt and ultimately break up democratic parties. They viewed domestic politics as a battle with no holds barred, including the arrest of their opponents. Even former members of the extreme right wing Arrow Cross Party were recruited and used to incite anti-Semitic disturbances and in some cases even to lynch political foes. Using threats and blackmail, the Communists exerted relentless pressure to oust their rivals from the parliament and the government. Hungarian democratic forces were divided and not resolute enough to withstand the tremendous pressure their opponents exerted on them. Clandestine Communists imbedded in rival parties increased confusion within the ranks of democratic forces. Some, like President Tildy did not think that resistance would pay off, partly because the Soviet position in Hungary was too strong. In addition, concessions to the Soviet Union were seen as the means to avoid full Sovietization even though each and every concession led to new demands. Many aspects of Communist politics had a broader appeal. There were not enough politicians in power positions that were devoted enough to multiparty democracy to make a strong stand for it. Some, like Tildy, and arguably even Ferenc Nagy, lacked the strength of character, or perhaps the sheer courage to stand up against the Communists and the Soviets. Revealingly, Tildy did not even try to defend his son in law, who was executed by the Communist government under the false charge of treason. Most importantly perhaps, foreign assistance, which was a crucial factor in places like Iran and Austria, where the local leaders resisted Soviet pressure, was lacking in Hungary.

The United States was undoubtedly the power, which could have provided that assistance. Military force was ruled out for political reasons and also because the Soviet Union enjoyed local military superiority. Diplomatic and economic pressure therefore remained the only option. Even this was problematic. Britain, the only remaining albeit weakened continental power aside from the USSR, had written off Hungary and refused to back strong U.S. pressure in Hungary's favor. Furthermore, Hungary was a former enemy that did not enjoy the sympathy of UN member states. Unlike Austria it was not in a geographically important position either. But the real problem was that the Soviets, instead of mollifying their policies under pressure, hardened them instead. The Western powers had almost no leverage on the Soviet Union when it came to the Soviet position in Eastern Europe. When faced with the choice of cooperating with the West or tightening their grip on their possessions, the Soviets invariably opted for the latter.

While the political tradition of disseminating good governance and democracy pulled Washington in the direction of intervention, political realism and the desire to maintain non-hostile relations with the former ally pulled it the opposite way. Eventually realism prevailed, leaving the U.S. scrambling to find the appropriate policy to undo what it conceded relatively easily after the war. In describing U.S. policy towards the Soviets in the immediate post war period, perhaps complacence is the most appropriate term to use. In theory Washington wanted a politically pro-Soviet, but economically open and pluralistic Hungary. In practice, however Hungary was relegated into the closed Soviet sphere, both economically and politically, with little resistance. Washington sent mixed signals. While George Kennan in Moscow threatened that the Soviet Union would be excluded from the new economic world order if the Soviets continued to destroy the Hungarian economy, Washington consistently refused to intervene in Hungarian politics, to give meaningful economic help or to provide trade opportunities. In fact, while policy planners talked of an open sphere in Eastern Europe, Hungary at least was surrendered to Soviet economic penetration. According to the standard explanation Eastern Europe was not important enough to confront the Soviets. Roosevelt consciously surrendered Eastern Europe for Soviet cooperation in world affairs, while Truman oscillated between writing it off and using Soviet cooperation in Eastern Europe as a test case in the relationship between the two powers. However, other factors were also at play. The liberal-internationalist impulse of U.S. foreign policy in the post war period was not extended to Eastern Europe. This was in part because the social-darwinistic doctrine of non-intervention as expressed by Minister Schoenfeld left it to the locals to achieve their democracy and independence without outside assistance, by their own courageous effort. In addition, Foreign Service officials collected evidence of Hungarian attitudes to reaffirm deeply engrained prejudices concerning the culturally inferiority of Eastern Europe, from which it followed that Hungary did not merit U.S. assistance the same way as for example Austria. It is easy to see the fallacy of the argument. Karl Renner in Austria stood up to the Soviets knowing that the Western powers of occupation supported him. Had the United States pursued a more active policy with regard to Hungary, such as the rapid extension of commercial ties, they may have made Soviet aims harder to achieve. Nevertheless, it is clear that Soviet, and not American policy determined the fate of Hungary and possibly of Eastern Europe as a whole.

Never in the period under discussion did the Soviet Union consider sharing control of Eastern Europe with the West. The Soviet Union enjoyed a hegemonic position in Eastern Europe, using Hungary as the other states of the region as imperial client states. The Communist regime in Hungary made sure that most Soviet economic and security demands were met. Stalinist dictatorships ensured unswerving loyalty to the Soviet Union's imperial aspirations. This does not mean that Soviet control on the Hungarian leadership was unlimited. In 1949 Hungary successfully resisted the integration of Hungarian economic planning into the Soviet system and preserved the independence of foreign trade and the financial system against Soviet encroachments. Because of its economic deficiencies, Hungary was incapable of fulfilling its export obligations to the Soviet Union. All in all the Soviet hold on Hungary was secure enough to keep it a useful client state. There was a crucial difference between the U.S. and the Soviet alliances. The U.S. transferred wealth to its allies by providing aid, loans and military assistance. In various ways, the United States provided more than 100 billion dollars in the form of bilateral credits and grants in the years from 1945 to 1965. From 1950 to 1962 Western Europe received 15 billion dollars in military assistance directly from the United States[2] in addition to the American nuclear shield. In contrast the Soviet allies transferred wealth to the dominant power through economic and trade arrangements as well as by sharing the costs of Soviet military build-up. Both the U.S. and the Soviet Union sought a leading role in their respective alliances, but with very different approaches.

In most cases the Hungarian leadership renounced sovereignty and invited the Soviet Union to participate in domestic politics. Moscow was seen as the legitimate leader of the world Communist movement, therefore Soviet and Hungarian interests were regarded as one and the same. Voluntary obedience, rather than an armada of Soviet advisors were the key to a relatively, although not wholly smooth relationship. Hungarian Communists appreciated the importance of Soviet military presence from the perspective of staying in power. Economic factors also played a role. The Hungarian economy came to rely on Soviet shipments of raw materials. Denial of them was an important tool of political coercion.

What really mattered from the U.S. perspective was the military aspect of the relationship: Soviet presence in Hungary contributed to the military threat in Central Europe. The elimination of Soviet presence in Eastern

Europe was one of the priorities of U.S. foreign policy in the first part of the 50s. In July 1956 for instance the NSC stated that a permanent Soviet presence in Eastern Europe "would represent a serious threat to the security of Western Europe and the U.S." Moreover, the NSC reaffirmed "America's traditional policy to recognize the right of all people to independence and the government of their own choosing. The elimination of Soviet domination of the satellites is, therefore, in the fundamental interest of the United States." The statement summed up the two basic impulses of U.S. policy: realism and idealism. Realism as expressed in the policy of nuclear deterrence; idealism as embodied by the Atlantic Charter or the Marshall Plan. In the aftermath of the war Washington was at a loss to square these components. After 1948, however, when the division of the continent into two opposing blocs became apparent, U.S. policy on Eastern Europe rested on a delicate balance between the urge to liberate Eastern Europe and the need to avoid a war resulting from recklessness. A middle-of-the road policy was needed that would work towards the retraction of Soviet power and the democratic transformation of dictatorships without provoking a Soviet military counter offensive. Even though the U.S. enjoyed clear nuclear superiority, the Soviets had the capability to overrun Western Europe with conventional forces.

Although the Truman administration is credited with the policy of containment recent research showed that it was bolder and more sanguine about the liberation of Eastern Europe than hitherto believed. Economic embargo was meant to hinder the consolidation of Communist regimes by creating shortages and to reduce the Soviet Union's military potential by denying strategic commodities and technology. Non-compliance by the allies reduced its effectiveness but even so the embargo was definitely a nuisance factor. Paradoxically Hungary procured some important raw materials for its program of industrialization and armament from the Western world in spite of the export controls. Aggressive psychological warfare, including subversion, sabotage, covert warfare and propaganda sought to undermine Communist regimes and counted even with military conflict with the USSR. Propaganda was the most effective tool, but it was fraught with a dilemma. While keeping hope alive behind the iron curtain that their would be no permanent peace until Soviet power retreated from Eastern Europe, radio broadcasts were not supposed to promise armed intervention, or incite armed rebellion. Aggressive psychological warfare was shielded by nuclear deterrence until the Soviet Union was able to deliver a crippling atomic blow against U.S. territory. At the end of the Truman era a reassessment of the strategy took place in the light of growing Soviet nuclear capability, which questioned the assumptions on which policy was based. It followed that American aggressive designs for the liberation of Eastern Europe were abandoned as being too dangerous to pursue. Eastern Europe became the captive of Soviet nuclear deterrence. Although the Eisenhower administration began with a strident rhetoric of liberation, within a year it returned to the doctrine of containment.

Stalin's death occasioned a new approach to solving the status of the eastern countries: negotiated settlement based on the concept of Finlandization. Although in 1955 the Soviets rejected talks on the status of the satellite states, the U.S. administration continued to look for a settlement of the Hungarian crisis on this basis. It was argued that the Soviets sought to control Eastern Europe because of security concerns, so if Soviet defense needs were guaranteed the continued occupation of Eastern Europe would become superfluous. Therefore, if talks were offered to the Soviets on this basis, an armed intervention could be forestalled and the status of Eastern Europe could be settled on a mutually acceptable basis. This was the idea behind the U.S. strategy to deal with the Hungarian crisis of October–November 1956. It is another matter that it did not work. Armed intervention was ruled out because it would have put all parties to great danger. In this respect the Eisenhower administration displayed prudent restraint. Up to November 2 Washinton thought that the strategy was working and events were going in Hungary's favor. Simultaneously there was a darker side to U.S. policy, one that could be plausibly denied later. This was aggressive propaganda, which incited the rebels to fight on in the hope of success. Aggressive propaganda was at least tolerated (although in Germany and Poland it was discouraged) even though U.S. officials believed that fighting the Soviets was suicidal. Torn between the desire to act and the fear of the consequences of an armed intervention, the U.S. pursued a policy that sent mixed signals. On the one hand the Eisenhower administration pursued talks with Moscow, seeking to alleviate Soviet fears that Washington was inciting or encouraging anti-Soviet protests. Simultaneously Radio Free Europe pursued an aggressive propaganda campaign designed to give hope to the revolutionaries encouraging them and even the Hungarian army to fight the Soviets with everything they had. This policy sabotaged the overall effort, since the harder the Hungarians fought the less chance there was for a peaceful resolution of the conflict.

John Lewis Gaddis has argued that the United States, on the whole, retained its idealistic, democratic values in dealing with its allies and this could be one explanation for its success. The U.S. never allowed itself to be like the enemy it was trying to cope with.[3] But the reckless propaganda campaign points to a cynical aspect of American policy. Although the chances for the success of the revolution were low, the Eisenhower administration may have perceived the rebellion as a low cost effort to destabilize the Soviet Union. If self-liberation failed, the U.S. could always disclaim responsibility, leaving the rebels to fend for themselves. When needed, the United States was ready to manipulate a small state, although in a less direct way then the Soviets. Ultimately, the U.S. acted purely in self-interest, as democratic and autocratic great powers alike have acted throughout history. Nevertheless, the United States remained the only Western power, which did not reconcile itself with lasting Soviet presence in Eastern Europe. The lessons of 1956 were learnt and instead of encouraging passive resistance, propaganda began to concentrate on the cultural penetration of the iron curtain. This strategy was more successful than the previous one and already in 1965 the Hungarian party leadership was forced to conclude that Western propaganda was winning the battle for the hearts and minds of the young generation. Increased trade helped drive Hungary into ecenomic bankruptcy and spread the culture of consumerism.

Strikingly, the Soviet records of the decision to crush the Revolution do not reveal any American influence on the Kremlin's decision-making process. This absence underscores the assertion that Soviet, and not American actions determined the fate of Eastern Europe. There were two immediate causes of the Soviet crackdown on Hungary. First, the bombing of Egypt, second the dramatic decline of Communist influence and what seemed to the Kremlin as the spreading of anticommunist violence. But it is doubtful that the Soviets would have allowed a significant change in Hungary's domestic or international condition in any case. Throughout the 1950s Hungary, as did the whole of Eastern Europe, provided important services to the Soviet Empire. In fact Hungary's condition as a non-sovereign supplier of imperial services provides helps understand why the Soviet system was imposed in Hungary in the first place. Beside the great difference between the personalities and political outlooks of Khruschev in the 1950s and Gorbachev in the late 1980s the chief difference between 1956 when the Soviets held on to Hungary and 1989, when they let it go, lay in Hungary's usefulness as a satellite. In 1956, despite its many problems Hungary was still an asset; in 1989 it was probably a liability. This calculus was an important determinant of Soviet presence—or absence—in Eastern Europe after 1945.

NOTES

1 For a discussion the cold war as a security dilemma see Robert Jervis, "Was the Cold War a Security Dilemma?" *Journal of Cold War Studies,* vol. 3 no. 1 Winter 2001. A recent appraisal of postwar Soviet policy talked about security through expansion. Levering et al., *Debating the Origins of the Cold War,* p. 148.

2 Geir Lundestad, *The United States and Western Europe since 1945* (Oxford, New York: Oxford University Press, 2003), p. 29; p. 71.

3 Gaddis, *We Now Know,* p. 288.

BIBLIOGRAPHY

Unpublished Sources

Arkhiv Vneshnei Politiki Rossiskii Federatsii, Moscow
Archives du Ministère des Affaies Étrangères, Paris
Magyar Országos Levéltár, Budapest
National Archives Washington D.C.
National Security Archives, Washington D.C.
Politika Történeti Intézet Levéltára, Budapest
Rossiskii Tsentr Hranenia i Izuchenia Dokumentov, Moscow
Történeti Hivatal, Budapest
Szegedy-Maszák Aladár gyűjtemény, Országos Széchenyi Könyvtár, Budapest
The Macartney Papers, Bodleian Library, Oxford

Published Sources

Balogh, Sándor, ed., *Nehéz esztendők krónikája, 1949-1953* (Budapest: Gondolat Kiadó, 1986).
Balogh, Sándor and Margit Földesi, eds., *A magyar jóvátétel és ami mögötte van... 1945–1949* (Budapest: Napvilág Kiadó, 1998).
Baráth, Magdolna, ed., *Szovjet nagyköveti iratok Magyarországról, 1953–1956 – Kiszeljov és Andropov titkos jelentései* (Budapest: Napvilág Kiadó, 2002).
Békés, Csaba, "Dokumentumok a magyar kormánydelegáció 1946. áprilisi moszkvai tárgyalásairól," *Régió – Kisebbségi Szemle*, vol. 3, no. 2, 1992.
Békés, Csaba, "Soviet Plans to Establish the Cominform in Early 1946: New Evidence From Hungarian Archives," *Cold War International History Bulletin*, no. 10, March 1998
Békés, Csaba, Malcolm Byrne and János M Rainer eds., *The 1956 Hungarian Revolution: A History in Documents* (Budapest, New York: CEU Press, 2002).
Cseh, Gergő Bendegúz, ed., *Documents of the Meetings of the Allied Control Commission in Hungary* (Budapest: MTA Jelenkor-kutató Bizottság, 2000).
Documents Diplomatiques Francais, 1956, vol. III.
Dokumentumok Zala megye történetéből 1944-1947 (Zalaegerszeg, 1995).
Foreign Relations of the United States, 1943, The Conferences at Cairo and Teheran.
Foreign Relations of the United States, 1944, vol. III.
Foreign Relations of the United States, 1945, The Conferences at Yalta and Malta.
Foreign Relations of the United States, 1945, vol. IV.

Foreign Relations of the United States, 1946, vol. VI.

Foreign Relations of the United States, 1947, vol. IV.

Foreign Relations of the United States, 1948, vol. IV.

Foreign Relations of the United States, 1950, vol. IV.

Foreign Relations of the United States, 1951, vol. I.

Foreign Relations of the United States, 1952–1954, vol. I.

Foreign Relations of the United States, 1955–1957, vol. XXV.

Gál, Éva, et al. eds., "A 'Jelcin Dosszié' – Szovjet Dokumentumok 1956-ról (Budapest: Századvég, 1956-os Intézet, 1993).

Haraszti-Taylor, Eva, ed., *The Hungarian Revolution of 1956. A Collection of Documents from the British Foreign Office* (Nottingham: Astra Press, 1995).

Izsák, Lajos and Miklós Kun, eds., *Moszkvának jelentjük: Titkos dokumentumok, 1944–1948* (Budapest: Századvég, 1994).

Juhász, Gyula, ed., *Magyar-brit titkos tárgyalások 1943-ban* (Budapest: Kossuth, 1978).

Kimball, Warren F., ed., *Churchill and Roosevelt – The Complete Correspondance* (Princeton, New Jersey: Princeton University Press, 1984), vols. 2, 3.

Kramer, Mark, ed., "The 'Malin Notes' on the Crises in Hungary and Poland," *CWIHP Bulletin*, issue 8–9.

Lázár, György, ed., *Szekfű Gyula moszkvai követ és a moszkvai követség jelentései* (Budapest: Magyar Országos Levéltár, 1998).

Murasko, Galina P., ed., *Vostochnaia Evropa v Dokumentakh Rossiiskikh Arkhivov* (Novosibirsk: Sibirsku Khronogaf, 1997).

Murasko, Galina P., ed., *Vostochnaia Evropa v Dokumentakh Rossiiskikh Arkhivov* (Novosibirsk: Sibirsku Khronogaf, 1998).

Ostermann, Christian, ed., "This is not a Politburo but a Madhouse—The Post-Stalin Succession Struggle, Soviet *Deutschlandpolitik* and the SED: New Evidence from Russian, German and Hungarian Archives" *CWIHP Bulletin* no. 10, 1998.

Ostermann, Christian F., ed., *Uprising in East Germany, 1953. The Cold War, The German Question and the First Major Upheaval Behind the Iron Curtain* (Budapest, New York: Central European University Press, 2001).

Pataki, István, ed., "Magyar–szovjet katonai egyezmények," *Múltunk*, 1995, vol. 40, no. 3.

Rainer M., János and Károly Urbán, eds., "'Konzultációk.' Dokumentumok a magyar és szovjet pártvezetők két moszkvai találkozójáról 1954–1955-ben," *Múltunk*, 1992, vol. 37, no. 4.

Resis, Albert, ed., *Molotov Remembers. Inside Kremlin Politics. Conversations with Felix Chuev* (Chicago: Ivan R. Dee, 1993).

Rzheshevsky, Oleg, ed., *War and Diplomacy. The Making of the Grand Alliance. Documents from Stalin's Archives* (U.K.: Harwood Academic Publishers, 1998).

Sereda, Vyacheslav and Aleksandr Stikalin, eds., *Hiányzó Lapok 1956 történetéből* (Budapest: Móra Ferenc Kiadó, 1993).

Sereda, Vyacheslav and János Rainer M., eds., *Döntés a Kremlben. A szovjet párt-elnökség vitái Magyarországról* (Budapest: 1956-os Intézet, 1996).

Szűcs, László, ed., *Dálnoki Miklós Béla kormányának minisztertanácsi jegyzőköny-vei* A kötet (Budapest, Magyar Országos Levéltár, 1997).

T. Varga, György, "Jegyzőkönyv a szovjet és magyar párt-és állami vezetők tárgya-lásairól – 1953 június 13–16," *Múltunk*, 1992, vol. 37, no. 3.

Vida, István, ed., "Iratok a magyar kormányküldöttség 1946. évi washingtoni láto-gatásához," *Levéltári Szemle*, 1978, vol. 48–49, no. 1.

Vida, István, ed., "K. J. Vorosilov marsall jelentései a Tildy kormány megalakulásá-ról," *Társadalmi Szemle*, 1996, no. 2.

Volokitina et al. eds., *Sovietskii faktor v vostochnoi Evrope 1944–1953* (Moscow: Rosspen, 1999), vol. 1.

Volokitina et al. eds., *Transilvanskii vopros vengero-ruminskii territornialnii spor i SSSR, 1940–1946, dokumenti* (Moscow: Rosspen, 2000).

Volkov, V. K. et al. eds., *Sovietski Soiuz i Vengerskii Krizis 1956 g. Dokumenti* (Moscow: Rosspen, 1998).

Zubok, Vladislav, ed., "CPSU Plenums, Leadership Struggles, and Cold War Poli-tics," *CWIHP Bulletin*, issue 10, 1998.

Books

Adomeit, Hannes, *Imperial Overstrech. Germany in Soviet Foreign Policy from Stalin to Gorbachev* (Baden-Baden: Nomos Verlagsgesellscaft, 1998).

Balogh, Margit, *A KALOT és a katolikus társadalompolitika, 1935–1946* (Budapest: MTA Történettudományi Intézete, 1998).

Balogh, Sándor, *Magyarország külpolitikája, 1945–1950* (Budapest: Kossuth Könyv-kiadó, 1988).

Barker, Elisabeth, *British Policy in South-East Europe in the Second World War* (London–Basingstoke: The MacMillan Press Ltd., 1976).

Barker, Elisabeth, William Deakin and Jonathan Chadwick, eds., *Political and Mili-tary Strategy in Eastern Europe* (New York: St. Martin's Press 1989).

Bak János et al. eds., *Évköny 1994* (Budapest: 1956-os Intézet 1994).

Berend Iván T., *A szocialista gazdaság fejlődése Magyarországon* (Budapest: Aka-démia Kiadó, 1974).

Bischof, Günter, *Austria in the First Cold War. The Leverage of the Weak 1945–1955* (London: MacMillan, 1999).

Bischof, Günter, Ambrose, Stephen, eds., *Eisenhower. A Centenary Reassessment* (Baton Rouge and London: Louisiana State University Press, 1995).

Bischof, Günter and Saki Dockrill, *Cold War Respite. The Geneva Summit of 1955* (Baton Rouge: Louisiana State University Press, 2001)

Bjornstad, Stein, *The Soviet Union and German Unification During Stalin's Last Years* (Oslo: Defense Studies, 1998/1).

Borbándi, Gyula, *Magyarok az Angol Kertben. A Szabad Európa Rádió története* (Budapest: Európa Kiadó, 1996).

Botting, Douglas, *America's Secret Army: The Untold Story of the Counter Intelligence Corps* (New York: F. Watts, 1989).

Bowie, Robert and Richard H. Immerman, *Waging Peace: How Eisenhower Shaped and Enduring Cold War Strategy* (Oxford: Oxford University Press, 1998).

Brand, H. W., *The Devil we Knew. Americans and the Cold War* (New York, Oxford: Oxford University Press, 1993).

Bull, Hedley, *The Anarchical Society. A Study of Order in World Politics* (New York: Columbia University Press, 1977).

Bundy, McGeorge, *Danger and Survival. Choices about the Bomb in the First Fifty Years* (New York: Vintage Books, 1990).

Cave Brown, Anthony, *Bodyguard of Lies,* Volume I (New York: Harper and Row Publishers, 1975).

Dallin, David J., *Soviet Foreign Policy after Stalin* (Philadelphia, Chicago, New York: J. B. Lippincott Company, 1961).

Davis, Lynn Ethridge, *The Cold War Begins* (New Jersey, Princeton: Princeton University Press, 1974).

Deane, John R., *The Strange Alliance. The Story of Our Effort at Wartime Cooperation with Russia* (Bloomington, London: Indiana University Press, 1973).

DeSantis, Hugh, *The Diplomacy of Silence. The American Foreign Service, The Soviet Union and the Cold War* (Chicago, London: The University of Chicago Press, 1979).

Dockrill, Saki, *Eisenhower's New Look National Security Policy, 1953–1961* (London: MacMillan, 1996).

Edmonds, Robin, *The Big Three. Churchill, Roosevelt and Stalin* (London: Hamish Hamilton, 1991).

Évkönyv V. 1996/97 (Budapest: 1956-os Intézet, 1997).

Évkönyv VI. 1998 (Budapest: 1956-os Intézet, 1998).

Feis, Herbert, *From Trust to Terror. The Onset of the Cold War, 1945–1950* (New York: Norton, 1970).

Feitl István ed., *Az Ideiglenes Nemzetgyűlés és az Ideiglenes Nemzeti Kormány, 1944-1945* (Budapest: Politikatörténeti Alapítvány, 1995).

Forland, Tor Egil, *Cold Economic Warfare: The Creation and Prime of CoCom, 1948–1954* (Oslo: Norwegian University Press, 1991).

Föglein, Gizella, *Államforma és államfői jogkör Magyarországon, 1944–1949* (Budapest: ELTE, 1994).

Frank, Tibor, *Ethnicity, Propaganda, Myth-Making: Studies in Hungarian Connections to Britin and America, 1848–1945* (Budapest, Akadémiai Kiadó, 1999).

Fülöp, Mihály, *A befejezetlen béke. A Külügyminiszterek Tanácsa és a magyar békeszerződés, 1947* (Budapest: undated).

Gaddis, John Lewis, *The United States and the Origins of the Cold War* (New York: Columbia University Press, 1972).

Gaddis, John Lewis, *The Long Peace: Inquiries into the History of the Cold War* (Oxford: Oxford University Press, 1987).

Gaddis, John Lewis, *We Now Know. Rethinking Cold War History* (Oxford: Clarendon Press, 1997).

Gati, Charles, *Hungary and the Soviet Bloc* (Durham, N.C.: Duke University Press, 1986).

Gilbert, Martin, *Road to Victory. Winston Churchill 1941–1945* (London: Heinemann, 1986).

Gilpin, Robert, *The Political Economy of Interational Relations* (Princeton, New Jersey: Princeton University Press, 1987).

Goncharev, Sergei, N. Xue Litai and John W. Lewis, *Uncertain Partners. Stalin, Mao and the Korean War* (Stanford: Stanford University Press, 1993).

Grose, Peter, *Gentleman Spy: The Life of Allen Dulles* (Boston: Houghton Mifflin Co., 1994).

Grose, Peter, *Operation Rollback: America's Secret War Behind the Iron Curtain* (Boston, New York: Houghton Mifflin Co., 2000).

Gyarmati, György, ed., *A Történeti Hivatal Évkönyve, 2002* (Budapest: Történeti Hivatal, 2002).

Hahn, Peter L., *The United States, Great Britain and Egypt 1945–1956: Strategy and Diplomacy in the Early Cold War* (Chapel Hill and London: The University of North Carolina Press, 1991).

Hammond, Thomas T., ed., *The Anatomy of Communist Takeovers* (New Haven: Yale University Press, 1975).

Hanhimaki, Jussi, *Containing Coexistence. America, Russia and the "Finnish Solution," 1945–1956,* (Ohio: The Kent State University Press, 1997).

Harper, John Lamberton, *American Visions of Europe. Franklin Delano Roosevelt, George F. Kennan, Dean G. Acheson* (Cambridge: Cambridge University Press, 1994).

Hixson, Walter, *Parting the Iron Curtain: Propaganda, Culture and the Cold War 1945–1961* (London: MacMillan, 1997).

Hogan, Michael, *The Marshall Plan. America, Britain and and the Reconstruction of Western Europe, 1947–1952* (Cambridge University Press, 1987).

Holloway, David, *Stalin and the Bomb. The Soviet Union and Atomic Energy, 1939–1956* (New Haven and London: Yale University Press, 1994).

Holsti, K. J., *International Politics. A Framework for Analysis* (Englewood Cliffs, New Jersey: Prentice Hall, 1967).

Immerman, Richard H., *John Foster Dulles: Piety, Pragmatism and Power in U.S. Foreign Policy* (Wilmington, DE: SR Books, 1999).

Immerman, Richard H., *John Foster Dulles and the Diplomacy of the Cold War* (Princeton, New Jersey: Princeton University Press, 1990).

Izsák, Lajos, *Rendszerváltástól rendszerváltásig, 1944–1989* (Budapest: Kulturtrade, 1998).

Izsák, Lajos and Gyula Stemler, eds., *Vissza a Történelemhez. Emlékkönyv Balogh Sándor 70. születésnapjára* (Budapest: Napvilág, 1996).

Juhász, Gyula, *Magyarország külpolitikája, 1918–1945* (Budapest: Kossuth, 1988).

Jervis, Robert, *Perception and Misperception in International Politics* (Princeton, New Jersey: Princeton University Press, 1973).

Kallay, Nicholas, *Hungarian Premier. A Personal Account of of a Nation's Struggle in World War II* (Westport, Conn.: Greenwood Press, 1954).

Kaplan, Karel, *The Short March. The Communist Takeover in Czechoslovakia, 1945–1948* (New York: St. Martin's Press, 1987).

Kárász, Artúr, *80 év alatt a föld körül* (Budapest–Paris, 1990).

Kolko, Joyce and Gabriel Kolko, *The Limits of Power. The World and United States Foreign Policy 1945–1954* (New York: Harper and Row, 1972).

Korom, Mihály, *Magyarország Ideiglenes Nemzeti Kormánya és a Fegyverszünet* (Budapest: Akadémiai Kiadó, 1981).

Kertesz, Stephen D. ed., *The Fate of East-Central Europe. Hopes and Failures of Amerian Foreign Policy* (Notre Dame In.: Notre Dame University Press, 1956).

Kertesz, Stephen D., *Between Russia and the West. Hungary and the Illusion of Peacemaking* (Notre Dame, London: University of Notre Dame Press, 1984).

Kissinger, Henry, *Diplomacy* (New York: Simon and Schuster, 1994).

Kovrig, Bennett, *The Myth of Liberation. East Central Europe in U.S. Diplomacy and Politics since 1941* (Baltimore and London: The Johns Hopkins University Press, 1973).

Kovrig, Bennett, *Communism in Hungary from Kun to Kádár* (Stanford University Stanford, California: Hoover Institution Press, 1979).

Kovrig, Bennett, *Of Walls and Bridges. The United States and Eastern Europe* (New York and London: New York University Press, 1991).

Krasner, Stephen D., *Sovereignty Organized Hypocrisy* (Princeton, New Jersey: Princeton University Press, 1999).

Kuniholm, Bruce Robellet, *The Origins of the Cold War in the Near East. Great Power Conflict and Diplomacy in Iran, Turkey and Greece* (Princeton, New Jersey: Princeton University Press, 1986).

Laquer, Walter, *Europe in Our Time, A History, 1945–1992* (New York: Penguin Books, 1992).

Leffler, Melvyn, *The Preponderance of Power. National Security, the Truman Administration, and the Cold War* (Stanford, California: Stanford University Press, 1992).

Leffler, Melvyn, *The Specter of Communism. The United States and the Origins of the Cold War, 1947–1953* (New York: Hill and Wang, 1994).

Levering, Ralph B., Vladimir O. Pechatnov, Verena Botzenhart-Viehe and Earl C. Edmondson, *Debating the rigins of the Cold War. American and Russian Perspectives* (Lanham, Boulder, Oxford, New York: Rowman and Littefield Publishers Inc., 2002).

Levinson, Sanford, *Written in Stone. Public Monuments in Changing Societies* (Durham, London: Duke University Press, 1998).

Lichtheim, George, *Imperialism* (New York, Washington: Praeger, 1971).

Lukes, Igor, *Czechoslovakia between Stalin and Hitler. The Diplomacy of Edvard Benes in the 1930s* (New York, Oxford: Oxford University Press, 1996).

Lundestad, Geir, *The American Non-Policy Towards Eastern Europe, 1943–1947* (Tromsö–Oslo–Bergen: Universitatsforlaget, 1978).

Lundestad, Geir, *The American "Empire" and Other Studies in U.S. Foreign Policy in a Comparative Perspective* (Oxford, New York: Oxford University Press, Oslo: Norwegian University Press, 1990).

Lundestad, Geir, *The United States and Western Europe since 1945. From "Empire" by Invitation to Transatlantic Drift* (Oxford, New York: Oxford University Press, 2003).

Luttwak, Edward N., *The Grand Strategy of the Soviet Union* (London: St. Martin's Press, 1983).

Mastny, Vojtech, *Russia's Road to the Cold War* (New York: Columbia University Press, 1979).

Mastny, Vojtech, *The Cold War and Soviet Insecurity: The Stalin Years* (New York, Oxford: Oxford University Press, 1996).

Márai, Sándor, *Memoir of Hungary 1944–1948* (Budapest: Corvina in association with Central European University Press, 1996).

Max, Stanley, *The Anglo-American Response to the Sovietization of Hungary, 1945–1948* (Ann Arbor, Michigan: Univesity of Michigan Press, 1990).

McCagg, William, *Stalin Embattled, 1943–1948* (Detroit: Wayne University Press, 1978).

Miscamble, Wilson D., *George F. Kennan and the Making of American Foreign Policy, 1945–1950* (Princeton, New Jersey: Princeton University Press, 1992).

Mitrovich, Gregory, *Undermining the Kremlin. America's Strategy to Subvert the Soviet Bloc* (Ithaca, London: Cornell University Press, 2000).

Morgenthau, Hans, *Politics Among Nations. The Struggle for Power and Peace* Revised by Kenneth W. Thompson (New York: Knopf, 1985).

Mravik, László, *The "Sacco di Budapest" and the Depredation of Hungary, 1938–1949* (Budapest: The Hungarian National Gallery, 1998).

Nagy, Ferenc, *Küzdelem a vasfüggöny mögött,* vols. I–II (Budapest: Európa, História, 1990).

Naimark, Norman, *The Russians in Germany: A History of the Soviet Zone of Occupation, 1945–1949* (Cambridge, Mass.: Belknap Press of Harvard University Press, 1995).

Naimark, Norman, Gibianskii, Leonid eds., *Establishment of Communist Regimes in Eastern Europe, 1944–1949* (Westview Press, 1996).

Nyaradi, Nicholas, *My Ringside Seat in Moscow* (New York: Crowell, 1952).

Okváth, Imre, *Bástya a béke frontján. Magyar haderő és katonapolitika 1945–1956* (Budapest: Aquila, 1998).

Paczkowski, Andrzei, *Fél évszázad Lengyelország történetéből* (Budapest: 1956-os Intézet, 1997).

Palasik, Mária, *Kovács Béla 1908–1959* (Budapest: Occidental Press, 2002).

Pelle, János, *Az utolsó vérvádak. Az etnikai és politikai manipuláció kelet európai történetéből* (Budapest: Pelikán Kiadó, 1995).

Perlmutter, Amos, *FDR and Stalin. A Not So Grand an Alliance, 1943–1945* (Columbia and London: University of Missouri Press, 1993).

Pető, Iván and Sándor Szakács, *A hazai gazdaság négy évtizedének története,* vol. I. (Budapest: Közgazdasági Kiadó, 1985).

Pécsi,Kálmán, *A magyar-szovjet gazdasági kapcsolatok 30 éve* (Budapest: Közgazdasági Kiadó, 1979).

Pruden, Caroline, *Conditional Partners. Eisenhower, the United Nations, and the Search for Permanent Peace* (Baton Rouge: Louisiana State University Press, 1998).

Raack, R. C., *Stalin's Drive to the West, 1938–1945* (Stanford, California: Stanford University Press, 1995).

Radvanyi, Janos, *Hungary and the Superpowers, The 1956 Revolution and Realpolitik* (Stanford Stanford University Press, 1972).

Rainer M., János, *Nagy Imre. Politikai Életrajz* vol. I (Budapest: Századvég, 1996).

Rainer M., János, *Nagy Imre, 1953–1958. Politikai Életrajz II* (Budapest: 1956-os Intézet, 1999).

Rainer M., János, *Nagy Imre* (Budapest: Vincze Kiadó, 2002).

Rákosi, Mátyás, *Visszaemlékezések 1940–1956* vols. I–II edited by Feitl István, et al. (Budapest: Napvilág Kiadó, 1997).

Resis, Albert, *Stalin, the Politburo, and the Onset of the Cold War: 1945–1946* (Pittsburgh: University of Pittsburgh, Center for Russian and East European Studies, 1988).

Révai, József, *Az ország újjáépítésének politikai előfeltételei* (Budapest: Szikra, 1945).

Ripp, Zoltán, *Ötvenhat és a hatalom* (Budapest: Napvilág Kiadó, 1997).

Romsics, Ignác ed., *Twentieth Century Hungary and the Great Powers* (Boulder, Colorado: East Euroean Monographs, 1996).

Sainsbury, Keith, *The Turning Point* (Oxford, New York, 1987).

Sakmyster, Thomas, *Hungary's Admiral on Horseback. Miklós Horthy, 1918–1944* (Boulder: East European Monographs, 1994).

Schmidl, Erwin, ed., *Österreich im Frühen Kalten Krieg 1945–1958* (Köln, Weimar: Böhlau, Verlag, 2002).

Schmidt, Mária, *Diktatúrák ördögszekéren* (Budapest: Magvető, 1998).

Seton-Watson, Hugh, *From Lenin to Khrushchev. The History of World Communism* (New York, Washington: Frederick A. Praeger, 1966).

Schöpflin, George, *Politics in Eastern Europe, 1945–1992* (Oxford, UK, Cambridge, Mass.: Blackwell, 1993).

Sherwin, Martin J., *A World Destroyed. Hiroshima and the Origins of the Arms Race* (New York: Vintage Books, 1987).

Stafford, David, *Britain and the European Resistance, 1940–1945: a Survey of the Special Operations Executive with Documents* (Toronto: Toronto University Press, 1980).

Standeiszky, Éva, *A magyar kommunista párt irodalompolitikája, 1944–1948* (Budapest: Kossuth Könyvkiadó, 1987).

Stark, Tamás, *Magyarország második világháborús embervesztesége* (Budapest: MTA Történettudományi Intézete, 1989).

Szakács, Sándor and Tibor Zinner, *"A háború megváltozott természete." Adalékok, tények, összefüggések, 1944–1948* (Budapest: Genius Gold Rt., Batthyány Társaság, 1998).

Szegedy-Maszák, Aladár, *Az ember ősszel visszanéz… egy volt magyar diplomata emlékiratából* (Budapest: Európa-História, 1996), vol. 2.

Szerencsés, Károly, *A kékcédulás hadművelet. Választások Magyarországon, 1947* (Budapest: Ikva, 1992).

Szurovy, Géza, *A kőolaj regénye* (Budapest: Hírlapkiadó Vállalat, 1993).

Thompson, Willie, *The Communist Movement since 1945* (Oxford: Blackwell, 1995).

Trachtenberg, Mark, *Constructed Peace. The Making of the European Settlement 1945–1963* (Princeton, New Jersey: Princeton University Press, 1999).

Ungváry, Krisztián, *Budapest ostroma* (Budapest: Corvina, 1999).

Urban, George, *Radio Free Europe and the Pursuit of Democracy: My War within the Cold War* (New Haven: Yale University Press, 1997).

Varsori, Antonio and Elena Calandri, eds., *The Failure of Peace in Europe* (London: Palgrave, 2002).

Vida, István, *A Független Kisgazdapárt politikája, 1944-1947* (Budapest: Akadémiai Kiadó, 1976).

Vida, István, *Koalíció és pártharcok* (Budapest: Európa, 1986).

Vígh, Károly, *Tildy Zoltán életútja* (Békéscsaba: Tevan kiadó, 1991).

Volokitina. T. V., G. P. Murasko, A. F. Noskova and T. A. Pokivailova, *Moskva i Vostochnaia Evropa–Stanovlenie politicheskikh rezhimov sovietskogo tipa, 1949–1953* (Moscow: Rosspen, 2002).

Williams, Appelman William, *The Tragedy of American Diplomacy* (New York, 1962).

Zadorzhiuk, E. G. and V.V. Marina, eds., *Febral 1948. Moskva i Praga* (Moscow, 1998).

Zubok, Vladislav and Constantine Pleshakov, *Inside the Kremlin's Cold War. From Stalin to Khrushchev* (Cambridge, Massachusetts, London, England: Harvard University Press, 1997).

Walt, Stephen, *The Origins of Alliances* (Ithaca: Cornell University Press, 1987).

Waltz, Kenneth, *Theory of International Politics* (New York: Random House, 1979).

Walzer, Michael, *Just and Unjust Wars. A Moral Argument with Historical Illustrations* (Basic Books, Third Edition, 2000).

Wight, Martin, *Power Politics* (London: Royal Institute of International Affairs, 1946).

Articles

Békés, Csaba, "The 1956 Hungarian Revolution and World Politics," *CWIHP Working Paper* no. 16 (Washington D.C.: Woodrow Wilson Center, 1996).

Carafano, James Jay, "Mobilizing Europe's Stateless: America's Plan for a Cold War Army," *Journal of Cold War Studies,* vol. 1, no. 2, (Summer 1999).

Critchlow, James, "Western Cold War Broadcasting: A Review Essay," *Journal of Cold War Studies* vol. I, no. 3, (Fall 1999).

Forland, Tor Egil, "'Selling Firearms to the Indians.' Eisenhower's Export Control Policy, 1953–1954," *Diplomatic History,* vol. 15, no. 2, (Spring 1991).

Gaddis, John Lewis, "The Emerging Post Revisionist Synthesis on the Origins of the Cold War," *Diplomatic History,* vol. 7, no. 3, (Summer 1983).

Gould-Davis, Nigel, "Rethinking the Role of Ideology in International Politics During the Cold War," *Journal of Cold War Studies,* vol. I, no. 1 (Winter 1999).

Göllner, András B., "Foundations of Soviet Domination and Communist Political Power in Hungary," *Canadian–American Review of Hungarian Studies,* vol. III, no. 2, (Fall 1976).

Gyarmati, György, "Harc a közigazgatás birtoklásáért, 1946," *Századok,* 1996, vol. 130, no. 3.

Gyarmati, György, "'Itt csak az fog történni, amit a kommunista párt akar.' Adalékok az 1947. évi országgyűlési választások történetéhez," *Társadalmi Szemle,* 1997, vol. 52, no. 8–9.

Hajdu, Tibor, "A Rajk-per háttere és fázisai," *Társadalmi Szemle,* 1992, vol. XLVII, no. 11.

Jervis, Robert, "Was the Cold War a Security Dilemma?" *Journal of Cold War Studies,* vol. 3 no. 1 (Winter 2001).

Juhász, Gyula, "A magyar–német viszony néhány kérdése a második világháború alatt," *Történelmi Szemle,* vol. 27, no. 2, (1984).

Kozma, István, "Család-név változtatás és történelem (1894–1956)," *Századok,* vol. 131, no. 2, 1997.

Kramer, Mark, "The Soviet Union and the 1956 Crises in Hungary and Poland: Reassessments and New Findings," *Journal of Contemporary History* vol. 33, no. 2, 1998.

Kramer, Mark, "New Evidence on Soviet Decison-Making and the 1956 Polish and Hungarian Crises," *CWIHP Bulletin,* no. 8–9 (Winter 1996/1997).

Kramer, Mark, "The Early Post-Stalin Succession Struggle and Upheavals in East-Central Europe: Internal-External Linkages in Soviet Policy Making" (Part 1) *Journal of Cold War Studies,* vol. I, no. 1 (Winter 1999).

Kramer, Mark, "The Early Post-Stalin Succession Struggle and the Upheavals in East-Central Europe: Internal-External Linkages in Soviet Policy Making" (Part 2) *Journal of Cold War Studies* vol. 1, no. 2 (Summer 1999).

Kramer, Mark, "The Early Post-Stalin Succession Struggle and the Upheavals in East-Central Europe: Internal-External Linkages in Soviet Policy Making" (Part 3) *Journal of Cold War Studies* vol. I, no. 3 (Winter 1999).

Loth, Wilfried, "The Origins of Stalin's Note of March 10 1952" *Cold War History* 2004, vol. IV, no. 2 (Jauary 2004).

Marer, Paul, "Reorientation and Commercial Relations of the Economies of East Central Europe," *A Compendium of Papers Submitted to the Joint Economic Committee, U.S. Congress,* 1972.

Marer, Paul, "The 'Soviet Bloc' as an Integration Model. Economic, Political and Cultural Aspects," in *Competing in One World* (Indiana University School of Business, undated).

Mark, Eduard: "American Policy Toward Eastern Europe and the Origins of the Cold War," *The Journal of American History,* vol. 68, no. 2 (September 1981).

Mark, Eduard, "The War Scare of 1946 and its Consequences," *Diplomatic History,* vol. 2, no. 3, (Summer 1997).

Mark, Eduard, "Revolution by Degrees: Stalin's National Front Strategy for Europe, 1941–1947," *CWHIP Working Paper* no. 31 (Washington D.C.: Woodrow Wilson Center, 2001).

McCauley, Brian, "Hungary and Suez, 1956: The Limits of Soviet and American Power," *Journal of Contemporary History,* vol. 16, no. 4 (October 1981).

Nevakivi, Jukka, "A Decisive Armistice 1944–1947: Why was Finland not Sovietized?" *Scandinavian Journal of History,* 1994, no. 19.

Pető, Andrea, "Átvonuló hadsereg, maradandó trauma, az 1945-ös budapesti nemi erőszak esetek emlékezete," *Történelmi Szemle,* 1999, vol. XLI, no. 1–2.

Romsics, Ignác, "A brit külpolitika és a 'magyar kérdés,' 1914-1946," *Századok,* vol. 130, 1996, no. 2.

Schlesinger, Arthur Jr., "The Origins of the Cold War," *Foreign Affairs,* October 1967.

Sipos, Péter and István Vida, "Az 1945 augusztus 27-én megkötött magyar–szovjet gazdasági egyezmény és a nyugati diplomácia," *Külpolitika,* 1985, vol. 12, no. 4.

Sipos, Péter and István Vida, "The Policy of the United States Towards Hungary During the Second World War," *Acta Historica Scientiarum Hungaricae,* 1989, vol. 35, no. 1.

Sipos, Péter, "A szovjetek és Magyarország, 1945," *História,* 1995, vol. 17, no. 2.

Spaulding, Robert Jr., "A Graduate and Moderate Relaxation: Eisenhower and the Revision of American Export Control Policy, 1953–1955," *Diplomatic History,* vol. 17, no. 2 (Spring 1993).

Standeiszky, Éva, "Antiszemita megmozdulások a koalíciós időszakban," *Századok,* 1992, vol. 126, no. 2.

Stikalin, Aleksandr, "A szovjet nagykövetség és az MDP-n belüli harc 1956 tavaszán-kora őszén," *Múltunk,* 1998, vol. 43, no. 2.

Szegedy-Maszák, Mihály, "The Rise and Fall of Bourgeois Literature in Hungary," *Hungarian Studies,* 1998/1999, vol. 13, no. 2.

Szűcs, László, "Magyarország és a Marshall Terv," *Levéltári Szemle,* 1998, vol. 48, no. 1

Tahnienko, Galina, "Atomia odnogo politicheskogo reshenia," *Mezhdunarodniaia Zhizn,* 1992, no. 5.

Urbán, Károly, "Révai József," *Párttörténeti Szemle,* 1978, vol. 24, no. 3.

Urbán, Károly, "Nagy Imre és G. M. Malenkov. Két miniszterelnök Sztálin után," *Múltunk* 1996, vol. 41, no. 1.

Varga, István, "A magyar valutacsoda," *Magyar Gazdaságkutató Intézet Közleményei,* issue 1 1946.

Weathersby, Kathryn, "Soviet Aims in Korea and the Origins of the Korean War, 1945–1950: New Evidence from Russian Archives," *CWIHP Working Paper* no. 8 (Washington D.C.: Woodrow Wilson Center, 1993).

Yegorova, Natalia, "The Iranian Crisis 1945–46. A View from Russian Archives," *CWIHP Working Paper* no. 15 (Washington D.C.: Woodrow Wilson Center, 1996).

Zielbauer, György, "Magyar polgári lakosok deportálása és hadifogsága, 1945–1948," *Történelmi Szemle,* 1989, vol. 31, no. 3–4.

Zinner, Tibor, "Az egyesületek és pártok feloszlatása Budapesten 1945 és 1948 között," *Politikatudomány,* 1988, vol. VI, no. 1.

Dissertations, Unpublished Manuscripts

Az állam biztonsága ellen kifejtett tevékenység és az ellene folytatott harc, 1949–1956, vol. 1–2 (unpublished manuscript, undated).

Baráth, Magdolna, *Gerő Ernő politikai pályája 1944–1956* (Ph. D. dissertation, 2002).

Bischof, Günter, *Between Responsibility and Rehabilitation: Austria in International Politics, 1945–1950*, part 2 (Ph. D. Dissertation, Harvard University, 1989).

Marchio, James, *Rhetoric and Reality: The Eisenhower Administration and Unrest in Eastern Europe, 1953–1956* (Ph. D. dissertation, 1990).

Okváth, Imre, A magyar néphadsereg háborús haditervei, 1948–1962 (Confrence Paper, Longyearbyen, 2003).

Preussen, Ronald W., *'Walking a Tightrope in the Twilight' : John Foster Dulles and Eastern Europe in 1953* (Conference Paper, Paris 1998).

Urbán, Károly, *Sztálin halálától a forradalom kitöréséig. A magyar-szovjet kapcsolatok története* (Budapest: unpublished manuscript, 1995).

Visuri, Pekka, *Finland in the Cold War. Why did Finland Remain outside the Soviet Bloc?* (Conference paper, Helsinki, 1998).

INDEX

Lieutenant-Colonel Riabchenko signs the Hungarian–Soviet Reparation Agreement (April 1945).

Meeting of the Smallholder Party (7 December 1945). From left to right: Ferenc Nagy, Kliment Voroshilov, Zoltán Tildy, Georgii Pushkin, B. I. Grigoriev and Vladimir Sviridov.

Vladimir Sviridov at ease with actors from Kiev.

Meeting of the Smallholder Party (7 December 1945). Talking and drinking from left to right: Kliment Voroshilov, Zoltán Tildy, Georgii Pushkin, B. I. Grigoriev and Vladimir Sviridov.

The arrival of the Hungarian delegation in Moscow (April 1946). From left to right: Vyacheslav Molotov, B. I. Grigoriev, Ernő Gerő, Ferenc Nagy, János Gyöngyösi.

Vladimir Sviridov presents Ferenc Nagy with the Soviet Union's gift, a ZIS Limousine (6 June 1946).

Hungarians in Washington (June 1946). At the front from left to right: Ferenc Nagy, Harry Truman, Mátyás Rákosi.

*The Soviet table at a reception in Park Club hosted by the U.S. minister
(13 July 1946). Vladimir Sviridov standing in the middle.*

Arthur H. Schoenfeld receives Zoltán Tildy (1946). Rákosi sitting on the right.

*Arthur H. Schoenfeld toasts Mátyás Rákosi
(28 May 1947).*

Mátyás Rákosi arrives from Moscow accompanied by his spouse (December 1947).

Liberation Day (4 April 1950). From left to right: Mikhail Suslov (with glasses), Mátyás Rákosi, Kliment Voroshilov.

Kliment Voroshilov greets a woman (1954).

Soviet delegation in Budapest about to lay a wreath on the Soviet memorial on Gellérthegy (1955). Andropov is in the middle with glasses.

A demonstration in New York for the Hungarian Revolution (September 1957).

Ingram Content Group UK Ltd.
Milton Keynes UK
UKHW021305140323
418559UK00036B/542

9 789633 861400